The Effective Use
of Reading

The Schools Council project The Effective Use of Reading was directed by Professor Eric Lunzer and Keith Gardner. It was based at the School of Education, University of Nottingham, from 1973 to 1976.

In addition to the honorary directors, the members of the project team were:

> Colin Harrison (1973–6)
> Terry Dolan (1973–4)
> Maurice Waite (1974–5)
> John Cole (1975–6)

The Effective Use of Reading

Edited by

ERIC LUNZER and KEITH GARDNER

Heinemann Educational Books
for the Schools Council

Heinemann Educational Books Ltd
Halley Court, Jordan Hill, Oxford OX2 8EJ
OXFORD LONDON EDINBURGH MELBOURNE
SYDNEY AUCKLAND SINGAPORE MADRID
IBADAN NAIROBI GABORONE HARARE
KINGSTON PORTSMOUTH NH (USA)

ISBN 0 435 10497 7 (cased)
0 435 10498 5 (paper)

First published 1979
Reprinted 1979, 1981, 1984, 1986, 1989

Printed and bound in Great Britain by
Antony Rowe Ltd, Chippenham, Wiltshire

Contents

Acknowledgements   x
Preface   xi

1 Introduction: Origins, Background and Development   1
Eric Lunzer and Keith Gardner

  I Origins and background   1
  II Development   4
III The form of the project report   5

2 From Learning to Read to Reading to Learn   7
Eric Lunzer

  I Introduction   7
 II From speaking and listening to writing and reading   8

   1 General considerations   8
   2 The settings of spoken language   9
   3 The setting of written communication   14
   4 Differences between spoken and written language 15
   5 The disadvantages of text, compared with the spoken
     word   17
   6 Permanence of text and its implications for a reader 24
   7 Overcoming difficulties in reading comprehension 29
   8 Summary   32

III Reading and the teacher   33

3 Comprehension and Comprehension Tests   37
Eric Lunzer, Maurice Waite and Terry Dolan

  I Is reading comprehension unitary or manifold?   37
 II Background   40

III Design of the inquiry 41
  1 Subjects 41
  2 Tests and procedures 43
  3 Grieg 46
IV Data analysis 49
  1 Reliability of the four tests 49
  2 The search for subskills 51
 V What can be tested? 63
VI What can be taught? 69
Appendix Brighty 70

4 Assessing the Readability of School Texts 72
Colin Harrison

 I Introduction 72
  1 The need for objective measures 73
  2 The need for new research 74
 II Assessing text difficulty — what can be measured? 76
  1 Legibility 76
  2 Linguistic variables 76
  3 Vocabulary difficulty 78
  4 The formulae used in the study 79
III The readability survey design 79
  1 Selection of schools 80
  2 Selection of text samples 80
IV The readability survey results 83
 V The cross-validation study 87
  1 The importance of motivation 87
  2 Criteria for establishing the validity of formulae 88
VI Results of the cross-validation study 90
  1 Age level, accuracy of formulae and subjective judgements 93
  2 Correlation with cloze readability scores 97
  3 Applying cloze readability scores in the classroom 97
  4 Are new formulae needed? 99
VII Conclusions 101
Appendix 1 The passages 104
Appendix 2 An example of a readability formula in use 106

5 The Incidence and Context of Reading in the Classroom 108
Terry Dolan, Colin Harrison and Keith Gardner

 I Introduction 108
 II The development period 109
III The general inquiry 115
  1 The selection of schools 115
  2 The population 116

3 Data collection		116
IV Results		117
1 Rationale		117
2 Time spent by teachers and pupils on the categories observed using the RBI		118
3 Types of reading and writing observed using the RBI		122
4 Patterns of continuous reading		124
V Additional primary school observation		126
1 The problem		126
2 Procedure		126
3 Discussion		130
VI Conclusions		134

6 Reading for Homework — 139
John Cole and Eric Lunzer

I Introduction	139
II Methods of inquiry	140
1 The questionnaires	140
2 The interviews	141
III Results	143
1 Amount of time spent on homework	143
2 Reading times	145
3 Reading purposes	148
IV Some examples	154
V Conclusions	158
Appendix Questionnaires used in surveys	160

7 Topic Work with First-year Secondary Pupils — 167
John Cole and Keith Gardner

I The problem	167
II The lessons we observed	167
III Methods of observation and results	169
1 Dominant activities during working sessions	170
2 The use of reading materials	172
3 The use of the library/resource area	174
4 Recorded interviews	176
5 The report-back session	184
IV Discussion	187
1 Introduction	187
2 Perspectives	187
3 An analysis	188
V Conclusions	190

8 Reading Laboratories — 193
Roy Fawcett

I Introduction	193

 II Background 194
 1 Rationale 194
 2 Previous studies 195
 III The main SRA experiment 198
 1 Design of the inquiry 198
 2 Subjects 198
 3 Procedure 201
 4 Results 204
 IV Subsidiary inquiries 212
 1 The SRA and Ward Lock Educational experiment 212
 2 Beyond laboratories 214
 V Evaluation 220
 1 Effectiveness of the SRA Laboratories 220
 2 Limitations 221
 3 Follow-up 223
 4 The way ahead 223
 5 The Bullock Report 224
 VI Conclusions 227

9 Improving Reading through Group Discussion Activities 228
Terry and Elizabeth Dolan, Vic Taylor,
John Shoreland and Colin Harrison

 I General introduction 228
 II A programme for improving reading, language and
 learning 233
 1 Background to the establishment of the programme 233
 2 Classroom organization and conduct of the programme 235
 3 Group discussion activities 235
 4 A note on material used in the activities 250
 5 General comments on the group reading activities and
 the reading programme in Pilot School 1 251
 6 Evaluative comments on the reading programme in Pilot
 School 1 255
 III Evaluation studies 258
 IV Conclusions 264
 Appendix Sample passages used for group discussion activities 265

10 What the School Can Do: Instances of Current Practice 267
Eric Lunzer

 I How the survey was conducted 267
 II Reading across the curriculum 269
 1 Teaching comprehension or bypassing it 269
 2 Reading in science 272
 3 Reading in mathematics 273

    4 Reading in the social sciences   274
    5 A policy for a school   276
  III Worksheets   280
      Example: Fold mountains   281
      Example: Working in the mill   281
      Example: The End of the Open Field System   283
      A combined-science course   285
  IV Sixth-form programmes   289
   V Case study   291
    1 Interview with headteacher   291
    2 Interview with Head of English   294
  VI Conclusions   297

11 Summary and Conclusions   299
    Keith Gardner

    I Introduction   299
   II Reading comprehension   299
  III Readability (Chapter 4)   301
  IV Classroom observation data (Chapter 5)   302
   V Reading for homework (Chapter 6)   304
  VI Reading in topic work (Chapter 7)   305
 VII An evaluation of SRA Laboratories (Chapter 8)   306
VIII Improving reading through group discussion activities
      (Chapter 9)   308
  IX Visits to schools (Chapter 10)   311
   X The way ahead   312

A Note on Statistics   314
Keith Selkirk

Bibliography   322
List of Tables   328
List of Figures   330
Index   331

Acknowledgements

The authors and publishers wish to thank the following for permission to reproduce copyright material:

Hamish Hamilton Children's Books Ltd for the extract from *Ice at Midsummer* by Alan Jenkins; Oxford University Press for the extract from 'Grieg' from *The Boyhoods of Great Composers* by Catherine Gough © Oxford University Press 1960; Janet Hitchman for the extract from her book *The King of the Barbareens*, published by Peacock Books; Evans Brothers Ltd for the extract from *Visual Biology* Book 2 by Michael Chinery: Board of Education of the City of New York for the table from *Curriculum Bulletin No. 6*, 1964; Manchester University Press and the authors for the graph from 'An experimental approach to the study of reading as a learning skill' by L. Thomas and S. Augstein in *Research in Education*: Rand McNally & Company for the extract adapted from *Brighty of the Grand Canyon* by Marguerite Henry, Copyright 1953.

They would also like to thank Maurice Waite for permission to reproduce the test using the extract from 'Grieg' in Chapter 3, and Roy Fawcett for permission to include in the book the chapter 'Reading Laboratories' which is adapted from his Ph.D. thesis *The Use of Reading Laboratories and other Procedures in Promoting Effective Reading among Pupils aged 9–15* (University of Nottingham 1977).

Preface

The topic of reading has been a central concern in education for many years. As a result, there is already an extensive literature which is directed mainly towards the teaching of young children, and the problem of pupils who fail to respond to such teaching. Indeed, the issue of reading failure has dominated public pronouncements to such an extent that we may easily forget that most of the pupils in our schools do in fact learn to read. It is to these pupils that this project is addressed. We have sought to enquire how average and above-average readers actually use reading in school, and what may be done to improve an existing competence.

This study required the co-operation of many people, and we would wish to acknowledge the help we have received both from Local Education Authorities and individual teachers. In particular, we would mention the willing assistance given by the Nottinghamshire, Derbyshire, and Lincolnshire Authorities. Through their senior officers we were able to identify and contact appropriate schools for our investigations.

Such work, however, rests ultimately on the decision of Head Teachers to allow research to proceed within their schools. Again we were fortunate, and we would record our appreciation of the support we received from our project schools. Beyond this, we are indebted to those schools which, although not included in the basic research, invited us to examine their own work in reading development.

Finally, mention must be made of the role of our Consultative Committee. A wide spectrum of interest was represented by its members and we are grateful for the guidance, both practical and theoretical, that we received.

E.A.L.
W.K.G.

1

Introduction: Origins, Background and Development

Eric Lunzer and Keith Gardner

1 Origins and background

This book is an account of the work undertaken in the course of a three year project funded by the Schools Council. It consists of a series of studies of pupils aged 10–15, who were average or above average readers, and these studies bear upon the capability of such pupils to use reading for learning, the factors that determine their success or failure, the effectiveness of the teaching they receive, and the conditions that appear to be paramount in ensuring an improvement in teaching approaches and pupil competence.

How did the project come into being, and what determined the course it took?

Its origins were twofold. One was immediate and accidental, the other less apparent to us at the start, but almost certainly more fundamental.

First, for reasons that were personal and anecdotal, we had been made aware that not all people approach the printed word in the same way. Some, and this includes a great many quite able pupils in the late years of secondary schooling, read every passage in the same way, without regard to the difficulty of the text or their own purposes in reading it. They read quite quickly and fluently (but silently and in their head), starting at the beginning and going on to the end. When, however, the going becomes too difficult, they merely give up. They have no alternative way of reading to fall back on. Others, and these would include our present readers, know how to vary the pace and style of reading to accord with both their personal purposes and the nature of the text. When they meet a difficulty, be it the intractability of the subject, the infelicity of a writer or ignorance of the background knowledge required to master a passage, they may pause to think. Or they may turn back and read over what was dismissed too lightly at first reading. They may skip a paragraph or two, knowing that they can return and backtrack if necessary. When they want to master the content of a passage in detail, or relish its style, they may read it over and over again. Or they may skim along to capture a general drift. In a word, their reading is flexible.

We believed that this flexibility is useful. It appeared to be the key to both learning from what we read, and to appreciating the 'sense of life itself' inherent in much great literature. It is a skill the effective reader has acquired, but we are not sure how.

From this, it seemed reasonable to believe also that a flexibility in reading style would be increasingly important to a pupil's learning as he progressed from primary to secondary school, and from the lower forms in the latter to the higher. But how would this need become manifest in lessons and homework? Could reading, in this sense, be taught? What efforts were presently made to teach it, and with what success?

With questions such as these in mind, an approach was made to the Schools Council in 1972. Some time was necessary to complete the detailed negotiations that were necessary for approval of the project. But there was ready acceptance of the idea. Indeed, the proposal was, in effect, a logical outcome of the current educational climate. The work of Bruner, Bernstein and many others had alerted educators to the crucial role of language in learning. Special mention should be given to the original and influential contributions of Halliday and Britton. The Schools Council had already funded projects concerned with spoken language (Wilkinson, Stratta and Dudley, 1974) and with writing across the curriculum (Britton et al., 1975; Martin et al., 1976). It was proper that attention should now be turned to reading.

The development of children's literary interests and appreciation was already being studied by Whitehead et al. (1974). Hence, a proposal that was focussed on reading for learning across the curriculum served to meet a need to study an area of language use in schools which hitherto had been largely ignored, and also offered an opportunity to complement work in other closely related topics.

At about the same time, an independent approach was made to Vera Southgate Booth, with a view to investigating the teaching of reading in the middle years of the junior school.[1] In the event, the two projects were run in harness, with much sharing of ideas, and a joint consultative committee.

By a coincidence which is probably not fortuitous, the Bullock Committee began its inquiries about a year before the two projects started on theirs. Its brief was, of course, wider than that of this project, since it included all aspects of language throughout the years of schooling.[2] Nevertheless, for the first time in an official inquiry considerable attention was devoted to reading beyond the initial stages.

There are other and more fundamental reasons for an awakening

[1] Extending Beginning Reading 1973–1977.
[2] Although whereas the Bullock Committee confined its attention to the English lesson, this project examines reading across the curriculum.

interest in reading for learning. They have to do with contemporary developments in British education.

Until quite recent times, the organization of education in Britain was frankly elitist. A strict selection procedure determined entry to secondary and higher education. As late as the mid-fifties, secondary education was based predominantly on a tripartite division of schools. Some 20 per cent of each age group were taught in grammar schools, while the remaining 80 per cent were taught in secondary modern schools or, more rarely, in technical schools. There were inequalities of opportunity, some arising out of the advantages or the disadvantages associated with social class, others due to the unequal provision of grammar school places in different regions. Nevertheless, a system of examinations which was as fair as it could be[1] (Vernon, 1957) ensured that, for the most part, those students who gained places in grammar schools were able to cope with the learning tasks that faced them. Perhaps even then it was a minority who could use books to full advantage, but the problems of learning were less acute, particularly as the system of entry operated in such a way as to exclude most of those pupils whose parents were themselves uneducated and who were, therefore, deprived of the opportunity of seeing books read and enjoyed by others outside of school (Wiseman, 1964). In any case, then as now a further and more restrictive selection limited entry to higher education, where learning through study would be even more essential.

By the early 1970s this situation had been changed drastically. The majority of secondary pupils were now being taught in comprehensive schools, and the tripartite system persisted only in a few areas. It is true that comprehensive education is still incomplete, as some independent schools and grammar schools have survived. There are still wide differences between the characteristics of different comprehensive schools due mainly to variation between neighbourhoods. Nevertheless, most secondary school teachers are now expected to teach students following an O-level and A-level curriculum as well as (and sometimes alongside) others who have only a minimal competence in literacy and numeracy.[2] In many schools, one finds some special provision for the most backward (DES, 1975). In the third form and beyond, there is often some degree of setting or streaming. But in the first two years there is a growing move towards teaching in mixed-ability groups.[3] In any case, the

[1] It was estimated, however, that some 25 per cent of pupils selected for grammar school placement were less able in their studies than the best pupils who were not selected.

[2] Literacy, in this context, is sometimes defined as the ability to read a popular newspaper; numeracy, less adequately, as the ability to carry out the four basic arithmetical operations on numbers of more than one digit.

[3] Since work on the project was completed, the 'Great Debate' has raised questions concerning mixed ability which may influence this process. But the general thesis put forward here remains unaltered.

teacher's own experience with the more able pupils presents him with a challenge – how is one to convey certain minimal elements of knowledge to all pupils, together with a positive attitude towards knowledge and some competence in the independent pursuit of knowledge?

It is generally accepted that the independent pursuit of knowledge entails the ability to use the written text. At the same time the necessity to provide opportunities for all pupils to progress at their own level despite wide variations among them will usually mean that some form of group or individual study will be employed, one which depends on written instructions and the use of written materials. In a word, changing approaches within schools have tended to emphasize the importance of reading for learning. Hence, the very attempt to provide comprehensive secondary education for all has made it more apparent that many pupils, perhaps most, need help and tuition to use written language, not just as writers, but also as readers and learners.

Education in the USA has long been less elitist than in Britain and it is no accident that a long tradition of teaching 'study skills', including especially the use of reading for learning, exists there. The teaching of reading in order to learn through reading is an essential consequence of the democratization of education. It is also significant that as we move towards a greater interest in 'teaching readers to read' in this country, ideas which were hitherto confined to a small body of specialists are gaining ground rapidly, chiefly through the work of the polytechnics and the Open University.

II Development

Once the original proposal to the Schools Council had been approved and the necessary funding obtained, a project team was assembled. It was necessary, immediately, to embark on three different operations. First, local schools had to be informed of our intentions, and groups of teachers formed who would act both as advisers and participants in fieldwork. Second, in consultation with these teachers groups, a preliminary programme for study and investigation was devised. Four main areas of inquiry were isolated:

1   An observational study of the use of reading for learning across the curriculum which, it was hoped, would provide a general picture of existing classroom practice.
2   A study of the nature of reading comprehension designed to clarify certain theoretical issues and provide a basis for proposals related to both assessing and improving reading comprehension.
3   An evaluation of existing classroom procedures which were aimed at the improvement of reading for learning.

4   An examination of the concept of readability, with special reference to the validity and usefulness of readability measures in the classroom.

Third, an extensive study of existing literature that bore upon the whole question of reading comprehension was undertaken.

In the event, the response of local teachers was both immediate and generous. In particular, headteachers were most willing to provide us with the facilities to embark on trials and pilot studies which were an essential preliminary to the various studies included within the project. Then, as work progressed it became evident that the four original areas of inquiry outlined above would require some extension.

Thus, classroom observation was expanded to encompass homework; a further inquiry concentrated on the special reading conditions which were assumed to exist in a project-based study; and in order to obtain a full picture of present efforts to improve reading for learning in the classroom, a nationwide sample of schools was visited.

It would, however, be misleading to leave a description of the project at this point. The resident team was not occupied entirely with observing pupils, carrying out research, collecting data and computing results. There was also a vigorous and continuing study of many issues related to the development of reading. In particular it was apparent that an understanding of the form of a communication system where a written code mediates between an author and a reader is crucial for an appreciation of the process of reading comprehension. Much time was spent considering this matter. It is appropriate, therefore, that our account of the work undertaken in the course of the project should open with a discussion which bears upon the question: How does a reader reconstruct the meanings which an author seeks to communicate through a written code?

III   The form of the project report

The report covers a variety of issues, some of which can be dealt with descriptively, but others require an explanation of statistical techniques and research design. It is inevitable, therefore, that the demands on a reader will vary from chapter to chapter We would suggest that some readers would find it useful to begin with Chapter 11 in order to gain an overall impression of the project. They might then be in a position to select those parts of the main report which will be of most interest to them.

The main report itself is arranged in the following way:

Chapters 2–4   A statement of the problem of reading comprehension. Chapter 2 is largely theoretical; Chapters 3 and 4 focus on separate issues of the problem of comprehension – comprehension in the reader and readability in the text. Both the latter are based, in the main, on our own investigations.

Chapters 5–7   Evidence of the present state of affairs in what we take to be a typical cross-section of primary and secondary schools. The topics covered here include an account of classroom reading (Chapter 5); a discussion of the role of reading set for homework (Chapter 6); and a description of observation work carried out in resource-based topic work (Chapter 7).

Chapters 8–10   A description and validation of some hopeful measures that are being pursued in selected schools. A rigorous inquiry into the effectiveness of reading laboratories is presented in Chapter 8; the use of a range of group discussion techniques is evaluated in Chapter 9; finally, a general view of the work we encountered during our visits to schools is outlined in Chapter 10.

The summary (Chapter 11) serves two purposes. First, it is a concise précis of the main findings of the project. Second, overall conclusions, taking every aspect of our work as a whole, are suggested.

2

From Learning to Read to Reading to Learn

Eric Lunzer

I Introduction

Learning to speak precedes learning to read. Hence, teachers of reading assume that young children have attained a certain language competence through listening and talking which will transfer readily to the reading situation. Indeed, such a competence is generally regarded as a necessary prerequisite for reading instruction (Downing and Thackray, 1971). Further, it has been assumed that meaning comes automatically with decoding. Because a child 'has language' the meaning is there, and can be transferred directly as the reader produces a phonetic transcription of a text (Callaway, 1970).

This simplistic idea, which implies that the teacher has little responsibility for fostering reading comprehension, except in so far as reading comprehension is a product of oral comprehension, is open to a number of objections. For instance, empirical studies of the errors made by young readers have confirmed that an attempt to preserve meaning is instrumental in determining what is actually read (Weber, 1968). Comprehension is not merely the outcome of a phonetic transcription of a written passage, rather it is present, at least in embryo, as reading proceeds. Meanings occur in the mind of the reader before words are decoded.

Also, it may be argued that the transfer of meaning from a phonetic transcription of a written text rests on an assumption that the spoken and graphic forms of language have sufficient communality to permit such a transfer to take place. This is open to question.

Written English is not a different language from spoken English. The two share what is essentially a common grammar as well as a common vocabulary. They differ at what Halliday, McIntosh and Strevens (1964) have termed the level of substance: the ultimate forms that carry meaning from one language user to another must be translated into patterns of sound or patterns of graphic signs. It is the two different coding systems and the different settings in which they are used that give rise to differing conventions between spoken and written language. In short, spoken language is immediate and, typically, improvised; written language is more 'edited'.

It may be mentioned in passing that when Bernstein (1971) draws attention to the variety of 'elaborated codes' that are accessible to the educated minority, he is alluding to the enrichment of the forms of spoken language by accretions from written language. When earlier (1961) he wrote of the 'public language' of the working class in contrast to the 'formal language' of the middle class, he was depicting spoken language in its purest form, as an immediate and almost gestural accompaniment to action. Thus, children whose experience of language is restricted in the ways described by Bernstein are doubly handicapped in their approach to written language.

The differences between spoken and written language are therefore central to a discussion of reading for learning, and it is worthwhile considering them in more detail because they constitute the principal background to all that follows in the present volume.

II From speaking and listening to writing and reading

1 General considerations

We would begin by referring to a conceptual distinction which is fundamental to any study of language. It is the distinction drawn by de Saussure between 'language' (*langue*) and 'speech' (*parole*). Language is what the language user knows; speech is what he does. Language consists of things like a vocabulary (or 'dictionary'), a grammar and a set of rules or habits for converting linguistic intention to linguistic substance. Speech is what is said or written. Language is the factory that produces the goods – or 'assays' them in comprehension; speech is the set of goods. Language changes slowly, even in individual users; speech is constantly created and decays in seconds (unless preserved in writing or on tape). Language is what we infer; it is speech that we observe. Nevertheless it is language which must be studied first, and the study of speech is secondary.

One might say that, apart from the conversion rules mentioned above, any spoken language and the corresponding written language are one and the same. For the basic rules and vocabulary are indeed the same.[1] But their characteristic output, speech or text, is usually very different, and the difference increases for the child when he passes from the study of beginning readers (learning to read) to the study of real text (i.e. text which assumes that he knows how to read).

[1] It seems to us that when Chomsky made the distinction between competence and performance, and elected (as he did at first) to restrict his analysis to the former, he was saying just this. But Chomsky's distinction is matter for argument (see Herriot, 1970); de Saussure's can hardly be questioned.

2 The settings of spoken language

We shall first consider what we take to be the key elements in a
conversational situation and their interrelation. They may be set out
in the following way:

1   Both speaker and listener share a common situation, to which
    they can refer by gesture as well as by word.

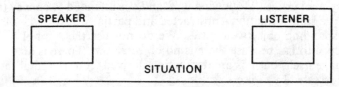

2   They also have experience of the outside world to which they may
    refer by speech, but not easily by gesture.

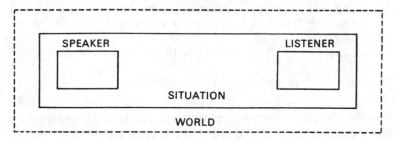

3   A message (M) is uttered by the speaker and heard by the listener.
    (In a physical sense it is a pattern of sound waves that passes
    between them.)

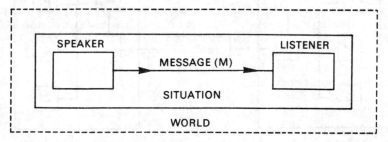

What must be assumed in the speaker and the listener to enable one
to utter the message and the other to understand it? We need to
consider four elements, all of which are somehow encoded in the
brain of each. In the speaker, they are:

1 his knowledge of the world upon which he draws (W');
2 his awareness of the common setting for a conversational exchange (this will include his impression of the listener himself) (S');
3 his ability to recall the context of his present utterance (what was said a moment ago and before that) (C');
4 his knowledge of the language he means to use (LK_1).

The symbol prime (') following W, S, and C is intended to convey that each is a transformation – abstracted and partially distorted – of the corresponding objective entities. We do not use the symbol ' with reference to LK, because there is no objective LK. There is an L, the language itself, but L is an abstraction derived from the total set of LKs possessed by its users.

The listener has a similar, but not identical set of impressions. That is:

1 a knowledge of the world (W");
2 an awareness of the common setting for a conversational exchange (S"), (this will include the listener's knowledge of the speaker);
3 an ability to recall the context of the utterances he is receiving (C");
4 a knowledge of the language being used (LK_1).

We have used the symbol (") to emphasize that the listener will, hopefully, share a common experience of events and language with the speaker, but will at the same time diverge from the speaker in certain respects.

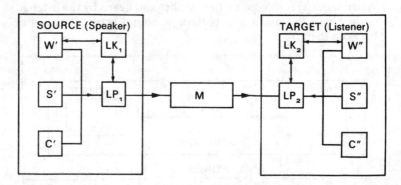

To account for the origin of the utterance or message we have assumed a further element in the speaker—a 'language processing unit' (LP_1) with a corresponding LP_2 in the listener. The distinction between LK_1 and LP_1 may seem a little artificial. In fact, it represents the capacity to select a relevant section of total knowledge for a specific purpose. In addition, it is necessary to represent the non-language elements in spoken communication. This is achieved by assuming:

1 a behaviour emitter in both speaker and listener (BE);
2 a behaviour interpreter in both speaker and listener (BI).

Non-language behaviour exhibited by speaker and listener along with the verbal message may then be indicated by the symbol (NLB).

All these elements have been included in Fig. 2.1 (p. 12) which is a diagrammatic representation of what we take to be the key elements in a conversational situation, and their interrelation.

The immediate occasion for an utterance is the speaker's intention to say something to the listener. It must arise out of his awareness: often c' when he responds to the other, often s' when his remark refers to the here and now, much less frequently to w' alone. It is of course a mistake to think of the function of speech as primarily informational. We will say more of this directly, but for the present it is well to remember that the most frequent exchanges are 'manipulative'—one of the parties is trying to get the other to do something, or 'interpersonal'—one or both parties are engaged in altering or maintaining some state of rapport between them, or both.

Although it is comparatively rare for an utterance not to have some reference to s and c, w' is nearly always involved. This is because of the close link between LK_1 and w', i.e. between our knowledge of language forms and our knowledge of the world. So close is this link that psychologists find it difficult to establish anything useful about how we organize our impression of things except by studying verbal behaviour and response to verbal messages.

Thus, in framing an utterance, LK_1 will draw in varying degrees on w', s' and c'. How this is done need not concern us here (fortunately—for it is the largest part of psycholinguistics). But it is important to note that the output of LK_1 is not just a string of words. The utterance always embodies a definite pattern of expression which is superimposed on these words. We refer to the rate of speech, to the distribution of pitch and stress, and to the incidence of pauses. All these carry meaning as importantly as the words themselves. For instance, the words 'You were right' can be altered from a statement (of approval) to a question (incredulity with continued disapproval) simply by a change in tonality.

Such considerations lead us to look at the lower half of Fig. 2.1, which is concerned with non-verbal behaviour.

There are two classes of non-verbal behaviour which help to further communication in face-to-face conversation: we may call these *mime* and *contact*. Mime is the use of movement or gesture to convey meaning. It is less common and pervasive in some cultures (e.g. England) than in others (e.g. Italy), and probably less frequent in

Figure 2.1   *The setting of spoken language*

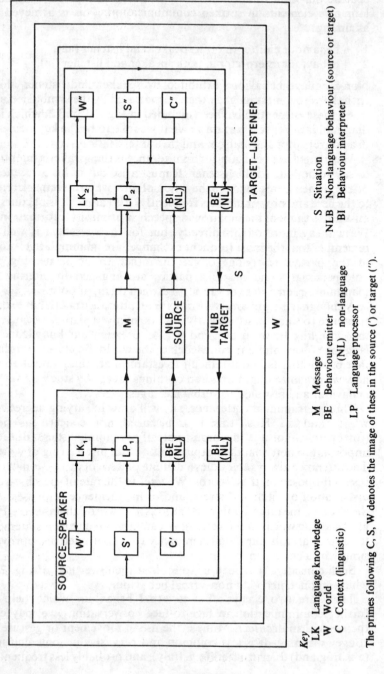

Key

LK   Language knowledge   M   Message   S   Situation
W   World   BE   Behaviour emitter   NLB   Non-language behaviour (source or target)
C   Context (linguistic)   (NL)   non-language   BI   Behaviour interpreter
                                    LP   Language processor   BE   Behaviour emitter

The primes following C, S, W denotes the image of these in the source (') or target (").

intimate dialogue than in rhetoric. But it is an important resource—
as in pointing. Contact is the use of fine movement to maintain or to
alter the state of rapport between the participants. Argyle (1969) has
shown how changes in eye-contact are used quite unconsciously to
signal the end of an utterance or an intention to continue, the
interlocutor responds either by taking over the role of speaker or by
continuing in that of listener. But there are many subtle ways in which
contact-behaviour aids communication, especially when it originates
from the listener. Changes in expression and posture signal
heightened or failing interest as well as comprehension or failure of
communication. The speaker senses these and, if he is wise, he reacts
appropriately, for example, by putting the thing another way when he
senses he was not understood the first time.

It is of course rare for both parties in a conversation to be talking at
once, and so we have cast one in the role of speaker, the other in the
listening role. But both parties emit non-verbal behaviour, and so
Fig. 2.1 indicates two streams of such behaviour, one originating
from the source (or speaker), the other from the target (or listener).
Each has its origin in the subject's changing response to the total
situation (s' or s''), and each is interpreted by the other and used to
modify his perception of that situation. As a result, communication
in spoken language is only partly verbal: it is eked out by non-verbal
communication, and it relies on this in ways which are not obvious to
the layman even though he is very skilful at exploiting them.

When is communication successful? One's first thought might be
to require some change in w'', bringing it closer to w'. If you
understand what I am saying, then your perception of things will be
more like mine. But such a restriction is inadequate on two counts:
first, because the function of communication is not always to convey
information from a speaker to a listener; and second because the
speaker's purpose may be more subtle, for example, to influence or
even to mislead. It is indeed reasonable to look primarily to changes
in w'' and in s'' when trying to gauge the success of the
communication. But we need to be more circumspect in saying just
what these changes should be. For the speaker, the communication
will have achieved its purpose if they are the sort of changes he
intended to produce in the listener. For the listener the same is true if
he is satisfied with the changes in his own perception of things, or of
the other, or of what he takes to be the other's perception of himself.

Before passing to a consideration of reading, it should be noted
that Fig. 2.1 is an abstraction of a particular episode in a
conversation. What usually happens is that the participants alternate
in the two roles: speaker becomes listener and listener becomes
speaker. This interchangeability of roles is a powerful aid to
communication. When there are only two participants there is
maximum provision for feedback. The greater the number of listeners,

the smaller the feedback—which is why a lecture should properly be thought of as midway between conversation and the use of text.

3 The setting of written communication

What has been discussed up to this point may seem a far cry from reading. However, our purpose in discussing spoken communication was precisely to illustrate the difference between written and spoken language. To this end we now consider the setting of written communication:

1   Unlike spoken communication there is no common situation (s) to which written communication can refer. The writer produces a message in one time and place and this is accessed by one or more readers in another. There is, however, a common experience of the world (w).

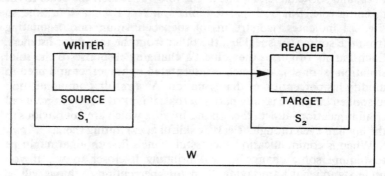

2   The product of communication (i.e. the text) is now permanent and not transient. This may be suggested by a double rectangle denoting the message (M).

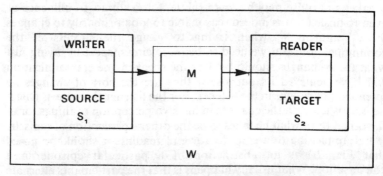

3   Because the communication is not face to face the verbal message cannot be supplemented, modified, or emphasized by non-verbal behaviour (i.e. there is now only a 'single path' message passing between source and target).

The setting of written communication may, therefore, be represented as in Fig. 2.2 (p. 16).

It may be pointed out that:

1   Because there are fewer resources to sustain the link between participants, the written setting is much less rich than the spoken setting.
2   Communication is weakened by the lack of a common situation and the absence of non-verbal support.
3   On the other hand, it is strengthened by the presence of a permanent text.

At the same time, the absence of a conversational setting produces a number of more subtle differences, and it is to these that we turn now.

4 Differences between spoken and written language

In principle, whatever can be written can also be said, while the converse is false. This is because spoken communication includes as an important part the quasi-gestural, that which sustains and makes for conversation itself, the interaction between two participants, as distinct from its content. 'Hello there', 'How do you do', 'Hey up', 'Yes', 'And then?', 'I see', 'Do you get my meaning?', 'What was that?', 'No, really', have as little part in written language as 'Pass the salt' or 'Give us a kiss'. All presuppose interaction. The former (but not, save indirectly, the latter) sustain conversation. By the same token, there might be nothing to prevent one saying what might be written, including the exposition of an argument (as in a lecture or tutorial) or the spontaneous aphorism or epigram (with embryonic poetry of a sort).

In practice, the situation is almost opposite. Whatever is said can also be written. But not without change. The last paragraph includes a string of speech tokens that 'cannot be written', but yet they have been. They appear in quotation marks, and that is the change. What is far more common is the re-creation of a conversation by an author to enable the reader to eavesdrop. Again, however, the conversation is in quotation marks. Usually, it is distorted; it is like conversation, but not exactly like it. There are no hesitations marked by *er*. There are fewer false starts and repetitions. More often than not, the 'conversation' is more coherent than true conversation. It sticks more to the point, even when it is a conversational point.[1] On the other hand, much that is written cannot be said unless one has first written it down. Poetic material requires too much rehearsal and correction

[1] The pastiches of Beachcomber and, especially, the plays of Harold Pinter are nice counterexamples. True conversation can be written or staged, but it is rare. So rare that one's first reaction is of disbelief. Because one looks in vain for the conventional disguise of written dialogue, one suspects that truth of being counterfeit.

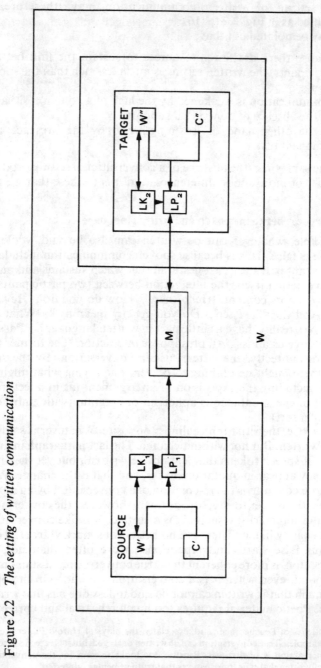

Figure 2.2 *The setting of written communication*

(For key see Fig. 2.1 and text.)

for one to deliver it *extempore*. (We use the term 'poetic' in the wider sense of Britton, to cover all material in which the form is an integral part of the 'statement', i.e. of what is conveyed.) Likewise, except for certain rare and well-rehearsed individuals, sustained argument demands too much thought and reference back for spontaneous delivery. Nor, for the same reason, can it be readily accepted by a listener. Thus in practice the domain of written language exceeds that of spoken language—and tries to include it.

To return to Fig. 2.2, the lack of a common situation is exacerbated by a restriction on the context (a restriction which cannot be shown in the diagram). The context is limited to what has already been introduced by the writer.[1] Hence the need for completeness and order. The writer must anticipate what knowledge (w″) he may assume in the reader, and supply all the deficiencies at the right moment. The reader cannot get back at him and ask for clarification, as a listener might do.

When a writer takes care to supply completeness (relative to the gaps in w″) and to order information, he is editing his thought. This is one aspect of editing. The other has to do with the form of the text, i.e. the language in which it is couched. Text is permanent. It is a 'statement'. It is evidence by which the writer will be judged. Nor will he be present to plead in his own defence. He will be judged by what he wrote, not by what he meant, if these are different. Therefore the written word is more grammatical than the spoken; it adheres more to the rules of grammar and usage.[2] When it is well done, it departs from these only by conscious intent (further editing), not by reason of the failure of performance relative to competence which is so characteristic of the spoken word (Chomsky, 1957).

5 The disadvantages of text, compared with the spoken word

If written language is more complete and more ordered and also less prone to error than spoken language, it should be easier to understand. When the matter is easy, for example, a simple story, and the reader is skilled, perhaps it is. But one suspects that there are more cases when the reverse is true, especially when the reader is less skilled. These contrasts are indeed substantiated by the available evidence (reviewed by Carroll, 1971 and by Howe, 1972). However, more often than not the relevant experimental work deals with differences in recall or between oral and visual presentations of the

[1] Sometimes, by accident, the necessary information occurs later. Sometimes the same is done by artifice, to convey a mood or to simulate an unfolding of the present. Sometimes it is done by an act of almost wilful obscurantism, as in certain official documents and in many computer training-manuals.

[2] It is true that it is more in accord with the prescriptions of those who write textbooks of grammar and of usage. But this is secondary. It is also more in accord with what is common to LK$_1$ and LK$_2$, i.e. the linguistic competence of language users.

same material. In other words, the student listens to a reading of the text or he is allowed to read it for himself. The former condition is not a true representation of the situation of the listener in conversation.

Why should the situation of the reader in Fig. 2.2 be more demanding than that of the listener in Fig. 2.1? We would suggest seven reasons—and there may be more.

(i)   There is no common situation. The 'situation' (or frame of reference) that is invoked is contained in the text and must be inferred from the text.

(ii)   The words stand alone. They are not supported by non-verbal behaviour (what we have called mime and contact-behaviour) or by verbal expression.

(iii) There is no opportunity of feedback to the source. If the writer's assumptions about the state of w″ were exaggerated, it is up to the reader to close the gap in whatever way he can.

(iv)   Reading is uninterrupted, monotonous. There is little opportunity for overt response on the part of the reader. If he makes some overt response (laughing aloud or jotting down a note, etc.) it is not immediately reinforced. The writer knows nothing of it.

(v)   The editing of text can stand in the way of comprehension. The very errors and hesitations of spoken language correspond to sticking points in the movement of the speaker's thought. They signal difficulties and offer time to overcome them—for the listener as well as the speaker.

(vi)   Because text is more complete than utterance, it tends to be more dense. To the immature reader, it is also unfamiliar in choice of words and in style: the language is his own, the style foreign.

(vii) The writer orders his material. But the order which he thought best may not be best for the given reader.

Let us consider these in turn.

(*i*) LACK OF COMMON SITUATION

This needs no amplification beyond what has already been said about the contrast between Figs 2.1 and 2.2.

(*ii*) TEXT UNSUPPORTED BY NON-VERBAL BEHAVIOUR

This limitation is overcome in part by punctuation and in part by syntactic rearrangement (e.g. 'Christopher Wren built this gazebo' versus 'It was Christopher Wren who built this gazebo' versus 'This is a gazebo and was built by Christopher Wren'—example adapted from Halliday, 1970). But punctuation is less 'eloquent' than spoken expression, and its significance needs to be learnt. The same is true of syntax. Indeed differences in the relative frequency of the various syntactic patterns constitute one dimension of 'register'.[1]

(iii) LACK OF FEEDBACK

Some false assumptions about the reader's pre-existing knowledge are inevitable. This is because the readership of a text is not known to the writer. At best, he is familiar with the class of individuals of which the reader is a member, and there may be wide variations within that class. There are two ways in which the resultant difficulty can be overcome: by consulting some other source (another book or another person), or by making inferences concerning what is assumed from what is actually said. The latter, especially, is demanding. To some extent, the teacher can try to minimize the problem for his pupils by careful selection of the texts which he recommends for their usage. This is a subject which will occupy us in Chapter 4.

(iv) MONOTONY OF READING

This presents a problem of motivation. One would expect the problem to be more acute for the extrovert reader than for the introvert, for the latter is better equipped to cope with a monotonous input (Eysenck, 1953). In time, no doubt, the experienced reader learns to internalize the response to his own response. Chapter 9 describes some methods for combining spoken language with silent reading. The expectation, which we have not proved, is that such experiences will tend to facilitate the interiorization of comment and feedback.

(v) EDITED TEXT CAN HINDER COMPREHENSION

One might devote an entire book to a commentary on this point. We will be content to make just three points.

First, there is a sound body of research into the causes of hesitation in speech (cf. Goldman-Eisler, 1958). Broadly speaking, apart from pauses corresponding to natural breaks of phrasing, hesitation signals some difficulty in making the right conceptual transition (what comes next), or in finding the right word or the right syntax for its formulation.

Second, although what passes between source and target in Figs 2.1 and 2.2 is a 'message', i.e. a form of words, what is intended by both is something quite different. It is a set of meanings, i.e. a substructure in w' and s' and also in w'' and s''. For the speaker, framing an utterance is an act of psycholinguistic encoding. For the listener and for the reader, it is a 'psycholinguistic guessing game' (Goodman, 1967; Smith, 1971). Perhaps, for the speaker, the sequence of encoding is from meaning, through vocabulary choice, to

---

[1] This is discussed more fully under section (vi), p. 21.

deep structure; thence, by transformation to surface structure, and finally by phonological transcription to utterance. Perhaps, although Chomsky (1965) is careful not to say so. What *is* certain is that the processing of the listener (or reader) is not in reverse order. What he does is to seize upon whatever cues he needs, whether in syntax or in words or in intonation, so as to reconstruct these meanings for himself. In order to do so, he must regenerate the message for himself, at least in part. Often he anticipates what is to come so closely that he shadows the speech he hears. We all know 'sentence finishers', who echo the last couple of words of anything that is said to them. It is therefore entirely natural for the listener to follow the speaker's thought as well as his utterance, not just in its finished form but in its actual framing.

Third, we have good reason to believe that it is one thing to follow an argument and quite another thing to understand an argument. When one 'exposes' an argument, one is bound to set it out in a logical order, for else it could not convince. But the construction of the argument involves much toing and froing. It is a matter of locating gaps in an unfinished outline, of dreaming up ways of filling these gaps, then testing them, and finally reordering the parts (cf. Bartlett, 1958). Recent work reported by Wason and Johnson-Laird (1972) offers several demonstrations of the difference between 'verification' (which corresponds to following an argument) and 'selection' (corresponding to understanding). To understand an argument one must retrace the steps of its proponent (less the 'dreaming-up'). The writer has no alternative but to edit. Here the editing is the final rearrangement—which has the unfortunate side-effect of concealing both the original problem and the psychological process of its solution. It takes a very perceptive writer to overcome the first bit of concealment. It is even more difficult to overcome the second. By contrast, when one talks one relives the solution process.

Certainly the above contradiction is most acute when the text takes the form of complex argument, and this is but one variety of content, which is not the most common. But one suspects that the same problem is present in less acute form whenever one is engaged in generalizing from instances. Much of the content of the secondary school curriculum is of this latter sort. No doubt this is one of the reasons underlying teachers' preference for the spoken word, a fact which was first made plain to us in the course of a preliminary inquiry (see section III), and amply borne out in the more systematic investigation of Chapter 5. No doubt we should have anticipated this, but one is wise after the event.[1]

---

[1] In fact this chapter could not have been written in its present form at the outset of our inquiry. Nor was it.

(*vi*) TEXT MORE DENSE THAN UTTERANCE

This is partly a comment on the differences in register that one might find as between spoken and written English. The term 'register' is rather a loose one and is used to designate 'the way in which language users tend to select certain forms conventionally in certain situations rather than other forms largely equivalent in terms of language content' (Phillip, 1969).[1]

It is true that children experience more than one register of spoken English and have to come to terms with several in the written language too, but even when what is said and the circumstances of its saying are the same, there will be differences due in part to editing and in part to convention. The written version may feel more foreign and will generally lack an element of warmth. There are some differences which are partly a matter of convention: *it is* versus *it's*, *however* or *but* versus *but* (only), *further* or *moreover* or *also* or *and* versus *and* or *also* (only), etc. But the boundary between convention and the effect of editing is not sharp. For instance, in the last two examples, the additional forms add elegance and variety to written language (they help overcome the monotony which comes from uninterruptedness). In speech they would seem pedantic and cold (edited speech approaches written language, and is associated with the impersonality of the public utterance). It is interesting to note that the very use of the words 'cold' and 'warm' in this context is a metaphor derived from the heat which is experienced when warm-blooded bodies are in contact (ultimately, mother and child). The impersonality of written language underlines the separation between reader and writer.

However, at least as important as any difference in idiom is a difference in 'intensity'. Some texts are certainly more dense, more elliptical, more compact than others. But consider the contrast

---

[1] It is in some ways an unfortunate term, since there are at least four dimensions of variation. They are: *field* (subject matter or specialization, e.g. legal English, advertising English, scientific English); *mode* (a term which corresponds exactly to our notion of 'editing'—but like editing, includes the difference between a speech or lecture, a conversation at a formal gathering of relative strangers and a conversation between friends, as well as that between written and spoken versions of the same theme, addressed to the same audience); *personal style* (formality or informality of language, contrasting diplomatic language at one extreme with the talk of intimates at the other— cf. Joos 1961), and *functional style* (variations associated with the interpersonal function of an utterance or a piece of writing, e.g. didactic, placatory, consolatory). Because it would be tedious to define 'a given register' in terms of all four dimensions, and because there are also areas of overlap, some writers (e.g. Davies, 1968, 1969) prefer to drop the term completely. However, if we did so we would still find ourselves hunting for a word to mean 'any set of determinants which continues in operation throughout a sequence of discourse and operates in such a way as to favour the selection of some lexical and syntactic options and the rejection of others that are semantically equivalent, where both sets of options are available to the user(s) and coexist within the same language'. (Our definition!)

between speech and unsophisticated writing in an example cited by Wilkinson *et al.* (1974).

> *The Pyrenean mountain dog (spoken)*
> this dog that I'm going to tell you about/lives along our lane/he's huge/and it has/long white hair coming over its face/and/its face is all squashed/as if someone had pushed it in/this dog's a Pyrenean mountain dog/it's very interesting the way the people who have it now/came to get it/you see/they read in the paper/that/this dog/had killed two alsatians/and the magistrate said it had to be destroyed/and they went up to the magistrate in court/and pleaded for it/and said/we live in the country/and/not many people come out there/so we'd be able to keep it/and so/that's what they did/
>
> *The 'Polar Bear' (written)*
> The 'Polar Bear' is a huge dominating Pyrenean mountain dog. It has a huge, ugly, squashed looking face which is covered by long white hairs. It lives down our lane most unfortunately and has a strange story behind it.
>   The people who have it now read in the newspapers that this dog had attacked and killed two alsatians, and therefore by order of the magistrate it had to be destroyed. The couple pleaded for it, and were allowed to keep it on the condition they kept it quiet.

This very nice example, here reproduced in part, is the work of a girl who is just under twelve years old. One would imagine that she has an ear for language and is a delight to her teacher. The second version is not dense in any ordinary sense. Yet it is only 88 words long as compared with 122 for the spoken version. We would signal the following three differences:

1   Several of the words used in the short written extract are less frequent. They are therefore less probable. From an information-processing point of view, they carry more 'information', being less predictable. Hence they impose a heavier load on cognition.

2   The phrasing of the spoken version is more simple. It is closer to the deep structure, especially in the matter of non-singular transformations, i.e. transformations which send two or more units in the deep structure to a single unit in the surface structure.[1] Since one must assume that the deep structure is itself a reflection of the thought structure (i.e. the associations in w'), it follows that, from the standpoint of transformational grammar, the written version must impose a heavier load on cognition. This is the same conclusion as that reached in 1 above, based on a different factor.

3   One side-effect of 2 is that the ratio of content-words to function-words is greater in the written version than it is in the spoken version. Since the former are less predictable, they carry more information. Once again, there is a greater load on cognition.[1]

[1] The grammatical structure of a sentence is a way of describing the relations of dominance-dependence between the words it contains. It can be represented in the form of a tree, e.g.

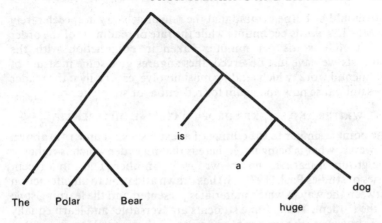

Theories of transformational grammar, of which the best known is that of Chomsky, suppose that, in addition to this structure, termed the surface structure, there is also a deep structure which brings out the functional relations between these words. In the sentence 'Iago persuaded Othello to suspect Desdemona', *Othello* is the object of *persuaded* and also the subject of *suspect*. The deep structure overcomes the problem by specifying two underlying sequences roughly corresponding to the two parts 'Iago persuaded Othello' and 'Othello suspected Desdemona'. The surface structure which appears in what is said or written is said to be derived from the deep structure by the application of transformations. Generally speaking, sequences which appear as discrete in the deep structure correspond to the underlying propositions. These in turn may be thought of as the parts of w′ which the speaker or writer seeks to transmit in the message. So the nearer the surface form to the deep structure, the less the task of the listener.

In the above passage, the written version has the sentence 'It has a huge, ugly, squashed looking face which is covered by long white hair'. The propositions that underlie this sentence are:

P1   IT (DOG) HAS FACE
P2   FACE (IS) HUGE
P3   FACE (IS) UGLY
P4   FACE LOOKS (= SEEMS) SQUASHED
P5   FACE HAS HAIRS
P6   HAIRS (ARE) LONG
P7   HAIRS (ARE) WHITE

Thus, seven propositions go to make up one written sentence. Corresponding to this, the spoken version has separate phrases: he's huge (SP1): it has long white hair coming over its face (SP2); its face is all squashed (SP3). The most complex utterance here is SP2, which is made up of the four propositions, P1, P5, P6 and P7. (Note that its 'face' *presupposes* P1.) SP3 relates to two propositions, P1 and P4. SP1 corresponds to only one proposition, similar to P2.

The greater length of the spoken version is due to the joint action of 2 and 3, since the greater abundance of simple phrases in the spoken version entails some repetition of content-words as well as the larger number of function-words.

It is worth noting that our own text in this passage is dense in quite a different sense. It passes quite rapidly from a reference to information theory to transformational grammar, with a little nod in the direction of general linguistic theory. We assume that many readers, but not all, will have at least some acquaintance with all three. When this is absent, the general sense will probably be clear enough—provided one stops to think.

It should be borne in mind that the rate of delivery in speech rarely exceeds 150 words per minute while the rate of reading is of the order of 250–400 words per minute. Taken in conjunction with the contrasts we have just observed, these figures give some measure of the 'mental work' which reading must involve, especially if the reader does not pause now and again for reflection, or simply for rest.

(*vii*) WRITER AND SPEAKER ORDER MATERIAL DIFFERENTLY

The point is similar to the editing of a text discussed under (*v*) above. However, what is being noted here is that an order which is right for one group of learners may be wrong for another. Thus, in a recent series of studies Pask (1976a, b) has drawn attention to an interaction between the way in which material is presented and the learning style of the student. While some students are 'versatile' and learn equally well however the material is given, others tend to be either 'comprehension learners' or 'operation learners'. Broadly speaking, the former thrive on a wholist approach, the latter on a step-by-step approach.

However, it should be added that these considerations would apply to any kind of presentation. Only under unfavourable circumstances would one expect them to be especially applicable to reading. But this would be the case where the reader is unsophisticated and there has been little preparation to guide his approach to the text.

6 Permanence of text and its implications for a reader

(*i*) THE NEED FOR FLEXIBILITY

We have so far noted six and possibly seven factors all of which tend to make it more difficult to learn from reading that it would be to learn from spoken discourse, especially if the latter takes the form of conversation, that is to say, if there are adequate opportunities for feedback from the listener. What then are the advantages to reading for learning?

There is, we would argue, one simple answer. Text is permanent, not transient like speech. The well-schooled reader is not paced by the material. He sets his own pace. It is with these considerations in mind that two arrows are shown from M to LP$_2$ in Fig. 2.2, in opposite directions. It is the reader who accesses the material when he wants to.

But, even if it is present, the reader will still want to stop and think. For in that case, he is likely to want to check that our understanding of the relevant theory agrees with his, and that our formulation is not in error. So, again, the text is demanding.

We apologize, but it helps to make a further point. The text is difficult not (or not only) because it is obscure, but because it is written at the level of interpretation and not at the descriptive level. But this is true of a good deal of the material that might be used in reading for learning. It is therefore not irrelevant to the present argument.

Therefore the arrow is from LP_2 to M. There must also be an arrow from M to LP_2, since he receives the 'message' when he reads it. Moreover, because the text is permanent, it can be returned to if desired to clear up ambiguity.

Finally, it can be accessed again and again and from any angle. The reader need not be constrained by the order of presentation, as is the listener. Because he can go over the text as often as he chooses, and in whatever order, he is in a better position to sort out the content from its manner of presentation. In effect, the reader can separate out informational content from interpersonal content.

Earlier it was noted that the written word constitutes a 'statement' (p. 17). A statement in this special sense (borrowed from aesthetics) is independent of its author, permanent, and liable to a kind of cross-examination.

Not all statements demand the same degree of cross-examination. In the world of art itself, it is often said that the best criterion of the merit of a product (statement) is the degrees of 'cross-examination' that it will bear. The best works are those that can be returned to again and again, in the confident expectation that they will reveal new facets, new modes of interpretation and fresh impulses for a distinctive aesthetic experience, all of which can coexist in complete harmony with the old. But our concern is primarily with objective texts or, in Britton's phrase, 'transactional material'. One should not press the analogy too far. No one would argue that a passage in a cookery book or in a physics textbook is most successful when it is most demanding. If anything the reverse is true. Given the limitations due to the complexity of the content itself, the most successful formulation is the one which imposes the least additional demands. It is the simplest and the most direct. What we have is a weak analogy. Like works of art, written texts can be looked at as often as necessary and in as much detail as is warranted. The need for cross-examination is a function of quite different factors, and in essence they are the factors we have just been concerned with, i.e. those that contribute to text difficulty for the given reader.

However, all our experience points to the fact that the untutored reader usually fails to take advantage of the permanence of text. His style of reading has been described in the last chapter. In a sense it is a carry-over from listener-behaviour. The listener is forced to interpret what he hears as and when he hears it. It is true that he can interrupt, but the effect of his interruption, if successful, is to elicit a new formulation or an amplification or an explanation from the speaker. The interruption results in a new message. 'Interruption' on the part of a reader cannot produce a new message. What he can do is to slow down or backtrack. These are habits that need to be learned.

Nor is the learning easy, for it involves a degree of unlearning. When he is learning to read, the pupil is handicapped by his own slowness. Due to insufficient mastery of the skills of word-recognition, his verbalization or audialization of the printed symbols produces a message which is both slower and less well-phrased for ready interpretation than the spoken word. Because of limitations of short-term memory, there is always a tendency for some part of the message to be 'erased' (forgotten) in the process of decoding the remainder, even when the message itself is short enough to be fully comprehensible when read to him by a fluent reader. There is therefore a sense of achievement in the attainment of fluent and rapid reading. With it goes the expectation that fluent reading is sufficient for reading comprehension, whatever the nature of the text. In the context of learning to read, slowness is an obstacle that must be overcome, and backtracking is of no advantage if the phrase has been read successfully.[1]

While there is general agreement that flexibility in reading pace is essential to profitable reading for learning, it is by no means easy to construct any adequate and reliable measures of this characteristic. This is largely because such measures are nearly always based on differences between an individual's performance on two texts (easy reading and difficult reading), and difference measures are generally unreliable. However, Rankin (1974), who has produced an excellent review of this area, was able to show by correlation that students who had undertaken a special course of instruction were better able to vary their rate of reading to suit the difficulty of the text. For these students, there was a high negative correlation between speed and text difficulty. This correlation was much lower for untutored (adult) students. The techniques that are described in Chapter 9 are particularly interesting in this context, since they provide a real incentive to 'use' the text in the fullest sense, instead of merely reading it at a standard speed, regardless of content or purpose.

(*ii*) READING STYLES

There are four styles of reading which can usefully be distinguished. They are: receptive reading, reflective reading, skim reading and scanning. Receptive reading is the most familiar and approximates to listener-behaviour. Reflective reading, as its name implies, is reading which is frequently interrupted by moments of reflection. Skim reading is a rapid style used mainly to establish what the text is about before deciding whether and where to read. Scanning is a kind of skimming, but it is skimming to see if a particular point is present in

---

[1] The pupil can often be helped by being asked to backtrack to the beginning of a phrase in order to obtain syntactic and semantic clues for the recognition of a difficult word. The practice of asking him to go back to a previous page to show him that he has met the word before is counterproductive. It interrupts the meaningfulness of his reading.

the text—or to locate it. Which of these styles is appropriate must depend on text difficulty and on the reader's purposes.

Difficulty of text is always relative to the pre-existing knowledge of the reader. The qualification is important. When he adjusts his rate of reading, he is effectively adjusting the rate of information-input. He is therefore reducing the cognitive strain in his interaction with the text. There are, of course, texts which are difficult for most readers. What this means is that they assume a considerable body of specialized knowledge. In our terms, they presuppose a high degree of structurization in some part of w". But if that situation already exists, the amount of 'information' contained in the message is not necessarily great. That is why the specialist has no difficulty in assimilating quite complex material in his own field.

However, the converse is also true. Even when the material is intrinsically easy, it may not be easy to the novice. The elements may be more or less familiar, but the interconnections that are imposed on them are not. In that case the existing linkages in w" do not coincide with those in w' or with those that are being put over in m. These pre-existing linkages may but interfere with the assimilation of the new information. Such might be the case in introductory courses in biology or history. For in both cases the learner already has experience—of animals and their habits, or of plants, or of the interaction between people. However, the way in which these things are being treated in his studies may differ from his own experience—of animals and plants and of people in relation to himself.

These considerations lead directly to the second factor which must determine rate of reading in the skilled reader. That is, his purpose in reading at the given moment. Consider the following situations:

(a) The reader wants to gain an overall impression of the passage upon which he is engaged. He wants to know what it is about, what kind of questions it deals with, what to expect.

(b) He wishes to follow the main lines of the argument, to follow the story, to gain some familiarity with the general outline of a process which is described in the text, etc.

(c) He wants to memorize the details of each example that is cited, to note the exact sequence of events that are related, to make sure of exactly what steps he must take to set up an experiment, etc.

(d) He wants to follow an argument which, to him, appears obscure in some part of the text, or he suspects a flaw in the argument.

(e) He wishes to verify whether a point that is made in one part of the text agrees or disagrees with one that he recalls having been made earlier in his reading.

The list is not exhaustive, but will suffice. To accomplish (a) the rate of reading will be rapid. Moreover reading will be highly selective, focussing on the beginnings and summaries of each section or paragraph, skipping most of what intervenes. This is the style we have termed *skimming*.[1]

The reading detailed under (b) is what was described as *receptive reading*. This is perhaps a misnomer, since the efficient reader is seldom wholly passive (unless, say, he is reading to try and get to sleep). The implication is that he is reading at a natural pace. However, that pace itself should not be constant, but adjusted to the rate of information-uptake as noted earlier, i.e. to the relative difficulty of the text.

Situations (d) and (e) involve the most demanding style of reading, sometimes termed 'critical reading', though we have preferred the term *reflective reading*. Such reading typically involves backtracking as well as pauses for reflection.

Situation (c) presents a somewhat different problem. In one sense, it stands midway between (b) and (d) or (e). But the added task is not one of comprehension, of coming to terms with the text, but rather one of learning in the sense of memorizing.

While these various purposes and kinds of reading have long been recognized, it must be admitted that there is still far too little hard evidence concerning the difference in processing that they imply. On theoretical grounds alone, we would agree with Smith (1973) that differences in rate of reading should not derive from a speeding up or a slowing down of audialization—or of finding the sense of each phrase in turn (if one is not an audializer, and most readers are). For optimal efficiency, the reading of each phrase should always be comfortably fast. The difference in rate is, or should be, due to the length and frequency of pauses between reads. For reading is not simply a matter of transcribing the written word, but also, and more importantly, a matter of assimilating its content. We would surmise that slowness in actual audialization would tend to have a soporific effect. It would therefore be counterproductive. However, the issue is open to research, albeit a different kind of research from that which has occupied us in the present volume.

There is one exception to the provisional maxim that all reading (in the strict sense) should be rapid. It concerns 'poetic material' in the widest sense. For it goes without saying that with this kind of text, the reader may well wish to relish the full flavour of the words, their sounds and their rhythm, and that too would be the writer's interest.

The different styles of reading that are appropriate to the different demands also underlie the best-known prescription for effective reading to learn. This is the SQ3R technique first propounded by Robinson (1946). The formula stands for Survey-Question-Read-Recite-Review. It is intended as a general scheme which can and

[1] The term *scanning* should be reserved for the process involved in trying to locate a specific topic within a text, for instance as a preliminary to (e).

should be applied to every text when reading is undertaken for the purpose of learning. For reading to be effective, i.e. to enable the reader to learn, he should place himself in the position of an active and interested listener. A preliminary survey (i.e. skim-reading, cf. (a)) is therefore undertaken to enable him to anticipate what sorts of things he will find out when he goes through the text using the receptive approach (b). However, before doing so he should anticipate the content at least to the extent of asking the questions which he has reason to believe may be answered in the text. Thus the initial S is followed by a Q phase, and this in turn by the first R (receptive read). Following on this reading, the student is required to recite, i.e. to go over the points he has established, so as to make sure he has indeed learnt from his reading. This is the second R. Finally, he should go over the main points again, review the material, paying particular attention to any points he has missed. This is the third R, and the student is advised to repeat the review at intervals to prevent forgetting.

It will be apparent that the SQ3R formula makes insufficient allowance for the kinds of distinction we have noted between types (b) and (c) or between types (d) and (e). Nor would it be appropriate to treat all transactional material in the same standard manner. Nevertheless, it has the advantage that it is a formula which can be understood and applied. It is less confusing than a general prescription to match reading style to reading purpose and text difficulty. The technique is given considerable emphasis in the *SRA Reading Laboratory* kits which are fully described in Chapter 8. The emphasis on SQ3R provides a clear and acceptable alternative to the listener-behaviour, which is so clearly inappropriate, but also the natural inclination of the untutored pupil. It may be, therefore, that this emphasis accounts in part for the success obained by the laboratory method as shown in Chapter 8.

7 Overcoming difficulties in reading comprehension

It has been suggested that the permanence of text enables the skilled reader to inform himself more effectively from the written word than he can from the spoken word, provided that he possesses sufficient flexibility of reading style, and knows how and when to use it. It remains for us in the present section to reconsider each of the disadvantages of reading as described in subsection 5, in the light of what has been said in subsection 6, with special reference to the pedagogical purpose of this work: how can we improve the pupil's reading for learning?

(*i*) LACK OF COMMON SITUATION

The function of the preliminary survey advocated by Robinson in the SQ3R formula is precisely to introduce a virtual common situation. It is to ensure that the reader is alerted to the kind of information, ideas, or argument he should expect. If effective, it produces a selective arousal of those parts of the reader's existing knowledge and experience (w'') that correspond to the effective 'world' (w') and situation (s_1) of the writer. When the material is objective or informational, the survey acts as an 'advanced organizer' in the sense of Ausubel (1968). It must be pointed out, however, that in imaginative writing the author prepares the reader through the gradual unfolding of events. The ordering of what is presented, like every other feature, is an integral part of the total message and contributes to its effect. SQ3R is, therefore, inappropriate to literary material.

(ii) TEXT UNSUPPORTED BY NON-VERBAL BEHAVIOUR

Although syntactic ordering, paragraphing and punctuation are designed to substitute for expression and gesture in spoken language, they are probably a good deal less effective, however skilled the reader. Nevertheless, in informational material this can be a positive gain, since the reader is more free to exercise his own judgement, being more immune to the 'manipulative' (Halliday, 1975), hortatory element that is unavoidable in any communication. As indicated earlier, he is in a better position to sift evidence from opinion.

(iii) LACK OF FEEDBACK

It is true that there is no feedback to the source. But the experienced reader is free to choose the kind of text that he can readily assimilate. In the case of the learner in school, one cannot expect that he will be able to make the choice for himself, since he lacks the necessary expertise. We have indeed produced some evidence for this in Chapter 7. It is for these reasons that we have devoted one part of our study to an examination of the texts used in schools and of the resources that are available to help teachers to make appropriate choices from the standpoint of readability. For the rest, the experienced reader knows how to search the text for additional clues to aid him in the understanding of a difficult passage, or if need be, how to find supporting material. Again, these are hard-won accomplishments, and the majority of students will almost certainly require help and guidance in their achievement. Above all, pupils in the early years of their secondary schooling need to be able to call on the assistance of the teacher to help them overcome any difficulties. Chapter 6 is an inquiry into the extent of reading involved in homework, with some reference to the amount of assistance given beforehand and the amount of follow-up.

(iv) MONOTONY OF READING

Reading is indeed a monotonous activity, so long as the reader adopts a style which he takes over from listener-behaviour. Experienced readers know that it need not be so. To them reading is often a kind of conversation with the text. As Robinson recognized, their reading suggests a flow of questions and preliminary assumptions to which they can find answers and confirmation (or contradiction) in the course of further reading. Such reading is not uninterrupted. It implies more or less frequent pauses for reflection (depending on the difficulty of the material), as well as backtracking or, more rarely, anticipation (skipping).

All that has been said so far would lead us to believe that such flexibility in reading needs to be learned. If the reader is to learn to ask questions, he must know what sort of questions it is appropriate to ask. One obvious technique is to provide the questions for him, as is done in comprehension exercises. But there are three objections to this method. First, asking the right questions is far from easy, especially if the questions are brought together at the end of the passage, or if they precede it. The questions we want the reader to ask are likely to occur at any point. Unless much thought is given to the formulation of questions, the majority of those that are set will be of a factual nature. They will tend to be of the sort that can be answered by scanning the passage to find the sentence which gives 'the answer'. Such behaviour is irrelevant to the aim of learning from reading. Second, ready-made questions may serve as examples, if they are searching questions. They are unlikely to give the pupil the incentive to ask his own, since they obviate the need to do so and positively distract him should he wish to do so. A true conversation implies the genuine participation of the listener as well as the speaker. Providing the reader with ready-made questions can produce no more than a pseudo-conversation, with the reader in the role of ventriloquist's dummy. Third, experienced teachers are aware that children rapidly learn to treat comprehension exercises for what they are: irrelevant chores that one must complete to satisfy someone else. There is little transfer to reading in subject areas.

We have experimented with two methods designed to alter the pupil's reading style. The first is the reading laboratory inquiry reported in Chapter 8. Reading laboratories include comprehension questions, but they differ from the comprehension exercise in a number of important ways. Perhaps the most significant is the emphasis placed on SQ3R. The second is reported in Chapter 9 and entails a combination of reading with group discussion. We have explored the potential of a variety of group assignments, each of which is designed to provoke a group discussion based on the text. In the course of the discussion students are led to formulate their own hypotheses and to search the text for confirmatory evidence. This technique seems to us to represent a promising approach to the teaching of reading for learning. It has been suggested that effective reading involves a process which is similar to conversation in that the reader is asking his own questions. For the independent, skilled reader, the conversation is covert. It goes on 'in his head'. In group discussion there is conversation based on the text, but the conversation is overt. And the process is far from monotonous.

(v) EDITED TEXT CAN HINDER COMPREHENSION

It would be foolish to argue that the printed word can substitute for the spoken. Indeed, it is possible that the immediacy of the oral presentation communicates to the listener in a way that cannot be achieved in an edited text. Some lecturers in institutions of higher education discover that the spoken presentation can communicate more than the circulated abstract or published text; and the seminar can be even more productive. But a discussion of the merits of spoken versus written situations may serve only to set up a false distinction. A pupil or student needs the printed word as an additional resource for learning. It is clear that this resource assumes increasing importance as study becomes more advanced. It is equally clear that it can never stand alone. For instance, it can never take the place of direct experience.

There is some support here for the recommendation contained in *A Language for Life* (DES, 1975) that learning to read effectively should be a subject-responsibility rather than the sole concern of an English department. At least this ensures that reading problems are discussed within the context of what is being studied.

(vi) TEXT IS MORE DENSE THAN UTTERANCE

Much of what has been said may be suggestive of ways of helping pupils overcome the pressure of a dense text. Our experience during the course of the project has indicated that a combination of a set reading strategy (e.g. SQ3R) and discussion approaches produces the conditions which encourage pupils to use texts with greater flexibility.

(vii) WRITER AND SPEAKER ORDER MATERIAL DIFFERENTLY

This is a complex problem. The study of learning styles is still in its infancy but it is probable that the optimal order of presentation of material is not the same for all learners. It follows that no single text will be appropriate for all learners. However, this is a problem that applies to all learning media, including practical experiment and the spoken word, as well as the written.

8 Summary

It has been suggested that:

1   There are differences between the spoken and written communication situations, and these were analysed.

2 It follows that comprehension is not transferred directly from the spoken to the written situation. Therefore, pupils require guidance which is directed towards the acquisition of reading styles, or strategies, which serve to overcome the problems posed by a written text.

3 The major obstacles to comprehension implicit in a text were described in detail. They stemmed in the main from the need, in writing, to overcome the absence of a common situation between writer and reader, and the lack of non-linguistic signals.

4 Finally, some suggestions were put forward which indicated how a reader might overcome the difficulties posed by a text.

III Reading and the teacher [1]

The arguments considered in the last section arise directly out of an analysis of reading in the light of language theory and some psychological evidence. However, it should be emphasized that taken together they constitute no more than a preliminary mapping of the field. Even if every point that is made has some basis in fact, we simply do not know what is their relative importance. We are not in a position to state clearly under what conditions a given factor is over-riding and when its effect is negligible. It seems to us to be self-evident that there is here a rich field of inquiry for specialists in psychology or in linguistics.

However, our own purpose in the present project was quite another. It was to explore the extent to which teachers used reading for learning across the curriculum, to discover how far children could successfully cope with tasks involving reading, and to establish what might be done to improve the teaching of study-reading and thereby help children to become independent learners.

The 'preliminary mapping' which we have undertaken constitutes a necessary background for our studies. While we cannot speak with certainty about the relative importance of the various factors, enough has been said to show that there is a real problem in progressing from learning to read to reading to learn. No doubt further research of a more fundamental nature can and will ultimately enable us to pinpoint the problems more exactly and to overcome them. In the meantime it was essential to engage in a programme of applied research, designed specifically to orient the progress of education in schools in the light of existing knowledge.

Information from previous research was slight and, to the knowledge of the project team, there had been no extensive empirically-based investigations in the United Kingdom. The

[1] I would like to acknowledge the collaboration of Terry Dolan in completing this section.

excellent publications emanating from the Writing across the Curriculum projects provided useful reference, and the comments of observers such as Douglas Barnes (1969) were valuable. Unfortunately, results of the survey carried out by members of the Bullock Committee were not yet available. The team had, therefore, to start by consulting teachers over a wide range of schools and subject specializations, and by carrying out a careful observational study of classroom practice.

One vital assumption made by the project team from the outset was that teachers have high regard for what children may learn from reading. Another was that this expectation would prove in many cases to be unrealistic. During the first few months of the project, members of the team spent some time in schools which had agreed to participate in the work, talking to pupils as well as teachers and librarians, and generally familiarizing ourselves with the problems as they appeared to those most directly involved. Much of the work that is reported in this volume stemmed from our desire to verify and to extend the impressions we obtained in these initial inquiries and at the same time to establish what changes might be most beneficial. It is therefore useful at this point to outline the principal findings of these pilot studies.

The following three questions were put through questionnaires and during interviews.

What and how much reading is involved in your subject?
Predictably, the amount of reading involved in lessons varied from subject to subject and from year group to year group, with considerable differences in the quantity and type of reading assigned to children. However, a few generalizations could be drawn from the many responses. Secondary teachers questioned by the team felt by and large that reading often plays an important part in their lessons, but they were reluctant to rely on it as the chief vehicle for learning. They suspected, no doubt rightly, that children in the lower years of the secondary school are not very skilled as readers. Nevertheless a sizeable vein of reading ran through many subjects, such as English and humanities. Teachers of science and mathematics generally reported that they did not consider that reading is a very reliable way to introduce their subjects. Some teachers drew attention to the fact that syllabuses are often so content-packed that they are compelled to 'feed' children with information rather than let them discover, perhaps through reading, under their own steam and at their own pace. Many stressed the transactional nature of the reading they set children, claiming that the chief purpose of reading is to enable pupils to 'do something' rather than to read 'merely for the sake of reading'. At the same time, a commonly-expressed point of view was that

reading alone constitutes one of the least effective ways for childre
acquire vital information.

*Are you always able to find suitable reading material, and if not, where
do you feel the present situation is inadequate?*

In general, teachers reported that it is not always easy to find suitable
reading material and very rare to find a single textbook which fills the
needs of a course. A frequent complaint referred to the impossibility
of finding a suitable course book to cater for the range of ability levels
in mixed-ability group situations. English teachers in particular
commented on the poverty of reading material with adult themes and
problems, presented in a simple but appealing format. Too often the
only suitable, readable books were those written for junior children,
and secondary children are reluctant to tackle such books with
enthusiasm. It is interesting to note that there was wide disagreement
among teachers about the content of some books, even when teachers
from within the same subject area were talking about the same book.
Some felt that explanations and descriptions were too wordy and
long-winded, while others considered the very same text to be terse,
cryptic and confusing. The most general complaint was of a lack of
funds to purchase sufficient supplies of up-to-date material.

*Do you feel that there are any special problems connected with the
reading specific to your subject and, if so, what are they?*

The most general problem was the specialist terminology and
vocabulary which children need to acquire. It was generally felt that
there is too little provision for a build-up of technical terminology
over the lower years in the secondary school—'too technical too
soon'. Leading children to grasp and acquire the vocabulary of a
subject is further complicated if children have a preferred meaning of
a word derived from its more common everyday usage, or when the
same word has different meanings depending on the subject, for
example 'solution', 'scale' and 'trace'.

Teachers were willing to try to teach techniques peculiar to their
own subject such as finding map references, the use of foreign
language dictionaries, reference keys and new symbols. However,
many claimed that proficiency in studying their subject depends to an
extent on the abilities and skills of another subject. Many secondary
teachers felt it a problem that they were untrained to teach children to
read and write. The teaching of literacy skills was often regarded as
the responsibility of the English department. It was therefore felt
unreasonable to expect a subject teacher to cope with a massive
syllabus at the same time as trying to develop tool-skills in the basic
subjects. Many teachers were irritated by having to spend time
correcting 'English' errors and one mathematician seemed to put his
finger on a commonly-held point of view: 'in the eyes of children,
mathematics is concerned with numbers. When there is a lot of

reading involved the children complain that words are English and English is not mathematics!'

Several teachers from across the subject range mentioned that, be it through lack of interest, motivation or ability, many children seem able to cope with reading at a decoding level but are quite unable to comprehend beyond a literal level. Teachers in general confessed that they do not really know what to do about this situation. The strategy of one mathematician seemed widespread. He felt ill-equipped to assist children who 'read' but did not 'understand' and his answer was to reproduce orally the mathematics contained in text in a simpler way, using the spoken word. By his own admission he was dodging the fundamental issue: in bypassing the need to deal with texts he was only delaying the problem both for himself and for the children.

Such then are the problems as they appeared to us at the outset, to which the present volume is addressed.

3

Comprehension and Comprehension Tests

Eric Lunzer, Maurice Waite and Terry Dolan

I Is reading comprehension unitary or manifold?

The effective use of reading calls for a good deal more than the ability to substitute the spoken form of words for their written form as one goes through the relevant print. Indeed there are those who maintain that effective reading requires not only the suppression of overt vocalization or lip-movements but also a more or less conscious elimination of covert vocalization or reading 'in one's head' (cf. Smith, 1973, pp. 77ff.). The present writers do not subscribe to the second of these principles, principally because the evidence for speed-reading (reading without covert vocalization) is far from conclusive (Gibson and Levin, 1975, pp. 342ff.). But it is clear that effective reading depends on comprehension in the first instance, and in the second on the application of appropriate study-skills.

The term 'study skills' as it is generally used is an all-embracing concept, and includes an analysis of the various modes of reading which the student can call upon when using some particular text, be it a book or an article or a hand-out. These modes: skimming, scanning, receptive reading and reflective reading (sometimes called 'critical reading'), are evidently procedures which need to be deployed effectively as a necessary condition for getting the most benefit from the act of reading. But the term 'study skills' also extends to such questions as how to take notes, how long and when to study, how to use works of reference, how to write an essay, and so on. This chapter will not touch on these wider issues, some of which are more relevant to the post-secondary student, while others are dealt with more fully in other publications.[1] Its brief is limited to an analysis of what is involved in reading for comprehension.

Comprehension means understanding. But there are at least two levels at which understanding may operate. At the lower level, it is sufficient that the reader satisfies himself that the matter which he

---

[1] The observations recorded in Chapter 7 are, however, very relevant to the consideration of note-taking at the secondary-school level.

reads makes some sort of sense. To do this he must know the meaning of most of the words and he must see that they hang together grammatically and conceptually. A reader who is operating at this level would accept and pass over

1   The Bedouins were a nomadic people who built many fine cities out of bricks and wood.

just as he would

2   The Bedouins were a nomadic people who built no cities.

or

3   The Greeks were a highly civilized people who built fine temples out of marble.

But he would reject

4   The Greeks built fine temples out of water.

or

5   The built fine Greeks out temples marble of.

since 4 makes no conceptual sense and 5 makes no grammatical sense.

This level of understanding is important and there are children who in much of their reading do not achieve even so much. But it is clearly far from sufficient to enable the reader to learn from what he has read, and the chief concern of this project is the use of reading for learning. To learn by reading, a student needs to penetrate beyond the verbal forms of the text to the underlying ideas. He must compare these ideas both with what he already knows and with each other, so as to pick out what is essential and what is new, and thereby alter his previous conception in line with this novel information.

These last two sentences may be taken as a definition of comprehension:[1] *to penetrate beyond the verbal forms of text to the underlying ideas, to compare these with what one already knows and also with one another, to pick out what is essential and new, to revise one's previous conceptions.* But none of these events is observable. How then are we to know as teachers and observers that comprehension has in fact taken place in the pupil? Whatever our own views about the nature of the learning process, teachers and educators are indebted to those workers in the behaviourist tradition, people like Skinner, Carroll, Bloom and Gagné,[2] in that they constantly alert us to the need to search for operational criteria of whatever it is we wish to promote. Operational criteria are such as can be formulated in terms of behaviour that is directly observable. In the context of education, these are termed *behavioural objectives.* To establish whether a given pupil has indeed understood a given passage, we need to set him one or more of a set of tasks: can he tell the meaning of the words in the passage? if a word is ambiguous

[1] This definition would need to be augmented if one wished to include what is needed for literary appreciation.
[2] See, for example, Skinner (1938, 1959), Carroll (1971), Gagné (1970) and, especially, Bloom, Hastings and Madaus (1971).

taken by itself, can he derive a particular meaning from its appearance in context? can he separate out the main themes in a paragraph from subsidiary points or examples? can he translate into direct terms ideas that may have been presented by metaphor? can he make such inferences as are essential to an intelligent reading?

Each of these last questions, and others like them, enable us to construct one or more 'comprehension items', based on the reading of a suitable passage. The answers that we obtain from our pupils will then constitute an operational criterion of their comprehension. If the passage has been well chosen and the questions were well devised, we can then make inferences about the pupil's ability to deal with other passages, those that he encounters in the course of his school work. What we have done is to translate a psychological or pedagogical goal (comprehension as defined) into a set of behavioural objectives.

Such is the rationale underlying the use of comprehension tests as a measure of effective reading. It is open to a number of *caveats*, and we will return to these at the end of the chapter. Anticipating, we may note in passing that the test situation is not the same as the general learning situation. The questions that we put will inevitably influence the behaviour of our pupil-reader. It was this last awareness which determined the writers in their choice of the particular kind of test used in the present study.

Its purpose is chiefly to inquire whether the several tasks which may be exemplified in comprehension-test items derive from distinct skills or subskills or whether comprehension is a unitary ability.

Both views are inherently credible. On the one hand one must acknowledge that it is not the same thing to decide, say, what is important or significant in a passage and to select among a number of different meanings of a word which one it is that is operative in a given context. If the same psychological processes are involved—formation of hypotheses, comparison of elements, verification—at the very least it must be acknowledged that these are adduced for different ends and in differing orders and with differing contents. On the other hand, it is clear that whatever native endowments and whatever experiences are conducive to hypothesis formation and retention, to comparisons and to verifications, must be common in large degree to the successful performance of any comprehension task. The question is therefore twofold: Is the manner of their deployment in different connections sufficiently distinct to allow of their independent evaluation? And are they sufficiently distinct to warrant the conclusion that a course of instruction (or a set of experiences) specifically designed to promote one of these will not be generalized to any of the others?

Both questions are open to empirical testing. Their importance is this. If it is indeed the case that the various tasks that one might set in a comprehension test derive from distinct subskills, it follows that teachers would be well-advised to establish which of these are deficient in their pupils so as to institute appropriate individualized remediation programmes. If this is not the case, then any attempt at the differential testing of comprehension is simply a waste of time, and any programme based on the results of such testing will probably be less beneficial than a more general programme.

The inquiry to be described is addressed to the first question: Can one reliably measure these several subskills? If the answer turns out to be negative—as indeed it does, with minor qualifications—then the second falls to the ground. For it would make little sense to test remedial programmes based on a meaningless assessment or on one that is quite unreliable.

II Background

It must be acknowledged at the outset that this is by no means the first contribution to this issue. However, the data that were to hand when we started our investigations were by no means conclusive. Also, the weight of opinion inclined to the first hypothesis, that comprehension involves a multiplicity of subskills, and such too was our own initial conviction.

By far the most ambitious study in this area is that conducted by Davis (1968). Davis constructed two forms of a 96-item test, each comprising eight subtests designed to measure distinct subskills. There were therefore twelve items in each form for each skill. Combination of the two forms produced twenty-four items per subtest and 192 in all. The subjects were 988 college students. The scale of this undertaking and the care in its execution command respect. Davis's own analysis of his data led him to conclude that he could reliably distinguish four skills rather than eight, and these he identified as: (1) identifying word meanings, (2) drawing inferences, (3) identifying the writer's technique and recognizing the mood of a passage, (4) finding answers to questions. A subsequent analysis of Davis's data by Thorndike (1971) produced only three factors, of which the first accounted for much the greater portion of the covariance while the other two did not admit of any clear-cut psychological interpretation.[1]

However, Spearritt (1972) re-analysed the same set of data using more sophisticated procedures and again found four correlated factors. These were similar to those originally described by Davis, except for the last, which was identified as 'the ability to follow the structure of a passage', this being quite different from 'answering questions'. It should be noted that correlations between factors were high, ranging from .75–.93, but generally lower than the reliabilities of the original tests.

[1] See A Note on Statistics, p. 314.

Davis's study is the largest and most careful, but there have been several others. Lennon (1962) gives a summary of twelve of these, and his work is further discussed by Farr (1969). Six of these twelve studies produced only a single general factor. Also, there is little agreement among the remainder as to the precise nature of the additional factors which they obtained.

Nevertheless, partly because of the weight attached to the work of Davis, and partly no doubt due to the attractiveness of the subskill hypothesis, it is this view which has tended to prevail among educationists (cf. Melnik and Merritt, 1972). Because it is typical of the thoughtful analyses of reading based on this assumption, and also because it has been particularly influential, it is interesting to note that several reading subskills are suggested in a publication by the New York City Board of Education, *Reading in the Subject Areas, Grades 7–8–9* (1964). These are shown in Table 3.1 (p. 42). The central items in this list, those headed comprehension, are most relevant to our present interest.

Readers who are concerned to explore the background further may wish to refer to the review provided by Farr. It should be noted that none of the previous studies can be taken as conclusive, nor is it easy to draw any inferences from the majority about the reading of school-age children, since they are based on data from adult readers.

III Design of the inquiry

1 Subjects

Nearly all of the data to be reported were obtained from a sample of 257 children in four primary schools. They were tested half-way through the first term of their last year, and were therefore aged 10–11 years. Two of these schools were in Nottinghamshire and two in Derbyshire. Taken as a whole, these schools formed a fairly representative sample of the kinds of school one would most often encounter in the east-Midland region, and the teachers in these schools used a diversity of teaching methods. Above all, they were interested in the work of the project, many attended our study groups, and all were willing to collaborate.[1] The 257 children represent the total population at the selected year group in these schools, less children who were absent on one or other of the testing sessions, and less those children whose reading level was so poor as to make any testing of little value.

The original intention was to obtain initial validation for a test suitable for top-class primary school pupils, and later to construct

[1] It should perhaps be added that obtaining a truly representative normative sample would have been very much a secondary consideration, nor does the present volume include a set of norms for the tests used in this inquiry.

Table 3.1   Reading in the Subject Areas, Grades 7–8–9
(from Melnik and Merritt, 1972: 23, in a chapter by Sidney J. Rauch;
reprinted from *Curriculum Bulletin No. 6* by permission of the Board of
Education of the City of New York.)

Reading skills	Language arts	Social studies	Science	Maths	Industrial arts
Word recognition					
1 recognize basic sight words	x				
2 use phonetic analysis	x				
3 use structural analysis	x				
4 use contextual clues for word meaning	x	x	x	x	x
5 use dictionary to check meaning	x	x	x	x	x
Comprehension					
1 understand word and sentence meaning	x	x	x	x	x
2 find main idea and related details	x	x	x	x	x
3 organize and classify facts	x	x	x	x	x
4 perceive sequence of ideas	x	x	x	x	x
5 draw inferences and conclusions	x	x	x	x	
6 understand problems	x	x	x	x	x
7 form judgements	x	x	x	x	
8 predict outcomes	x		x	x	
9 read critically— distinguishing fact from opinion	x	x	x		
10 read for appreciation	x				
11 understand relationships	x	x	x	x	x
12 follow directions	x	x	x	x	x
Work study					
1 understand parts of a book	x	x	x	x	
2 understand the index of a text	x	x	x	x	
3 use of the dictionary	x	x	x	x	
4 use of the encyclopedia	x	x	x		

5 understand library techniques	x	x	x		
6 interpret maps	x	x	x	x	
7 understand charts	x	x	x	x	x
8 interpret graphs	x	x	x	x	
9 understand diagrams	x	x	x	x	x
10 adjust reading rate—skimming	x	x	x	x	x
11 select and evaluate information	x	x	x	x	x
12 use techniques of retention and recall	x	x	x	x	x

(The x under each subject area indicates that the reading skill is relevant to that particular subject.)

similar tests for use with pupils in the mid-secondary year groups. The data obtained from this first study were found to be such as to reduce the importance of a similar undertaking for the secondary level, having regard to the broad objectives of the project as a whole as described in Chapter 1. Such a programme remains a possibility for the future, but it is not seen by us as having a high priority. It should be added that the tests to be discussed were found to yield satisfactory discrimination even at the fourth-year secondary level, and were therefore used as additional measures in the SRA experiment which is described in Chapter 8.

2 Tests and procedures

Four separate tests were constructed with a view to fulfilling the two main aims of this inquiry. These were (1) to resolve, if possible, the issue raised in section I (i.e. is comprehension a composite of a multiplicity of distinct subskills) and (2) to make available to teachers a new and more challenging form of comprehension test than any that is currently available. These tests were developed over a period of a year, mainly by Maurice Waite, a junior-school headteacher of considerable experience, but in consultation with the project team as a whole and also with the many teachers who took part in our study groups and in the extensive trials that were found to be necessary.

Each of the tests has two distinctive features: it consists of an extended passage followed by nearly thirty questions, and the questions themselves are divided into eight subgroups corresponding to certain hypothesized subskills. The first of these features may be defended both on scientific and on pedagogical grounds. The study of an extended passage corresponds closely to the task which a pupil will face when engaged on topic work (cf. Chapter 6) or in preparation and revision. Such a test should therefore be more valid (*prima facie*). At the same time it was felt that to ask pupils to think hard about the content of a single passage in a number of ways is to provide a challenging and educationally relevant experience. The same cannot be said of a series of disconnected short paragraphs, each followed by a short question, or of a test that can be answered by repeatedly scanning the passage to 'find the answers'. The second feature, i.e. grouping of questions, was of course essential to the inquiry. Moreover, if the result had turned out to be positive, the profile which emerged would constitute a diagnostic tool.

In describing the eight question types below, it is useful to refer to the relevant instances in the first test, *Grieg*, which appears in full on pp. 46–8. In addition, the reader may wish to refer to the nearest corresponding category in the comprehension section of the New York List shown in Table 3.1 (p. 42). For greater convenience, the initialized headings only will be used in the remainder of this chapter.

1 *Word meaning* (W) (Item 1; NYL 1)
2 *Words in context* (WIC) Deriving the appropriate meaning of an ambiguous word from the context in which it appears. (Item 2; NYL 1)
3 *Literal comprehension* (L) Finding the answers to questions when these can be obtained directly by reference to a phrase or a sentence in the text. (Items 3, 4, 5, 6, 9; NYL 1, 2)
4 *Drawing inferences from single strings* (ISS) A *string* is an uninterrupted sequence of words, usually a phrase or a short sentence. Questions in this category require the reader to draw an inference from such a sequence as opposed to deriving its literal meaning. (Items 7, 8; NYL 5, 7)
5 *Drawing inferences from multiple strings* (IMS) These tasks are similar to ISS, save that the necessary information for making the inference cannot be found by reference to one phrase but must be deduced from a comparison of two or more facts appearing in different parts of the text. (Items 10, 12, 13; NYL 3, 5, 7, 11)
6 *Interpretation of metaphor* (M) These questions require the reader to show an understanding or appreciation of meanings that are given indirectly by use of metaphor. (Items 15a, 15b; NYL 7)
7 *Finding salients or main ideas* (S) Self-explanatory (Items 17, 19; NYL 2, 3)
8 *Forming judgements* (J) This category was originally thought of under the heading of 'evaluation'. However, while the items clearly require the reader to go beyond the text, he is not asked to make a value-judgement about the worthwhileness of the passage or of its presentation but rather to offer an intelligent interpretation of ideas contained in the text or implied by it in the light of his own knowledge of related matters. (Items 11, 14, 16, 18, 20; NYL 6, 7)

While most of the NYL categories do have some counterpart in ours (the exception being categories that are specific to a particular kind of passage), the correspondence is far from one to one. This is deliberate. The NYL categorization, and others like it, seemed to correspond to differences in the content of questions rather than differences in the thinking processes required in the reader. If there are differences in process (and this is precisely the point at issue in the present inquiry), then many of the NYL items seem to call for different mixes of the same set. The present categorization was conceived of as partly hierarchical (cf. L, ISS, IMS), and partly corresponding to very clear differentiations (cf. W, WIC, M). If there are different subskills, then a categorization like the present one is more likely to uncover them.

The decision to use four texts was not taken *a priori*. It was hoped initially that a single test, *Grieg*, would produce reliable results as well as a reliable differentiation of the relevant subskills. Subsequent analysis of the data yielded by a trial sample of 199 children (not included in the final sample) showed minimal evidence of differentiation. However, such negative evidence could not be accepted at face value: it could be due either to the paucity of items in any one category, unavoidable in relation to a single passage, or to the simplicity of the passage itself (*Grieg* is a prosaic sort of piece), or to both. The second passage, *Brighty*, adapted from the Scott Foresman *Reading Systems Programme*, was more demanding in style. Results obtained from nearly 300 children (again not included in the final sample) produced just three factors, only one of which loaded on items from both tests. At this point, it was argued that the marked contrast between the two passages (one factual, the other literary) might operate in such a way as to mask the differentiation into item types for which evidence was sought. The third and fourth tasks were therefore constructed to parallel each of the first two—in content, in interest level, and in format. *Alistair*, like *Brighty*, was adapted from the Scott Foresman Programme. *Jane* tells the story of the childhood of an imaginary female painter, a tale which bears a striking resemblance to the boyhood of Grieg! It was specially written by the team, with one eye on the passage which it was designed to parallel.

None of these tests was easy to construct. In each case the items went through successive revisions, following on a series of trial runs conducted with samples of 12–15 children. These numbers were deliberately kept small to allow for discussion of items with the children as well as their teachers. In the case of the first test, *Grieg*, no fewer than nine revisions were made before the test was considered satisfactory, taking into account facility levels, ease of marking, adequacy of distractors, and so on. By way of example, item 1 (w) initially took the form of open-ended questions: *Write the meaning of — in your own words*. This produced many problems, including the child who wrote: 'I no it but I carnt rite it'! The experience gained in the construction of items for the first two tests proved beneficial in producing the others. While no fewer than ten versions were made for *Grieg*, and eight for *Brighty*, *Alistair* went through only five versions and *Jane* was produced in three.

Each of the tests was designed to be completed by nearly all children in the space of one lesson (35–40 minutes). Extra time is allowed if required. The tests are not timed.

3 Grieg

We present this test in full to enable the reader to assess the adequacy of our claim to have produced useful measures and potentially discriminating items. The second passage *Brighty* (but not the test) is shown in the Appendix (p. 70). All of the passages, tests and instructions for scoring are available from the writers.

Grieg[1]

If you draw a line from the Shetland Islands to the north of Scotland, across the North Sea, it comes to the town of Bergen in Norway. Bergen is a fishing port, with a big harbour full of boats. You can see the masts showing above the roofs from every part of the town. Down on the quay the fishermen spread out their nets to dry. Close by is the fish market. The whole town smells of the sea, and tar, and fish.

Two hundred years ago a man sailed across the North Sea to Bergen from Scotland. His name was Alexander Greig. He liked Bergen, and made up his mind to settle there. But he found that the Norwegians mispronounced his name. So he changed Greig to Grieg, and then they said it the right way.

Alexander Grieg began sending lobsters to Scotland for people to eat. It was not long before he became rich, and the family moved into a big house. Soon the Griegs felt they were Norwegians rather than Scotsmen. Alexander's son and grandson both married Norwegian girls.

This grandson (another Alexander) was the father of the composer. He too lived in Bergen, and he carried on the family business. Both he and his wife were fond of music. Alexander could not play himself, but his wife was a fine pianist. She even took part in concerts in Bergen.

After they were married they set up house near the harbour. They had five children, three daughters and two sons. Edward was the younger of the two boys. He was born a little over a hundred years ago. He had large blue eyes and thick fair hair, and was a dreamy-looking little boy.

Edward loved looking at the boats in the harbour. He used to walk along the quays among the nets and the baskets of fish. Often he watched the boats put out to sea and vanish beyond the horizon. If the weather was wet, he had to stay indoors instead. One rainy day he thought he would like to try and play the piano. He started by playing one note, and then another with it to make a chord. All the time he listened very carefully to the sound. At first he only played with one hand. Then he found he got a richer sound by using both hands together.

His mother was very glad to hear him playing. Because she loved music

[1] Gough, C. (1960) *Boyhood of Great Composers* London: Oxford University Press

so much, she had always hoped that her children would be musical. When he was six she decided he was old enough for piano lessons. She taught him herself. She was a strict and careful teacher. Edward had to practise a great many scales and exercises each day. He found these boring and used to hurry over them: it was much more fun to play tunes. But he knew his mother always listened while he practised. She used to call out from the kitchen when he played a wrong note.

Once a week friends came to the Griegs' house to play and sing together. There were very few concerts in Bergen, so people had to make their own music. Edward's mother played the piano at these musical evenings. Edward was too young to join it, but he sat in a corner and listened. He heard a great deal of music in this way.

When Edward was nine his grandfather died. The old man had been very important in the town, so he had a big funeral. His parents took Edward to it. An army band played a special march, and Edward found the slow, sad music very moving. In fact he remembered it for the rest of his life.

The corresponding test was as follows (entries in the right-hand margin denote subscale, F and r_{it} as in Table 3.2, p. 50).

1 Underline one meaning from those on the right which is nearest in meaning. *Use the story to check your answers.*

(a) vanish	appear, fade, faint, end, disappear.	W, 90, 32
(b) composer	conductor, pianist, bandsman, writer, violinist.	W, 61, 34
(c) mispronounced	wrote wrongly, missed, spoke wrongly, made fun of, spelt wrongly.	W, 79, 48
(d) quay	landing-stage, sea-shore, port, goods-yard, beach.	W, 35, 32

2 Now do the same for these words as they are used in the story:

(a) exercises	body-movements, practice-tests, stretching, running, skipping.	WIC, 45, 28
(b) chord	length of string, thin rope, piano keys, high notes, notes played together.	WIC, 49, 45
(c) scales	climbs, musical term, weighing instrument, the covering on the skin of a fish.	WIC, 56, 45

3 Where is Bergen?	L, 81, 33
4 Who sent lobsters to Scotland?	L, 91, 37
5 Why did grandfather have a big funeral?	L, 72, 46
6 Where in the town was the Griegs' house?	L, 53, 44
7 In what year did Alexander Greig sail from Scotland?	ISS, 52, 52
8 How did Edward know that his mother listened whenever he practised?	ISS, 63, 55
9 What did Alexander Greig change his name to?	L, 75, 53
10 What do you think Edward did for a living when he grew up?	IMS, 71, 54

11 There was a smell of tar in the town. What would tar   J, 18, 33
    be used for?

12 What did Edward's father do for a living?   IMS, 45, 35

13 Not all men in Bergen could be fishermen. Name two   IMS, 46, 51
    other jobs, apart from fisherman and musician, that a
    man might have done to earn a living.

14 How is it possible to draw a line across the North Sea? J, 20, 50

15 *Use your own words* to explain the meaning of:
    (a) 'He found he got a richer sound'   M, 28, 53
    (b) 'Edward found the slow, sad music very moving'   M, 16, 45

16 Which *three* of the following fish would the fishermen J, 65, 48
    of Bergen *not* be able to catch? Underline those you
    choose: cod, plaice, pike, roach, herring, trout.

17 Which *four* words from the following list do you think S, 58, 57
    are most important to the story? Underline the four
    you choose: Bergen, concert, teacher, piano, harbour,
    Scotland, funeral, Grieg, horizon, child.

18 Edward's mother was a good teacher and the boy grew   J, 54, 54
    up to be a famous man. From what you know already
    and from what you have read in the story, decide
    which two of the following statements are true and
    underline them:
    (a) Some famous musicians have had good teachers.
    (b) Good teachers make all their pupils famous.
    (c) Hard practice makes all pupils famous.
    (d) Many famous musicians did not need a good
        teacher.

19 Using what you have learnt from the story about   S, 50, 54
    Grieg's home and family, underline *three* sentences
    from the six below which best seem to fit a story with
    the title 'A Winter Evening at the Griegs' Home'.
    (a) Edward sat alone in the house with nothing to do.
    (b) The room appeared cosy and warm in the light of
        the oil-lamps.
    (c) The house was soon to be filled with the sound of
        music.
    (d) Edward's mother was baking in the kitchen while
        the rest of the family sat reading.
    (e) The breeze from the window was very pleasant.
    (f) The Grieg family sat by the log fire awaiting the
        arrival of their friends.

20 From the following, pick out the *two* things you think J, 74, 54
    had most to do with Edward learning to play the
    piano.
    (a) the weather
    (b) an interested mother
    (c) a rich family
    (d) grandfather selling lobsters
    (e) the beautiful countryside and the boats in the
        harbour
    (f) a love of music

IV Data analysis

1 Reliability of the four tests

Table 3.2 (p. 50) provides a breakdown of the facility levels and discriminatory efficiency for each of the items in the four tests. Where an item is either right or wrong, the F index is simply the percentage of boys and girls who chose the right answer. When two or more answers are called for, the value for F has been averaged. For a test to be effective, these values should not be very high or very low: to know that a pupil passes on an item which is passed by nearly everyone else tells us very little. (And vice versa for difficult items.) Not all items need have an F of 50, but the majority should fall between 20 and 80, as they do—and the more items with F values of 35–65, the better the discrimination of the test.

But it is not sufficient for an item to discriminate absolutely; it should also be relevant in the sense that those children who pass the item should by and large be better at comprehension than those who fail. The index of discrimination (in this restricted sense) used here is the correlation (r) of the item with the total score for the test of which it is a part. It is clearly an index of the homogeneity of the test. Those rs which fall much below .40 are unsatisfactory. Items with very low or very high Fs rarely achieve a high r. This is inevitable, but a few may be tolerated since they increase the range over which the test can be expected to discriminate. Further, in the present case at any rate, we would not wish to have too many rs very high, i.e. above .6. This is because, hopefully, the tests should also provide differential discrimination for the eight subareas. The table shows that any failure to do so is not due to over-high values of r. Some are too low, but overall the values of F and r testify to the care taken in item-development.

It is interesting to note some trends in these F levels. W and L items tend to have high F levels and the Fs for L, ISS and IMS items tend to be in that order (from easy to difficult). This is a built-in feature of these tests, and validates the hierarchy in the categorization of items. But the gradation is far from perfect. We will return to this point in section V. One may note that even seemingly easy WIC items have only intermediate F levels: many children are prepared to argue that when the young Grieg was practising scales, he was dealing with the covering on the skin of a fish, presumably because Bergen is said to be a fishing town. Few teachers will be surprised, but those who care will not be happy. This is what the project is about. The very low F levels for M items in the upper-junior age range testifies to the difficulty of any form of abstraction and its affinity with Piaget's 'formal reasoning', these being issues which the first writer has discussed elsewhere (Lunzer, 1960, 1965, 1978). Finally J items can be pegged at any level, depending on what pre-testing knowledge they call for.

Table 3.2   The four tests: summary of item analysis (n = 257)

	Grieg		Brighty		Jane		Alistair	
	F^1	r_{it}*	F	r_{it}	F	r_{it}	F	r_{it}
W	90	32	85	37	84	48	74	38
	61	34	51	28	47	55	74	53
	79	48	89	41	77	62	61	58
	35	32			54	35		
WIC	45	28	29	30	64	52	64	47
	49	45	21	21	50	55	30	26
	56	45	58	24	40	49	52	52
L	81	33	79	27	84	36	79	30
	91	37	53	42	80	45	52	60
	72	46	72	49	96	32	76	44
	53	44	77	50	52	35	81	57
	75	53	64	59	73	56	57	53
ISS	52	52	25	31	65	44	44	40
	63	55	30	52	75	52	9	25
			47	38			47	22
			55	39			33	14
IMS	71	54	35	47	33	56	52	35
	45	35	49	72	44	60	54	74
	46	51	40	21	54	67	38	31
			58	50			63	48
			60	43			25	26
			16	41			6	35
M	28	53	47	49	46	42	28	41
	16	45	53	65	21	36	54	57
			39	68			26	50
			29	20			25	17
S	58	57	69	67	67	40	64	56
	50	54	45	71	54	21	46	68
J	18	33	52	39	17	31	66	50
	20	50	23	21	39	61	65	39
	65	48	51	33	78	53	72	54
	54	54			59	53		
	74	54			77	55		

[1] F, facility, i.e. % correct answers
* r_{it}, correlation of item success with score on total test, decimals omitted

The data shown in Table 3.3 (p. 52) relate to the reliabilities of these tests as wholes. Entries in the first column are estimates of reliability based on the internal consistency data given in Table 3.2. The remaining values are taken from the tests administered to the pupils in the course of the SRA study reported in Chapter 8. The sample was a little smaller (n = 212) than the main sample of the present study (n = 257), but its composition was otherwise similar.

One may assume that the alpha values give a slight overestimate, since they include an element of specificity inherent in the fact that all the items in any one test relate to a single passage. *Alistair* is marginally less good than the other three tests. But all have parallel-test reliabilities (the most demanding and satisfactory criterion) of around .80. This is a shade low for a satisfactory measure. Combining two tests raises the reliability of measurement to .86 or more, which is acceptable. Combining all four tests produces a correlation of .89 with the Edinburgh Reading Scales. It would not be easy to raise this figure (by extending the testing and/or refining the items), and it is one which compares favourably with most of the best existing tests of reading.

The last figure is also a cross-validation index, since the Edinburgh Scales were constructed on very different principles and standardized on a quite different (Scottish) population.

2 The search for subskills

There are a number of techniques which might help to determine whether all of the tests in a battery are measuring the same thing or whether they indicate more than one ability, aptitude or skill. Factor analysis will generally be the first choice, since this technique was devised with this specific end in view. Factor analysis does two things. It provides a convenient summary of a set of correlations between tests, showing how they cluster, i.e. which tests go most nearly with which other tests. When the number of measures is at all large (say eight or more), this cannot be done by inspection. Factor analysis also affords a method whereby the performance of each individual on every one of the measures can be expressed more summarily by calculating his performance on each of the underlying factors. Obviously, this is helpful only if the following two conditions are fulfilled: the number of factors must be appreciably less than the number of tests from which they are derived; and the nature of these factors is such that they admit of a ready psychological interpretation.

The first condition is largely assured by the mathematical procedures that are used in the derivation of factors. But the character of the original data constitutes a limiting constraint: if the original measures are really quite disparate, they will not produce a small set of factors, save by chance. If the factors are mainly due to

Table 3.3 Reliability of the four tests

	Cronbach-Alpha	Brighty	Jane	Alistair	G+B	J+A	G+B+J+A	Edinburgh
Grieg	83	79	79	73	(94)	81	(90)	81
Brighty	83	—	81	78	(95)	85	(93)	83
Jane	85	—	—	74	85	(92)	(91)	83
Alistair	84	—	—	—	80	(94)	(90)	79
G+B	90	—	—	—	—	88	(97)	86
J+A	91	—	—	—	—	—	(97)	86
G+B+J+A	—	—	—	—	—	—	—	89

Decimals omitted from all correlation values.
n = 257 for values in the first column
n = 212 for all the other columns
Bracketed values are of limited worth, since they are 'contaminated'. (They represent correlations of half or quarter scores with whole scores.)

chance, two things are likely to happen: they will not account for much of the covariance (or communality) of the original data (as indicated in the matrix of their correlations—see A Note on Statistics, p. 319), and they will not admit of any psychological interpretation.

This brings us to the second condition. The psychological interpretation of factors depends on three things: on how well one can 'read' the pattern in a table like Table 3.4 (this is fairly trivial, and mainly a matter of practice); on the strength of one's psychological insight; and above all on the adequacy of the data themselves. The latter is a matter of the acumen which one has exercised in selecting the original measures. Generally speaking, factor analysis is most powerful when (a) it is used to test an initial hypothesis about the way in which the measures should group, and (b) two or more related measures have been included which were deliberately designed so as to point up each of the factors one is looking for—on the assumption that the initial hypothesis is correct. The rest is standard scientific procedure. To the extent that the factors are found as predicted, they confirm the hypothesis; to the extent that they do not, they indicate that it must be revised or even abandoned.

Mention was made of chance. The operation of chance or of errors of measurement in educational and psychological testing is a topic which often receives less than adequate treatment in introductory textbooks. This is because the writers of such texts are generally much better at noting the peculiarities of trees than they are at characterizing the configuration of woods. For the present it may be sufficient to note that it is not easy to separate out the effect of the following:

(a) errors in scoring and transcribing (i.e. human error which can be minimized but cannot be eliminated);
(b) variability of assessment both within and between markers (wherever the scoring is not fully constrained or mechanical);
(c) occasion-to-occasion variability of performance (the pupil may vary in his concentration at any given moment);
(d) occasion-to-occasion variation in the accessibility of strategies to the pupil (there is often more than one way of tackling a particular question and one may be quicker and less error-prone than another; an individual may for any reason hit upon one of these rather than another, even though he has the necessary knowledge to do either);
(e) item specificity (this is related to (d): however careful one may be in item construction, it is inevitable that some items will more readily evoke the strategies one hopes to measure than others);
(f) between-individual variance in the strategy-evoking potential of differing items (some feature of any given item may for any

reason suggest a way of answering the question to one individual but not to another).

Since none of these effects can be controlled for (although by the exercise of due care, several can be minimized), and none can be eliminated, they are all confounded in what is termed error-variance or chance effects.

Equally germane to the present discussion, the effects of (d), (e) and (f) will tend to be much greater in a test of reading comprehension than in a test of mathematical aptitude. This is because mathematical performance relies heavily on the availability of algorithms or routines or drills which the good student must know and which any student can be taught. To a greater or lesser extent, the form of the question evokes the routine.[1] This is why tests of mathematics can aspire to reliabilities of the order of .95 while one is more than satisfied with a reliability of .90 in a test of reading comprehension. It is also why one is often satisfied with a reliability of .70 or less in a test of attitude. It also explains why the average intelligent human being is better at the interpretation of text than even the best and most elaborate computer programs (at the time of writing), while quite run-of-the-mill programs are daily constructed to solve complex mathematical problems more swiftly and more surely than any computational genius.

Further narrowing this discussion, all of the effects (c) to (f) are compounded in the measure that the items in a test are inter-dependent. This obtains in some measure in our own tests, since all of the questions in each test bear on the reading of a single long passage. We have deliberately chosen to make a sacrifice in the reliability of our measures in the interest of enhancing their validity.

There are several methods of factor analysis. But given a sound body of original test data, they usually lead to quite similar results when one takes the final step of psychological interpretation. The method chosen for the present inquiry is that of Kaiser (1970), which yields an interpretation in terms of factors which are oblique, i.e. the factors themselves are correlated, and sometimes strongly correlated with one another. There are three reasons for this choice:

1   Such factors are generally easier to interpret because the relation between each and a few selected tests is clearer.
2   Such factors are more psychologically credible. One might expect literal interpretation to be distinct from inference, but one would not expect the two to be unrelated.
3   We are impressed that the same statistician who was mainly

---

[1] This is also the greatest pitfall in the construction of mathematical tests: the temptation to over-rely on items which are maximally reliable but which make a minimal call on mathematical inventiveness.

responsible for the popularization of *varimax*, formerly the most popular orthogonal procedure (leading to uncorrelated or independent factors), has gone on twenty years later to perfect the present technique, which he deems superior. Also two of us have had extensive experience of both techniques and are able to confirm the efficiency of Kaiser's 'Little Jiffy' from the standpoint of an unsophisticated user.[1]

So much by way of necessary introduction. In seeking to test whether there are several skills of comprehension, the procedure described in section III aspires to the ideal mentioned on p. 53. Each of the four tests produces a subscale total on each of the eight putative subskills. If the hypothesis of their distinctiveness is to be upheld, the matrix of their intercorrelations should produce eight factors, which may however be correlated with one another.

As already noted, the table of correlations cannot be interpreted by simple inspection. There are thirty-two measures. While it is not worth reproducing, it should be noted that the level of correlation between pairs of measures is similar to the values of r_{it} in Table 3.2, save that their dispersion is smaller: there are fewer .8s or .7s and also fewer .3s and .2s. Most of the correlations are 'moderate', in the range of .4–.6.

The results of the factor analysis are shown in Table 3.4 (p. 56). The matrix yielded six significant factors.[2] These have been 'rotated' for maximum clarity of interpretation, using Kaiser's criterion (which is mathematical and objective). The intercorrelations of these factors are shown in Table 3.5 (p. 57).

Because Table 3.4 is still quite indigestible, its main features have been summarized in Table 3.6 (p. 57). It is clear that there is no support for the subskill hypothesis. The most that can be said is that (a) two of the factors relate more or less exclusively to *Brighty* and *Alistair* and two others to *Grieg* and *Jane*, and (b) neither w nor s have loadings on the first and most general factor. But the correlations among the factors themselves are such as to weaken even the most putative interpretation: factors 1–4 form a cluster, factor 5 is simply a less potent (more specific) contributor to the same hierarchy, and the independence of factor 6 defies any interpretation. We would offer it as a general rule for the interpretation of oblique factors that the greater the correlations between factors, the stronger should be the psychological rationale for identifying their separate meanings. The distinction between language and operativity found by Lunzer, Wilkinson and Dolan (1976) is a positive example of the application of this rule. The present results are a negative example.

[1] Cf. Lunzer, Wilkinson and Dolan (1976): Lunzer, Dolan and Wilkinson (1976).
[2] Factors having eigen values greater than 1. Any further factors would account for less of the communality than the average original measurement!

Table 3.4 Factor analysis, four tests

		1	2	3	4	5	6
Grieg	W	−13	−07	93*	02	01	−00
	WIC	49*	16	15	−11	−09	10
	L	08	05	19	09	52*	−04
	ISS	26	01	31	−02	20	−02
	IMS	95*	−17	−21	−04	20	07
	M	29	17	08	28	−25*	02
	S	23	11	09	06	−11	44*
	J	45*	05	31*	−06	01	16*
Brighty	W	−15	−01	03	82*	05	08
	WIC	07	−09	33	44*	−28*	−21*
	L	15	09	−02	50*	15	−14*
	ISS	48*	26	25	−39*	−10	−29*
	IMS	40	38	−04	−13	−05	−07
	M	70*	04	−13	12	−07	−04
	S	09	81*	−11	00	01	−01
	J	40	82*	27	−16	03	09
Jane	W	00	−03	83*	02	05	02
	WIC	56*	08	10	03	−07	10
	L	19	04	06	06	55*	−07
	ISS	21	−02	10	20	30*	−01
	IMS	95*	−11	−11	−10	17	02
	M	15	13	−09	53*	−21	04
	S	15	06	16	05	−14	48*
	J	62*	03	23	−10	−07	09
Alistair	W	−07	−00	03	80*	00	06
	WIC	23	−06	20	46*	−30*	−19*
	L	09	15	−01	47*	18	−11
	ISS	15	36	41*	−41*	−19	−31*
	IMS	40	39*	−19	12	−00	−08
	M	75*	−00	−13	15	−19	−07
	S	−01	85*	−09	03	−02	−04
	J	−37	78*	01	11	13	15
Per cent of common variance		31.20	21.00	18.30	18.10	7.30	4.10

Decimals omitted.
Asterisks indicate salient values for interpretation.

However, the separation of *Grieg* and *Jane* from *Brighty* and *Alistair* indicates the need for a further statistical test. It is by no means unexpected, since it was built into the construction of the battery and corresponds to Britton's distinction between transac-

Table 3.5 Intercorrelation of factors shown in Table 3.4

	2	3	4	5	6
1	79	85	80	47	−02
2	—	73	78	43	−05
3	—	—	81	43	00
4	—	—	—	44	−03
5	—	—	—	—	−14

Decimals omitted.

tional and poetic texts (1971). One would not be surprised to find that some children will be more receptive to factual material while others are more receptive to fictional writing. Is this bifurcation so strong as to mask the separate roles of subskills? If so, the distinctiveness of the latter should appear more clearly when the results of these four tests are analysed in separate pairs.

This has been done in Table 3.7 (p. 58), which shows the results of factor analyses carried out on the data for *Brighty* and *Alistair* and for *Grieg* and *Jane* taken separately. Also shown are the results for the *Brighty* and *Alistair* data taken from Fawcett's SRA study relating to the same age group (Chapter 8). Each of the analyses yields two factors but none of the pairs correspond, i.e. each of them draws its principal loadings from a different set of 'subskills'. Only

Table 3.6 Summary of Table 3.4

(a) *Distribution of significant loadings*

	Grieg	Brighty	Jane	Alistair
W	3	4	3	4
WIC	1	4	1	4
L	5	4	5	4
ISS	3, 1	1	5, 1	3, 4
IMS	1	1	1	1, 2
M	5, 1	1	4	1
S	6	2	6	2
J	1, 3	2	1	2

(b) *Identification of factors by the subscales and tests to which they relate*

Factor	Subscale	Tests
1	IMS, ISS, M, WIC, J	G, B, J, A
2	S, J	B, A
3	W, ISS, (J)	G, J, A
4	W, WIC, L, M	B, A, (J)
5	L, ISS	G, J
6	S	G, J

Table 3.7   Factor analyses: two tests

		Brighty and Alistair				Grieg and Jane	
		Main sample n = 257		SRA sample n = 212		Main sample n = 257	
		1	2	1	2	1	2
Brighty	W	15	30	43	− 02	32	20
	WIC	− 26	64*	25	− 09	33	20
	L	42	28	81*	− 12	03	63*
	ISS	17	44*	84*	− 21	48*	20
	IMS	34	32	51*	21	30	27
	M	76*	− 08	50*	14	61*	− 03
	S	82*	− 08	− 02	73*	68*	− 13
	J	78*	− 48*	− 27	85*	68*	− 01
Alistair	W	12	55*	54*	03	46*	28
	WIC	− 19	79*	58*	− 08	64*	00
	L	49*	22	62*	03	− 18	77*
	ISS	34	05	46	− 00	− 04	66*
	IMS	50*	20	45	25	27	44*
	M	− 02	64*	48	14	63*	− 15
	S	45	22	10	64*	72*	− 42
	J	66*	− 17	07	61*	74*	− 07
Percentage of common variance		60.20	39.80	59.90	40.10	65.00	35.00
		$r_{1,2} = .95$		$r_{1,2} = .95$		$r_{1,2} = .93$	

The rotated labels *Grieg* and *Jane* appear in the Grieg and Jane section between the two blocks of rows.

Decimals omitted.
* Indicates those loadings which are salient for identifying the relevant factor.

one interpretation remains: each of these analyses is trying to make sense of 'error' as defined on p. 53. Because a theoretical model which is different for every sample tested is no model at all. The results of factor analysis must be replicable or they are worthless.

But suppose the original grouping into subscales was wrong, might there not be some other grouping which would be theoretically and empirically justifiable? As a test of this further possibility, we conducted several factor analyses on the several items in each test, taking each separately, later in pairs, and finally all together (112 items). Not surprisingly, these attempts proved a dismal failure. The intercorrelations of item pairs are low, of the order of .1 or .2, and the application of factor analysis to the resultant matrices simply produces a large number of 'factors' which defy any but the most *ad hoc* interpretation. We freely acknowledge that such data-dredging is nearly always to be deplored. There were sound reasons for positing the putative subskills in the way that we did, and correspondingly little reason to believe that some better rationale would emerge from the data.

At this point a discerning but inexperienced reader might well object: if the original items are indeed so unreliable that their correlations are as low as stated, then the fault lies in the construction of the tests themselves. Not so. A strong element of 'error' as defined is intrinsic to this kind of test. But what is common to all the effects of error is that they tend to be random, and therefore self-cancelling. The surest way to overcome their effect is to increase the number of items: what is left after averaging out error is, or approximates to, the true variance of whatever is tested. That this has been achieved has already been shown in the first part of this section.

One may now press the argument one step further. What if subscale totals are averaged out over all four tests, so minimizing the error due to the small number of items in each subscale when the tests are taken separately? The results of this analysis are shown in Table 3.8 (p. 60). All the correlations are of the same order. They produce one common factor which accounts for 71 per cent of the total variance (and 100 per cent of the usable common variance). The last column is particularly revealing, showing the high degree of accuracy with which the results for any one subskill can be predicted from a knowledge of the pupil's performance on the remainder. This is essentially the technique used by Davis (1968).

Suppose, finally, that one were to use some quite different method of identifying subskills, using different passages and different item types for each putative subskill? The *Edinburgh Reading Test (Stage 3)* constitutes just such a measure. It consists of five separate subtests, each using a consistent question mode, each bearing on two or three different short passages, and purporting to measure, respectively, facts, sequences, main ideas, viewpoints and vocabulary.[1] This kind of test maximizes the chance of obtaining distinct factors, inasmuch as the effect of item formulation (which is standard for each subskill) is, illegitimately, compounded with that of item content. This set of scales was given to the SRA sample of 212 children already referred to. The results as shown in Table 3.9 (below) indicate very high correlations between the five Edinburgh scales and a single common factor.

The single factor accounts for 81 per cent of the total variance. Thus one must reject the hypothesis that the several tasks used in tests of reading comprehension call on distinct subskills which can be differentially assessed and taught. There remained the possibility of a

---

[1] Moray House College of Education (1973) *Edinburgh Reading Tests (Stage 3)* London: University of London Press

Table 3.8 Correlations and factor analysis for subscale totals derived from the complete battery

Subscales	WIC	L	ISS	IMS	S	M	J	Unique common factor	SMC*	RMS**
W	66	68	66	66	65	68	63	77	61	78
WIC	—	64	66	66	64	64	60	75	57	76
L	—	—	69	72	65	66	69	80	65	81
ISS	—	—	—	73	68	68	65	80	65	80
IMS	—	—	—	—	72	73	69	83	70	84
S	—	—	—	—	—	70	68	79	64	80
M	—	—	—	—	—	—	72	81	68	82
J	—	—	—	—	—	—	—	79	63	80

* Squared multiple-correlations of the raw variable with the remaining variables.
** Square root of the above (calculated on four significant figures).
Decimals omitted.

Table 3.9 The Edinburgh Reading Test Stage 3: intercorrelation of scales
(n = 212)

| | Correlations | | | | Loadings on |
	2	3	4	5	single factor
1 Facts	75	74	79	77	83
2 Sequences	—	76	76	79	84
3 Main ideas	—	—	72	81	83
4 Viewpoints	—	—	—	77	83
5 Vocabulary	—	—	—	—	87

Decimals omitted.

much weaker hypothesis: that there exist two levels of reading comprehension: a lower level requiring only recognition of the meaning of words and literal comprehension of phrases and sentences, and a higher level which is essential for inference, establishing salients and so on. Certainly the facility levels shown in Table 3.2 indicate that, given similar passages, tasks that require lower-level processing in this sense are indeed more readily solved than those which demand further thinking. But this is partly a matter of the way in which texts are written and the kinds of questions that they permit. For it goes without saying that children who are above average relative to the discrimination of a particular test will tend to do well on the easier items and more poorly on the harder. If our weaker hypothesis is to be meaningful it needs to be formulated more precisely: *That there exists an identifiable group of pupils whose performance on higher-level tasks is defective to a degree which would not be predicted on the basis of their performance on lower-level tasks.*

To test this hypothesis, it was necessary first of all to establish the existence of groups of pupils on the basis of their performance on the four tests. To this end a cluster-analysis procedure was applied to the data. This had the effect of grouping the children in such a way as to maximize differences between groups and to minimize differences between the members of each group, such differences being stated in terms of their profiles on the thirty-two subscales derived from the original four tests (with n = 257). The analysis yielded three clusters: children who were generally successful on all subscales, those who were generally poor, and children whose performance was intermediate. The average scores obtained by each of these groups on each of the eight question-types are shown in the left-hand column of Table 3.10 (p. 62). These scores are expressed in the form of deviations from the overall mean in standard units or sigma scores (i.e. $(X-\overline{X})/\sigma$, where X is the obtained score and $\overline{X}$ is the population mean for the relevant row).

The next step was to calculate the 'expected score' of each pupil on each of the five high-level items based only on his average performance on the three lower-level items, i.e. W, L and ISS. These predicted scores were then subtracted from the obtained scores on the left of Table 3.10 to yield residual scores. The average residual scores for the three groups are shown in the right-hand column of Table 3.10. These are the data that are critical for the two-level hypothesis.

Had the hypothesis proved correct, the residual scores of the intermediate group (poor on high-level tasks *relative to their performance on low-level tasks*) should have been strongly negative, while one or both of the other groups would obtain positive residuals on these tasks (to compensate, since the mean residual for the population is always set to zero). Clearly this is not the case. What

Table 3.10 Comparative performance of three groups on harder and easier sections of the tests

	Mean sigma scores Group			Residual scores (see text) Group		
	I	II	III	I	II	III
W	− 1.01	+ .03	+ .54	not calculated (approximately zero)		
WIC	− .83	− .12	+ .57	− .18	− .09	+ .19
L	− 1.14	− .22	+ .64	not calculated (approximately zero)		
ISS	− .85	− .16	+ .62	not calculated (approximately zero)		
IMS	− .93	− .21	+ .72	− .30	− .40	+ .54
M	− .81	− .27	+ .71	− .16	− .20	+ .29
S	− .85	− .09	+ .56	− .36	− .10	+ .30
J	− .81	− .15	+ .56	− .37	− .23	+ .44
n	54	103	100	54	103	100

one observes is that the high-scoring group had higher scores than predicted. Conversely, both the low-scoring and intermediate-scoring groups showed poorer scores than predicted.

The evidence suggests that the five subscales which acted as criteria seem to be more discriminating than the three which were used as predictors. Even this may be a statistical artefact, inasmuch as the three clusters were generated from all eight subscales, not five. Hence a prediction derived from any subgroups of the eight, in our case the three less-demanding ones, may be expected to include an element of error, with consequent regression to the mean. Thus the results would seem to be entirely consistent with a hypothesis of a unitary aptitude of comprehension and do not conform with the hypothesis of two levels of comprehension skills.

V What can be tested?

Most of the findings that have been considered in section IV relate to a battery of four tests which were especially constructed with two aims in view:

1 To provide a measure which could be used in British schools in order to provide a differential diagnosis of the comprehension skills that are available to each of the pupils in our classes. Such a measure would offer a basis for tailor-made teaching programmes, whether these would use individualized learning or group activities.

2 To provide a form of testing which could be shown to have satisfactory reliability and validity and which can also be commended to teachers as a worthwhile learning experience in its own right, instead of being an intrusion on teaching time.

We believe that the second aim has been realized. The first aim has clearly not been realized and we would further maintain that it is probably incapable of realization because it is founded on (our own) misconception.

There is little need to enlarge on the tests themselves. They have been shown to have quite high reliabilities (about .8 for a single test, .86 or better for two tests and .9 for all four, even within a single age group, and with some under-representation of the extremes of the ability range). Their validity, measured against the Edinburgh Reading Scales, is of the same order. They were constructed by teachers for teachers. Whether or not they commend themselves to teachers is not for us to say. But they do approximate to real teaching-learning situations.

The tests have not been standardized, and no norms are offered whether in the form of age-related percentiles or of reading quotients. These could be obtained with a sufficient expenditure of time and money (little effort is needed). But one may well ask to what end. A teacher may wish to provide an exercise at the beginning of the school year and again at the end in order to verify the progress that has been accomplished under his guidance. How much will he gain from knowing the standing of each pupil relative to some normative population? If he does require this additional knowledge, there is no dearth of quick economical tests which would fulfil his need.

To revert to the principal theme of this chapter. The problem was formulated at the outset in the form of two quite opposite hypotheses: that reading comprehension can be broken down into a number of distinct subskills or, alternatively, that it constitutes a single aptitude or skill, one which cannot usefully be differentiated. The evidence that has been adduced strongly supports the second hypothesis. In the course of this inquiry, a third alternative was examined, that some pupils might 'possess' lower-order skills but not higher-order skills. We found no support for this hypothesis either.

We conclude that individual differences in reading comprehension should not be thought of in terms of a multiplicity of specialized aptitudes. To all intents and purposes such differences reflect only one general aptitude: this being the pupil's ability and willingness to reflect on whatever it is he is reading.

It should be added that this is not at all a case of the researcher setting out to prove a point and using statistics to justify whatever he wants to find. The reverse is true. With varying degrees of commitment, every member of the research team had embarked on the exercise with the aim of isolating the ultimate constituents of comprehension in the form of subskills. It is the data that proved resistant.[1]

Finally, when we use the word 'aptitude' to describe the pupil's ability and willingness to reflect on text, we are clearly not referring to some fundamental characteristic of his nervous system. What we are saying is that differences in ability and in motivation and the particular circumstances of life experience have combined to bring about a certain level of facility in interpreting the printed word which should be accepted as a point of departure for further teaching and does not stand in need of further diagnosis, especially into constituent subskills.[2]

How far can one be certain in rejecting the subskill hypothesis? There are three answers to this question. First, complete certainty is too high a requirement. One cannot presume to prejudge the outcome of further investigations, new modes of inquiry and new ways of formulating the problem. The judgements that one makes are made in the light of existing knowledge. Second, the present findings are

---

[1] It is interesting to note an exactly similar experience in a research recently reported on the opposite side of the Atlantic, in the form of an ERIC abstract: *The Assessment of Fundamental Skills Involved in Reading Comprehension* by Anna Miars Bezdek. This study examined the nature of reading comprehension to determine if the process is best described as a unitary ability or in terms of multiple skills that can be identified and measured. Test items were constructed to measure each of the comprehension skills selected for investigation: (1) remembering word meanings, (2) inferring word meanings from the context, (3) understanding content stated explicitly, (4) weaving together ideas in the content, (5) making inferences about the content, and (6) recognizing the author's purpose and point of view. After trial testing, the items were analysed and a final form of the test was administered to 369 fifth-grade pupils who were slightly above average in intelligence and general reading achievement. The results of the analysis of the intercorrelations among the skill measures indicated that the coefficients ranged from .61–.75. These findings indicate that the subtests were not assessing separate unique aspects of reading comprehension and that one factor, tentatively identified as general reading comprehension, accounted for nearly 73 per cent of the total test variance. Thus, the results support the theory that reading comprehension is a unitary ability.

[2] Of course we recognize the importance of interest and knowledge in the comprehension of a particular test, but these are not reading skills as such.

consistent with most other work in the field, including the Davis data (which was certainly not clear to ourselves at the outset). It will be argued, too, that if more careful work along similar lines to our own were to result in the vindication of subskills, they would not be usable. (This is not meant to exclude the possibility of a genuine breakthrough.) Third, and most important, the thesis as stated, that comprehension draws on the ability and willingness to reflect, is one that would in any case follow from what is to us the most plausible psychological approach to the relevant phenomena. This too was not evident to us at the start of our inquiry.

The first point is a platitude which need not be laboured. The second may seem surprising. Much of the appeal of the subskill theory derives from the authority which attaches to the Davis study, because it is the most careful in the field. But if one pauses to consider exactly what it is that Davis found, the case becomes much weaker. The subskills which he looked for were not unlike those that we hoped to find. The factors that he found were very different. The first was a vocabulary factor, the second an inference factor, and the third was the ability to identify the writer's technique and recognize the mood of a passage. The fourth factor is a questionable one, since two analyses of the same data do not agree (see p. 53). Now there are good logical grounds for regarding the ability to recognize word meanings as an essential element in comprehension. But there are equally good psychological grounds for saying that this is a prior knowledge which the reader brings to the comprehension task. Davis's second factor is central and corresponds fairly closely to the view of comprehension that is argued here. (One notes, however, that it is strongly correlated with vocabulary.) His third factor is really a content factor. It will be recalled that Davis used different passages for each type of question (as indeed have nearly all other researchers). It has already been noted that some students are more likely to excel at literary appreciation while others will incline more to scientific material. If the former produces a specific factor, it is not one that is universally applicable, like reflection itself.

To this we would add that in Davis's study, as in our own, the intercorrelations between factors were as high or nearly as high as the reliability of each. What this means is that even if one accepts the evidence of significant differentiation at its face value, one is still not in a position to capitalize on the pattern of scores obtained from each individual so as to prescribe appropriate treatment. This is because a profile is really a set of difference scores, based on the differences between a pupil's score on each of the scales or factors. But any difference measure incorporates test error from both scales involved, and the greater the correlation between the two scales, the more the true component of each will be included in a (notional) portion of score which is common to both. Inevitably then, any difference in scores will be mainly due to the two error components.[1]

However, if one considers what goes on when a student reads and what happens when he completes a comprehension test, one will find little to support the notion of subskills. Early in this chapter, we acknowledged a debt to those who have stressed the importance of requiring objective behavioural criteria to support one's intuitions about curricular aims and to test the efficiency of the methods one may choose in order to achieve them. This is a justification for the retention of comprehension tests as part of the back-up available to the teacher for the purpose of assessing the effectiveness of his teaching. It also gives a sanction for some expenditure of effort directed to the improvement of such measures. But it is a very serious mistake to suppose that the completion of a test and comprehension in reading are one and the same thing. How a student completes a test is an *index* of his capacity to comprehend; it is not the capacity itself and still less is it the comprehension itself.

When a student reads intelligently he understands ('comprehends'). But what is he actually doing? It seems reasonable to argue that the things that he does form a sequence which is repeated as he goes through the text. Not all the elements in the sequence need be present at each repetition. For instance, the sequence includes questioning and judging, and these two things are necessary from time to time, but it would be ridiculous to seek to question and analyse every phase or sentence one reads. Also, it is possible (but not certain) that some of these things can go on simultaneously. Certainly, not all of them are conscious. The sort of sequence we have in mind is represented by the rows of Table 3.11 (p. 67): decoding, making sense, questioning, judging, revising one's notions.

Each of these things can be described at any level, with greater or lesser certainty, depending on the state of the relevant psychological research. Three of these levels are indicated in the columns of Table 3.11. The first is the commonsense level. It is the most superficial level, but also the most generally useful. One knows what it means, and unless one is a specialist, there is no need for further analysis. The second is the level of initial analysis: spelling out what is meant, but still in layman's terms. The third is the level of functional psychological description: it is an attempt to list the kinds of functions that need to be performed by operations in the reader's brain. The nature of these operations is not specified, nor is their structure. A more detailed, structural analysis of these operations would make a fourth level (this being the most fundamental for psychological research), while their physiological realization would

---

[1] Sad but true. In advancing this argument, as we must, we are reminded of the only jeweller in a small town addressing a nervous bridegroom: 'This is an excellent ring: genuine 18 carat gold. Cost you £10. If you don't believe me, you've still got to pay me a tenner for it. It's the only ring I have, and I see the young lady is seven months gone!'

Table 3.11 The process of reading: three levels of description

Level 1	Level 2	Level 3
Decoding print	identifying letters, words, phrases	scanning, fixating, anticipating, categorizing testing, matching, verifying
Making sense	assigning meaning to phrases and sentences	anticipating syntactic and semantic categories, matching, verifying
Questioning	noting discrepancies between different statements or between what is read and what is known	retrieving material from long-term memory, comparing, inferring
Judging	weighing evidence, reconciling discrepancies, hypothesis-testing, deciding	retrieving, comparing, re-formulating, re-ordering, accepting, rejecting
Revising notions	accepting, rejecting	modifying semantic structures in long-term memory

be a fifth. These levels are not explored in the table, and they are irrelevant to our purpose.

Now the first point to note is that the term 'comprehension' or 'understanding' does not appear in any column or row. It is not very difficult to see why. Comprehension is not a label or a description of anything that the reader actually does; it is a statement about how well the thing is done. And it relates to the whole. Gilbert Ryle referred to this sort of word as a 'got it' word as opposed to a 'doing' word. It does not describe an event in time; it characterizes an achievement. In the same way one can describe what a man does when he runs a race, one can break down the sequence of actions he performs, and one can describe these at any level. Both the running and the actions (raising and lowering legs, etc.) are events in time. But what about winning a race? One can say, 'He won the race in four minutes' and the meaning is clear enough, but it makes no sense to go on, 'Ah, but all those four minutes were spent running, how much time did he spend winning and when did he actually do this bit of winning?' (cf. Ryle, 1949).[1]

The second point to note is that the descriptions in Table 3.11 contain no reference to the subskills in Table 3.1 or to those on p. 44. This is because they are not really a part of reading nor are they

---

[1] 'Learning' is in the same category.

different kinds of reading. They are different 'comprehension tasks'. In other words, they describe the sort of questions that one can and should include in a varied and interesting comprehension test. But completing a comprehension test is not itself reading, though it always requires either prior reading or reading to refer, or both. It is an indirect measure of the adequacy of reading. If the description in Table 3.11 is at all correct, then the elements in the sequence will be the same whatever the question the student is set to answer, although it is true that some questions are more taxing than others, and so require more 'questioning' and more 'judging'.

In the same vein, it is easy to see why analysis fails to show even a broad grouping in terms of high-level and low-level skills, or a group of students who are successful at the latter but fail with the former. What we have called 'inference from multiple strings' (IMS) would clearly be a high-level skill while 'literal interpretation' (L) would be lower-level. But consider the following passage with the IMS questions that follow:

> John and his cousin Michael were great friends. They were nearly twins, but not quite. Michael was just one day older.
>
> Our story begins with Michael's birthday. Michael was seven. John was excited. He had a present for Michael, a train set. He knew that next day Michael would have one for him. What would that be? At Michael's party they played many games. Billy was sick because he ate too much icecream. Lizzie cried because she didn't win at musical chairs. But John and Michael had a great time.
>
> That night John couldn't sleep, thinking about the day and also about the morrow. Next morning, he woke at six. It was Wednesday, and it was his own birthday.
>
> Question 1: How old was John?
> Question 2: What day of the week was Michael's birthday?

Both questions require 'inference from multiple strings' (IMS). One would guess they would be correctly answered by most children of eight or even younger.

By contrast one might ask the reader to refer back to the last two sentences in the first paragraph on p. 62 and answer the following question: Does a higher *residual* score correspond to a higher *raw* score: always/sometimes/never? This question calls for a literal interpretation of 'residual'. But it is not an easy one.

These examples are surely not unique. One must conclude that the relative difficulty of a question or of an interpretation is mainly due to the difficulty of the text on which it bears. It is not due to some hypothetically-distinct differences in the thinking process associated with the question type.

Of course, it remains true that with any given passage the relative difficulty of questions will tend to conform with what we found from *Grieg, Brighty, Alistair* and *Jane*.

VI What can be taught?

The fact that one cannot reliably measure different skills in comprehension does not mean that comprehension cannot be taught. Nor does it mean that comprehension tests are useless. Indeed the negative finding about skills is quite consistent with the view that comprehension tests may serve a useful purpose and also that the best tests of comprehension will include a variety of tasks similar to those incorporated in the present inquiry.

A good comprehension test is a (necessarily indirect) measure of a pupil's ability to reflect on what he is reading. It is also a stimulus for such reflection. But to provide that stimulus one must give precise tasks. It is not enough to say: 'think'. Also, it is obviously desirable to include a variety of tasks. And, finally, in order to provide a challenge and an opportunity to all the members of a group, whatever their ability, one would want to include the easier w and l items as well as more demanding ims, m and j items (in relation to the given text). A bad test is one that can be answered without prior and thorough reading of the text, simply by 'looking up' the right phrase or sentence to answer each question. Such a test offers little stimulus for reflection.

Nevertheless it is well to bear in mind that the conventional comprehension test or exercise is not the only way to stimulate reflection nor, perhaps, is it the best. This is because, however realistic the exercise, it is still different from the real thing: reading for a purpose and understanding what one reads. In a comprehension exercise, the questions are provided for the pupil and his task is simply to answer them.

Comprehension tests have also been criticized on the grounds that many questions are assessed on the basis of previous knowledge or of indirect clues given in the questions themselves. Thus Tuinman (1973) showed that results of replies to comprehension tests were well above chance accuracy even when the subjects had never seen the passage on which they were based. However, he did find a doubling of mean scores when the readers had seen the passages. Moreover correlations between seen and unseen scores were low. But it remains possible that comprehension tasks measure a very specialized skill.

There is certainly some danger in an over-reliance on the comprehension exercise as a means of improving reading, as is well brought out in a recent paper by Thomas and Augstein (1972) who found that reading a passage in the expectation of a request to write a summary produced better results than reading the same passage in the expectation of a comprehension test. Students who were told they would have to produce a summary are superior on a subsequent comprehension test (unexpected) as well as in the quality of their summaries (expected).

However, the question of what can be taught and how it can be taught is taken up more fully in the last four chapters of this volume. The present chapter was concerned with the theoretical analysis of comprehension, which is why it has been put at the beginning. Its findings can be summed up quite simply:

1   It is not possible to provide a reliable differential test of comprehension skills.
2   One can construct useful, acceptable and reliable measures of comprehension.
3   Even the best tests of comprehension have their limitations, and such tests or exercises should not be used as the sole means of improving reflective reading.

Appendix

Brighty

1   Brighty the mule ran soundlessly through the trees and just at sunset came upon his own little piece of meadow nestled deep in the forest. It lay in a pool of shadow with only shafts of gold where the sun pushed through the trees. It smelled of the sweetness of wet earth and new grass.

2   With tired feet, Brighty tested the welcoming green carpet. His hoofs sank deep. He doubled his long legs and fell into its softness. For a long time he lay still, then he began rolling blissfully, enjoying the springiness of the soft grass after his rocky mountain beds. At last he rose to crop the juicy blades as the sun dipped low and darkened the shadows across the meadow. Soon he had eaten his fill of it. Now to find his secret cave, and sleep.

3   A full moon danced its beams along the path from the meadow to Brighty's cave. With a grunt of happiness, he trotted along the path until it opened out into a black cavern. Nature had built a huge shelter in the side of the cliff. It had a wide, sandy floor, but what Brighty loved most of all was the pool of clean, clear water near the back of the cave, and the thick bed of ferns to lie in.

4   He buried his muzzle in the pool and drank deeply. Then he settled down in a clump of ferns and opened his mouth in a wide, stretching yawn. Everything was just as it had been many times before, even the ghost-white tree standing at the mouth of the cave. He lay among the ferns watching the sailing moon until his eyelids drooped and sleep overcame him.

5   Night wore on and soon the only sounds were Brighty's little snorings and the water tinkling into the pool from the roof of the cave.

6   Then, far below the mouth of the cave, a wildcat in search of food came slinking forward, her tawny coat mixing with the lights and shadows of the rocks. Her huge eyes gleamed golden-green in the dark as she crept nearer to the old dead tree. She halted there a moment, then hooked her claws into the trunk and climbed swiftly until she was level with the mouth of the cave.

7   At first Brighty lay undiscovered in the ferns, but soon her searching eyes fixed upon his white belly. For a long time she lay watching him, her tail swishing and her mouth partly open, showing her white fangs.

8   At last she stole forward on a long branch, testing it first with her forepaws and then with her whole body. It bent under her weight but she steadied herself,

balancing like a diver. Then with one powerful leap she launched herself down into the ferns. At that very moment Brighty was snuggling deeper into the ferns and she landed short of her mark. Cruel claws intended for his head and neck, ripped his forelegs from shoulder to hoof. Instantly he was awake and on his feet squealing in terror as he faced the hissing wildcat. He pawed wildly, trying to kick her over the edge of the cave, but cunningly she rolled underneath him, stabbing with her claws. Brighty backed away, rearing as he did so and flailing with his hoofs. Once he landed on the cat's muscled body but she rolled out from under him.

9   Suddenly she turned and with a bound was up in the tree. She tried a second spring down on him and this time she landed on his back. Down they both went onto the floor of the cave, snarling and grunting as they rolled across towards the pool. Brighty struggled to shake free of the claws stabbing into his shoulders, but they only dug deeper. Now they grappled on the very edge of the pool until they finally went spinning into the icy water. Still the wildcat would not let go. With a scream of pain Brighty rolled over on his back, pinning her beneath him in the water. For long minutes he held her there, until gradually the claws eased and at last they fell away. Slowly and painfully Brighty struggled from the pool.

4

Assessing the Readability of School Texts

Colin Harrison

If a teacher is to plan individual instruction to meet specific needs, her first task is to assess the attainment level of every child and provide each with reading material of the right level of readability.
A Language for Life 17.19

The effect of modern approaches in many subjects is to put a higher premium than ever on the ability to read. There is increasing use of assignment cards and worksheets. All too often these and the tasks they prescribe make no allowance for individual differences in reading ability, and the advice given to subject departments [by a suitably qualified member of staff] should include a concern for readability levels in the material being used.
A Language for Life 15.8

I Introduction

The quotations given above from *A Language for Life* (DES, 1975) serve as a bridge from the previous chapter to the present one. In Chapter 3 an account has been offered of the nature of reading comprehension, and this establishes a theoretical framework upon which many of the suggestions for developing responsive reading which occur later in this volume will be based. The potential value of a book or worksheet in the classroom is determined by at least three groups of factors: the ability of the children to read and understand; how the teacher presents the text within a lesson; factors associated with the text itself, notably the extent to which it is legibly and attractively produced, and clearly or simply written. The first group of factors has been introduced in Chapters 2 and 3, and the second group, those relating to how texts are used, will be discussed most fully in Chapters 5, 7 and 10. While both will be referred to in the present chapter, it is on the third group of factors, those relating to the text itself, that our attention will be focussed.

INTRODUCTION 73

1 The need for objective measures

The need for the teacher to consider carefully the nature of the demands made by any book is emphasized in a number of sections of the Bullock Report. The problem for the teacher is how to determine 'the right level of readability' for each child. Even if the teacher has a reasonable knowledge of the reading ability of a child, there remains the difficulty of deciding which factors need to be taken into account in deciding whether a text is suitable or not, and which ones are most important. Most teachers feel that they are far from being experts in matters connected with teaching or developing reading, and while they need to make judgements every day about whether or not a book will suit a certain group, they would often welcome an assurance that their judgements are sound ones. Normally this assurance would be sought from a colleague, but this is not always practicable, particularly when work is being planned outside school. Similarly, a perfectly valid method of assessing whether children can cope with a particular book is to give it to them and monitor their response carefully. Clearly the problem with this method is that it takes time, and if the results are negative then that time will have been used unprofitably, and possibly a good deal of money will have been mis-spent. What seems to be needed is a more objective method of predicting text difficulty.

The potential value of such objective methods has also been implied in certain research studies of the reliability of individual teachers' judgements. A number of studies have found that while pooled teacher-judgements are extremely reliable and consistent, the opinions of individuals may vary wildly in relation to particular books or passages. In a series of four experiments carried out at Nottingham University as a part of in-service workshops on readability, experienced teachers were asked to write down the age at which they thought 'an average child' could read and understand two printed passages (see Appendix 1, p. 104). The passages had not been chosen with the aim of presenting the teachers with difficult decisions, but Passage A was from an autobiographical novel and Passage B was from a biology textbook, which made it unlikely that many teachers would feel completely confident about both assessments. On each occasion, a range of between six and nine years was noted for Passage A, and on three of the four occasions a range of between six and eight years was noted for Passage B. Similarly, there was a good deal of disagreement about which was the more difficult of the two passages: in each group about one third thought that B was the more difficult to read, some felt that there was little to choose between them, and half assessed Passage A as the more difficult. When the scores were averaged out, however, a much clearer picture emerged.

As Table 4.1 (p. 74) shows, the pooled scores of different groups of teachers were much closer to each other than were the estimates of individual teachers. Equally, although the pooled group-2 scores are lower than those of the other groups for both passages, all four groups assessed Passage A as the more difficult. It is interesting to compare these results with the predicted reading level obtained from the best-known readability formula, that devised by Rudolf Flesch in 1948. Using a conversion table, his formula yields a reading-age level of 13.95 for Passage A and 12.32 for Passage B. These figures are remarkably close to the overall mean scores of our teachers' groups, which were 13.22 and 12.42 respectively.

The suggestion that in estimating text difficulty individual experts'

Table 4.1   Mean estimates of teachers of age at which 'the average child' could read two passages with understanding; Flesch formula readability scores given for comparison

	Passage A				Passage B			
	mean	lowest	highest	s.d.	mean	lowest	highest	s.d.
Group 1 (n = 17)	13.24	10	19	2.4	12.70	9	17	2.5
Group 2 (n = 22)	12.38	9	15	1.6	11.95	8	14.5	1.5
Group 3 (n = 22)	13.90	11	18	1.7	12.70	9	16	2.1
Group 4 (n = 12)	13.50	10	17	1.8	12.40	11	14.5	0.9
Average teachers' score (n = 73)	13.22				12.42			
Reading level (obtained from Flesch formula)	13.95	.			12.32			

judgements are often unreliable has been made by the greatest authority on this subject, Professor George Klare of Ohio. He has reported experiments with teachers, librarians and others which have given similar results to those given in Table 4.1. One would not want to infer from this, however, that anyone is suggesting that teachers are wholly incapable of choosing suitable material for their students to read. It is rather that in this important task there are certain measures available which can assist the individual teacher by offering an objective index of the prose difficulty of the passage.

2 The need for new research

It seemed in the light of such evidence that the Effective Use of Reading project team should investigate which of the many methods of predicting text difficulty seemed likely to be most useful to teachers. Most of the research into the readability of school texts has been conducted in the USA, and comparatively little is known about the validity of using predictive formulae in British schools. Two further issues which seemed worthy of investigation were the extent to which formulae seemed more effective with one age range rather than another, and the extent to which formulae were accurate in predicting the difficulty of texts in different subject areas. The cross-validation study which was initiated to obtain this information will be described in detail later in this chapter, but it only represents one part of the research into readability which the project team carried out. In addition to considering which formulae could be most useful to teachers, we also wished to apply the formulae themselves to texts in use in schools in order to examine the reading levels in different subject areas and age groups.

During the course of the project team's visits to a number of local authorities, discussions with teachers indicated that many were concerned about the inability of children to cope with the reading demands of specific subject areas. Secondary school heads of mathematics and science departments informed the team that in the lower years a transition to mixed-ability grouping and individualized learning was extremely difficult when many children did not possess the reading skills to allow them to work independently from a workcard or worksheet. It was also widely felt that in some science and mathematics CSE courses there was a much heavier emphasis on verbal concepts than used to be the case, and that as a result some children who were poor readers but were otherwise good in these subjects were unable to cope with the textbooks for the course and examination questions which tested what had been learned from it.

This kind of debate has immediate relevance for the classroom teacher, but it tends to rely on subjective evidence. It is not easy to judge whether texts are more difficult or demanding than they used to be, nor whether those in one subject area are more difficult than those in another. The second part of our readability study, therefore, was to attempt a survey of the difficulty levels of printed texts in use in a number of subject areas. Since it was at secondary level that such information seemed to be most needed, the survey focussed on first- and fourth-year groups, and as in the classroom observation study, the subject areas examined were English, mathematics, science and social studies. The decision to have the two rather broad categories of science and social studies was forced upon us by the multiplicity of curricular groupings in the schools themselves: only within these fairly broad categories could we pool data and examine overall trends.

II Assessing text difficulty—what can be measured?

Having made the initial decision to undertake two related studies, one into which measures seem potentially most useful and another applying such measures to data gained from a survey of texts in use in schools, it was necessary to decide which types of measure should be considered for inclusion in the study. As noted in the previous section, the way in which a book is written is by no means the only factor determining its acceptability and usefulness in the classroom. As librarians know, a colourful cover with an intriguing illustration will encourage a reader to open and begin reading a book which would otherwise lie on the shelf. As heads of English departments know, the title of Poe's *Tales of Mystery and Imagination* has tempted many a 'reluctant reader' who would not normally tackle nineteenth-century stories. Illustrations within a book can give crucial information to enhance understanding of the text and help the poorer reader. Unfortunately, however, the effect of all these variables is extremely difficult to quantify, and for this reason it would be difficult to include them in a large-scale study.

1 Legibility

By contrast, research into legibility of print has been undertaken on a fairly large scale, although paradoxically the results of much of the research are inconclusive. In their concise review of this field, Watts and Nisbet (1974) report the pioneering studies of Burt, Miles and Tinker, but conclude that the usefulness of many results is diminished because of a failure to control the many variables which can affect legibility. Among those, for example, are type font (i.e. the particular style of type used by the printer), type size (e.g. 8-point, 12-point), the size of spaces between words, lines, or paragraphs, the width of margins, the nature of the ink used for printing, and the texture, colour and reflective qualities of the paper. The problem for the researcher is that most studies only report on a small number of these variables, and others on which no data is given could have had an important effect on the outcome of the experiment. It was therefore decided that although format and legibility must be recognized as important in determining how a reader will cope with a text, these aspects would not be included in our own study. This was also because it was intended to look at texts already in use, and it seemed most unlikely that there would be sufficient overlap between samples to allow useful general points to emerge.

2 Linguistic variables

We return, therefore, to how a text is written, and the factors which appear to make it more or less readable. If a layman is asked what tends to produce readable prose, he might suggest 'simple English' or 'not too many long words'. This commonsense view has a good deal to commend it, and it has been regularly established that vocabulary and sentence structure are the two most crucial determinants of text difficulty. Attempts to quantify linguistic variables, and to combine these into a formula for predicting the difficulty a reader is likely to have in reading a particular passage, go back to 1923. George Klare, in his authoritative reviews of readability research (1963, 1974) gives an account of the historical development of formulae which would be out of place here. A more readily obtainable general introduction to the field is that written by Jack Gilliland (1972).

As an example of one of the dozens of formulae which are available, we shall use that of Rudolf Flesch, which first appeared in 1948. It is probably the most widely known in the USA, and has the advantage that it was designed to cope with adult reading matter, rather than the prose of the junior school primer. It is the grade score conversion of this formula which is used in Table 4.1 earlier in this chapter. The Flesch formula takes the form of a reading ease score (RE):

$$RE = 206.835 - (0.846 \times NSYLL) - (1.015 \times W/S)$$
where NSYLL is the average number of syllables per 100 words and W/S is the average number of words per sentence.

The RE score is in fact a notional comprehension score out of 100. A US school-grade score is derived from a conversion table.

The above formula is typical of most of those used widely today. It was produced following a good deal of research into the factors which were associated with comprehension of prose passages. After analysing many linguistic variables, Flesch found (using a multiple regression technique) that two in particular seemed to correlate most highly with difficulty. These were the average number of syllables per word, and sentence length. Now many long words are known to even beginning readers ('elephant' and 'aeroplane' are examples) and most adults would find it difficult to define 'palp' and 'khor', but in general the average number of syllables per word in a passage turns out to be a fairly good predictor of the overall level of vocabulary difficulty. Similarly, a long sentence need not be complex, but in practice measures of grammatical complexity whether in terms of subordinate clauses or more intricate linguistic measures have been found to correlate extremely highly with straightforward sentence length. Bormuth, for example, found a correlation of .99 between a count of words per sentence and an extremely complex syntactic variable, the Yngve 'word-depth' index (Bormuth, 1966). There are in fact certain readability formulae which measure grammatical complexity using some syntactic variable such as clause structure, number of T-units per sentence, or percentage of propositional phrases. However, partly because not all teachers are reliable in terms of their knowledge of English grammar, and partly because such variables present the computer programmer with massive difficulties, the formulae included in the present study only use sentence length as a variable to estimate grammatical complexity.

3 Vocabulary difficulty

For estimating or predicting vocabulary difficulty, most of the formulae use a measure of word length, such as the average number of syllables per word, or the average number of polysyllabic words per sentence. The choice of one variable rather than another is partly determined by the type of reading material from which the formula was originally derived. For example, in infant-school primers, the proportion of monosyllabic words might correlate most highly with the scores of passage difficulty based on what the children could read and understand. With adult prose, however, this variable could be less crucial, and the proportion of three-syllable words might be a more useful variable to include. As Zipf's (1935) law[1] demonstrates, word length is inversely correlated with word frequency, and a measure of word length is thus an indirect measure of frequency. The Dale-Chall formula is an example of one which measures this variable more directly. Their formula uses the percentage of words in a passage which are on a list of 3000 familiar words as an indicator of vocabulary difficulty. The idea is that the greater the proportion of infrequently used words, the more difficult the reader is likely to find the passage. This formula therefore neatly bypasses the problem caused in the other formulae by the fact that some long words are used frequently and many monosyllabic words are used very rarely.

The Dale-Chall formula has been proved in a number of cross-validation studies (reported by Klare, 1963 and Chall, 1958) to be one which is most accurate in predicting difficulty, but unfortunately it has one great drawback—the formula is very tedious to work out. Each word in a sample passage needs to be checked against the 3000 word list, and there are approximately thirty rules giving details of how suffixes, irregular verb forms, abbreviations and proper nouns are to be treated. Sue Davies, computing assistant in the Education Department at Nottingham University, has written a computer program which works out the Dale-Chall formula score, and which can be readily adapted to cope with any other word list. The scope of her task can be estimated from the fact that it took over six months part-time effort to produce a working program, whereas the program which works out nine other formulae was written in two days by Graham Walker, who at the time was a trainee programmer at the Cripps Computing Centre. Their valuable efforts have not only assisted the Effective Use of Reading project, but have led to the

[1] The results of statistical analysis are applied to problems in linguistics.

dissemination of a readability analysis package which is currently in use in six other universities.

4 The formulae used in the study

The criteria for including a readability formula in the study were not simply those related to ease of application, or convenience for computer programming, as the inclusion of the Dale-Chall formula demonstrates. A survey of the relevant literature in this country and the USA was undertaken, and formulae were included either because they had a good record in reliability and validity studies, or because they were already in fairly wide use in this country, irrespective of whether data on reliability or validity were available. The formulae used in the study were the following: Mugford (1972), Flesch Reading Ease (1948), Flesch Grade (this is a transformation of the Reading Ease score which suggests a US school grade at which the average reader should be able to understand a passage), Fog (Gunning, 1952), Smog (McLaughlin, 1969), Smog-X (the Smog formula involves the teacher in making an approximation to a square root—in this computer version the exact square root is used to produce the Smog index), Powers, Sumner and Kearl (1958—this is a recalculation of the Flesch formula, and is most effective with junior-school passages), Farr, Jenkins and Patterson (1951—this too is a reworking of the Flesch formula), Forcast (*sic*) (Sticht, 1973—this is the formula devised for US Army research into literacy problems; for ease of application it does not incorporate a sentence-length variable), and finally the Dale-Chall formula (1948).

If this emphasis on the objective and quantifiable leads the reader to feel that a rather narrow perspective on reading difficulties is being offered, then perhaps a cautionary note should be sounded. Like all tools constructed by educational researchers, readability formulae results are not meant to displace the teacher, nor relieve him or her of the need to make judgements. Readability formulae offer, in exchange for some rather tedious arithmetic and word-counting, an objective estimate of text difficulty which it might be even more difficult to obtain by another method. This information can then be used as one factor in the decision about whether or not a book or passage is likely to cause problems for a particular class or group. It is incumbent upon the teacher to use such information profitably, and to be aware of its limitations.

III The readability survey design

Having made the decision about which formulae were to be included in the cross-validation and readability survey studies, it became clear that the logical order in which to carry out the two pieces of research was the reverse of that originally planned. If we carried out the survey first, this would provide us with a subset of data on which to make comparisons between readability-formulae scores and judgements of difficulty made by a separate group of experienced teachers which were to be the basis of the cross-validation study. We would then be in a position to re-analyse the complete survey data using the formula or formulae which correlated most highly with the criterion of pooled teacher-judgements. For a number of reasons, which are given in a later section, the formula which on balance appeared to be the most valuable was the Flesch grade score, and accordingly it is used in the present section in reporting the results of the readability survey.

1 Selection of schools

In planning the survey we began by approaching Nottinghamshire LEA with the intention of establishing a population of secondary schools which would offer a representative range of catchment areas and types of schooling. In the event, thanks to the generous assistance and support of Mr A. K. Harrison, then adviser for English in Nottinghamshire, every school in one county district (population 200,000) agreed to take part in the sampling exercise. The district contained ten secondary schools in all, of which three were fully comprehensive. There was one large grammar school, two mixed secondary and four single-sex secondary schools. In terms of catchment area the district included one of the most favoured suburbs of Nottingham, a densely-populated town five miles from the city, a number of mining areas and two semi-rural areas.

The headteachers of all these schools were visited, and it was made clear that our intention was not to make inter-school comparisons but to gain information about the type of reading materials in use in different subjects, and to examine their difficulty levels. Rather than ask teachers in the schools what they normally used, it was decided to simply choose one week in the spring term, and to collect text samples for analysis based on what was actually in use in the classroom during that week. This method of data collection was chosen because it was less likely to tempt those cooperating to name books which were in the department's stock, but which were rarely used and read by the children. It also is rather more reliable than a method which requires a hard-pressed teacher to recall over a busy term which books have or have not been used.

2 Selection of text samples

In each school a single member of staff undertook to distribute to colleagues in English, mathematics, science and social studies departments a brief form which was to accompany each text sample. Staff who taught first-year and fourth-year groups were asked to supply at the end of the designated survey week, copies of any books, worksheets or other printed materials which they had used in class.[1] These were collected from the schools, the pages cited in the forms were photocopied, and the texts were returned within three days.

The text samples were then punched onto computer cards for analysis, together with details of source, subject, age group, type of material (i.e. textbook, reference book, worksheet, etc.) and whether the text was used in a supported or unsupported context. This final category was to differentiate between reading undertaken when the text was discussed with the teacher, or at least the teacher's support was available, and those occasions when the reader was working on his or her own with no direct support available. The length of text samples varied a good deal. The range was 102–810 words, with a mean of 399 words. The wide range was a necessary part of the research design. Usually in readability research a great deal of care has to be taken in establishing sampling reliability. For example, it is not very useful to announce that the reading level of a book is 10.5 years, if this has only been determined on the basis of a single hundred-word sample of text, when scores from other samples within the same book may differ from the first sample by three or four years either way. Some books do vary a great deal, and may have sections written by different authors included in them. For this reason it was decided so far as possible to analyse the whole of a passage which the teacher supplied. This may indeed have only been part of a chapter of one book, but it did at least represent what the child had been required to read. To this extent, therefore, the issue of sampling reliability within a text does not arise. We are not suggesting that each passage score represents that which would be obtained for the whole of the book from which it was taken, but that it does at least indicate the difficulty level of the sections read by those children during that week.

Not every school supplied samples of text for each subject and age group. No doubt this was partly due to organizational problems within the school, but it probably was also related to the absence of printed sources in the classroom in certain instances. As reported elsewhere in this volume, the use of printed sources in some subjects is rather limited. On our local authority visits there were a number of occasions on which heads of science departments informed us that no textbooks were used with some lower-secondary forms. This was usually either because it was claimed that no suitable book existed, or because the department could not afford to buy one which was available. The problem associated with isolating samples of prose in mathematics texts are rather different. A readability formula cannot cope with mathematical expressions very effectively. We therefore

---

[1] The teachers were asked to give samples of texts used with groups reckoned to be of 'average' ability by the school's own standards. In a three-form entry streamed school this meant B forms, and in comprehensives the middle 'band' of three.

Table 4.2   Flesch formula grade-scores for readability survey passages
(reading level = grade score + 5)

	1st-year passages			4th-year passages		
	Number of texts	Reading level	Standard deviation	Number of texts	Reading level	Standard deviation
English	17	12.4	1.2	23	12.9	1.4
Mathematics	5	11.3	0.6	15	12.7	1.7
Science	9	13.5	2.3	12	14.0	1.8
Social studies	22	13.0	2.3	22	14.1	2.2
Population means	53	12.73		72	13.60	

included in the analysis more lengthy verbal questions and expository prose, and ignored expressions such as 'p ⊃ q', 'F ∈ G', or 'Expand $(a+b)^3$'. Altogether 125 passages with a total length of over 49,000 words were analysed.

IV The readability survey results

Table 4.2 (p. 82) shows the number of text samples collected from each subject and age group, and the average reading level of the texts in each group as derived from the Flesch formula, together with the associated standard deviation for each group, which is a measure of how much variation in difficulty there was in the group. The term 'reading level' is used in preference to the more usual 'reading age' because the latter phrase is sometimes interpreted in unfortunate ways. A child who has a chronological age of eight and a 'reading age' (as derived from a standardized test) of ten is a very different reader from a fifteen-year-old with a 'reading age' of ten. The term 'reading level' is used to avoid this connotation; it should be taken to suggest the age at which those children whose reading competence is about average for their age should be able to cope with the passage.

The results are given in terms of the Flesch formula grade scores since this formula is quite widely known, and was shown to be the second most consistent in the cross-validation study which will be referred to below. Dale-Chall formula scores were better in terms of correlations with teachers' judgements, but these were felt by the authors to be rather lower than the true reading levels, and need to be corrected using a conversion table (*vide* Klare, 1963). A number of interesting points emerge from these results.

Overall, texts used in English departments do not vary greatly in terms of average difficulty-level between year groups. It must be noted, however, that within every group there was a good deal of variation between texts. One would not want to suggest that English teachers are failing to give fourth-year students reading which will make a demand on the intellect. A number of interacting factors must also be considered.

The fourth-year English passages included a number of samples of that ubiquitous species the gritty northern novel, in which short sentences and racy dialogue might well produce a low readability score. Many first-year stories, however, are fairly demanding. A Leon Garfield book, for example, might well be expected to pose problems in terms of its prose complexity, and while its hero may be an adolescent, the book may be much more difficult to read than the John Wyndham novel encountered in the fourth-year CSE course. One would suggest that the implication for English teachers is not so much that the reading tasks of the fourth form are too easy, but that those given to first formers would appear to be only marginally easier than those given to fourth formers. Another factor which will have had the effect of lowering the fourth-year scores is the fact that they include a number of works of poetry. For completeness the computer analysis included extracts from Shakespeare's *Macbeth* and Eliot's *Journey of the Magi*. As it happens both of these came out with a reading-level score of approximately 12.5. The reaction of an English teacher to this would be surprise, since neither work is easy reading for twelve-year-olds. The reason for the low scores is that both extracts contain some fairly brief sentences, and these depressed the overall result in each case. In a sense it seems irrelevant to ask whether a poem is comprehensible in the way we would ask that question of a novel or textbook. There are certainly occasions when partial comprehension is not only acceptable but positively expected within the context of an English lesson. The analysis of poetry using measures of readability is not wholly invalid, nor without precedent. Allard (1946) used nearly 700 poems in a study of the reading preferences of 50,000 elementary school pupils. Not surprisingly, he found that children's preferences were inversely correlated with vocabulary difficulty. However, most readability formulae would fail to register any extra difficulty associated with unusual sentence structure or compression of language, which are common in poetry.

The levels of difficulty associated with mathematics textbooks and worksheets were low. Mathematics texts were also more even in difficulty than any others. One problem, however, that has been pointed out to us by mathematics teachers is that by training they are inclined to prefer terse and condensed prose to that which might be written by word-spinning humanities teachers. This could well produce low readability scores, but could still mask problems for readers unfamiliar with the subject. Also many of the sentences analysed in mathematics texts were brief instructions, rather than expository prose. This too might tend to lower the reading-level score. A further point is that, as with worksheets, instructions for a task ought to be in simpler prose than anything else a child reads. Normally comprehension is a building up of meanings from the text, and partial understanding can be coped with. In the case of intructions this is not so: any failure to comprehend is likely to leave the reader in a situation which can only be resolved by the teacher.

An interesting study which sheds further light on the problem of highly compressed prose has been conducted by van der Will (1976). She ran two versions of an experiment in which junior school children had to obey a taped instruction (for example, to draw a blue circle and a cross next to it). The instructions to do the task were presented in one of four forms. The longest of these consisted of two sentences, the second of which was periodic, with two simple main clauses joined by 'and'. The versions became more compressed, the hardest being composed of a single sentence with a main clause, a subordinate adverbial clause, and an adjectival phrase. The fourth version was highly compressed, and would have been assessed as easier than the first on most readability formulae. Nevertheless, in the first experiment the children needed to have a number of repetitions before they could obey the compressed instruction, whereas no repetitions were necessary for those who heard the first, and longer, version. In her second experiment no repetitions were allowed, and those children who received the compressed instructions were significantly less successful in completing the task.

Lest it should seem that the case in favour of readability formulae has been irreparably damaged, one should point out that van der Will's longer instructions are not typical of most prose. As has already been emphasized in reference to Bormuth's work (1966), longer sentences generally do tend to suggest complex sentence structures, and not simple ones, and thus are more difficult to comprehend. The periodic sentence structure of van der Will is a comparative rarity among textbook authors.

In both year groups, science and social studies (which includes history, geography and environmental studies) contain the most difficult texts, with first-year science standing out as particularly difficult. It is slightly disturbing to note that seven of the nine samples of first-year science prose were from teacher-produced worksheets. Some of these had prose which was as difficult as the standard O-level physics textbook. In a sense this is not surprising, since most textbooks are written by teachers, and scientists will tend to prefer a certain type of prose. Nevertheless, since the worksheet is essentially an instructional leaflet which should allow for individual and independent progress, a reading level two years above the pupils' average age does suggest that the children have to cope with difficulties associated with the way in which the text has been written, as well as those associated with the task itself and the scientific concepts involved.

These findings are consistent with a number reported by Klare (1963) in which social studies and science texts are rated as rather too difficult for most of the children who are required to read them. One can accept that conceptual difficulties are a part of all school subjects, but these are not what a formula purports to measure. Subject specialists are trained to use linguistic conventions of their discipline, and it is extremely difficult to judge the extent to which this form of expression is crucial to the subject. The question of what is acceptable is just as important as what is comprehensible.

The different patterns of integration of science subjects in each school at both first- and fourth-year level made it impossible for comparisons to be drawn within the scientific disciplines, but one accepts that particularly in chemistry and biology, the high number of specialist technical terms creates special difficulties for the reader.

The different headings under which history, geography and social studies are taught in various schools also precluded differentiation by subject, although again one must note that geology was a subject which seemed to have a particularly high number of unfamiliar and difficult words.

As has already been suggested, the difficulty level of a book is not the only determinant of how successfully it can be approached by a reader. The way in which it is used is also an important factor. We have already made the distinction between using a source in class, when problem words or passages can be discussed with the teacher, and using it in a situation such as for homework or for reference when no teacher-support is directly available. American researchers have suggested that a book used in an unsupported context should have a reading level approximately two years lower than that which a reader can cope with when the teacher's help is available. We controlled for this variable and found a slight negative correlation ($r = -0.07$) between passage difficulty and use in an unsupported context. In other words, the texts set by teachers to be read by children on their own turned out to be slightly more difficult than those used in class. This finding was related to the way in which science and social studies teachers used textbooks. As we learned on the LEA visits, the need felt by teachers to deal with practical work and give notes did not always allow time for reading in class, and therefore it tended to be relegated to homework. Often the task is not a reading homework as such, but one in which the student takes home the textbook for reference or note-making. At the very least, therefore, one should emphasize that the books which are the most difficult to read and understand in the whole school are given to children with the least support from the teacher. It seems clear that the implications of this should be considered carefully by our science and social studies colleagues.

Following the initial analysis of the data reported in Table 4.2, tests of statistical significance were applied, but with little in terms of conclusive results. A two-way analysis of variance failed to show any significant differences between the prose samples in different groups, but this should not be interpreted as implying that the results are unreliable, or indeed in the general sense non-significant. As teachers we should perhaps be a little surprised to learn that the reading demands we make of first formers at secondary level are *not* significantly different from those related to CSE and O-level courses.

An analysis of texts in terms of type (i.e. textbook, reference book, fiction or poetry, workcard or worksheet, and pamphlet or brochure) revealed one significant finding, which was that reference books tended to be harder to read than all the other types of text. This finding is not surprising, since reference books contain much specialist information, and would thus present the reader with unfamiliar vocabulary, but it reinforces the point made above concerning the need for alertness on the teacher's part if the most difficult reading tasks are undertaken in an unsupported context.

V The cross-validation study

The other aim of this readability study was to examine which of the many formulae currently available are potentially most valuable to the practising teacher. The cross-validation study was therefore planned to provide information about how closely each formula agreed with pooled subjective assessments of difficulty, and with actual comprehension scores on the passages in question.

In order to establish a basis on which subjective judgements could be compared with formulae scores, a random sample of passages was selected from the original set which were collected during our survey. A group of experienced teachers assessed each of the passages, and estimated its reading level. Since interest and motivation are vital in reading the teachers were also asked to estimate on a four-point scale whether the children at the age level they specified as appropriate would find the passage interesting or boring.

1 The importance of motivation

The importance of motivation in reading, more particularly the reader's level of interest in the content of what he is reading, has come to be regarded more and more seriously by researchers into readability. Teachers would tend to agree that often a child who is not a particularly good reader can surprise us by reading with comprehension as well as enthusiasm a book which seems far too dense in terms of vocabulary and grammatical complexity compared with what he can normally manage. When this happens the reason tends to be related to a high level of motivation. Firm evidence of this phenomenon is found in a study reported by Shnayer (1969). He took a group of nearly 500 eleven to thirteen-year-olds, gave them a standard test of reading comprehension, and on the basis of it split the subjects into seven notional ability-groups. He then gave each subject a number of comprehension tests on passages which had been assessed by the Dale-Chall formula as two grade-levels above the children's own age level. As well as completing comprehension tests, the subjects were asked to rate the interest level of each passage on which the test was based. There were a number of interesting findings, but the central one was that except for the lowest-ability group (which clearly contained subjects who had fundamental problems at the decoding level), there were no significant differences between ability groups in comprehension of stories rated as 'high interest'. Another important finding was that poorer readers did comparatively worse on passages they rated as uninteresting; in other words the high-ability students were less affected by low interest level.

2 Criteria for establishing the validity of formulae

In his review of previous cross-validation studies of readability, Klare (1963) refers to nineteen cases in which the criteria of pooled subjective-judgements are compared with formulae results. Usually teachers or librarians provide the assessments, but occasionally the views of students have been sought. The general trend has been that correlations of .60–.90 have been found between estimates of passage difficulty and readability formulae scores, irrespective of whether teachers' or students' ratings have been used. In our own study we wished to compare the judgements made by the pupils with those of teachers, and accordingly arrangements were made for children to assess the difficulty and interest levels of the passages.

These data would give us two perspectives on the difficulty level of passages against which we could assess the formulae scores: one from teachers and one from pupils. Both of these have the disadvantage that they are subjective and do not attempt to measure the actual level of understanding of a group of readers. Another method of examining the validity of the formulae scores would be to compare them with comprehension test results based on the passages in question. The problem with this method has naturally been the time and effort involved in preparing reliable comprehension tests on a large group of passages. For this reason a standard set of passages from a large-scale test, the McCall-Crabbs *Standard Test Lessons in Reading*, has been used in a large number of American validation studies. Since the early sixties, however, the use of multiple-choice comprehension tests has become less frequent, and cloze procedure scores are now much more commonly used as a correlate of the readers' comprehension. In comparative terms cloze tests, involving the deletion of every nth word (usually fifth, seventh or tenth) in a passage, are much quicker to prepare, and offer the researchers none of the problems of item construction and development associated with a normal comprehension test.

In a cloze test the reader's task is to work out from the surrounding context which word has been omitted, and to insert the one which seems most appropriate in each blank space. The proportion of correctly-guessed words gives an indication of the extent to which the reader has understood the passage. The scores a reader obtains on a number of passages will vary according to how difficult each one is to comprehend, and they enable the researcher to rank the passages in order of difficulty. The rationale behind this method of testing comprehension is discussed in papers by Bormuth (1967, 1968a), and it is now widely accepted. Nevertheless, as will be emphasized later in this chapter, while one might endorse a wider use of the technique, caution is needed in interpreting cloze test results.

The forty passages for the analysis were a stratified random sample from the 127 passages which had been collected for the readability level survey. The stratification was by age and subject grouping, to ensure that samples of materials from English, mathematics, science and social studies were represented at each age level. In the event, due to an error in cloze-tests administration, one passage was dropped from the analysis, and the two groups of texts comprised 23 first-year and 16 fourth-year passages. These were printed in booklets with randomly ordered pages. The teacher raters were twenty-four experienced teachers on advanced diploma or higher degree courses at Nottingham University. They were given all the passages to assess, and were not informed that the texts had been taken from only two year groups. The student raters were 175 children (85 first-year and 90 fourth-year) from a different school district from that in which the samples had been collected. They were given similar booklets and asked to make judgements about difficulty and interest level 'as if they were a teacher'; they were only required to rate the passages which had originally been used with their own year group, but of course they were not informed of this.

The cloze tests were given to 200 first- and fourth-year children in a third school district. Again, students were only required to tackle the set of passages originally obtained from their own year group. The rate of deletion used was every tenth word, beginning at or beyond the fiftieth word in the passage. All ten possible versions of each passage were produced using a computer program; this had the disadvantage of upper-case (capital letter) printing throughout, but the advantage that every passage was presented in a uniform manner. Mean passage-length was just under 400 words, so the passages contained on average about thirty-five deletions.

On the important issue of deletion rate, one should note that although the work of MacGinitie (1961) and Fillenbaum et al. (1963) has indicated that fifth word deletion is quite satisfactory for cloze testing, there are reasons for using lower rates. The belief that the percentage of cloze items correct does not rise significantly with a deletion rate below one in five has been challenged by independent studies by McNinch et al. (undated) and Klare et al. (1972). These studies suggest that depending upon the nature of the material, the deletion pattern which will produce the highest cloze scores may be every seventh, ninth or tenth word. In our own study it was felt that although fifth-word deletion might increase reliability of scores, it would have a considerable dampening effect on motivation, bearing in mind that some of the passages had readability scores suggesting a very high difficulty level.

The scoring of the cloze test answers was done on a verbatim basis; that is a word was scored as correct only if it was the exact one which had appeared in the original passage. Minor mis-spellings were disregarded, but otherwise the word had to be that which the author had written. This practice is now the established one in readability research, since a number of independent studies have demonstrated that the enormously lengthy process of using a scoring system which accepts synonyms as correct produces only a minimal increase in the correlations with passage difficulty (Bormuth, 1968b).

VI Results of the cross-validation study

Since the pooled teacher-judgements were based on the whole set of thirty-nine passages, it is to these that we turn first in considering the correlations with readability formulae. The central aim of the cross-validation exercise was to isolate that formula (or those formulae) which would be the most appropriate to use in analysing the difficulty levels of the survey passages.

As Table 4.3 (p. 91) shows, the highest correlation was with the Dale-Chall formula ($r = .77$), but nine of the ten formulae included in the study gave correlations of .68 or above. The only exception is that of the US Army Forcast formula, which is different from the others in that it does not employ a sentence-length variable. In addition the Forcast formula variable of proportion of monosyllabic words is one which we would expect to have a higher correlation with elementary-school passages than with those from a secondary school. From the top section of the table we can see that two indices of vocabulary complexity, i.e. the percentage of words on Dale's 3000 list, and the mean number of syllables per word in a passage, both give higher correlations with the criterion of teacher-judgements than the Forcast formula.

If we take the data in Table 4.3 as determining which formula is most appropriate for widespread use, then the Dale-Chall formula would seem to be the one since it correlates most highly with our criterion. There are, however, other factors to be taken into account: first, the Dale-Chall formula is not widely available in the UK, and more importantly neither is the Dale 3000 word list. Second, the formula takes a great deal of time to compute for more than a small number of passages, since it involves the rater in establishing whether each separate word is or is not on the list. Third, Dale and Chall give thirty rules for exceptions in determining whether or not a word is to be regarded as familiar for the purpose of computing the formula score. Thus there is a danger that these rules may be applied unreliably or even not applied at all, making Dale-formula scores much less reliable as predictors of difficulty.

The second best correlate of difficulty, the Flesch Reading Ease score, also poses problems, since it produces not a grade score but a notional comprehension score out of 100, which is uninterpretable to

Table 4.3 Correlation of linguistic variables and readability formulae with criteria of pooled teacher-judgements of passage difficulty

(based on 39 passages assessed by 24 judges)

Percentage words on Dale's 3000 list	.68**
Average number of syllables per word	.68**
Average number of letters per word	.53**
Average number of letters per sentence	.50**
Average number of words per sentence	.35*
Dale-Chall	.77**
Flesch—Reading Ease	.74**
Powers-Sumner-Kearl	.73**
Smog (McLaughlin)	.71**
Smog (using exact square root)	.71**
Flesch—Grade	.69**
Fog (Gunning)	.69**
Farr-Jenkins-Patterson	.68**
Mugford	.68**
Forcast (Sticht)	.60**

* Significant at .05 level.
** All correlations significant at .01 level.

an English teacher without reference to other scores or a transformation table. The third best correlate, the Powers-Sumner-Kearl formula, raises another crucial question. Although correlations are high, the actual grade scores given by the formula exhibit a marked ceiling effect. While most of the formulae suggest a gap of two years on grades between first-year and fourth-year passages, the Powers-Sumner-Kearl formula only gives a jump of .65 of a year. This is not entirely surprising, since this formula was developed for application particularly with primary-school passages, and it discriminates much more effectively below the fourth-grade level.

The next highest correlations in Table 4.3 relate to the Smog formula. The correlation of .71 is in fact slightly higher than that obtained by McLaughlin in his own validation study. Why then do we not accept his as the most useful predictor of difficulty? The answer is that the Smog formula has a standard error nearly twice as great as that associated with most other formulae. For most formulae the standard error associated with the regression equation is fairly low, and in the region of plus-or-minus .7–.85 of a school year, which gives a range of up to 1.7 school years within which the true difficulty score is likely to lie. The Smog formula has a standard error of plus-or-minus 1.5 school years, which suggests a range of three years. This was the price McLaughlin paid for having the neatest formula in use. In fact, we would normally only expect two-thirds of the scores computed to be accurate to within the range of the standard error. To

Table 4.4   Means of readability scores over 40 passages

	1st-year passages (n = 24)	4th-year passages (n = 16)
Pooled teacher-assessments	11.30	13.14
Flesch—Reading Ease	78.31	66.78
Powers-Sumner-Kearl	5.09	5.76
Smog	8.23	10.12
Flesch—Grade	7.23	9.21
Farr-Jenkins-Patterson	68.89	59.43
Mugford	11.50	13.59
Fog	8.95	11.37
Forcast	8.76	9.46
Dale-Chall	6.88	8.04

put it the other way round, we may expect one in three true scores to be outside a three-year age range. One is therefore inclined to feel that this range of potential error is too great for reliable classroom use, when exact grading rather than ranking is the important criterion.

It was for these reasons that the Flesch Grade score was the one chosen for use in the readability level survey. First, as Table 4.4 shows, the reading levels (i.e. the grade levels + 5) are similar to those from which the sample passages were actually taken (12.23 for first form and 14.21 for fourth form). Second, the scores are derived directly from the Flesch RE formula, which was the second best overall, and the lower correlation is essentially related to a rounding effect in the transformation formula. Third, many teachers do have access to the Fry Readability Graph, and in a pilot study (Harrison, 1974) we showed that Fry graph scores correlated extremely highly with Flesch RE scores. In other words, this non-arithmetic aid can be said to give scores which would be as valid as those obtained from the Flesch formula.

1 Age level, accuracy of formulae and subjective judgements

Further examination of Table 4.4 raises the question of why the teacher judgements, and most readability formulae, show a gap of two years in predictions of text difficulty over a three-year age range. There are a number of possible reasons for this.

It could be simply a statistical or sampling weakness which has isolated for analysis simpler texts than those in normal use at fourth-year level. Alternatively, it could be that both teachers and formulae are giving artificially low scores, because of some kind of ceiling effect at fourth-year level. Finally, it could be that the sampling is adequate and there is no ceiling effect in scoring, which would imply that either first-year texts are comparatively difficult, or fourth-year texts slightly easier than one might have expected.

The first suggestion, that our sample texts are rather simple, is not supported by corroborative subjective evidence obtained by teachers at a National Association for the Teaching of English conference. Many teachers claimed they were 'horrified' at the difficulty of the reading material children had to face, particularly in certain subject areas in the fourth year. The second suggestion of a ceiling effect may apply, since it is clearly evident in the case of some formulae, and is not a topic on which there is much research evidence available. Against this is the point that the two-year gap is not only present in readability-formula scores, but may also be seen in the pooled teacher-judgements, and certainly the method of data collection was designed to avert the possibility of a ceiling effect in the normal sense (the estimates of passage difficulty offered an age range of below six to over eighteen years). There are reasons for suggesting that the third suggestion is correct, namely that although certain texts are very difficult, the spread of difficulty was less than one might expect. Notwithstanding the difficulties of O-level and CSE textbooks, one can suggest that the gap in reading level between first and fourth year is in reality less than three years. In English, for example, there is a tendency to offer quite difficult Puffin books at first-year level, while motivation to read is fairly high, while at fourth-year level in an endeavour to encourage reading, writers such as Barry Hinds or John Wyndham, with a simple or racy prose style, may be more in evidence. One could suggest further possible causes, but for the time being it must at least be noted that the problem of pinpointing the actual reading level of a book or text is a very delicate one, and one which at best is only solved in part by evidence of correlations in a cross-validation study.

Table 4.5 (p. 94) gives two groups of intercorrelations: the results

Table 4.5   Intercorrelations of variables in cross-validation study

	T-DIFF	T-INT	CLOZE	C-DIFF	C-INT	WDS/SEN	SYLLS/WD	MUGFORD	FLESCH-RE	FOG	DALE/WDS
T-INT	39										
CLOZE	51*	09									
C-DIFF	86**	29	64**								
C-INT	55**	78**	10	31							
WDS/SEN	11	10	16	24	15						
SYLLS/WD	70**	50*	55**	78**	47**	18					
MUGFORD	69**	63**	44**	69**	63**	07	88**				
FLESCH-RE	62**	44*	61**	64**	38	31	81**	81**			
FOG	38	26	51	34	23	76**	57**	57**	83**		
DALE/WDS	56**	54**	53**	65**	44*	28	86**	79**	69**	30	
DALE/FM	56**	69**	45*	58**	56**	22	82**	79**	68**	34	93**

1st-year passages (n = 23)

Table 4.5—continued

		T-DIFF	T-INT	CLOZE	C-DIFF	C-INT	WDS/SEN	SYLLS/WD	MUGFORD	FLESCH-RE	FOG	DALE/WDS
	T-INT	48										
	CLOZE	69**	35									
	C-DIFF	82**	46	50*								
	C-INT	30	80**	48	20							
4th-year	WDS/SEN	74**	21	61*	37	16						
passages	SYLLS/WD	50*	29	32	61*	07	13					
(n = 16)	MUGFORD	56*	21	35	64**	09	14	90**				
	FLESCH-RE	71**	33	51*	68**	12	37	86**	86**			
	FOG	81**	36	57*	67**	21	70**	75**	75**	94**		
	DALE/WDS	63**	39	40	83**	18	15	87**	91**	82**	72**	
	DALE/FM	82**	48	58*	86**	29	43	76**	84**	83**	82**	94**

All values of r given as positive; decimal points omitted.
* Significant at .05 level.
** Significant at .01 level.

T-DIFF	Pooled teacher estimates of passage difficulty
T-INT	Pooled teacher estimates of passage interest level
C-DIFF	Pooled children's estimates of passage difficulty
C-INT	Pooled children's estimates of passage interest level
WDS/SEN	Mean number of words per sentence
SYLLS/WD	Mean number of syllables per word
DALE/WDS	Percentage of words not on Dale 3000 word list
DALE/FM	Dale-Chall readability formula

for first-year and fourth-year passages are presented separately, since the student ratings and cloze tests were different for each age group. Perhaps the first point to note is the very high correlation ($r = .86$ and $r = .82$) between teacher- and student-ratings of passage difficulty. The strength of correlation is of course partly related to the fact that the ratings of difficulty were obtained in almost identical ways. Nevertheless, it does seem that at both age levels teachers and pupils are in agreement about what is difficult and what is easy to read. It is not surprising then that the correlation of both sets of judges with readability-formulae scores are broadly parallel within each age group.

There are however marked differences between age groups in the correlations with readability formulae. At fourth-year level, correlations with readability formulae are higher for all except one formula. There is a causal explanation for this in statistical terms which at least gives a partial account of why this comes about. If we look at the first-year level, we see that the correlations between judgements of difficulty and the words-per-sentence variable are very low. Since this variable is normally given a high weighting in a readability formula it is not surprising that correlations with the formulae are lowered. Probing a little further, it would seem, in this study at least, that syntactic complexity (as measured by sentence length) was not a crucial determinant of passage difficulty at first-year secondary level.

By contrast, the vocabulary variable—syllables per word—which is used in a number of formulae, has very high correlations with subjective assessments of difficulty at first-year level, and slightly lower ones at fourth-year level. Against teachers' judgements the figures are $r = .70$ at first year and $r = .50$ at fourth year. The most stable formula, in terms of both year groups, is that of Flesch, and this presents further support for the decision to use the Flesch formula in our related study of the difficulty level of a large number of passages from different subjects and age groups.

If we turn briefly to the interest-level variables, we again note very high level of agreement between teachers and students about what would be found interesting or boring in the classroom. We did in fact control for sex in the students' ratings and found a number of statistically significant differences which were highly subject-specific and replicated across age groups, with boys tending to assess English texts as rather boring, and girls consistently rating science and geography texts as boring. Often a passage rated as difficult was also assessed as being of low interest. This might not surprise us, but it is worth noting that a higher correlation between prose difficulty and interest level was found with our first-year passages ($r = .64$ for Flesch) than with the fourth-year passages ($r = .12$). It would be dangerous to generalize from a single study, but a possible interpretation is that at fourth-year level content rather than prose difficulty is playing a greater role in determining the reader's response in terms of interest level, and passage content is not measured directly by the formulae we have used.

2 Correlation with cloze readability scores

Finally, we must consider the correlations of our subjective variables with the cloze test scores. At each age level, correlations between the cloze criterion and readability formulae are rather lower than those which have been found in certain other studies. Bormuth (1966) and more recently Miller (1974) have found correlations as high as .8–.9 between cloze scores and the same formulae used in the present study. One possible reason for this discrepancy would be unreliable cloze results in our own study, but other explanations can be offered. It may be, for example, that at fourth-year level interaction with interest level (which we have already seen is not highly correlated with readability formulae scores) has affected the cloze results. This line of argument is supported by a study of Schlief and Wood's (1974) who found very poor (.28) or even negative correlations between the cloze scores of children and nine readability formulae. Their work used magazines and newspapers, rather than passages from reading tests or carefully-prepared 'Readers' Digest'-type passages of what might be called 'pseudo-information'. In our own study the passages were not chosen to represent a carefully-balanced group of information-giving passages. Some were from novels, others from textbooks, while a good number were from teacher-produced worksheets, giving instructions on how to carry out a task. Very little evidence is available at present about the differential performance of children on cloze passages of such different types. In the context of the classroom, teachers want help in selecting suitable materials for their students in every reading task, and at present it may well be that we still know far too little about how readability measures of all kinds function with different types of text. It seems clear that on the individual level, cloze answers give us some idea of how the reader is responding to the text, and equally the pooled scores of large numbers of children on cloze tests have been found to correlate highly with other estimates of passage difficulty in many studies, though by no means all.

3 Applying cloze readability scores in the classroom

However, in considering the classroom applicability of cloze techniques as a measure of readability a number of problems arise. Bormuth (1967, 1968a) has reported that if a child scores 38 per cent on a cloze test, then this suggests he or she is coping reasonably well with understanding it. In the latter of the two studies referred to, he suggests an alternative criterion of 44 per cent. Both figures have been used by teachers in helping to make judgements about the difficulty levels of materials. Bormuth's findings were based on large-scale research studies, each involving a hundred subjects, and his figures of 38 per cent and 44 per cent were the average scores on a cloze test which were associated with a certain degree of success on a multiple-choice comprehension test. The problem for the teacher is whether the cloze test scores of a small group would be a reliable indication of the difficulty level of the passage. In large-scale research it is generally considered essential to use each possible version of a passage in a cloze test; thus if seventh-word deletion is being used, one version might begin at the first word, and every seventh after that, the next version would begin with the second word in the passage, and so on. Only in this way could the researcher be certain that every word in the passage was taken account of, and that an unreliable result had not been obtained by a single version which happened to delete a particularly difficult (or particularly easy) set of words.

Another problem for a teacher wanting to use average cloze scores as an indication of the difficulty level of a whole book is that of sampling reliability. Most readability formulae require that a number of samples of prose are assessed and the results averaged in order to obtain a more reliable score. Normally a minimum of three such samples are taken, but five or more are sometimes recommended, depending on the nature of the formula and the accuracy required by the teacher. If an estimate of the difficulty level of a book as a whole is required, then this suggests that a number of cloze tests should be constructed and the results averaged, and this is indeed the approach recommended by Rankin and Culhane (1969) in their account of how cloze techniques might best be used to assess readability. These considerations seem to suggest that unless they are used with great care and in a systematic way, cloze scores as indicators of readability levels may be unreliable and potentially misleading. It may be that at present teachers would be advised to continue using cloze results as an indication of the level of an individual's response, but should beware of pooling data from comparatively small samples and making judgements about the readability levels of texts. To reinforce this warning one should report that in our own study we found individuals in the same class scoring 0–100 per cent on the same passage. The standard deviations in our cloze study were generally about 9 per cent, and those in Bormuth's were 17 per cent. The reason those in our study were comparatively small was that our subjects were only required to deal with texts which had been used with their own year group (by teachers in another school district); Bormuth used texts of different levels and with a wider age range. Nevertheless, the size of the standard deviations in our study is quite large in relation to the range of mean scores which was obtained overall. The average score on our easiest first-form passage was 56 per cent, and that for the most difficult was

27 per cent. The average for all first-form passages was 41 per cent, and this means that on an averagely-difficult passage we should expect two-thirds of individual cloze scores to come within the range 32–50 per cent. In other words, we could expect the individual results on an average passage to have a good deal of variation, and to approach both ends of the difficulty range obtained in our survey. Clearly, if only a small group of children perform the cloze test it is unlikely that the result would be a reliable one.

4 Are new formulae needed?

To sum up, our findings do not suggest that there is a need for new formulae to measure prose difficulty in terms of vocabulary and sentence-structure. The two best-known formulae in the US, the Flesch and the Dale-Chall, proved best on cross-validation with teachers' judgements. Our own British product, Len Mugford's formula, was about as good, and in fact was extremely close in pinpointing the actual age level derived from the pooled teacher-estimates. The issue of interest level is clearly one which must be controlled for in further studies, particularly when a number of passages are being compared. Lastly, we would suggest that although it offers an attractive window into the reader's response, the use of cloze tests as a measure of readability still requires a fair amount of fundamental research. J. B. Carroll made exactly this point in a seminal survey published several years ago (1971), but while many researchers are using cloze as a variable because scores are so readily obtained, there remains a good deal of doubt about what precisely cloze procedure is testing. When we have a fuller answer to this question it seems likely that cloze will be a more valuable instrument in examining the nature of the reader's response. On the crucial issue of the reliability of individual teacher-judgements of text difficulty, numerous studies (*vide* Klare, 1975b; Harrison, 1977) have concurred in finding that they can be much less reliable than pooled judgements. The implication of such research is clearly that teachers should endeavour to discuss the selection of texts with their colleagues, and to approach a consensus view of what their pupils can read with understanding. In our own survey, the number of teachers used as a criterion group in assessing the difficulty levels of passages was comparatively small (twenty-four), and yet their pooled results were very reliable. Only three individuals had poor correlations with the pooled scores (i.e. below .6); all the others were in the range $r = .68–.88$. Another indication of their reliability was that when the teachers' individual scores were included in a stepwise multiple-regression analysis (Youngman, 1975), using their pooled scores as a criterion, a multiple correlation of $R = .995$ was obtained using only twelve of the twenty-four teachers. In other words, the scores of the most consistent twelve teachers took account of 99 per cent (i.e. R^2)

of the overall variation in scores, and enabled us to reconstruct the pooled scores of the whole group of twenty-four.

The question of what makes a teacher a reliable judge of readability is a complex one. Of the three teachers who had poor correlations with their colleagues' scores in our own study, one was not a native English speaker, but the other two were remedial specialists, and knew a good deal about the problems of poorer readers. The passages in out study were taken from normal lessons in first and fourth year, and included extracts from some CSE and O-level textbooks. It could be, therefore, that a secondary teacher with a wide general acquaintance with several curriculum areas would be in a better position to judge the passages than a remedial specialist whose skills are used over a narrower area, and who concentrates mainly on basic literacy and number work. The scale of the present study was not large enough to allow a thorough investigation of what makes for a reliable judge of readability, although it would be interesting to know whether as a general rule teachers in some subjects tend to be more skilled than others, both in relation to judging their own subject areas and those of others. At present such information is not available, and one is inclined to recommend what will be suggested elsewhere in this volume, namely that within their own schools teachers should attempt to familiarize themselves with the language demands of other subjects as well as their own. A teacher who is aware of the extensive range of demands made by texts on children at different age levels is likely to be in a much stronger position to make a reliable judgement about potential difficulties.

The need for this awareness is perhaps particularly great when the interests of different subjects are joined in interdisciplinary work, whether in science or humanities. Collaborating teachers may find it extremely difficult to evaluate the books from another subject area, and objective measures of readability may therefore be particularly helpful in assessing the relative difficulty of texts. This is not to deny the value of the opinions of non-specialist teachers: indeed these are to be valued precisely because such teachers may have insights into the problems of the child which the specialist would not readily appreciate. In this context one must also endorse the appointment in certain schools of 'floating' remedial specialists whose role is to sit in with normal classes and assist children with learning difficulties. Apart from giving valuable support to the notion that learning difficulties are not encountered solely by one group of children, such teachers can fulfil two important functions which relate to the use of texts in the classroom. Firstly, they can monitor the use of books and worksheets and offer the teacher another perspective on which passages or topics are causing particular difficulty; secondly, they can mediate between the text and the pupil, not simply by paraphrasing or explaining difficult sections, but also by encouraging more careful and more responsive reading.

VII Conclusions

In this final section, we are not suggesting that readability formulae should be applied indiscriminately to everything a student is likely to read—apart from being totally unrealistic in terms of the time this would take, it would also be inappropriate in some cases and potentially harmful in others.

We are not suggesting that textbooks with a high readability index should be scrapped—in these times of economic restraint this would be folly. What we would suggest is that the results of our research, taken together with parallel findings from similar studies, give firm evidence that many students, perhaps even most students, learn less than they might otherwise do from school texts, and this is because texts are presenting difficulties not just in terms of conceptual content, but because of the way in which they are written.

The implications for us as teachers are therefore:

1 We must be more alert to which of the books we use are likely to be causing extra problems; for example, we should not expect children to work effectively on their own in the library if the reference book we send them to is likely to be harder to read than most other books in the school.
2 We should pay special attention to the difficulty level of books in the content areas when the student's intrinsic motivation to read is likely to be low, because it is precisely when motivation is low that high level of prose difficulty is likely to lead to non-comprehension.
3 We must look with particular care at textbooks, worksheets and workbooks which give instructions for a task. Very often these will relate to work which the student is to tackle on his or her own, and for which anything less than full comprehension will mean that no progress can be made. In our own study we found that teachers tended to assume that this failure implied that the task itself was too difficult. It needs a high degree of professional skill to observe all the students in a class and to decide in particular cases whether a workcard is causing problems because of its content, or simply because of the way it is written. Nevertheless, at a time of increasing usage of individualized learning materials, it is a skill which we must foster.

Does readability level make a difference? The answer to this question has been demonstrated in a number of carefully-controlled studies conducted by George Klare (1975a). He has shown that if you take two groups of readers who are equal in reading ability and give them exactly the same comprehension test, those given a more readable version of the test passage will learn and understand more. He prepared two versions of the test passage—the original one, and another which had been rewritten in simpler prose—and found that significantly higher comprehension test scores were obtained by the group which was given the passage with a lower readability score.

In making the assertion that children can learn more from more simply written texts it is important to include a cautionary note regarding the use of readability formulae at the stage of textbook authorship. As has been pointed out consistently in readability research, there is no causal relationship between difficulty level as predicted by a formula and the actual difficulty a reader is likely to encounter. Formulae simply measure certain correlates of text difficulty; they do not measure that difficulty directly. The formulae were designed to be applied *post hoc* to samples of prose, and it is invalid to assume that they can be used as an infallible guide for authors. As long ago as 1947 Gunning attacked this simplistic misconception and the short-sentence mania which he felt it had caused (*vide* Klare, 1963). He also repudiated the idea that in order to write readable prose authors should adopt a stereotyped technique.

The dangers of writing to a formula have been experienced by the Resources for Learning Development Unit based in Avon, which has used readability formula scores to assist them in producing materials aimed at different reading levels for mixed-ability groups. Initially the formula results were a valuable guide, but gradually the writing team became aware of what factors they could alter in order to affect the measured readability score, and gradually the team realized that they were tending to write stilted and incoherent prose. These prose passages conformed to the age levels required, but this was by no means enough, and the team soon recognized that while formula results can assist in pinpointing difficult passages, a low score does not guarantee a good style, nor a discernible flow of argument. A passage initially rated as 'difficult' may have contained a number of long sentences with subordinate clauses because this was the most appropriate mode of expression. Indeed, it might well be that to artificially lower the readability index by rewriting the passage with shorter sentences could actually make it more difficult to read. This could come about, for example, if the rewritten version extended the distance between complex ideas which had been closely linked in the original structure, but it could also happen if the short sentences of the rewritten version were awkward and disjointed.

As we have attempted to stress from the outset, measuring or predicting readability is a complex matter, but providing care is taken, objective measures of readability can be of value to classroom teachers as well as to educational researchers. As will be reported in later chapters, our project has found that in many cases teachers tend to have low expectations about the use children can make of books in their learning. If the texts given to children are too difficult, then naturally the response of the reader will be a limited one. The findings reported in this chapter strongly suggest that in science and social studies in particular, the demands made of children by the texts currently in use are excessive, particularly in the lower years of secondary schooling. Our conclusion is that children can be helped to use books and other printed resources more effectively than they do at present, and although one should not overestimate their potential, measures of readability can be used to help in this important task.

Appendix 1

The passages[1]

Passage A

APART FROM THE SANATORIUM, GIMINGHAM HALL WAS THE
LARGEST HOUSE I HAD EVER LIVED IN. IT WAS REPUTED TO HAVE
BEEN BUILT ON THE SITE OF A CASTLE ONCE OWNED BY JOHN OF
GAUNT (HENCE MY DRAMA) AND IT WAS SAID THAT A TUNNEL RAN FROM
THERE TO THE RUINS OF BACTON PRIORY. AS BACTON WAS WELL OVER
FIVE MILES AWAY THIS WAS QUITE IMPOSSIBLE, BUT I BELIEVED IT
THEN, AND FOR MANY YEARS DID THE EQUIVALENT OF 'DINING OUT'
ON THE STORIES I MADE UP ABOUT THIS TUNNEL AND MY ADVENTURES
THEREIN, ALTHOUGH IN ACTUAL FACT I WAS TERRIFIED OF GOING
MORE THAN TWO STEPS DOWN THE CELLAR STAIRS. IT WAS NOT AN
OVER-LARGE HOUSE, BUT IT WAS FULL OF ODD LITTLE ROOMS AND
CORNERS. WITH THE PERVERSITY OF CHILDHOOD I WAS REASONABLY
HAPPY THERE, WHERE BY ALL THE LAWS OF PSYCHOLOGY AND WHAT-NOT I
SHOULD HAVE BEEN MOST MISERABLE. WHEN I WAS GROWN-UP I TRIED
TO DISCOVER FROM THE MINISTRY OF PENSIONS WHY I WAS SENT
THERE, BUT THEY WERE NONCOMMITTAL, AND THE OFFICER I QUESTIONED
WAS OBVIOUSLY AFRAID I MIGHT MAKE A FUSS.
I AM INCLINED TO THINK THAT MY AWKWARD QUESTIONS MAY HAVE
LED TO THE PREMATURE DESTRUCTION OF MY FILE.
I BELIEVE IT WAS A GENUINE MISTAKE. AT SEETHING HALL,
MISS HUNTLEY HAD RUN A HOME FOR DIFFICULT CHILDREN WITH SOME
SUCCESS, AND WHO WAS MORE DIFFICULT THAN I? WHEN SHE MOVED
TO GIMINGHAM THE LANDLORD HAD REFUSED TO ALLOW BOYS ON THE
PREMISES, SO THEY HAD TO GO, AND GRADUALLY I SUPPOSE THE
CHARACTER OF THE PLACE CHANGED, FOR THE GAPS WERE FILLED BY
ELDERLY AND MIDDLE-AGED GENTLEWOMEN, ALL A BIT 'GONE' IN
THE HEAD. THEY WERE, I EXPECT, MORE PROFITABLE AND LESS
TROUBLE THAN CHILDREN, AND THOUGH NONE OF THEM WAS RAVING
MAD THEY WERE THE SORT OF RELATIONS ONE WOULD RATHER NOT SEE,
ESPECIALLY IF ONE HAD A TITLE OR HIGH POSITION. ALTHOUGH
I DID NOT OF COURSE REALISE IT THEN, THE PLACE IN MY TIME WAS
DEFINITELY A PRIVATE MENTAL HOME, AND REGISTERED AS SUCH
WITH THE BOARD OF CONTROL. WHENEVER THE BOARD'S INSPECTORS
CAME DOWN I WAS ALWAYS SENT FOR A WALK WITH MISS GARNER, AND MISS
HUNTLEY WAS ALWAYS REFERRING TO ME AS THE ONLY 'NORMAL'
GIRL THERE. THERE WERE ABOUT TWENTY-FIVE INMATES, MOST OF
THEM BETWEEN FORTY AND SIXTY. THERE WERE A FEW TEENAGE
GIRLS, AND CISSIE WHO WAS ELEVEN AND MYSELF, THEN NINE AND
A HALF. MISS HUNTLEY WAS ALWAYS REFERRED TO AS 'MA'AM'
AS IF IT WAS HER NAME. MISS GARNER WAS HER PARTNER, AND
SHARED HER LIFE IN THE DRAWING ROOM, BUT MISS DENNY, WHO WAS
A KIND OF HELP, LIVED WITH US.

[1] See Table 4.1, p. 74.

Passage B

BLOOD CONSISTS OF A WATERY LIQUID CALLED PLASMA IN WHICH THERE ARE VAST NUMBERS OF TINY CELLS CALLED CORPUSCLES. UNDER THE MICROSCOPE (SEE A) IT CAN BE SEEN THAT MOST OF THE CELLS ARE LIKE TINY RED PLATES. THESE ARE THE RED CORPUSCLES THAT GIVE THE BLOOD ITS COLOUR. THERE ARE SMALLER NUMBERS OF WHITE CORPUSCLES OF IRREGULAR SHAPE.

THE WORK OF THE BLOOD. THE BLOOD SYSTEM IS THE BODY'S TRANSPORT SYSTEM, CARRYING MANY SUBSTANCES FROM ONE PART OF THE BODY TO ANOTHER. OXYGEN FROM THE LUNGS IS CARRIED ROUND THE BODY IN THE RED CORPUSCLES. DISSOLVED FOOD FROM THE DIGESTIVE SYSTEM PASSES INTO THE PLASMA. IT IS CARRIED FIRST TO THE LIVER AND THEN TO THE REST OF THE BODY. THE ACTIVITIES OF THE CELLS PRODUCE A NUMBER OF WASTE PRODUCTS. THESE DISSOLVE IN THE PLASMA AND ARE CARRIED AWAY BEFORE THEY CAN POISON THE CELLS. CARBON DIOXIDE WASTE IS REMOVED BY THE LUNGS AND OTHER WASTES ARE TAKEN FROM THE BLOOD IN THE KIDNEYS.

THE WHITE CORPUSCLES HELP OUR BODIES TO FIGHT DISEASE BECAUSE THEY CAN DESTROY GERMS AND THE POISONS THEY MAKE.

THE CIRCULATION OF THE BLOOD. BLOOD TRAVELS ROUND THE BODY IN A SYSTEM OF TUBES THAT BRANCH MANY TIMES AND REACH ALL PARTS. IT IS PUMPED ALONG THESE TUBES BY THE HEART, WHICH IS THE 'ENGINE' OF THE BLOOD SYSTEM. THE HEART HAS THICK MUSCULAR WALLS AND IS DIVIDED UP INTO FOUR SECTIONS (SEE B).

THE TUBES THAT CARRY BLOOD AWAY FROM THE HEART ARE CALLED ARTERIES. THEY HAVE THICK WALLS WHICH WITHSTAND THE PRESSURE ALONG THE ARTERIES AND BY TAKING SOMEONE'S PULSE (SEE C) YOU ACTUALLY FEEL THE STRENGTH AND FREQUENCY OF THE HEART BEAT.

IN THE ORGANS OF THE BODY THE ARTERIES DIVIDE UP INTO MANY TINY TUBES CALLED CAPILLARIES. THESE HAVE VERY THIN WALLS AND THEY PASS ALONG THE CELLS OF THE BODY. FOOD AND OXYGEN PASS OUT OF THE BLOOD AND INTO THE CELLS. SOME OF THE PLASMA ALSO LEAKS OUT OF THE CAPILLARIES AND BATHES THE SURROUNDING CELLS. AFTER PASSING THROUGH THE TISSUES, THE CAPILLARIES JOIN UP AGAIN TO FORM VEINS WHICH CARRY THE BLOOD BACK TO THE HEART. VEINS HAVE THINNER WALLS THAN ARTERIES AND THE BLOOD IN THEM HAS LOST MOST OF ITS PRESSURE. IT FLOWS GENTLY BACK TO THE HEART, HELPED ON ITS WAY BY GENERAL MOVEMENTS OF THE BODY. SMALL VALVES PREVENT IT FROM FLOWING THE WRONG WAY.

Appendix 2

An example of a readability formula in use

As an example of a readability formula in action the Flesch Reading Ease score has been worked out for the passage below which is taken from a fascinating document of modern history—the 1908 Sears, Roebuck mail order catalogue. Suppose a teacher wished to gauge the age group below which the reading demands of Sears's prose would be likely to prevent a child from profiting from the book. Clearly he could look at the catalogue himself, ask colleagues, or ask some children, but this would not give him an objective indication of whether the level of prose difficulty is much greater than, for example, his normal history textbook.

For convenience, a single passage of almost 300 words has been selected, but it would be reasonable and in certain cases judicious to take three 100-word samples from different places in a book and average them before calculating the Reading Ease score.

It is a well-established fact that the finances of a church or Sunday school depend largely upon the attendance of its members. One church has evolved a plan by which the punctual attendance of its Sunday school members has been brought about in a very interesting manner. They purchased a dozen sets of our 'Holy Land' views, including the stereoscopes, and on the first morning their attendance was only about twenty-five at the opening hour. The announcement made was as follows: 'Every scholar who arrives before the opening of the school at 9.30 will be given a colored stereoscopic view free. If you arrive after the school has commenced you do not get a stereoscopic view. When you have fifteen of these colored stereoscopic views, you will then be given a beautiful stereoscope free, which will complete your set and enable you to enjoy your collection of views.' This plan aroused such interest and enthusiasm among the young people that the next Sunday the attendance was over forty when the school opened. The following Sunday the attendance was greater yet, and over sixty views were needed to supply those present at the opening hour. The attendance rapidly increased, and with this increase of attendance came a corresponding increase in the collection, so that the cost of these views was rapidly made up in this manner. There was another very important effect which this plan produced. It stimulated a real interest in the lessons of the day, for everyone in the family, from the old folks to the children, take an interest in these wonderful colored stereoscopic views, and home study is developed to a greater extent and made far more interesting and helpful than by any other plan that has ever been devised.

The Flesch score combines two variables—syllables per word and words per sentence—in a formula, so it is first necessary to count words, syllables and full stops.

Number of words = 294
Number of syllables = 461
Number of sentences = 10

If you have taken the trouble to count the syllables in this passage you may well have arrived at a number other than 461. Counting syllables is not always a reliable business, even among relative experts, and there are often difficult decisions. In the present case 'opening' has been scored as three syllables and '9.30' as only one. The rationale for the second decision is that numerals do not serve the same function as normal words, and they are often capable of being pronounced in more than one way. For consistency, therefore, numbers are counted as single-syllable words.

The resulting figures for the average number of syllables per 100 words and words per sentence are 156 and 29.4 respectively. Included in the Flesch formula (see p. 77) they give a Reading Ease score of 45.0. Flesch produced a transformation table which allows us to interpret the score in terms of a reading level in years (by adding 5 to the US school-grade score) as follows:

Flesch Formula Score	Estimated Grade Level	Age Level
90–100	5	10
80–90	6	11
70–80	7	12
60–70	8–9	13–14
50–60	10–12	15–17
30–50	13–16	18–21
0–30	College or above	

On the basis of this table the age-level of the passage is approximately 18. Using a more complex algorithm borrowed from the Nottingham computer program an age level of 19.3 is obtained. This compares with an average reading level for fourth-year social-studies materials on our survey of 14.1 years, so a teacher could assume that for the average fifteen-year-old the catalogue would be very difficult going. Clearly the length of Sears's sentences has had an influence on this Flesch score: an average of 29.4 words per sentence is extremely high by contemporary standards and no doubt this would have an effect on the reader's ability to comprehend the passage. It would then be up to the teacher to use this information sensibly—not necessarily to reject the book, but in order to decide how he could best mediate between the reader and the text. In a case such as this, two other crucial factors are the teacher's view of the purpose of the reading and the likely level of the reader's motivation. Readability measures must never be considered as alternatives to subjective judgement; it is more profitable to look on them as a useful extension of the teacher's own judgements.

5

The Incidence and Context of Reading in the Classroom

Terry Dolan, Colin Harrison and Keith Gardner

I Introduction

Although reading is usually regarded as fundamental to learning in the classroom, at the inception of the project there was little information available concerning the actual reading tasks a pupil undertakes during the school day. Opinions and impressions abounded, but we lacked objective information to answer such questions as: How much reading does a pupil attempt? How does such reading fit into the context of other activities? What is the relative importance of reading in different areas of the curriculum?

It appeared essential that the project should attempt a descriptive analysis that would go some way towards providing teachers with a picture of existing classroom practice. This would serve at least to

1 illuminate a discussion among teachers as to the use made of reading and writing in the classoom;
2 shed some light on the issue as to whether or not existing practice provided an appropriate context for promoting effective reading in all areas of the curriculum.

Such was our intention. In the event, the translation of intent into action proved a formidable task. It would have been comparatively simple to have designed questionnaires to obtain information. Two main considerations deterred us from relying completely on this approach. First, the Bullock Committee was in being and it was known that a substantial survey of the use of language activities in schools was taking place. There was little point in attempting to replicate this work. Second, the project team were determined to avoid the weaknesses inherent in a complete dependence on the impressions of pupils and teachers as to the real nature of what really happens from hour to hour in the classroom. Therefore, a decision was made to embark on an observational study. This meant that a complete strategy for evolving a reliable and objective procedure had to be designed, piloted and validated.

The project was fortunate in that other research areas within the

University of Nottingham School of Education were concerned with various aspects of classroom observation. Hence, a large amount of existing expertise was readily available. Nevertheless, it was inevitable that the energies of the project had to be concentrated on this aspect of its work for a considerable time.

II The development period

In essence, we wanted to observe individual pupils and teachers throughout a school day, recording every relevant activity. The first task was to define what we were going to observe and record. Initially, the research officers who were appointed at the beginning of the project (Terry Dolan, Colin Harrison and Dr Paula Allman) sat in on a variety of lessons and made observations on an unstructured basis. The notes from these informally-recorded sessions were compared, and following discussions on what information would be most useful a preliminary Reading Behaviour Inventory was drawn up. This was refined in field trials over a six-month period, during which the team profited from the advice of the teachers who were involved in the project, and from two authorities on classroom observation research: Professor E. C. Wragg of Nottingham University, and Mr Sid Hilsum, who was the senior author of the NFER study *The Teacher's Day* (Hilsum and Cane, 1971). The team considered a number of possible approaches to recording data, and the decision to construct and validate a new instrument was not taken lightly. Consideration was given to classroom-interaction analysis systems such as that of Flanders (1970) and systems of recording the language activity of the classroom, notably that devised by Bellack *et al.* (1966), but none of those available allowed for the concurrent emphasis on content and form which we wished to obtain.

Of recent research undertaken in the United Kingdom into the patterns of classroom activity in our schools, perhaps the study which in methodological terms related most closely to our own was *Teaching English in the United Kingdom* (Squire and Applebee, 1969). This important book has perhaps received less attention than it deserves because it was written for an American audience and published in America, but it offers a wide-ranging and challenging description of English teaching at secondary level in a variety of schools. The overlap between this study and our own is limited to a single subject area; the observations in the Squire and Applebee study were made in 1967 and ours were made seven years later; nevertheless, the wish to examine quantitatively the content of lessons and the methods used in presenting that content to children was common to both projects, and although a detailed comparison of the findings of the two projects will not be possible within this chapter, some points of interest will be raised in later sections.

After the fieldtrials the final form of the Reading Behaviour Inventory (or RBI) was determined. We should state at this point that for observation purposes the definition adopted for 'reading' was 'fixating a printed or written source'. This must not be regarded as a simplistic definition of the reading process, but rather as a convention to allow for reliable data collection.

Another set of problems emerged from a consideration of how the behaviour of both teacher and pupil should be observed and recorded. Clearly, some system of time-sampling had to be employed. In its final form the Inventory allowed for the following:

1   a minute-by-minute time-sampled record of the incidence of the specified classroom activities of (a) one pupil and (b) the teacher;
2   a record of how the class was grouped (i.e. whether the pupils were working independently, in small groups, or all engaged in the same activity);
3   a record of the total amount of reading observed minute by minute on a 1–4 scale, together with details of the text in use. The scale was as follows:
     $1 = 1 - 15$ seconds $2 = 16 - 30$ seconds
     $3 = 31 - 45$ seconds $4 = 46 - 60$ seconds
4   a record of the amount of writing done, recorded on a similar 1–4 scale, together with details of the type of writing task.

The categories under which the teacher's and the pupil's behaviour were to be observed are given below:

Category	Definition/example
Teacher	
Administrating	Marking register; taking in marks; talking to colleague who enters during lesson.
Supervising	Walking round generally keeping an eye on the class; calling class or a pupil to order.
Informing	Talking to whole class—imparting information *ex cathedra*.
Discussing	Engaging in a question-and-answer session with whole class or group.
Individual tuition	Directing the work of a single pupil; non-public conversation.
Reading	Reading aloud or silently; reading a book or a child's writing.
Writing	On blackboard; in an exercise book.
Pupil	
Administrating	Getting books out, sharpening pencil, going to toilet, walking to resource area, etc.
Waiting attention	Waiting with arm raised for teacher's attention or queuing to see teacher.

Category	Definition/example
Not involved	Chatting about non-relevant matters; disruptive activity; doodling.
Listening	To the teacher; to a tape or record; to a child or group speaking or reading.
Observing	Watching an experiment, film or drama.
Practical	Painting, drawing, cutting out; doing an experiment.
Discussing with teacher ⎫ Discussing with child ⎭	Private or public discussion, but content of discussion is task-orientated.
Deliberating	Pausing for thought during sustained activity (common in maths and scored reliably by observers).
Writing ⎫ time-sampled Reading ⎭	At the time-sampled instant the child was writing.
Calculating	Working on written calculation.

Reading and writing activities

Reading

Textbook	Includes workbooks.
Reference book	Observer uses own judgement; generally a bound book used by child doing 'research' work.
Library book	Includes classroom library books and personal 'reader'.
Exercise book	Children spend a good deal of time reading their own—or others'—exercise books.
Blackboard	or other temporary handwritten display.
Other printed matter	Generally a teacher-produced worksheet or booklet.

Writing

Copying	Direct from book or blackboard; making fair copy from draft.
Reference work	Making own notes by summarizing writing of another; usually done from printed source.
Personal	Essay, poem, personal account, diary; child writes up something his own way.
Answering	Answering specific questions; comprehension test; quiz.

Such were the basic mechanics of handling the Inventory and a situation was reached where the project officers were able to operate independently with a high level of agreement between the observations of different observers. As well as discussing the Inventory during a number of meetings with the project directors, interobserver reliability was established using a videotaped lesson which was scored and then discussed, and by a system of paired observations in which observers sat side-by-side and recorded the activities of a single child for comparison later. However, it was also necessary to ensure the validity of the instrument, in that the pupil being observed did not change his, or her, behaviour due to being aware that some form of assessment was taking place. The normal procedure adopted was as follows.

Having obtained the permission of the teacher to observe his or her lesson, the observer would then ask whether there were any children in the group who were poor readers, and would arrange to be alerted if he sat near such a child, since the aim was to focus on an average or above-average reader. The teacher would be given the opportunity to introduce the observer as a 'visitor who is learning about how our school works', and usually the children would be asked to help the observer by answering any questions he might put. The observer was generally taken to be some kind of assessor of the teacher, or possibly a student-teacher who was not yet ready to be entrusted with a class of his own.

Normally the observer would sit towards the back of a room, and appear to watch a child about eight feet away and in front of him. In fact, the child chosen would be one much closer, possibly to the left of and slightly behind the observer. It was very rare for the child under observation to display any signs of self-consciousness, but this did occur at times with the 'decoy'. In general, it took a very short time for the observer to achieve the 'wallpaper effect', and for the children to accept him as a non-threatening part of the environment.

The activities of the teacher and the selected child would then be annotated for the whole session using the RBI. This basically provided an analysis based on one-minute time-sampling of what activity each was following, and the materials in use. Notes were made on the content of the lesson, and specific details kept of any printed matter read by the child or teacher.

In order that readers of this report may have a clearer picture of the nature of the information gained from the classroom observation study, a sample Reading Behaviour Inventory protocol is reproduced in Fig. 5.1 (p. 113). This looks dauntingly complex to the uninitiated, but to the trained observer it offers a quantitative record of the amount of time devoted to various activities, and it also allows one to examine the sequence of activities, and how these are related to the teacher's role and the way in which the class is grouped.

Each of the forty columns represents a single minute, and at specified times during each minute the observer records the activity in which the teacher is engaged with a tick, and that of the pupil with a circle. The categories are not mutually exclusive, as is demonstrated in the thirty-third minute, during which the pupil is logged as listening and writing concurrently. In the first minute the teacher was giving information about the tasks to be undertaken, and the pupil

Figure 5.1 Reading Behaviour Inventory

11.20 a.m.

	1	2	3	4	5	6	7	8	9	10	11	12	13	14	15	16	17	18	19	20	21	22	23	24	25	26	27	28	29	30	31	32	33	34	35	36	37	38	39	40
Teacher administrating	✓	✓																														✓	(T₂)							✓
supervising														✓																							✓		✓	
informing	✓			✓	✓																		✓										✓	✓	✓		✓			
discussing			✓	✓		✓	✓	✓	✓	✓	✓	✓	✓		✓	✓	✓	✓	✓	✓	✓	✓	✓	✓	✓	✓	✓	✓	✓	✓	✓							✓	✓	✓
indiv. tuition																																								
reading																																								
writing																																								
Pupil administration																																								
waiting att'n																																								
not involved								o	o																															
listening	o	o	o														o	o	o	o	o	o	o						o	o	o	o	o	o	o	o				
observing													o																											
practical																																								
discussion t.c.								©																												©				
deliberating																																								
writing t.s.										o	o	o	o																				o	o	o					
writing time				3	3	1	1			2	4	3	3		1	4								2	3	1	2	2					3	2	2	3		2	1	
writing c r p a					c					c	c	c	c	c	c									c	c	c							c	c	c			c	c	
reading time				3	3	1	1			1				1	4	1					2	1		2	1	1	2	2												3
reading t.s.				o	o	o	o			o											o	o		o			o	o												o
Materials book t.r.l.			①	①																																				
ex. book, etc.					o										o	o											o	o												
printed matter					o	o	o			o	o	o	o	o										o									o	o	o			o	o	
blackboard																																								
apparatus																																								
Group whole class	o	o	o	o	o																																			
groups				o	o	o	o	o	o	o	o	o	o	o	o	o	o	o	o	o	o	o	o	o	o	o	o	o			o	o	o	o	o	o	o	o	o	o
individuals																														o	o	o									

Pupil copies out poem → Teacher fetches new group for talks → Pupil reads friend's exercise book → Pupil reads friend's poem card → Copies second poem → Second teacher (T₂) enters to give out maths homework → Pupil copies hwk., returns to poem

Case no. 1103 (Girl)
School 01
Observer 2
Age group 4th Yr. Sec.
Activity English:

Pupils each asked to write a two-minute talk on a book they have read or are reading. These will be given in groups of 3–4 plus Teacher. (Girl under observation had prepared hers in advance.) Asked then to copy out a chosen poem from poem card and write thoughts for homework.

was listening. The fourth time-sampled activity was reading (indicated by the heading *reading t.s.*), and in the *Materials* section of the Inventory a further circle in the *book t.r.l.* section indicates that either a textbook, reference book or library book was being read (the letter inside the circle indicates which). The numeral in the *reading time* category refers to the total amount of reading which took place during the time-sampled minute, which in this case was estimated as between thirty and forty-five seconds. In the fifth minute there was a similar amount of reading, but this time there was also some writing. This is shown by the numeral in the *writing time* category, which shows that the total amount of writing during the preceding minute was less than fifteen seconds, and by the *c* in the *writing c r p a* category, which indicates that the writing was straightforward copying, and not reference work or note-making, personal or free writing, or writing down answers to questions. The circles in the *Group* category show that for the first five minutes the pupils in the class were all engaged on the same activity (namely listening to the teacher's intructions). The pupil under observation spent the remainder of the lesson working in a small group, except for the time during which a second teacher came in to give homework for mathematics. One further symbol which needs explanation is the circled letter *c* which occurs twice within the category *discussion t.c.* It will be recalled that we wished to differentiate between a child's private chatter, task-orientated discussion with another child, and task-orientated discussion with a teacher. These are coded respectively as *not involved*, and within the *discussion t.c.* category a circled letter *c* and a circled letter *t*. It is worth mentioning that the pattern of the child's activities which can be deduced from the time-sampled minutes and the arrowed notes is only loosely related to the teacher's aims and the overall lesson description which are given below them. This fact stresses the value of such detailed observations, and demonstrates the information which may be lost if details about lessons are gathered solely from reports offered by classteachers.

Another set of problems was posed by the necessity of observing both primary and secondary school classrooms. In general, secondary schools operated a more or less rigidly timetabled system; primary schools a more flexible regime. It was desirable to obtain some comparison between pre-secondary and secondary pupils, yet at the same time do justice to the more integrated work of the primary school. In the event, a compromise solution was arrived at.

Observations were centred on selected secondary schools and divided between four main areas of the curriculum: English, mathematics, science, and humanities. Experience during trials indicated that little relevant information could be obtained from other lessons and the use of observer-time was critical. Then in order to obtain the necessary comparisons, similar observations were made in the largest primary schools which sent their pupils to these secondary schools. It was realized that there were two possible weaknesses in this procedure: (1) while the secondary schools were specifically chosen to provide a reasonably representative sample as regards type, size and catchment area, the primary schools might not represent such a carefully stratified sample as the secondary schools; and (2) in order to make comparisons with secondary lessons it was necessary to impose a framework of subject discipline on the primary school lesson-periods. The observer classified the occupation of the pupil as English,[1] mathematics, science or humanities, and this was not always a simple decision in a school without a formal timetable. Therefore observations of a second selection of primary schools were arranged in order to obtain further information about the primary sector, children's activities being monitored for the entire school day.

III The general inquiry

1 The selection of schools

The sixteen schools in Nottinghamshire and Derbyshire in which the project team made their observations were selected as follows: the project directors discussed with LEA advisers the best ways in which to establish a population of schools such that, as far as possible, different types of school were represented. On the basis of that advice the directors made contact with eight secondary schools, seven of which subsequently agreed to take part in the observation study. Four of these were purpose-built comprehensives: there was one mixed grammar school, a girls' secondary modern and a grammar school which had recently gone comprehensive, in which all year groups but the first were based on a selected intake. The nine primary schools which took part in the study were all feeder schools for those in the secondary sample. The secondary schools were asked to name their largest contributory primary schools and of the ten approached initially all but one agreed to assist us. Once the headteacher had given general approval the team sought an opportunity to explain to individual teachers what was envisaged, and asked their permission to sit in on a small number of lessons. Naturally some teachers had misgivings, particularly in those secondary schools where there was no experience of team-teaching, and the presence of an extra adult in the classroom was unusual. In all cases the observer made it clear that our inquiry was essentially concentrated on the child rather than the teacher, and in the event teachers were extremely cooperative in allowing their lessons to be observed. The lessons were usually

[1] Although few primary teachers would consider 'reading' a different subject from 'English', it was not unusual to see 'reading' and 'English' as separate subjects on the timetable.

selected by prior agreement with the classteachers, although the observers made it clear that they did not wish to see specially staged lessons nor necessarily ones in which reading was crucial. In the whole study the lessons of over 100 teachers were observed, and there was only one teacher who did not wish to be observed in any lessons. It must be pointed out that the aim in selecting for observation a number of different types of school was essentially to make our data more representative, and not in order to make comparisons between schools or types of school.

2 The population

Observations were carried out in:

1   top junior-school classes;
2   first-year secondary school classes;
3   fourth-year secondary school classes.

In all cases the pupils observed were, in the opinion of the teacher, of average or above-average reading ability.

3 Data collection

Between September 1974 and April 1975, a team made up of four project officers[1] collected data on 202 sessions, most of which were of double-period length. The total length of time represented was 9990 minutes, which was divided fairly evenly between each year group and subject group. The only category with a comparatively low representation was top-junior science, which was not taught as a specific subject in many schools.

The number of minutes observation in each of the subject areas for the three age groups was:

	English	Mathematics	Science	Social studies	Totals
Top junior	1215	725	431	624	2995
1st-year secondary	814	845	851	794	3304
4th-year secondary	751	867	1005	1068	3691
			Total observation time		9990

Mean duration of each observation session 49.5 minutes[2]
Standard deviation 18.9 minutes

[1] After the pilot phase, and before the main observation study, the team lost the services of Paula Masterman, but gained those of Maurice Waite. John Cole, who joined the team in January 1975, took part in the primary-school observations.
[2] It is interesting to note the relative rapidity with which the concept of the 40-minute lesson has been jettisoned in favour of 60- or 80-minute periods. In 1967 Squire's and Applebee's team logged mean lesson-length of 39.1 minutes (1969: 51).

IV Results

1 Rationale

The tables in this section constitute a summary of the data obtained from our classroom observations. It will be appreciated that these do not purport to show what happens in a 'normal' lesson in the subject areas observed, but rather give the overall picture that emerges from a large number of lessons observed in a carefully selected sample of schools. No two lessons are alike, but in most subjects there are certain types of lesson which recur, and the aim in our sampling was to ensure that the final results reflected the overall pattern of activity associated with the equivalent of three or four weeks' work in a subject.

Because of the unusual nature of the data a reliability check using techniques such as odd-even, split-half procedures would have been misleading. Inter-rater reliability of observations had been established during the time that the inventory was being developed. As an additional check, each lesson was assigned at random to one of two groups. T-tests were then used to examine whether any significant differences occurred between the two halves of data for each of the categories recorded in each cell, top junior, first-year and fourth-year secondary. The results were encouraging: the frequencies of observations suggested unreliable results in a very few cells only, and these were mostly cells in which an activity occurred so rarely (in junior science for example) that no clear pattern of incidence could emerge.

Data from the observation inventories were analysed using a computer program B.I.D.A. (Behaviour Inventory Data Analysis) written by Colin Harrison. This program standardizes the scores to take account of variable lesson length prior to testing for significant differences between groups and between subject areas. It is not advisable to use t-tests to test for differences when pairings of more than two groups from the same population are being tested. Consequently, Scheffé multiple-comparison tests were applied in addition to the standard one-way analysis of variance test. The Scheffé test is extremely stringent, however, and the number of categories attaining statistical significance on the basis of this analysis is smaller than might be expected. Had the two pairs of adjacent year groups—top juniors and first-year secondary, and first-year and fourth-year secondary—been compared separately using t-tests alone, the number of significant categories between group differences would have doubled.

2 Time spent by teachers and pupils on the categories observed using the RBI

Table 5.1 (p. 119) shows the overall percentage of time spent by teachers on the activities noted on the Inventory. Table 5.2 (p. 120) shows the overall pattern of percentages of lesson time spent by children on the activities.

1   There are some clear indications of differences between teacher and child activity at junior-school level as compared with both age groups at secondary level. Teacher informing, for instance, which accounts for 3 per cent of teacher-time at junior level and occupies fifth place in the time scale, rises to second place in the secondary school, with percentage times of 17 and 23. This is balanced by a large proportion of time spent by junior school teachers in giving individual tuition, which does not fall below 43 per cent in any subject, and reaches 59 per cent in maths and social studies. The means for each year group in this category were:

Juniors 51 per cent
First-year secondary 35 per cent
Fourth-year secondary 22 per cent.

Thus, there is a clear indication of a pattern of change in the type of lesson that dominates the junior and secondary school day.

2   This pattern of change is reflected in our observations of children's activity (see Table 5.2). Attention is drawn particularly to the *Listening* category. Our definition of listening does not include listening to a teacher or a fellow pupil during the transaction of a private conversation. This would be classified as 'discussion'. Hence, *listening* indicates a situation where a pupil is receiving 'a single stream of sound' either from the teacher, another pupil (e.g. when reading a novel round the class), or possibly from a tape or gramophone recording. At junior level, pupils spent 10 per cent of lesson-time listening; at the secondary stage this rose to 26 and 29 per cent respectively for the two age groups observed.

3   A further category in which there is a marked difference between age groups is *pupil writing*. In bald terms, junior pupils spent 15 per cent of lesson-time writing, which was only 2 per cent short of the figure for fourth-year secondary pupils who were following CSE and O-level courses, while the mean figure for first-year secondary pupils dropped to 9 per cent. It must be pointed out that we did not isolate statistically significant differences between individual subjects, despite variations of up to 8 per cent between groups. This finding relates to the large within-group variation. In English at top-junior level, for instance, the mean proportion of time spent writing was 18.8 per cent of a session, but the standard deviation associated with this figure is 19.2 per cent. In other words, there was often a heavy emphasis on writing in some lessons and little or no writing in others.

Table 5.1 The percentage of teacher's time spent on various activities

		Administrating	Supervising	Informing	Discussing	Individual tuition	Reading	Writing
Top juniors	English	13	24	4 – –	10 –	43 + +	5	0 –
	Maths	13	12	2 –	11	59	0 –	2
	Science	21	7	4	8	57	0	1
	Social studies	12	20	2 – –	6	59 +	1	0
	For all lessons	14	19	3 – –	9 –	51 + +	3	1 –
1st-year secondary	English	15	23	16	21	11	13	5
	Maths	11	5	11	8	54	6	4
	Science	15	12	21	14	37	4	3
	Social studies	12	12	21	16	39	3	4
	For all lessons	13	13	17	15	35	7	4
4th-year secondary	English	14	16	11	22	19	19	2
	Maths	13	14 +	17	15	35	2	8
	Science	13	9	37	14	23	2	8 +
	Social studies	18	17	23	17	13 –	8 +	3
	For all lessons	15	14	23	17	22 –	7	5

Levels of significance

These have been computed using the very stringent Scheffé test, in which levels better than .1 may be regarded as significant.

+ = < .1 level   + + = < .05 level
– = < .1 level   – – = < .05 level

The percentages signalled as significant are based on comparisons between two groups: top juniors versus 1st-year secondary, and 1st-year secondary versus 4th-year secondary. In each case the + and – signs indicate whether the difference is significantly greater or smaller than the corresponding figure in the 1st-year secondary results.

Table 5.2 The percentage of pupil's time spent on various activities

		Calculating	Reading (time sample)	Writing (time sample)	Deliberating	Discussing with child	Discussing with teacher	Practical	Observing	Listening	Not involved	Waiting attention	Administrating
Top junior	English	0	16	19	3	10	2	7	3	15 –	16	2	10
	Maths	26	6	5	7	11	5	4	4	9	7	9+	8 –
	Science	0	6	22	3	11	5	28	0	7 –	7	2	8
	Social studies	0	9	13	3	17++	3	18	1	3 – –	11	3	15
	For all lessons	5	11	15+	4	12+	3	10	2	10 – –	12	4	10
1st-year secondary	English	0	22	13	1	6	2	3	2	38	11	2	6
	Maths	13	10	5	6	10	3	13	3	16	10	3	12
	Science	1	9	11	1	9	4	23	7	26	8	3	9
	Social studies	0	15	9	1	6	5	18	4	26	13	3	10
	For all lessons	4	14	9	3	8	4	14	4	26	10	3	9
4th-year secondary	English	0	29	13	1	5	3	0	5	42	14	0	3
	Maths	23	8	11	6	10	3	5	7	18	17	1	8 –
	Science	3	10	20	2	7	4	11	8	31	10	0	5 –
	Social studies	0	16	21+	1	8	4	9	3	24	11	1	8
	For all lessons	6	15	17+	2	8	3	7	6	29	13	1 –	6 –

Levels of significance
See note to Table 5.1.

Also it should be noted that the overall session-time taken up by whole-class discussion and listening to the teacher at first-year secondary level would leave less time available for writing.

4   The *reading* category indicates that less time was spent on this activity in each subject area in the junior classes than in the counterpart at both secondary age levels. The differences signalled were not significant, but some further comment is necessary. First, it will be recalled that for various reasons a separate inquiry into reading activities in junior classes was carried out, and an analysis of this additional work is set out later in this chapter. Second, whatever the position regarding differences between junior and secondary school, it is quite clear that reading at secondary level, outside of English lessons, takes up a stable, if small proportion of lesson-time throughout the pre-examination courses. Our figures for reading of 22 and 29 per cent of lesson-time in English at first- and fourth-year secondary level are much higher than those given by Squire and Applebee (1969, p. 56), who reported 7 and 2 per cent at the respective age levels. This great discrepancy is largely due to the differing schemes of categorization; Squire and Applebee included a category called *literature* which was a separate activity from *reading*, and the percentage of time devoted to this general area was 23 per cent at first-year level and 36 per cent at fourth-year level.

5   No set of statistics provides a total picture of the dynamics of a classroom, but some comments based on our observation of actual classroom behaviour may serve to illuminate the figures. It appeared that reading does play a different role in junior lessons from that in secondary lessons. The situation in which the whole class follows a passage which is being read aloud is much less common in top-junior lessons than in those at secondary level. In secondary English and social studies particularly, it was not uncommon for a good part of a lesson to be based on a passage being read aloud, usually with each child following the text from a book or worksheet. This is shown in full in the figures for *teacher reading*. A crucial difference at junior level was that *teacher reading* was accompanied by *pupil listening* rather than pupil following the text. Equally, the practice of group reading of a play, poem or novel, is not found frequently in the junior school, where activities were much more individualized. Thus secondary school figures for *reading* are likely to be boosted by such activities, but the actual involvement of the pupil in reflective reading may be questioned. This could be as near to 'mechanical' reading as one would be likely to get. On the other hand, the observed reading of junior pupils was often associated with accomplishing tasks for which reading was essential.

6   Further analysis of Table 5.2 indicates that the salient language activities which emerged from each age group were:

Top junior   writing and discussion with other pupils

First-year secondary   listening and reading
Fourth-year secondary   listening, writing and reading.

3 Types of reading and writing observed using the RBI

A consideration of time spent on reading and associated activity provides some information about the role of the written word in classroom work. The overall time spent on writing and reading can be further divided among (a) different types of writing, and (b) different reading sources. This information is given in Table 5.3 (p. 123). The definition of the various categories used in this table were outlined on pp. 110–11.

(i) WRITING

1   Britton *et al.* (1975) drew attention to what they considered to be an excessive amount of time spent by children, including those at first-year secondary level, on writing for an ill-defined purpose and for a narrow implied audience. It may be thought that our figure of 9 per cent of total lesson time spent on writing at first-year secondary level hardly supports this contention. However, our definition of writing was very rigorous. A pupil had to be physically putting pen to paper. Thus, it would not be inconsistent for a pupil to describe a complete lesson as 'writing' while we would record some instances of 'writing' interspersed with 'deliberating', 'not involved' and 'discussing'. Now it is reasonable to assume that the most concentrated periods of writing will fall within the category of 'personal writing' and reference to Table 5.3 will show that at first-year secondary level the proportion of personal writing in English lessons is lower than in any other age group. Therefore, our low estimate of total writing time at first-year secondary level is accounted for partly by our definition of 'writing', and partly by the decrease in personal writing in English lessons which led to a reduction in the incidence of continuous writing. In short, we would not argue that our findings necessarily conflict with those of Britton and his associates.

2   Copying direct from a source is more common in subjects which have a particular emphasis on factual knowledge. While there are clear reasons as to why this should be, it should be noted that one effect may be to limit the purposes of reading. A pupil who transfers information mechanically from source to textbook is not encouraged to exercise reflective reading, and a subsequent reading of the textbook is likely to be for retention rather than for reflection. Thus, a circular action is set up where, in both reading and writing, memorization takes precedence over thinking. When this approach dominates a particular subject certain questions should be posed concerning the opportunity given to pupils to experience a reflective use of language to establish principles and ideas.

Table 5.3   Overall percentages of types of writing and reading material in the 4 subject areas for each year group

	English			Mathematics			Science			Social studies		
	Top juniors	1st-year secondary	4th-year secondary	Top juniors	1st-year secondary	4th-year secondary	Top juniors	1st-year secondary	4th-year secondary	Top juniors	1st-year secondary	4th-year secondary
Writing												
Copying	12	8	16	10	50	60	60	46	56	30	33	13
Reference	3	22	27	0	0	0	0	0	19	39	3	17
Personal	46	34	44	0	0	5	20	29	8	22	37	45
Answering	38	36	13	90	50	36	21	25	17	8	27	26
Reading												
Textbook	17	66	71	32	37	59	0	30	13	11	34	42
Ref. book	12	5	16	0	0	0	31	7	1	54	25	7
Library	34	1	5	2	0	0	0	0	1	0	3	0
Ex. book	14	15	5	2	12	23	27	14	43	24	16	10
B'board	2	12	1	59	4	18	15	22	25	2	13	6
Other	22	0	3	5	47	1	27	27	18	10	9	36

(*ii*) READING

1   The reading section of the table shows an increasing use of the textbook related to the age of the pupil. The only exception is fourth-year secondary science where, apparently, the pupil's own exercise book and the blackboard are the main reading sources in lesson time. Equally, the use of reference and library sources in secondary science and social studies appears to be rather limited. It may be concluded that pupils have few opportunities to compare and contrast sources in these areas. The major role of reading is either to provide instructions for written or practical work, or to provide a set of basic facts.

2   The use of the workcard or worksheet is represented by our classification *other*. It features strongly in English at junior level, mathematics at first-year secondary level, all science courses, and fourth-year secondary social studies. Generally, this stimulus for reading is devoted more to ordering or controlling pupil action than to any other purpose.

4 Patterns of continuous reading

A further attempt to provide some qualitative data on how children use reading in school is shown in Table 5.4 (p. 125). Each time an observer saw that a pupil under observation did some reading, even if it was only to glance at some instructions, a record was made at the end of the time-sampled minute of the estimated total amount of all reading during that minute.

1   Approximately half of all classroom reading occurs in bursts of less than fifteen seconds in any one minute. However this is interpreted it is impossible to escape the conclusion that a large amount of classroom reading is fragmented in nature.

2   To carry the analysis further, it is useful to consider the opposite viewpoint. Outside of English lessons a very small amount of observed reading took up a complete minute in any one minute of observation. A nil return from mathematics might have been expected, and it occurred. In science, however, 1 per cent at first-year secondary and 3 per cent at fourth-year secondary is a clear indication of the type of reading which is pursued in these lessons. Equally, the highest figure under social studies was 5 per cent.

3   If reading in the classroom is largely fragmentary, what kind of reading are pupils asked to undertake? Teachers will readily recognize certain standard classroom procedures which give rise to a preponderance of 'short-burst' reading, such as:

A pupil reads a short question from a textbook, workcard, or the blackboard, prior to answering it.

Using resource materials, a pupil will fixate on a key phrase or sentence which is copied into an exercise book or project file. The

Table 5.4 Patterns of continuity in reading for each age and subject group, given as a percentage of the overall reading time recorded for reading in the group

		Type 1	Type 2	Type 3	Type 4
English	Top juniors	46	29	11	13
	1st-year secondary	53	27	10	10
	4th-year secondary	34	25	14	27
Maths	Top juniors	41	47	11	0
	1st-year secondary	70	22	8	0
	4th-year secondary	72	24	4	0
Science	Top juniors	69	26	5	0
	1st-year secondary	75	21	3	1
	4th-year secondary	57	36	4	3
Social studies	Top juniors	60	28	8	3
	1st-year secondary	60	28	8	3
	4th-year secondary	44	42	9	5

Type 1 Total reading during time-sampled minute was 1–15 seconds.
Type 2 Total reading during time-sampled minute was 16–30 seconds.
Type 3 Total reading during time-sampled minute was 31–45 seconds.
Type 4 Total reading during time-sampled minute was 46–60 seconds.
  Thus Type 1 represents only intermittent reading, and Type 4 continuous reading.

search is rapid, the process of copying involves frequent short references to the original material.

Answering literal questions can result in a similar reading strategy. The pupil skims a text to find appropriate answers.

4 It is unlikely that 'short-burst' reading provides pupils with an adequate means for developing a critical or evaluative approach. Even in English lessons only 10 per cent of reading observed at first-year secondary level would meet a minimal criterion for being termed 'continuous'. At fourth-year level the figure is 27 per cent. Thus, there is evidence that continuous reading in the classroom is limited largely to English lessons, and its role is limited at the beginning of secondary education. Therefore, even if some form of developing reading for learning is attempted in secondary schools, it seems that pupils will have few opportunities to exercise or practise abilities related to reading for learning, unless changes in classroom procedures also take place.

V Additional primary school observation

1 The problem

It will be recalled that the decision to carry out an additional and extended observational study in primary schools rested on two main considerations which related to:

1   the sampling of schools;
2   the suitability of the method of recording data employed in the main study when applied to the relatively flexible classroom organization found in the junior school.

Therefore, the observation study described here both extends the number of primary schools studied, and utilizes a modified procedure which permits a closer examination of the classroom activities followed by the pupils. At the same time, sampling of lessons was no longer selective in that the entire day's activities of children under observation were recorded. By this means we are able to test the major findings of the original junior-school survey.

2 Procedure

Experienced primary teachers on full-time Diploma in Education courses at the University were trained using video-recorded lessons to use the Reading Behaviour Inventory. Headteachers of schools which fed project secondary schools were approached and permission sought for the study. Observers then visited schools which offered to accommodate the survey and spent at least one day familiarizing themselves with the Inventory, introducing themselves to staff, meeting children and explaining more fully the schedules to teachers. As a result of these precautions classteachers were at ease with observers, and observers knew sufficient about pupils to avoid selecting children of below-average reading ability.

Fourth-year children from seventeen schools were observed over two periods of time, fifteen pupils in a summer term and seventeen in a spring term. In some schools children were seen from three separate classes and in all data were gathered for thirty-two children. Data for a further two children were discarded when two observers considered that one school had deliberately arranged a programme which was especially dense in reading-related activities. All other observers felt reasonably certain that they had seen fairly routine sessions which were usual and typical for the classes participating. Indeed, a frequent comment from classteachers was that they were too busy to 'lay on' display lessons specially and, in any case, they couldn't be bothered to maintain the pretence for an entire day.

Pupils were randomly selected for observation from those in clearest view from the observer's vantage point. In general, children were unaware that they were under observation but on occasions when children asked the observer what he or she was doing, they were told in the vaguest terms that the observer was interested in what the group were doing. As far as possible observers stayed with children for the entire school day with instructions to continue observation in recreation time during bad weather or when children continued working or stayed indoors to finish assignments. Such occasions were rare and there were no wet playtimes during the period of observation. A total of 9464 minutes (157 hours 44 minutes) of school time was observed over the thirty-two days with a daily average of 296 minutes (4 hours 56 minutes).

Table 5.5 (p. 128) presents a summary of the time spent on the various lesson-activities observed over the thirty-two days. Some subjects did not occur very often whereas others were seen daily. English has been broken down into its various aspects so as to provide a clearer picture. Four major activities seem to dominate in terms of time, and between them they account for three-quarters of all observations. There were ninety separate sessions of one or other aspect of English, each averaging 30 minutes per session and between them accounting for 28 per cent of every day's work. An average of one hour was spent every day on mathematics and this took a further 20 per cent of the day. At least one aspect of humanities (topic, project, history, geography, RE) was seen daily, averaging 52 minutes and occupying 17 per cent of the day's work. Finally, there were twenty-three PE or games sessions over the thirty-two days, each lasting an average of 51 minutes and averaging out at a further 12 per cent of the day. Apart from these activities, one is struck by the variation in the range of the sessions which constitute the remainder of the day, a reflection perhaps of the difference in types of classroom regime observed.

Turning to the activities specified on the Behaviour Inventory, it is informative to look at each one in terms of the four periods of time which make up most primary school days. Table 5.6 provides a convenient summary with details expressed as percentages for an average of the total daily recordings. For the teachers there is a predictable drop in administration after the first session in each half of the day. Other statistically-significant findings relate to the decrease in informing and rise in supervision between morning and afternoon sessions. It is interesting to note the variation in the distribution of the incidence of individual tuition of pupils. At least a quarter of session-time is spent with individual children except in the case of the first session in the morning. Here one notes more administration and group- or whole-class informing. Many of the findings in relation to children's activities are again quite predictable, with significantly more calculating, reading and writing in morning sessions and more practical work (art, craft, PE, games) in the

Table 5.5   Activities observed over the 32 days

Activity	Minutes observed	Average session length	Average daily length	Number of sessions
Administration	171	9	5	18
Assembly	624	28	19	22
Art, craft	418	46	13	9
Topic, project	950	34	30	28
PE, games	1168	51	36	23
Broadcasts	138	23	4	6
French	198	49	6	4
Geography	240	60	7	4
History	259	43	8	6
Music	372	46	12	8
Religious Education	209	42	6	5
Science	116	58	4	2
Writing/news, diaries	898	39	28	23
Comprehension, spelling	877	36	27	24
Reading	519	26	16	20
Between-session reading	41	7	1	6
Tr. reads to class	56	14	2	4
Discussion	144	14	4	10
Poetry, drama	143	49	5	3
Mathematics	1918	55	60	35

Summary				% of day
Mathematics	1918	55	60	35	20
All English	2683	30	84	90	28
Humanities	1658	39	52	43	17
Reading	560	21	17	26	6

afternoon. One notes a gradual decrease in time spent on language-related activities over the day with 54 per cent of all recorded activities consisting of one or other aspect of language in the first morning-session, falling off to 38 per cent by the last session in the afternoon. Time spent listening tends to follow the pattern for teacher informing/discussing during the day.

A summary of lessons in which any reading was observed over the thirty-two days is presented in Table 5.7 (p. 131). Columns 6 and 7 express these findings in terms of hypothetical forty-minute lessons. Pupils spend time reading in all subject areas, particularly English and music. The extraordinary amount of time spent reading in the latter seems quite anomalous at first sight but it has to be pointed out

Table 5.6   Percentage of time spent on activities recorded on the RBI across the average school day

	am		pm		am	pm	Daily	am v. pm	Over-all
	1	2	1	2					
Teacher									
Administration	25	18	17	13	22	15	19	**	**
Supervision	26	27	36	38	26	37	31		
Indiv. tuition	18	33	24	26	24	25	25		
Informing	16	14	11	11	16	11	14	**	**
Discussion	9	8	12	7	9	10	9		
Writing	2	5	2	2	3	2	2		
Reading	3	3	3	3	3	3	3		
Child									
Administration	12	10	13	10	11	12	11		**
Not involved	11	12	9	8	11	9	10	**	*
Waiting att'n	3	3	3	3	3	3	3		
Practical	16	22	30	40	19	35	26	*	
Observing	3	1	3	1	2	2	2		
Calculating	6	8	1	1	7	1	4	**	*
Listening	18	13	19	13	16	16	16		**
Discussion	8	8	8	7	8	8	8		
Writing	15	11	9	10	14	9	12	**	**
Reading	13	15	11	8	14	10	12	**	*

** Difference significant at .01 level.
* Difference significant at .05 level.

(N.B. The figures are an expression of the percentage of time spent on each activity over the session length: activities are not exclusive in that a child may be recorded as performing two activities at the same instance, e.g. 'observing' and 'listening' when viewing a schools' TV broadcast. Consequently, the sum of percentages in any one column may exceed 100.)

that figures refer to reading executed at singing pace—ten lines may take only two minutes in a song of lively tempo, but considerably longer in the case of slow songs or in ones with choruses.

The incidence of reading within different types of English lessons is not uniformly distributed as may be seen in Table 5.8 (p. 132) which focusses on English. About one third of English time involved children writing up newsbooks, diaries, etc., or doing essays and creative writing. In terms of a hypothetical forty-minute lesson, there were only three minutes reading recorded and these were of the work actually written. A further third of English time was taken up with comprehension, grammar and spelling work. This type of lesson called for children to read for a fifth of the lesson time. About 20 per cent of English time logged over the thirty-two day period was spent reading library books in class, sometimes in specifically timetabled sessions and sometimes when children were encouraged to read after completing assignments. Children didn't appear to need much encouragement to read in these sessions and several observers commented on children's irritation when they were asked to put away their books in order to commence another activity.

One of the most important objectives in conducting the survey was to produce information about circumstances of prolonged reading in the classroom. It was hypothesized that prolonged reading of continuous prose would involve a different reading approach than would reading one or two words or lines out of a text. In an effort to obtain information about prolonged reading, minute-by-minute recordings were made of all reading and a summary of the results as they relate to subject areas is presented in Table 5.9a (p. 133). Continuous (non-stop) reading was only seen in any substantial amount in English and music sessions. As indicated earlier, the findings in relation to music are accounted for by the nature of the task and the tempo of the songs. Leaving aside English, it can be seen that 93 per cent of reading in mathematics and 88 per cent of reading in social-studies sessions was in bursts of under half a minute. Even in English this pattern is not broken except in the case of actual reading sessions (see Table 5.9b).

A daily average of 33.4 minutes of reading was recorded during the thirty-two days observation. Well over one-third of this was private reading of library books during set reading periods or on occasions when children read between lessons. The only substantial amount of prolonged reading recorded was seen during these reading sessions. Although there was reading in the context of subject lessons in the primary schools observed, by far the greatest incidence of continuous reading took place when children were reading privately to suit their own purposes rather than to complete an assigned learning task.

3 Discussion

The major findings of the main survey are sustained. It is apparent that reading is centred on 'English' work, and that 'short-burst' reading dominates most lesson-time. However, this follow-up survey has enabled us to bring into focus an important aspect of the junior school regime which has been underestimated up to this point. The common practice of encouraging pupils to read between activities appeared to produce the most intensive reading we observed. Certainly this type of reading resulted in continuous attention to print which was observed only rarely on other occasions. The pupils were finding both pleasure and absorption in their chosen task.

Whether such private reading disappears in the secondary school because pupils change or because a less flexible classroom

Table 5.7 Summary of observed reading

	Minutes observed	No. of sessions	Reading time samples	Average no. of time samples per session	Average daily length in minutes	% of lesson	Minutes in a 40-minute lesson
English	2683	90	660	7.3	84	25	10
Maths	1918	35	126	3.6	60	7	3
Assembly	624	22	32	1.5	19	—	—
RE	209	5	22	4.4	6	10	4
Music	372	8	154	19.25	12	41	17
French	198	4	12	3	6	6	2
Topic/proj.	950	28	73	2.6	30	8	3
History	259	6	28	4.7	8	11	4
Geography	240	4	33	8.25	7	14	6
Science	116	2	22	11	4	19	8

Table 5.8 Reading in English lessons

	Minutes observed	No. of sessions	Reading time samples	Average no. of time samples per session	Average length of session in minutes	Average in 40-minute lesson	% of 40 minutes
News, diaries, creative writing	898	23	68	3	39	3	8
Comprehension, grammar, spelling	877	24	184	8	36	8	21
Reading	519	20	337	17	26	26	65
Reading between activities	41	6	35	6	7	34	85
Poetry/drama	148	3	16	5	49	4	11
Teacher reading to children	56	4	—	—	14	—	—
General discussion	144	10	—	—	14	—	—

Table 5.9   Estimates of continuous reading

	Minutes observed	Minutes involving reading	1	2	3	4
(a)						
Maths	1918	359	235 (66)	95 (27)	19 (5)	10 (3)
English	2683	1109	482 (44)	238 (22)	111 (10)	278 (25)
Social studies	1449	279	157 (56)	90 (32)	17 (6)	15 (5)
Music	372	140	53 (38)	46 (33)	31 (22)	10 (7)
(b)						
News, diaries, creative writing	898	160	85 (53)	56 (35)	13 (8)	6 (4)
Comprehension, grammar, spelling	877	432	290 (67)	103 (24)	28 (7)	11 (2)
Reading	560	490	90 (18)	76 (16)	67 (14)	257 (52)
Poetry/drama	148	27	17 (63)	3 (11)	3 (11)	4 (15)

Notes
Figures in brackets indicate the reading recordings expressed as percentages of the total recordings in each category.
1 = 1–15 seconds of reading in the minute
2 = 16–30 seconds of reading in the minute
3 = 31–45 seconds of reading in the minute
4 = 46 seconds to the entire minute

organization is employed, it is difficult to say. We are able to record, however, that the junior school pupils we observed did enjoy personal reading during the school day. We suspect that opportunities for such reading are less frequent in the secondary school day.

On the other hand it may be argued that personal reading, of the kind we are now discussing, has little to do with reading for learning. It is reading to pass the time, or escape from reality; it is indulgent reading unrelated to the harsh business of disciplining eye and brain for more pragmatic purposes.

This is not entirely true of the pupils we observed. Personal reading was often linked to an interest or a topic which was being actively pursued, but, and this is the point at issue, the topic itself was probably chosen by the learner, not set by the teacher.

We could conclude that teachers experience difficulty in creating opportunities for continuous, reflective reading in lesson-time, both at junior and secondary levels. In the top-junior classes we observed we have firm evidence that pupils utilized their free time for intensive personal reading, and such free time was a normal part of the school day, but we cannot say that the abilities, attitudes, and intentions present in the content of personal reading were transferred to 'set' reading.

VI Conclusions

It is not our purpose to criticize teachers, apportion blame for apparent faults, or make superficial judgements. Rather we wish to describe what is happening in the classroom now, and from this information draw out those elements that will illuminate a discussion concerning the improvement of our pupils' capacity to use reading effectively.

We have provided some supporting evidence for the opinion that the transfer from primary to secondary education involves pupils in an adjustment to unfamiliar classroom procedures and methods. In particular we found that there was a distinct shift from individual guidance to 'teacher informing'. One effect of this was to relegate a great deal of classroom reading to the role of controlling pupil action either through answering written questions, or following in-structions.

On the general question of primary-secondary transfer we would not attempt any judgement. The reactions of teachers offer two quite opposing views. On the one hand, there are those who believe that secondary education should be different, and that pupils should be motivated by new challenges. On the other, there is the firm belief that, in the lower school at least, pupils should be offered an approach that develops naturally from the primary-school régime.

It seems to us that either view is valid, providing the essential continuity of reading development is recognized, but our study indicates that, for average and above-average pupils, the experience of meaningful reading across the curriculum becomes stabilized, or even regresses, at first-year secondary level, and has a low priority throughout the pre-examination years. There are many reasons for this. Contrary to our expectations, teachers appear to be pessimistic about the virtues of reading for learning. This may well be a pessimism born out of experience—pupils may not show a high degree of proficiency in handling the printed word. However, where the reaction to this has been to limit the role of reading in lesson-time, the very means of effecting improvement have been ignored. To quote from another part of this report, we cannot achieve better reading by retreating from print. Also, teachers regard reading in lesson-time with some degree of suspicion. They feel uneasy if pupils are 'only reading'; they consider they may be regarded as inefficient if a visitor to a lesson finds a substantial number of pupils merely gazing at books or resource materials; they admit to being able to identify the inattentive listener more easily than the careless reader.

It seems, therefore, that in the discussion of a language policy which is proceeding in many schools, a fundamental decision must be made. One could make a case for frankly admitting that the printed word is an inefficient medium for both acquiring information and promoting thought. If this is the decision then viable alternatives must be sought. The retreat from print should be an organized withdrawal, not a rout. But if the decision is to make a determined effort to teach more efficient reading, then we would urge a close scrutiny of the role reading plays across the curriculum. A fundamental necessity is to provide the pupils with a meaningful experience of reading in science, social studies, mathematics and English.

At this point, it must be emphasized that our study embraced only junior and secondary schools. Our observations did not extend to a middle-school system. There is the possibility that a different pattern of transfer and reading development might emerge in this situation.

To return to the implications of our observations, we consider that our findings would generally support the view that some form of writing is a frequent outcome of classroom reading. A great deal of this writing can be categorized as copying or answering. A question now arises as to the extent to which such reading outcomes invite pupils to reflect upon their reading. No precise answer is possible, but it is important to consider the effect of solitary reading, followed by solitary writing. Too often a pupil may be denied a real opportunity for partaking in a discourse which illuminates reading.

It would be completely unrealistic to suggest that every reading situation in the classroom should allow for a full opportunity to reflect, discuss and formulate ideas. However, in the consideration of a language policy we would urge teachers to note that when curricular and timetable pressures result in a succession of lessons in which time to talk about reading is at a premium, then effective reading is likely to be a casualty. Immediate objectives run counter to long-term aims. One possible solution would be the injection of discussional reading sessions into the major subject teaching areas, and ways and means of achieving this are discussed in Chapter 9.

Such a suggestion meets the Bullock Committee's recommendation that reading should not be the sole concern of the English department. However, the view that reading cannot be taught in isolation is supported by few subject teachers. They feel that reading should be the concern of a specialist, and they should be free to concentrate on their own subject. We would respond that whether or not the development of reading is a specialism in itself, pupils still require the experience of reflecting upon reading: hence there is still the necessity to build in a meaningful approach to reading in some class lessons across the curriculum.

Much of what has been said above is heightened by our analysis of patterns of continuity in classroom reading. The incidence of 'short-burst' reading is very high. It might be argued that we have overstated the case here. A pupil who 'reads' for thirty seconds could, in fact, be studying a passage of some 60–150 words, depending on reading speed. The breaks in this reading could represent thinking and deliberating. The point is well made, but it does not reflect what we observed. If it did, then our category—deliberating—would show up more strongly than the 3 per cent of lesson-time recorded at first-year secondary level and 2 per cent at fourth-year level. Equally some commentators have suggested that a lesson employing cloze procedure would be recorded as 'short-burst' reading using our method of observation. Apart from the fact that this is not a common lesson strategy, especially in lessons outside of English, the fact remains that 'discussion' and 'deliberating' would have become substantial components of our observations. Therefore we are emphatic: what we term 'short-burst' reading is not some kind of continuous, reflective reading, which has been misrepresented by the methodological constraints of our observations.

We would be encouraged if teachers would test our assertion, for the issue is extremely important. The project has developed and validated an appropriate observational instrument; the process of observing pupils is not difficult. Or, at another level, we would ask merely that what and how pupils read in lesson-time should receive closer scrutiny.

In our seminars, which ran concurrently with the project, it was also argued that our conclusions on 'short-burst' reading were based on the observation of traditional lessons, and a different pattern would have emerged if we had considered resource-based lessons. If traditional-type lessons have dominated our observations then it is because such lessons figure more frequently in secondary schools than self-learning or 'guided discovery' situations. We would accept that our data do show the prominence of teacher-dominated lessons in secondary schools, but our schools were a representative sample. Further we are far from convinced that many resource-based lessons do, in fact, deny the statement that very little continuous reading is used in lesson-time. We have observed pupils engaged in topic work who treat their reading in a way which suggests that their main objective is to transfer the words of an author into their own books or files. This observation does not conflict with the experience of those teachers with whom we have discussed this matter. Verbatim copying from written sources in topic work is a widespread and major concern. Indeed in general the pupils we observed seemed unable to discard the reading habits of the traditional classroom when the wider scope of the resource area was made available to them.

We strongly suspect that changing the reading environment alone will not produce more effective reading. More direct and purposeful action is required. Equally, it seems that children do not reveal and display to secondary-school teachers abilities which have been acquired in the more flexible junior-school classrooms. Thus, it is our impression that the effort to introduce more open teaching into secondary education, however praiseworthy in itself, is unlikely to produce better reading unless it is supported by a programme of instruction and counselling designed to help pupils to use reading sources efficiently.

Our observations were, in this instance, limited to the classroom. It might be argued that the experience of continuous, reflective reading, which we claim is limited in lesson-time, takes place at home. This point is taken up in Chapter 6. Here we would stress that even though there is substance in the argument, the fact remains that pupils reading at home are denied immediate access to advice and guidance. The teacher is not available. Thus when pupils are actually engaged in a crucial reading task, they cannot immediately ask for help, nor can the teacher observe their approach and intervene. Hence, we are convinced that homework assignments cannot be used as a substitute for classroom reading.

At the outset of this project we believed that reading was widely used in the classroom and that teacher expectations of possible reading outcomes would probably be high. What we have found tends to deny both these hypotheses. In most lessons, reading for learning seems to have a relatively minor role. Equally, teachers are generally realistic. They know that many of their pupils gain little from unsupported reading and they are more surprised by the successful reader than the unsuccessful. What emerges here is direct evidence that the Bullock Committee's conclusions concerning reading standards were well founded. The argument about comparative standards is sterile; the fact of pupils experiencing difficulty in using reading for learning is a present reality. It is our hope that our observations will serve to illuminate discussions regarding the role of reading in the classroom.

6

Reading for Homework

John Cole and Eric Lunzer

1 Introduction

The observations reported in the last chapter suggest that when pupils engage in reading it is usually a fragmented and intermittent activity. They are rarely expected to inform themselves by reading a part of a book. The principal source of information may be the spoken word of the teacher, or it may take the form of direct practical experience, or of observation through visual aids. While these may appear in any combination, textual material tends to be used as an incidental aid to learning or as a stimulus for writing down what has been learnt. Thus reading episodes were quite generally limited to durations of less than thirty seconds, they were often associated with writing, as when the pupil is required to read in order to answer a written question, and reading from the blackboard or from the pupil's own exercise book figured prominently in some instances, though not in all.[1]

However, lesson observation cannot give a complete picture of the pupils' uses of resources for learning. The common experience of teachers might suggest that a study of homework requirement could produce a different result. While some assignments might still require the reading of short fragments (e.g. a problem in mathematics), others might call for more sustained reading, as when the student is asked to revise a lesson from a textbook or to prepare for one in advance. The present chapter is based on two separate inquiries designed to establish the extent and kind of reading required as part of homework.

The first of these studies was based on two questionnaires designed to be completed by pupils and by teachers respectively. The second, involving fewer subjects, was limited to pupils but was based on a structured-interview schedule. Thus the results of the latter could be used to amplify the findings of the questionnaire, as well as providing

---

[1] Teachers of science appear to make less use of textbooks in the fourth year than they do in the first (see Table 5.3, p. 123).

an independent check on their accuracy. Both studies were carried out in ten secondary schools in the East Midlands region, all of which were already associated with the work of the project.

II Methods of inquiry

1 The questionnaires

A pilot survey was carried out in three secondary schools in the early part of the summer term of 1975. This provided an opportunity to test the questionnaire forms which had been drawn up in the light of the developing concerns of the project team, and to improve on a number of questions. Thus, the earlier forms were found to give insufficient indication of the kind of reading engaged on and of its quality.

In their final form the questionnaires to pupils and teachers were closely parallel and each consisted of four sections. The first of these called for classificatory information—initials, age, sex, etc. The second called for a brief outline of the homework assignment to which the questionnaire related, and for the details of any reading undertaken. These included the source of the text, the total time spent on reading, and the largest continuous interval spent on reading. The next section, which was brief, asked for a statement of the purpose or purposes of the reading. Here the respondent was required to circle one or more such purposes from a list of eleven.[1] The fourth section was designed to produce information concerning the context of the homework and included questions relating to the preparation and follow-up given in school as well as the amount of help or discussion sought from parents or from friends.

Each completed questionnaire related to a specific homework assignment. However, the distribution of the relevant forms to teachers and pupils was designed to obtain a reasonable coverage of the homework which would normally complement the teaching of subject groups examined in Chapter 5. Thus, for every one of the subject areas identified—English, mathematics, science and social studies—two teachers in each of the ten schools were asked to collaborate by filling in the teacher's questionnaire and obtaining completed pupil questionnaires from a representative group of students. The questionnaires were designed to cover all of the assignments in these subjects set for the relevant classes during the second week in October 1975. For any one subject area, one class in each school was chosen from the first year and the other from the fourth, this pattern being repeated to yield a theoretical total of 80

[1] See Appendix section C, pp. 162 and 165. In the event, this part of the pupil questionnaire was found to be of limited value, for reasons given below, p. 149. Teachers' responses are discussed on pp. 148ff.

teacher-respondents and 960 pupils, since the recommended group-size was twelve. It was anticipated that some teachers would wish to set more than one homework for the relevant group in the chosen week, and where this happened, separate forms were made available both to pupils and to teachers.

The teachers were approached after consultation with relevant heads of department. Choice of pupils was left to the teachers themselves who were asked so far as possible to make their selections in such a way that the same pupils would not be completing questionnaires in more than one subject. However, if two pieces of homework were set in the same area, two forms would be completed by each member of the group. To conform to the terms of reference of the project as a whole, teachers were asked to choose pupils of average or above-average ability. The term 'average' was defined so as to include all but the weakest students, i.e. pupils who might be expected to obtain CSE at grade 4 or above in the subject concerned. However, no ceiling was specified and the abler respondents would include potential strong O-level candidates.

In the event, it was found that one of the schools did not set homework in the first year, with the result that nine schools contributed to the first-year results and ten to the fourth. In many cases more than one homework was set. In some, none was set or the teacher concerned failed to return the completed forms for himself and his group. The total eventual return proved to be 1186 forms representing 94 assignments. The distribution of these is shown in Table 6.1 (p. 142).

2 The interviews

An interview-schedule was developed by one of the project officers (John Cole) following an extensive series of preliminary trials. The schedule was designed to replicate and amplify the information already gained from the questionnaires and contained similar questions. However, since the interview is an individual procedure, the number of respondents was necessarily more limited. Nevertheless, it was found possible to obtain information relating to no less than 693 assignments from a total of 158 respondents.

The same ten schools were represented. In each of these, eight children were interviewed in the first form and eight in the fourth. These had been selected at random within the school from those who had completed a questionnaire (approximately forty-eight in each year group). The design of the interview, however, differed from that of the questionnaire in one important respect. Whereas each completed questionnaire related to one assignment only and in general no pupil was asked to complete questionnaires in more than one subject area, the interviewers were asked to elicit all the information about the homework set on three occasions in a given

Table 6.1   Distribution of questionnaires returned by pupils and teachers

Subject	Year	Teachers	Boys	Girls	All pupils
English	1	15	89	89	178
	4	8	49	66	115
Maths	1	12	54	78	132
	4	15	80	96	176
Science	1	9	48	52	100
	4	11	71	45	116
Social studies	1	8	41	51	92
	4	16	78	105	183
Totals		94	510	582	1092

Table 6.2   Frequency of assignments reported in interviews

	Year 1		Year 4	
	Boys	Girls	Boys	Girls
English	33	28	26	37
Maths	27	24	28	60
Science	26	17	48	32
Social studies	34	31	48	39
Art and craft	9	3	11	12
Languages	65	35	15	25
Home economics	0	0	0	19
Other	2	3	3	10

week. All of the interviews were held on a Wednesday and questions were asked about homework set the night before, the night before that (Monday) and the preceding weekend. On any one of these occasions, one, two, or three homeworks might have been set. In the event, the 79 first-formers produced information on 280 assignments while the 79 fourth-formers yielded 413 records.[1] These were distributed as shown in Table 6.2.

It will be apparent that all of the homework reported during an interview was included in the interview records. Thus these data are

[1] Although reserves were listed in each of the schools, two were not found.

not limited to the four subject-groups listed in Chapters 4 and 5 and in the questionnaire. The biggest additional grouping is modern-language studies, especially in the first year. This group was excluded from the remaining sections of the inquiry principally because reading in a foreign language is very different from reading in one's own tongue, especially when one is a beginner.

For the most part, the questions asked in the interview paralleled those appearing in the questionnaire (see Appendix). However, with the exception of the general questions comprising the first section, the list of questions was repeated as often as necessary to cover each of the assignments done on any occasion. As in the questionnaires, information was sought about the nature of the assignment, the time it took, the amount of reading required, the purpose of such reading, the source of the text, etc. One point of difference should, however, be mentioned. All the questionnaires were given out before the homework and for the most part they were completed just after the homework itself. One of the key questions was: Indicate the longest time you have spent in continuous reading. Such a question would have been inappropriate in the interview, when respondents were being asked to talk about what they had been doing the previous night or on any more distant occasion, particularly as they were not given any prior notice that they would be selected for interview.[1] Instead, the formulation used in the interview was: Did you read in long chunks of a page or more at a time?

Each interviewer visited two of the ten schools on two separate occasions, speaking to four pupils in the first school and four in the second. Nineteen of the twenty interviewers were graduate students in the School of Education, all of whom had volunteered to participate in the inquiry and who had been trained in the course of three meetings. The training included viewing a video recording of a specimen interview and completing a schedule. The specimen interview was conducted by John Cole, who also acted as the twentieth interviewer.

III Results

1 Amount of time spent on homework

Table 6.3 (p. 144) constitutes a summary of the replies to the question: How long did the homework take in all?[2]

In most secondary schools first-year pupils are generally expected to spend about thirty minutes on any one homework assignment

---

[1] This was deliberate, since forewarning might have produced a special effort to comply with the supposed wishes of the interviewer.

[2] For the teacher questionnaire 'did' became 'should'.

while fourth-year pupils are expected to spend 30–45 minutes, depending on the school and the subject. These expectations which no doubt correspond to school policy are clearly reflected in the data. In all subjects more 'long' homeworks are reported in the fourth year than the first and this holds true in all three sources of information.

Teachers' estimates of expected duration fall into the intermediate categories (21–40 minutes) more often than do the estimates of actual duration reported by the pupils. The latter are more liable to claim 'long' periods of work, as well as 'short' ones, especially in replies to the questionnaire. Such a pattern is entirely in accordance with expectation, since the teachers' estimates are estimates of a mean.

Finally, the estimates given by pupils in interview are in general lower than those given in the questionnaire and also lower than those

Table 6.3   Duration of homework

Year 1	English			Maths			Science			Social studies		
	S	M	L	S	M	L	S	M	L	S	M	L
T	7	67	27	34	66	0	33	55	11	38	25	38
Q	26	42	33	58	32	11	50	35	15	36	35	29
I	40	38	22	43	49	8	32	42	27	28	48	25
Year 4												
T	0	38	62	7	81	13	18	54	27	13	31	57
Q	10	30	60	25	56	20	52	23	26	8	19	75
I	24	32	45	33	36	30	40	30	30	16	30	55

Categories	Source of data
S (short) 20 mins. or less	T teacher
M (medium) 21–40 mins.	Q pupil questionnaire
L (long) 40 mins. or over	I pupil interview

given by teachers. This discrepancy is not necessarily an indication of unreliability, since the assignments reported in the interview are different. However, the uniformity of this trend is striking. Perhaps pupils did in fact spend longer on an assignment when required to complete a questionnaire on the work they were doing. Neither teachers nor pupils were given notice of the interview in time to alter their normal practice.

There are striking differences between the different subject groups. Homework assignments take longer in English and in social studies than in mathematics and science, especially in the fourth year. Pupils report longer sessions and the expectations of their teachers are also greater. We have no evidence that these differences were offset by the degree of concentration demanded by the task, but it is a possibility that one would not wish to rule out.

2 Reading times

Table 6.4, below, shows the distribution of replies to the question: How much time was spent in reading? The figures are percentages and relate to estimates of the total time spent in reading in the course of each assignment. Reading was defined for both teachers and pupils as 'looking at written or printed words'. Needless to say, this definition would be highly misleading in any other context and was chosen only to secure some uniformity and relevance in the answers given to questionnaires and interviews.

While there are considerable variations within all subjects both in the first year and in the fourth, the distributions in the three columns—

Table 6.4   Duration of reading

Year 1	English			Maths			Science			Social studies		
	T	Q	I	T	Q	I	T	Q	I	T	Q	I
0–5 mins	20	29	51	65	84	56	66	64	37	13	28	32
6–10	14	25	14	25	14	34	11	16	24	—	26	29
11–15	27	12	11	8	3	6	—	8	21	38	17	16
16–20	20	9	7	—	—	2	11	3	5	25	11	5
21–30	13	16	14	—	—	2	11	3	8	13	17	16
31 +	7	10	4	—	—	2	—	6	6	13	3	2

Year 4	English			Maths			Science			Social studies		
	T	Q	I	T	Q	I	T	Q	I	T	Q	I
0–5 mins	13	15	24	61	53	57	18	48	29	—	11	14
6–10	13	30	16	27	26	20	27	20	30	6	23	21
11–15	25	19	16	13	14	10	36	9	21	31	22	21
16–20	25	13	3	—	5	5	—	5	5	44	13	7
21–30	13	19	15	—	4	4	9	9	9	13	24	24
31 +	13	4	28	—	1	3	9	11	6	6	11	13

T teacher.   Q pupil questionnaire.   I pupil interview.

teacher questionnaire, student questionnaire and student interview— are in broad agreement in most cases. One may conclude that the replies give a reasonably accurate representation of the incidence of reading in the course of homework assignments. Taken as a whole, the amount of reading is clearly by no means negligible. Thus in English nearly 50 per cent of assignments entail more than ten minutes of reading in the first year, as do 60 per cent or more in the fourth year. The figures for social studies are similar. Assignments that demand considerable amounts of reading are less frequent in science, but they do occur quite regularly in the fourth year and sporadically in the first. First-year mathematics rarely involves any considerable amount of reading, but by the fourth year students are reporting that nearly 50 per cent of assignments involve them in more than five minutes of reading.[1]

In view of the wide distribution within subjects already referred to, such differences as appear between the three classes of response are rarely of any significance. Perhaps the only point worthy of note is the tendency for teachers of social studies to expect large amounts of reading, even in relation to the quite lengthy times reported by their students.

Table 6.5 (p. 147) provides information about the kinds of reading involved in these assignments. More specifically, the table shows how often students were required to read fairly continuously, as must be the case when reading is a central part of the learning process, as opposed to more circumscribed episodes, as when the student looks for a specific question or an answer that may occupy no more than two or three lines of text. The form of question used in questionnaires to students and teachers allowed for such a quantification of continuous reading when it was present. Thus it seems reasonable to suppose that when the duration of the largest uninterrupted 'read' was greater than five minutes, such reading was central to the learning. The relevant data are recorded in columns 5–8, with the last two of these indicating homeworks which clearly involved quite considerable periods of study reading. Similarly, the first four columns indicate the amounts of reading involved in the remaining assignments. Reading episodes of one minute and less can hardly involve the student in any demanding study of text, and when these are the maximum reported by students or teachers it is reasonable to conclude that the reading was not central to the learning. Episodes of 2–5 minutes form a more doubtful category, with perhaps a preponderance of non-study reading. In this connection it should be recalled that if the relevant episode was indeed a continuous period of study reading, readers are far more likely to overestimate the time spent in reading than to underestimate it. It is true that there are occasions when an observer would note that no more than two minutes were spent in quite careful perusal of a page of moderately difficult text, followed by one minute or less of re-reading or reflection. But it is highly probable that on nearly all such occasions the reader himself would claim in good faith to have spent five to ten minutes in reading.

It was unreasonable to ask respondents to the interview to give a specific estimate of the longest time they had spent reading continuously in each of the homeworks they had recently done. They

[1] The 2–5 per cent of responses indicating fifteen minutes or more spent in reading mathematics are probably due to an over literal interpretation of the working definition, 'looking at words'!

Table 6.5 Longest period of uninterrupted reading[1]

	0–1 mins.		2–5 mins.		6–15 mins.		16+ mins.		% 'long chunk'
	T	Q	T	Q	T	Q	T	Q	
Year 1									
English	20	24	34	32	26	18	20	28	1
Maths	75	68	24	29	0	2	0	0	68
Science	22	46	77	37	0	13	0	5	37
Social studies	13	24	38	23	51	28	0	24	52
Year 4									
English	13	2	51	49	13	30	26	20	81
Maths	27	50	67	37	7	12	0	1	19
Science	18	33	54	43	9	13	18	12	45
Social studies	0	12	64	31	19	38	19	21	56

[1] All figures are percentages of all homeworks in their relevant category. Abbreviations as on Table 6.3. See text for interpretation of last column.

had not been prepared for the interview, and would therefore have had difficulty in making a usable estimate of the exact amount of time taken up by any one part of a homework. However, the chief interest lay in the centrality of the reading. This question could be tackled directly in the interview by asking the pupil if most of the reading was continuous, did it involve 'reading long chunks of a page or more at a time'.

It is interesting to note that once again there is considerable agreement between replies to interview and questionnaire. The complement to the percentage given in the last column of Table 6.5 is nearly always between the corresponding percentages in the second and fourth and somewhat nearer the latter. There is also a broad similarity in the trends indicated by teachers and students when reporting the relative demands for study reading of different subjects in the two relevant year groups.

Taken together, the results given in Tables 6.4 and 6.5 show that continuous reading is a frequent part of the homework task. It is nearly always required in English, while in social-studies subjects it occurs in more than half the assignments that are reported either in interview or in questionnaires. In science, too, although the frequency is less, study reading in some form appears to be characteristic of more than a third of all homework. Mathematics requires less reading, presumably because most mathematics homeworks involve the student in working examples or in solving problems.

3 Reading purposes

Both teachers and children were asked to indicate why reading was required in any given assignment by circling one or more items in a list of possible reading purposes. The list is given in section C of the questionnaire (see Appendix) and is reproduced in the first column of Table 6.6 (p. 150).

Every teacher concerned was given an explanation of the intended meaning of each of these terms. Thus *test preparation* referred to a particular test normally given during the period immediately following the assignment, while *revision* related to a larger section of the subject, without necessary reference to a test or an examination. However, both purposes might apply to one and the same assignment. Similarly, *to do questions* would be appropriate to reading a problem in mathematics as a necessary first step to its solution, whereas *to find out answers* would imply some kind of search through a more extensive section of the text as in a standard comprehension exercise in English or in certain types of science worksheets. Here too both purposes might be circled, as when a mathematics teacher expects his students to refer back to an example in the text once they have read the problem which they were set for homework.

Although teachers were asked to explain these definitions to their pupils, it was clear in the event that the children had great difficulty in completing this part of the questionnaire. In general, their answers failed to agree either with one another or with the purposes named by the teacher. Moreover, while the latter were usually consonant with the nature of the work prescribed as shown elsewhere in the questionnaire, the purposes given by children often bore little relation to what they were actually required to do. The present account is therefore limited to the information given by the teachers. The distribution of these replies is shown in Table 6.6.

A comparison of the entries in the main body of Table 6.6 with the numbers given in the bottom row shows that teachers indicated a total of 232 purposes for reading in 94 homeworks. In other words the average assignment was thought to satisfy two or three of the purposes given in the list. Moreover, it will be seen that five of the eleven possibilities account for 177 of the total selections (72 per cent): (3) to do questions, (4) to find answers, (5) to prepare for a lesson, (6) to make notes, and (10) to follow-up a lesson. A preliminary inspection of the table shows that these purposes are unequally distributed across the four subject areas. Thus purposes (3) and (4) predominate in mathematics and in social studies, while (5) appears most frequently in English and in social studies; (6) is again used by social-science teachers and also by science teachers.

In themselves these distributions are not unexpected. They confirm the anticipation that reading in mathematics arises most often in the context of problem-solving, and that teachers of science and of social studies not infrequently require pupils to make notes for homework, whether from a textbook or from a worksheet. This requirement figures less often in English homework, but teachers of English are more likely to ask their pupils to prepare for a lesson, for example by reading a chapter in a book, as also are teachers of social studies. Purpose (10), lesson follow-up, appears with comparable frequency in all subjects.

The data in Table 6.6 give a complete picture of the purposes named by teachers for each subject. However, since in general several purposes were named for any one assignment, they do not enable one to categorize the individual assignments in terms of the kinds of reading which they required. Thus, one of the most significant questions raised by the present survey concerns the incidence of study reading for homework. More specifically, is there any relation between the amount of time spent in reading and the nature of the reading required? It was shown in the last chapter that the reading that occurred in lesson-time was most often fragmented. In the last section of the present chapter, it appeared that reading for homework

Table 6.6 Purposes of reading for homework as stated by teachers
(Absolute frequencies)

Year	English 1	English 4	Maths 1	Maths 4	Science 1	Science 4	Social studies 1	Social studies 4	All subjects
1 Test preparation	1	0	1	0	0	1	1	2	6
2 Revision	1	1	4	5	0	3	0	2	16
3 Questions	4	3	10	14	5	7	5	6	54
4 Supply answers	3	3	8	3	4	4	6	7	38
5 Prepare for a lesson	6	4	0	0	2	0	3	4	20
6 To make notes	1	1	0	0	5	6	3	6	21
7 To check work	3	1	0	0	2	0	0	0	7
8 To do corrections	2	0	0	0	1	0	0	0	3
9 For pleasure	6	1	0	1	0	3	0	0	12
10 To follow-up a lesson	6	3	6	6	7	5	3	8	44
11 Other	3	2	1	0	0	1	2	2	11
Number[1]	15	8	12	15	9	11	8	16	

[1] The numbers appearing in this row are invariably below the relevant column totals due to the fact that teachers frequently specified more than one purpose for an assignment.

was far more often sustained. One might hypothesize that an assignment that required longer periods of reading usually involved sustained reading, while shorter periods of reading were more often associated with the use of text for a limited purpose such as the completion of an exercise.

To establish whether this prediction was indeed confirmed, it is essential to group the reading purposes of Table 6.6 in such a way as to place each assignment in one of a few mutually-exclusive categories, based on the distinction between sustained reading or study reading on the one hand and intermittent reading or reading for a limited purpose on the other. It was therefore decided to allocate to the first category s (*study reading*) all homeworks circled for one or more of purposes (5) *lesson preparation,* (6) *making notes* or (10) *lesson follow-up.* Homeworks circled for purpose (3) *to do questions* and/or (4) *to find answers* are categorized as E (*exercise reading*). Some homeworks were scored in both categories and these have been categorized as ES, while those to which some other purpose was assigned have been categorized as N (neither). Such homeworks were circled only for the remaining purposes, namely (1), (2), (7), (8), (9), or (11). Table 6.7 (p. 152) shows the distribution of these homeworks in terms of the named categories across the four subject areas with a further partitioning of results based on the length of time spent in reading (using the teacher estimates as measure). The first column in this table, headed O, contains those homeworks for which teachers stated that no reading was required.

Of the 30 homeworks which demanded less than 10 minutes of reading, 15 were categorized as E and 1 came under N. Only 3 were categorized as s only. At the opposite extreme, 28 homeworks were thought to require 20 minutes of reading or more, 13 of these appearing in the s column and 11 in ES. The data for the intermediate block confirm these indications that the more reading the teacher requires, the more likely he is to stress purposes which imply that the reading is fairly central to the homework rather than merely instrumental to something else. It is interesting that, outside of mathematics, teachers generally confine their selections to s categories or to E categories and rarely included the purposes in both these groups.

Taken as a whole, these data confirmed the impression that whereas the teachers whom we observed did not rely on reading for learning in lesson-time, the present sample (which included the same schools together with six others) did expect considerable amounts of reading as homework, especially in social studies and in science. Homework set in English also demanded considerable periods of sustained reading, often including an additional written element such as answering comprehension questions or preparing a summary.

Reference to Table 6.8 (p. 153) shows that in most cases the

Table 6.7 Purposes of reading for homework (from teacher questionnaires)
(Absolute frequencies)

	1–9 mins.				10–19 mins.				20 mins. or more				T
	E	S	ES	N	E	S	ES	N	E	S	ES	N	
Year 1													
English	1	1	0	0	2	2	1	0	1	4	0	1	15
Maths	5	0	2	1	0	0	3	0	0	0	0	0	11
Science	1	1	4	0	1	0	0	0	0	1	1	0	9
Social studies	1	0	0	0	1	1	1	0	1	1	2	0	8
All year 1	8	2	6	1	4	3	5	0	2	6	3	1	43
Year 4													
English	0	0	0	0	0	3	0	0	0	1	3	0	8
Maths	5	0	5	0	2	0	3	0	0	0	0	0	16
Science	2	1	0	0	1	1	4	0	0	2	0	0	11
Social studies	0	0	0	0	2	2	2	0	0	2	5	1	16
All group	7	1	5	0	5	6	9	0	0	7	8	1	51
All E	1	1	0	0	2	5	1	0	1	5	3	1	23
All M	10	0	7	1	2	0	6	0	0	0	0	0	27
All Sc	3	2	4	0	2	1	4	0	0	3	1	0	20
All SS	1	0	0	0	3	3	3	0	1	5	7	1	24
All	15	3	11	1	9	9	14	0	2	13	11	2	94

Key
E exercises ES both categories S study N neither of these T total.
(For definitions see text.)

passages read for homework were taken from textbooks or from worksheets. In addition, many assignments involved writing, and pupils needed to read what they themselves had written, whence the frequent appearance of the pupil's own exercise book as a source of text for his reading.

It should be pointed out that the categorization of this table was made not by the respondents themselves, but by the principal research officer concerned (John Cole) on the basis of the more specific information contained in the questionnaire to pupils. Dictionaries and encyclopedias were coded as reference works and the latter account for most of the 26 per cent of texts coded as R for science homework in the first year. In this same category, the comparatively high percentage for social studies homeworks may be partly attributed to the inclusion of atlases and maps under the

Table 6.8   Sources of text read as part of homework

	Year 1					Year 4				
	T	R	L	E	W	T	R	L	E	W
English	38	6	8	46	26	60	2	10	28	21
Maths	50	—	—	30	36	59	—	—	20	24
Science	12	26	4	56	6	71	1	—	23	35
Social studies	13	46	1	24	48	51	19	3	28	32

Key:
T   textbook
R   reference book
L   library book
E   exercise book
W   worksheet/card
 Figures are percentage of responses in each cell.

general heading of reference material. The distinction between the T and L categories is not between fiction and non-fiction but between books used by nearly every member in a group for a given assignment and books used by one or two pupils only. Thus an English novel would appear under category T if, as happens most often, it was a set text for the whole class, although of course it would appear as L if it was an individual selection.

Two features of these data merit some comment. The first is the relatively rare appearance of entries under the category L. Perhaps this reflects a fairly general expectation among teachers that unless a homework assignment is fairly narrowly structured, with specifications of just what the pupil is to read, there might be too much uncertainty about the outcome. The second relates to the last category W. It was noted that worksheets were used in clusters: in some departments their use was rare, yet they were used more widely than any other reading material. There were indeed schools where a reliance on worksheets seemed to be a feature of general school policy. While there are strong arguments that could be urged in support of such a policy, there are also a number of dangers attendant to its adoption. The problem is discussed more fully in Chapter 10.

IV Some examples

The detailed tabulations given in the last section indicate quite an extensive demand for reading in homework. However, with the exception of Table 6.7, the data for length of assignment, amount of reading required, type and source of reading, and purposes of reading have all been dealt with separately. Also, the figures contained in this last section give little or no indication of just what it is the pupils were required to do.

The present section is designed to provide some amplification of the quantitative data by furnishing all of the more important indices pertaining to each individual assignment together with a brief description of what the students were asked to do. For the sake of brevity, the number of examples has been limited to eight, i.e. one in each subject area in the first and fourth years respectively. However, the examples are fairly typical and illustrate the quite demanding tasks that pupils are often set for homework and the not insignificant role of reading in many of these.

In each of the tables that follow, all estimates of duration are in minutes. The letters T.R.T. denote total reading time while L.C.R. stands for longest continuous read. Numbers listed against *Purposes* denote the corresponding categories as shown in Table 6.6, while *Sources* are shown by letters corresponding to those used in Table 6.8.

ASSIGNMENT A   FIRST-YEAR ENGLISH

| | Teacher estimate | Pupil estimates | |
		Median	Range
Total duration	30 mins.	30 mins.	15–90 mins.
T.R.T.	5–10 mins.	5 mins.	1–60 mins.
L.C.R.	5 mins.	5 mins.	1–20 mins.
Purposes	2, 3, 7		
Sources	W	W(L)	

The children were required to produce a short piece of writing— either a conversation or a description of a pleasurable experience. The stimuli provided were class discussion before the homework was attempted and a worksheet which the children were to read before attempting the task. The group, a mixed-ability class, varied widely in the times claimed for all aspects of the assignment, but a glance at the questionnaires confirmed that the longest times were not in fact claimed by the ablest children. One member of the sample claimed to have read a library book in addition to the worksheet, which was read by all. All said they had spent more time in writing than in any other activity. One notes that this is an instance of an assignment in English in which none of the purposes cited for reading has been categorized as 'study reading'. As in most such homeworks, the total reading time was comparatively short.

ASSIGNMENT B   FIRST-YEAR MATHEMATICS

	Teacher estimate	Pupil estimates Median	Range
Total duration	25 mins.	20 mins.	10–45 mins.
T.R.T.	3 mins.	3 mins.	1–10 mins.
L.C.R.	1 min.	1 min.	1–4 mins.
Purposes	3, 4		
Sources	T	T	

This was a fairly typical mathematics assignment, and as was often the case, the amounts of time claimed for reading are small. The children were required to calculate the volume of wood needed to make up a closed or open box-shape. This exercise was taken from a standard mathematics textbook. All pupils judged that most of their homework time had been spent 'calculating or thinking' and in the teacher's view most pupils completed the homework 'satisfactorily'. It is perhaps surprising that the teacher stated that there had been no class discussion of this task either before the homework or after it, although he did discuss the work afterwards with some individuals. Quite properly, *lesson follow-up* is not given as a reading purpose, although it was clearly a purpose for the homework as a whole.

ASSIGNMENT C   FIRST-YEAR SCIENCE

	Teacher estimate	Pupil estimates Median	Range
Total duration	20 mins.	20 mins.	10–30 mins.
T.R.T.	2 mins.	5 mins.	0–10 mins.
L.C.R.	2 mins.	2 mins.	0–5 mins.
Purposes.	3		
Sources	W	W	

The task set by the teacher was to draw a diagram to illustrate the method of collecting gas over water and to answer a question on safety on an accompanying worksheet. Disappointingly, none of the seven pupils who completed the questionnaire made any reference to the purpose of the experiment illustrated by the diagram. However, one mentioned safety and three referred to the bunsen burner. Amounts of time claimed for reading are small and children found the homework very hard to categorize. On the questionnaire form the children were asked to indicate how they had spent most of their time by circling one item in a list consisting of *writing, calculating or thinking, reading,* and *other.* Only one pupil circled *other,* although drawing must have taken up much of their time. For the rest, the responses were variously split between *writing* and *calculating or thinking.*

ASSIGNMENT D   FIRST-YEAR SOCIAL STUDIES (GEOGRAPHY)

	Teacher estimate	*Pupil estimates*	
		Median	*Range*
Total duration	45 mins.	30 mins.	20–45 mins.
T.R.T.	20 mins.	10 mins.	1–15 mins.
L.C.R.	5–10 mins.	5 mins.	1–10 mins.
Purposes	3		
Sources	W	W	

The task was to fill in missing words in a passage dealing with the distribution of tropical rain forests and their characteristics. The pupils were required to copy the passage from their worksheet, using a list of words given in random order at the bottom of the sheet to fill in the gaps, together with a map which they had drawn in the previous lesson. The teacher found it hard to estimate the likely reading time since the homework involved copying, which meant 'alternate reading and writing in short bursts'. As has been noted above, this is typical for 'exercise reading'.

ASSIGNMENT E   FOURTH-YEAR ENGLISH

	Teacher estimate	*Pupil estimates*	
		Median	*Range*
Total duration	45 mins.	45 mins.	25–60 mins.
T.R.T.	15 mins.	15 mins.	7–30 mins.
L.C.R.	10 mins.	10 mins.	5–15 mins.
Purposes	10, 11		
Sources	W, E	W, E	

The previous lesson had featured class reading and discussion of two extracts from the novel *Walkabout* by J. V. Marshall. One passage was omitted in class and reproduced in the worksheet given out for this homework assignment. The pupils' task was to read the passage and then, in their own words, contrast the upbringing of the aboriginal boy with that of the white children. Under the heading *Purposes* the teacher had included 'lesson follow-up (coded 10) and to abstract information and reproduce it as part of a piece of continuous, imaginative writing'. It may be assumed that this task was a demanding one. The teacher concerned described the reading as 'difficult', but the pupils rated it as easy or of little difficulty.

ASSIGNMENT F   FOURTH-YEAR MATHEMATICS

	Teacher estimate	Pupil estimates Median	Range
Total duration	60 mins.	40 mins.	25–63 mins.
T.R.T.	20 mins.	15 mins.	10–35 mins.
L.C.R.	5 mins.	5 mins.	1–9 mins.
Purposes	3, 5		
Sources	T	T	

The task here was to complete a number of questions on a set portion of the SMP text. The source was Book 3 and the reference was Chapter 3, pp. 32–4, being an introduction to matrix multiplication (combining row and column matrices). The pupils were set four questions, but all of these were in several parts, and the tasks were probably demanding.

Three of the ten respondents estimated that most of their time was spent in reading and seven reported that reading was the main part of the homework. Clearly, most of the time was spent in thinking about what to do in the light of the information given in the book and comparatively little in computation or writing. It is interesting to note that both teacher and pupils rightly include the time spent in reflection about the text as part of the reading time.

ASSIGNMENT G   FOURTH-YEAR SCIENCE

	Teacher estimate	Pupil estimates Median	Range
Total duration	20 mins.	20 mins.	10–190 mins.
T.R.T.	15 mins.	5 mins.	2–60 mins.
L.C.R.	15 mins.	2 mins.	1–10 mins.
Purposes	3, 4, 10		
Sources	R	E	

The pupils were given a list of metals and asked to arrange them in order of reactivity. The teacher here expected pupils to refer to general reference books as well as their previous year's notes. He indicated that the work was discussed before its execution and again when it had been completed. In the event all pupils (only seven completed questionnaires were received) reported using exercise books only. Two of the girls gave aberrant times for homework and reading, but here as elsewhere these wide deviations did not affect either the medians or the means for the group.

ASSIGNMENT H   FOURTH-YEAR SOCIAL STUDIES (GEOGRAPHY)

	Teacher estimate	Pupil estimates	
		Median	Range
Total duration	60 mins.	45 mins.	30–60 mins.
T.R.T.	15 mins.	6 mins.	3–15 mins.
L.C.R.	5 mins.	2 mins.	1–5 mins.
Purposes	3		
Sources	W		W, E

This assignment was fairly demanding. The pupils were following a Schools Council geography course, continuously assessed, leading either to Mode III CSE or to an O-level. They were required to complete a table in a worksheet by carrying out various calculations based on data gathered on a field excursion in the previous week. Some of the necessary information could be had from their textbook, which also included a worked example. Most of the respondents found difficulty in estimating T.R.T. for this homework because, typically, 'the reading was all in small bits'. Nevertheless all claimed that the reading was either 'essential' or 'important' to the homework.

V Conclusions

The studies reported in this chapter complement the evidence contained in Chapter 5. Taken as a whole, they indicate that reading forms an appreciable component in homework assignments both in the first year and in the fourth, especially in English and in the social studies. Reading demands in science are somewhat smaller, and they are least in mathematics.

The evidence was obtained from questionnaires completed in ten schools and involving a total of 94 assignments distributed more or less evenly between the four subject areas. Each of these was reported on by a teacher and 7–12 pupils. Additional and corroborative data were obtained by structured interviews with a total of 158 pupils bearing on 413 different assignments.

The replies given in interview suggest that 70–80 per cent of homeworks in English required at least some reading in 'long chunks', i.e. sustained reading whether for study or for literary appreciation. The percentage for social studies is approximately 50, while in science it is 37 per cent for first-year pupils and 45 per cent for fourth-year pupils. Even in mathematics these indices are 10 per cent and 19 per cent (Table 6.5). Both the corresponding questionnaire responses and the remaining data cited in the chapter bear out the impression that reading plays a far more significant role in the work done by these pupils at home than it does in their classwork.

In conclusion, the following points merit consideration.

1   One is not surprised to find that reading plays a more significant role in homework than it does in classwork. The face-to-face situation provides an opportunity for varied and stimulating learning experiences, including teacher-explanation, teacher-led discussion, practical experimentation, visual, audial and audio-visual representations, fieldtrips, visits, and doubtless others besides. The printed word is a resource for information and a possible vehicle for conveying instructions, but in neither role is it the sole or need it be the principal source. By contrast, the pupil working in his own home is cut off from the teacher and his fellow pupils, nor does he have access to a resources centre.

2   Even at the level of tertiary education, it is often thought that reading becomes more meaningful when preceded by an oral presentation in which the lecturer sets out a general framework together with an indication of the lacunae which the student must supply for himself, and how he can best do so.[1] Reading is less demanding in the secondary school and very much more closely directed. Nevertheless, it seems not unreasonable here for the teacher to introduce a topic by some other form of presentation and use the printed word only as a follow-up.

3   If we were to take the pupils' own reports of their reaction to the printed word as they encountered it in their homework assignments, there would be good ground for approval of the system: in nearly all cases they reported that the reading was easy or that it was of no particular difficulty. Similarly, the teachers were generally well satisfied with the work that they received.

4   Nevertheless, there is reason to believe that in relegating the use of reading for learning to homework, we are not giving our pupils the help they need, especially the help that they need in learning how to read. The universality of the report that the reading was easy carries little conviction for it is often the mark of the poor reader that he is unaware that he has made little sense of the text in front of him, so long as he knows the words or at least knows how to pronounce them.

The apparent failure to understand the purpose of the experiment studied as a science homework by a group of first-year pupils is one instance and the evidence is not conclusive. Nevertheless, experience tells us that pupils can often complete the written work which they are required to do without understanding the passage they have been asked to read, by simply scanning for the 'answer' given somewhere in the text. Also, in most comprehension exercises, students can answer questions with well above chance accuracy even when they have not read the passage (Tuinman, 1973).

Such factors would sufficiently account for the general satisfaction of teachers with the quality of the work handed in, especially when

[1] For a fuller discussion of these issues see McLeish, 1976.

one recalls that the subject teacher is rarely concerned with reading for its own sake and that it is an ungracious teacher who is less than satisfied when more than half the pupils obtain more than half marks in the exercise which they have been set.

5   The cogency of the above arguments should not be allowed to obscure the conclusion that the present study provides little direct evidence about how well these children were able to comprehend what they were reading for homework and how much profit they derived from it. Had time permitted, we would certainly have sought further evidence by questioning a sample of children about the passages which they had read, asking them to explain the meanings of difficult words in such passages, to paraphrase any passages that were superficially ambiguous, and to summarize the gist of the passage or of a paragraph within it. Answers to such questions would have provided direct evidence for or against the considerations urged above. It may be that some teachers will wish to try such techniques themselves as and when the opportunity allows.

Appendix

Questionnaires used in surveys
Pupil

Section A
Initials: Boy 1   Girl 2 (please circle number)
1 *School* (please circle number) e.g. 05
                                                01
                                                02
                                                03
                                                04
                                                05
                                                06
                                                07
                                                08
                                                09
                                                10
2 *Year group* (please circle number)
   First year 1   Fourth year 2
3 *Day homework was set* (please circle number)
   Monday   1
   Tuesday   2
   Wednesday 3
   Thursday   4
   Friday   5

4 *Day homework was done* (please circle number)
Monday   1
Tuesday   2
Wednesday   3
Thursday   4
Friday   5
Saturday   6
Sunday   7
5 *Place homework was done* (please circle number)
In school 1
At home   2
Other   3

Section B
1 *What was the homework set?*...
....
....
....

2 *Did the set homework involve any reading at all?* (please circle number)
Yes 1   No 2
If YES, please continue:
Book(s) used (if any)

Author or Editor	Title	Chapter/ Section	Page number (if specified)

Details of other things you read, e.g. worksheets, own exercise books, etc.
....
....
....
....

3 *Length of homework*
Please indicate
(a) total time spent on all homework .... mins.
(b) total time spent on reading .... mins.
(c) longest continuous time you spent reading .... mins.
4 *Type of reading*
Most of the reading time in this homework was spent in (please circle
number)
(a) reading continuously   1
(b) reading in frequent short intervals   2
(c) reading only occasionally   3

To estimate the total time spent on reading (3b above) was (please circle number)

(a) very difficult   2
(b) fairly difficult   2
(c) reasonably easy   3

If (a) please state why ....
....
....

5 *Type of homework*

I spent most time this homework in (please circle number)

writing   1
calculating or thinking   2
reading   3
other   4

Was reading the main part of this homework? (please circle number)

Yes 1   No 2

Was the reading in this homework done to enable you to do another task? (please circle number)

Yes 1   No 2

Section C

1 *Purpose of the reading* (please circle as *many* as necessary)

Test preparation	01	To make notes	06
Revision	02	To check work	07
To do questions	03	To do corrections	08
To find out answers	02	Pleasure	09
To prepare for lesson	05	To follow-up lesson	10
		Other	11

(If 11 please specify ....
....)

Section D

1 Did any of your reading involve you in having to find out answers to questions? (please circle number)

Yes 1   No 2

If YES did you find out what you were supposed to find out?

Yes 1   No 2

2 How did you find the reading? (please circle number)

Very difficult   1
Difficult   2
Of no particular difficulty   3
Easy   4

3 How important was the reading to the homework? (please circle number)

Essential   1
Important   2
Not really important   3
Unnecessary   4

4 I discussed this homework *before* I did it with (please circle as many numbers as necessary)

a teacher 1
another boy or girl 2
another adult 3

I discussed this homework *while* I was doing it with

a teacher 1
another boy or girl 2
another adult 3

I discussed this homework *after* I had done it with

a teacher 1
another boy or girl 2
another adult 3

5 What you had to read was (please circle box)

Very interesting 1
Fairly interesting 2
Dull 3
Very dull 4

6 Was the reading you had to do enjoyable? (please circle number)

Yes 1　　　No 2

Teacher

TO THE TEACHER

The aim of this research is to establish how much reading is generally involved in homework, the purpose of that reading, and its outcome.

'Reading' can be defined as 'looking at written or printed words'. Clearly, the use of this definition implies that 'reading' will be a part of the homework task in maths and sciences as well as in English and the humanities.

The project team will therefore be particularly grateful to those teachers who attempt the very difficult task of applying the precise meaning of 'reading' to all questions.

Your pupils will need guidance in order to complete their questionnaires. It will be much appreciated if you will set aside time to show them *how* to fill in the form. It will be *very* much appreciated if you can resist the temptation of setting aside time to tell them *what* to put!

Thank you for taking part in this research. Homework is a prominent feature in the lives of many schoolchildren, and yet very little is known about it. It is hoped that this research will cast some light onto a fairly murky area.

Section A
Initials ....
1 *School name* (please circle number), e.g. 01

                          01
                          02
                          03
                          04
                          05
                          06
                          07
                          08
                          09
                          10

2 *Year group* (please circle number)
  First year 1   Fourth year 2
3 *Day homework was set* (please circle number)
  Monday   1
  Tuesday   2
  Wednesday 3
  Thursday   4
  Friday   5
4 *Day homework should be done* (please circle number)
  Monday   1
  Tuesday   2
  Wednesday   3
  Thursday   4
  Friday   5
  Saturday   6
  Sunday   7
  Any time at weekend   8
  Any time before time for handing in 9

Section B
1 *Brief outline of homework set* ....
....
....
....
2 *Did the set homework involve any reading at all?* (please circle number)
  Yes 1   No 2
  If YES, please continue:
  Please give details of book(s) to be read for homework:

Author or Editor	Title	Chapter/ Section	Page number (if specified)

Please give details of any other reading materials, e.g. worksheets, exercise books, etc. ....
....
....

3 *Duration of homework*
Please indicate
(a) total time needed for all homework .... mins.
(b) total time needed for reading.. mins.
(c) longest continuous time you would expect a child to spend reading
.... mins.

4 *Type of reading*
The homework compelled the child to spend most of the reading time (please circle number)
(a) reading continuously   1
(b) reading in frequent short intervals   2
(c) reading only occasionally   3
To estimate the length of time needed for reading was (please circle number)
(a) very difficult   1
(b) fairly difficult   2
(c) reasonably easy   3
If (a) please state why ....
....
....
....

Section C
1 *Purpose of the reading* (please circle as *many* as necessary)

Test preparation	01	To make notes	06
Revision	02	To check work	07
To do questions	03	To do corrections	08
To find out answers	04	Pleasure	09
To prepare for lesson	05	To follow-up lesson	10
		Other	11

(If 11 please specify ....
....
....)

Section D
1 Estimate of reading difficulty (please complete only if the pupil was required to read print). The reading in this homework was (please circle number)
very difficult   1
difficult   2
of no particular difficulty   3
easy   4
2 All pupils completed the homework   1
Most pupils completed the homework   2
Some pupils completed the homework   3
Few pupils completed the homework   4
(please circle number)

3 All pupils completed the homework satisfactorily   1
   Most pupils completed the homework satisfactorily   2
   Some pupils completed the homework satisfactorily   3
   Few pupils completed the homework satisfactorily   4
   (please circle number)
4 *Discussion* (please circle number)
   (a) Was there class discussion of the set task *before* the homework?
       Yes   1   No   2
   (b) Was there class discussion of the set task after the homework?
       Yes   1   No   2
   (c) Was there discussion of the set task with individuals *before* the homework?
       Yes   1   No   2
   (d) Was there discussion of the set task with individuals *after* the homework?
       Yes   1   No   2

Thank you again for completing this questionnaire. It is hoped that you have not found it too burdensome.

7

Topic Work with First-year Secondary Pupils

John Cole and Keith Gardner

1 The problem

The results of the classroom observation work described in Chapter 5 showed the amount of time spent on various activities in normal lessons across the curriculum. While this inquiry was fundamental in order to obtain a general picture of classroom practice, the project team was aware of its limitations. In particular integrated studies were not strongly represented.

It might be argued that where a school had adopted an approach based on individual assignments rather than class lessons, the reading demands on pupils would be greater, and the experience of using reading for learning more extensive. There was a need to test this hypothesis.

Unfortunately, pressure of time made it impossible to replicate both the scale and rigour of the original observations. In the event it was decided to study one project in one school in some depth rather than attempt a wider and perhaps a less informative survey. This decision meant that this aspect of our work would have to be regarded as a pilot study rather than a definitive statement. What is offered is an account of one project extending over one half-term. It is therefore an example, not a norm.

II The lessons we observed

We approached one of our project schools with a request for facilities to observe topic work in the first year. The cooperation of head and staff was both immediate and enthusiastic.

Our choice of school was determined by a number of factors. Previous contacts with the staff enabled us to be accepted as colleagues, and the members of the project team were no strangers to many of the pupils. The school, an 11–18 comprehensive, created five years earlier by the amalgamation of a mixed grammar school and a girls' secondary school, had a purpose-built lower-school unit separate from the main school, but on the same campus. This unit had some traditional classrooms, but most important from our point of view there were also open-plan working areas grouped mainly about a central and accessible library/resource area. In many ways, therefore, the physical conditions were ideal for our purpose.

In the lower school, there existed a team of teachers led by two committed enthusiasts, who ran an established topic-based course which occupied all pupils for twelve periods in every forty-period week. Again, this seemed to meet the requirements for the type of activity we wished to observe.

The course itself rested on the following principles:

1   pupils should work in mixed-ability groups,
2   the staff contribution should be through team-teaching,
3   an emphasis should be placed on resource-based learning,
4   pupil participation should be a fundamental aim,
5   staff and pupils should work within the framework of a structured, pre-planned, project.

It may be claimed, therefore, that the situation we selected for scrutiny represented a 'progressive' development within secondary education. Our purpose was not to make comparisons between such an approach and more traditional methods, but to describe the use made of reading and allied skills during the normal operation of a structured project.

A first-year intake of some 360 pupils was divided into three 'bases' with about 120 pupils in each base. Every effort was made to achieve a reasonable balance of ability-range within each base. The bases were, in turn, subdivided into four classes where again every effort was made to distribute pupils of high, average and lower ability in each group. We were satisfied, therefore, that within the limitations of any selection procedure we would have the opportunity to observe genuine mixed-ability groups. The method of observation that we adopted was similar in many ways to that described in Chapter 5.

The integrated-studies course was based on topics selected by the teacher which were pursued for about one half-term. These topics were usually centred in the first instance on school-produced pamphlets or booklets which were intended to serve as no more than an initial stimulus. The booklets, pamphlets and key lessons were designed to lead the pupils towards the use of the well-stocked library area, which had special collections of books, filmstrips, tapes and other resources relevant to the topics being studied at any one time.

Each topic was studied through three separate kinds of lesson: the key lesson, the working session, and the report-back.

The key lesson was presented by one or two of the teaching team to a complete base of 120 pupils. Its purposes were to introduce the main topic, or that part of it which was to be subjected to more particular study, to define areas for further exploration, to lead in to the tasks to be completed by the pupils, which were listed in a Pupils' Guide, and to provoke interest in the work to be covered. The methods of presentation varied. Overhead-projector slides, tapes, records, and filmstrips were used to supplement and illustrate a presentation prepared by the teachers. The pupils were expected to make notes, and usually there was an opportunity for discussion based on question and answer. Each key lesson observed in this study occupied a full seventy-minute session.

Pupils spent the greater part of the course in working sessions. A typical week took the following form:

Monday	1.30 p.m.–2.40 p.m.	key lesson
Tuesday	9.30 a.m.–10.40 a.m.	working session
Wednesday	9.30 a.m.–10.40 a.m.	working session
Thursday	1.30 p.m.–2.40 p.m.	working session
Friday	1.30 p.m.–4.00 p.m.	working session and report-back

The working sessions involved pupils in pursuing individual and group assignments. It was in these sessions that the teachers expected most of the ground to be covered, and most of the work to be done. Hence, our observations were concentrated on these periods, during which the pupils were called upon most frequently to use reading for learning.

Reporting-back sessions, like the key lessons, involved the whole base. On these occasions, groups of pupils gave an account of their activities and findings to the remainder of the base.

In essence, our study describes some of the activities of 120 pupils engaged in a topic 'Ancient Civilizations' over a period of six weeks in the spring term of 1976. Six teachers were involved in the course, which was the third element of an integrated study extending over the school year. The earlier topics studied were 'Creation and Evolution' and 'Stone-Age Man'.

III Methods of observation and results

One project officer (John Cole) designed and took charge of the observations. He was assisted by three Advanced Diploma students from the University of Nottingham, each of whom had a special interest in observational work.

Information, both quantitative and qualitative, was obtained by the following procedures:

1 A descriptive account of each session attended by members of the team was produced daily. This provided a general overview of the total operation.

2 The dominant activity of individuals within groups was sampled

randomly, care being taken to ensure that the pupil under observation was unaware of the observer's interest. Some examples of work completed by pupils under observation were collected and photocopied.

3 A record was kept of the reading materials used by some groups of pupils. These groups were selected purely on the basis of ease of observation because it was vital to preserve the essential features of work in an open-plan area. Interference with normal work was kept to a minimum.

4 The behaviour of pupils using the library area was sampled by direct observation.

5 A series of tape-recorded interviews with selected pupils was carried out to throw further light on their methods of study.

6 Further recordings of report-back sessions were made to obtain evidence of the response of the pupils to the topic being studied.

It was hoped that, taken together, these procedures would provide adequate pictures of the pupils' reading strategies, their reactions to resource-based activities, and their use of language.

1 Dominant activities during working sessions

Each observer carried out a minute-by-minute observation of individual pupils working in small groups. The categories employed in the schedule designed for classroom observation were modified in pilot work to meet the special requirements of surveying project work in an open teaching area. In this study the observers judged and recorded the dominant activity of each pupil in a working group. For instance, in any one minute of observation a pupil writing with occasional reference to a source, or occasional pause for thought, would be recorded as 'writing', regardless of what he happened to be doing at the end of that minute. Observations were recorded on eleven separate occasions spread over three weeks and they totalled 1468 minutes of scrutiny.

The results are summarized in Table 7.1 (p. 171). The figures represent the proportion of time spent in various activities over a period of time rather than a typical session. Indeed, individual sessions varied considerably. The category *drawing and tracing* emerged as the fifth largest category, yet it was not noted at all in five out of eleven observation sessions.

Writing emerges as the salient activity. The reason is that most of the tasks set in the Pupils' Guide demanded a written response, and the completion of a 'folder' was the evidence that a topic had been studied. Observers were able to make subjective judgements regarding the nature of this writing. Most of it was copying or near copying. Note-taking was also prominent, but this consisted mainly of transferring short passages from a source to a rough book.

Reading was clearly a less time-consuming occupation, but it was evident that some reading was required of all pupils in most assignments. What is crucial is the nature and purpose of such reading. It was obvious that the pupils were reading mainly to answer questions, and these answers had to be written. Here it is interesting to note that reading and writing concurrently made up only 1.8 per cent of activities recorded. This confirms an impression gained by the observers concerning the strategy adopted by pupils. While much of the writing was classified as copying, it was not word-by-word copying. Rather, the pupils tended to memorize a phrase or a sentence and then refer briefly to their text for confirmation of a word or a spelling. The important point is that the main purpose of observed reading was to remember something that had to be written in order to answer a set question.

There is little doubt that when teachers design a project of the kind we observed, their intention is that pupils should obtain information by using the available resources. In order to help pupils in their 'research', some guidance was offered on how to find suitable sources and on how to collate or record the information so obtained. What we observed was that, again and again, individuals and small groups of pupils adopted strategies of their own for a very specific purpose: to maximize short-term recall, and to bypass reflection. It cannot be denied that these strategies were often successful in enabling them to reach the overt goals set by the teachers. What of the overall gain? We must defer an answer to a later section, when we can consider the results of our report-back sessions and of individual interviews.

The figure for 'discussion' was the third highest category, but even this does not reflect the amount of talk that took place for it omits the

Table 7.1 Dominant activities

Category	Time observed (minutes)	Percentage of total time
Writing	447	30.4
Reading	126	8.6
Discussion of work	160	10.9
Checking work	50	3.4
Deliberation	64	4.4
Pupil or group working with teacher	30	2.0
Not involved	241	16.4
Writing and reading concurrently	27	1.8
Administration	87	5.9
Departures to resources	54	3.7
Drawing and tracing	126	8.6
External distraction	56	3.8

casual comment made, for instance, during the dominant activity of writing. There is here a real difference between the pattern of activity reported in Chapter 5, and the form of the project periods we are now considering. Verbal interchange was more pronounced both between pupil and pupil, and between pupil and teacher.

Finally, the amount of time during which pupils were 'not involved' requires some comment. It is the second highest category, and the conclusion may be drawn that the pupils spent one-sixth of lesson-time doing nothing. But one might also say that they spent five-sixths of their time working, and that with a minimum of supervision. Would an observation of any office or assembly line produce a very different picture?

One can only speculate about the relative value of learning under direct supervision in a classroom lesson, where 'not involved' is less frequent, and learning in a self-determined way when, apparently, 'not involved' is more prominent.

2 The use of reading materials

What children actually read in the course of the project was of great importance. In order to gain this information an observer surveyed a chosen area for scrutiny. Normally, this area would be occupied by ten to twenty pupils. Every three minutes the situation in the area was recorded under the following headings:

1 time of observation,
2 number of pupils in the area,
3 number of pupils using their own notes for reference,
4 number of pupils using school-produced materials,
5 number of pupils consulting books,
6 the titles of books being used,
7 page references, where appropriate.

An example of a completed schedule is provided as Fig. 7.1 (p. 173). Column 2 indicates the number of pupils occupying the area under observation; column 5 shows the number of pupils using books, and the titles of these books are listed in column 6. A total of 130 separate three-minutely observations were made and 884 pupils were observed.

In the course of these observations it became clear that the pupils spent a considerable amount of reading time referring to their own notes. This is shown in Table 7.2 (p. 174).

What kind of reading did this referring back to 'own notes' involve? In the main, pupils were preparing to make a fair copy from their rough book, or were checking over their final presentation.

By and large the books used for reference purposes were few in number. During the period when the whole base was studying 'The

Figure 7.1 *Behaviour in library area*

Group A1   Max. no. present 12   Date: 12 January 1976   Observer: A.D.   Reading Record (1)

Time	No. of pupils in survey	No. using own notes	No. using teachers' guide	No. using books	Book titles	Comments
1.42	12	2	3	6	*Out of the Ancient World* (×5) *Ancient Sumer* (×1)	1 gone to fetch paper
1.45	12	4	2	5	Dictionary (×2) *Out of the Ancient World* (×3)	1 to map
1.48	12	1	3	7	*Out of the Ancient World* (×7)	1 about to start colouring
1.51	12	3	1	6	*Out of the Ancient World* (×6)	1 with teacher 1 thinking
1.54	12	4	0	5	*Out of the Ancient World* (×5)	1 thinking 1 with teacher 1 about to start writing

Table 7.2   Percentage of reading time distributed by type of text being used

Pupils' activity	Week 1	Week 2	Week 3	Week 4
Using own notes	47.5	33.3	25.3	35.5
Using school-produced materials	11.3	8.3	3.4	0.9
Using books	11.3	24.4	12.9	22.7
Not reading	29.9	34.0	58.4	40.9

Birth of Civilization' only five different titles were noted during the observation periods. These were:

1   *Out of the Ancient World*—the basic reference book
2   *Ancient Sumer*
3   *The Cradle of Civilization*
4   *The History of the World*—used only for tracing
5   A pocket dictionary used by two pupils to find the meaning of one word: *cooperation.*

When the base began to study different aspects of the general topic, twenty-one further titles were used in the teaching area.

Whether or not the recourse to books for information was sufficient for the purposes of the project we were studying is an open question. The number of titles considered is no indication of the quality of information gained. What should be noted, however, is that few pupils appeared to avail themselves of the full resources at their disposal.

3 The use of the library/resource area

For this aspect of the inquiry, the observers used informal contact with pupils to gain information about how they used the well-stocked resources that had been organized for topic work. It was apparent that the resource area was visited frequently, and most pupils had at least some knowledge of what they were expected to do. One typical response which was recorded was:[1]

> Well if you don't know where the books are, there's a little booklet which has all the names of the books. Then you have a code number beside it, then you go to the shelf, that'll say so-so number, then you look on the shelf until you find the book.

In fact only a minority of pupils appeared to go so far. Generally an acceptable source book was found from the project shelf. It is fair to say that the first book which contained something that could be noted served the pupil's needs.

Some picture of the way in which the pupils worked in the resource

[1] The full transcript of this interview is given on pp. 180–2.

area can be communicated by reproducing a chart of one observation period. Table 7.3, below, shows the grouping and activities of children noted at five-minute intervals in the course of one such period.

There was an ever-changing pattern, but two points of interest emerge. First, working groups normally gathered in twos and threes and discussion took place within which it was usual for a dominant figure to direct operations. Second, searching often appeared to be a random sampling of books from the shelves rather than a purposeful inquiry. Although the pupils could explain how to find an appropriate book, they appeared reluctant to put this theory into practice.

The modes of searching individual books for the required information were varied, but there was little evidence of a widespread use of table of contents, index or chapter headings. Often an arresting illustration became a focus of attention and acted as a kind of trap. To give some point to these general comments, here is a single case study of the progress of a girl of average ability. She was responding to a question in her Pupils' Guide: *Describe Roman homes, mentioning buildings, food, clothing, furniture, heating and other*

Table 7.3   Library/resource area grouping and activities

Time	No. of groups working together	No. of pupils in each group	Individuals working alone	No. of pupils 'searching'	Total no. of pupils in area
1.50	7	3, 5, 4, 3, 2, 4, 2.	4	10	37
1.55	8	2, 2, 5, 4, 3, 2, 2, 2.	2	9	33
2.00	7	3, 3, 3, 2, 2, 2, 2.	3	13	33
2.05	8	2, 2, 2, 3, 2, 4, 2, 2.	4	13	36
2.10	6	3, 2, 2, 3, 2, 2.	4	6	24
2.15	8	4, 3, 2, 2, 2, 3, 2, 2.	1	9	30
2.20	6	3, 2, 2, 3, 2, 2.	1	9	24
2.25	6	3, 3, 2, 2, 4, 2.	0	3	19
2.30	5	3, 3, 2, 4, 2.	1	6	21
2.35	6	2, 2, 3, 2, 4, 2.	1	6	22

comforts. What difference would there be between the homes of rich men and craftsmen? The girl seized on the word 'building' and, when asked what she was looking for replied, 'Something about Roman building'. She browsed through some books randomly and eventually selected *How They Lived in Ancient Rome.* An illustration of the Forum had engaged her attention, and she decided to work from that source although the amount of information about domestic life was unpromising. She then began her assignment by paraphrasing the legend of Romulus and Remus. When questioned about this she replied that she was preparing a proper introduction. It appeared that she thought she was following the technique employed by her teachers in their key lessons.

A study of three girls working together as a group, but using only one source book, serves to illustrate another way in which questions from the Pupils' Guide were answered. The girls were searching for information to reply to the question: 'Try to describe the land of Sumer as it looked in 300 B.C.'. The book in use was *Ancient Mesopotamia and Persia.* When questioned, the girls insisted that they had looked at the chapter headings to find what parts of the book would be useful to them. The observer was doubtful if this had actually happened. At least it was established that the pupils knew what they had been told to do. One girl read out aloud the passages she thought were relevant, and all three girls made notes in rough books. These 'notes' were near copies of the originals.

Various structures were noted, but common to many groups was the dominant figure who made the rules and carried them through. It must be pointed out that while some of the practices adopted by these small cooperatives seemed to be of doubtful value as study techniques, they were partly successful within the context of the groups we observed. The pupils were involved, and had developed their own strategies for 'finding answers'. What is more they seemed to enjoy doing it.

4 Recorded interviews

Three taped transcripts of some selected interviews are reproduced below. They are drawn from three levels of ability. The first is from an able pupil; the second from an average pupil; and the last from a less-able pupil. We present them without comment. The children speak for themselves.

INTERVIEW WITH FELICITY

DH What school did you go to before you came here?
F   (Child names school.)
DH When you were at that school, did you do topics?
F   Yes.
DH What topics did you do?

F   We did a topic on a television programme called *A Year's Journey*. We used to watch and make notes, and then we had worksheets throughout the week and then we watched the programme.

DH   Did your teacher tell you how to do it, or did you go and work on your own?

F   Work on our own mainly, because the worksheets we could work through at our own pace.

DH   Did you use the books and other things as well?

F   Yes.

DH   When you came here and you came to do Integrated Studies, had you ever done anything like that at your junior school?

F   Not really.

DH   What's different about this to what you used to do in your junior school?

F   We have a booklet to read before we start, and then a booklet with questions in, and a resource centre with filmstrips and slides which we didn't have in our old school.

DH   When you go into the resource centre do you ever use the filmstrips and slides or do you usually or nearly always use books?

F   I mostly use books, but I do use filmstrips sometimes.

DH   Have you used any on this particular project?

F   I don't think so, but I was going to look at some this afternoon.

DH   When you did your last project, did you use filmstrips then?

F   Yes, I think I did.

DH   How do you use them? What do you do with them?

F   I didn't use the filmstrip, I used some slides and you put them in the projector and there's a small screen attached to it and it shows up on that.

DH   And what does that tell you in fact?

F   There's a picture there and some writing underneath, and there's a booklet that comes with it and you can read what the picture's showing.

DH   When you're doing your project ... 'Ancient Egypt' ... what books have you used to help you so far?

F   Quite a lot out of the resource centre and then there are some class books that you can get in a large quantity.

DH   What sort of books have you used in the resource centre? Can you tell me some titles?

F   *Ancient Egypt*. There are two books called *Ancient Egypt* and *Out of the Ancient World*.

DH   Are they from the resource centre or are they in the classroom?

F   They're in the classroom.

DH   What have you used from the resource centre so far?

F   I think there's *Ancient Egypt* and one called *Egypt, Rome and Greece*. I can't remember any of the others.

DH   Tell me how you go about doing it. What's the first thing that you do when you've got a new project, what's the first thing that happens?

F   We'd have a key lesson from the team leader, that's when we all get together and gives us a lecture about the subject.

DH   What's the use of the key lesson?

F   Well you make notes and it's to tell you what you're doing about. Because if he said, right, go through the Pupils' Guide and do all the questions, you just wouldn't know what they were about.

DH   Do you find the key lesson useful?

F   Yes.

DH   And what's the next thing you do yourself when you've had your key lesson?

F   We get a Pupils' Guide and read a booklet that we're given or a sheet and as soon as we understand it, we can start on the questions.

DH   When you've got a question, how do you go about answering it? What's the first question? Can you remember what it says?

F   It's a map. We have to draw a map so we usually do it as a class, if it's a map. If it's about question 2 we ...

DH   What's question 2 then, tell me what that was.

F   It's write about ...

DH   Can you remember? Can you remember any of the questions that you've done?

F   Well there are certain plays, but I haven't got up to them yet.

DH   No. I mean can you remember the sort of things the other questions say?

F   Write about things like 'How civilization got there in Egypt'.

DH   If you had to do that, how would you go about doing that?

F   Well, I'd look in as many books as I could and find as much information as possible.

DH   How do you find the information?

F   From resources.

DH   How do you know what book to find though?

F   Well, there's a book in resources, a couple of them, and you look through them and you look for the subject, rather like a dictionary, and when you find the subject that you want, it's got a number by the side of it. So you look round the resource centre for the number and it will say the number on the shelf. So you look through that shelf.

DH   Good. Do you sometimes get books off the first-year project shelf?

F   Yes.

DH   They've got them all drawn out together then, but sometimes you look for the number and find other books besides?

F   Yes.

DH   Now you've got your book and found the right page you want to look at presumably, what do you do then?

F   You can't take project books back to the classroom and so you're meant to make notes and take your rough book up.

DH   How do you makes notes? What do you do when you're making notes?

F   I sort of read through the paragraphs and the ideas, dates and things that are in it you just write down in the book.

DH   Do you write it in sentences or do you just put down ...

F   I just put down any words to remind me.

DH   So that if I read it, it probably wouldn't mean anything to me, but it would to you?

F   Yes.

DH When you've done that, you've made your notes, what do you do next? How many books would you read? You might do two or three at once or just one?

F   Yes. Perhaps. But it depends how much information you get out of one book.

DH I see, sometimes you get a lot from one book. And you've got all your information, what's the next thing you do?

F   Well you take it back to the classroom and then you write it up in best onto the file paper.

DH Good. Do you like IS? You might not like it? Do you like it? What do you like best about it?

F   Yes. Well, I like the report-backs 'cos they're seeing how other people get on in their work and then I like just using the books and writing and doing charts and pictures.

DH Do you like doing that especially because it's on your own, or would you prefer it if you were having to work together as a class all doing the same?

F   I wouldn't like it if we have to work in a class because you couldn't work at your own pace. The teacher's telling you everything to do and you've just got to do the same and everybody's work is the same.

DH Did you used to work as a class in your junior school?

F   Well we had the same worksheets but we could work at our own pace.

DH Have you ever had to work as a class? Can you ever remember having to do it, or do you have certain lessons here as a class?

F   Yes we do things like science.

DH And you don't like doing that as much as when you can do it on your own?

F   No.

DH So you tried working in a class to see. What don't you like about them? Is there anything you don't like about IS or which could be changed to make them better?

F   I think it could be changed a bit. I don't know whether it could be, but the only thing I think is wrong is that people could just do about two questions in half a term, 'cos the teacher's just waiting for you to do the work and get on with it yourself and you could get away with not doing any work.

DH I don't quite understand.

F   If I was given a booklet, I could easily . . . 'cos we work through it say for about half a term or four weeks, and then we could easily . . . we're just told to work through the book and I could easily work at my own pace and do a very slow pace and not do much work at all.

DH You mean it's very difficult for the teacher to know whether you're doing . . . whether you're working as hard as you can do? Do you always? Or do you sometimes not try as hard as you could?

F   Sometimes I don't, but I usually try. I do work at home as well.

DH Do you think most people work as hard as they could? Or do some people not?

F   I think most people do, but some people just don't think. . . . There's not a job like when you grow up, so you might as well not learn it.

DH You mean now they think learning about Ancient Greece or Egypt has got nothing to do with real life?

F Mm. They think it's got nothing to do with the job you're going to get when you grow up.

DH Do you ever think now about the job you're going to do when you grow up?

F Yes. I think I want to be a doctor, I think.

DH And you're thinking about it already?

F Yes. I've had it in mind for ages ... for years. I've always wanted to be something.

DH Have you? Why is that?

F I don't know, but my mum works in a hospital and I'd like to 'cos I think it's just a nice job to do. You meet other people and it's a good job and you get good pay.

DH And do you think what you're doing here now will make a difference to getting a job when you finish school?

F What, to be a doctor?

DH Yes.

F Not really but I still like to study it 'cos I might not be able to get a job as a doctor.

DH What do you think we're doing?

F I don't know.

DH Haven't you even thought about it?

F No.

INTERVIEW WITH PHILIP

DH What junior school did you go to?

P (Child names school.)

DH When you were there, did you ever used to do topics?

P Yes.

DH What sort of topics did you do there?

P Well, we had television programmes and worksheets.

DH Did you do them on your own or did the teacher make you do them as a class or what?

P When I came to the school the headteacher had twenty-two more children than he should have had, so he made up three classes and we had three topics and you could choose which one you wanted to do.

DH I see. And then you did it on your own did you?

P Well the teacher made out the worksheets.

DH When you came here and you did Integrated Studies, were the topics you did like the things you do here in IS or were they different? Did you go about it in a different way?

P Yes we did.

DH What's different about this IS to how you used to go about doing topics?

P Well, now you're left to your own than. .... We had more help from teachers.

DH When you're starting a project in IS, what's the first thing that happens?

P Well, we're usually given a key lesson.

DH What's the purpose of that? What's it for?

P   Well, usually the team leader or another teacher, he tells you about what we're going to do.

DH And what's that for? What does that tell you?

P   That's to give you a head start.

DH And then what do you do next? You've had your key lesson . . . what's the next thing you do?

P   Well, usually handing out books and other things . . . that usually takes up a lesson.

DH What do you do with the books? You mean Teachers' Guide . . . Pupils' Guide . . . what do you do with them?

P   The Pupils' Guide is usually the questions.

DH What do you do with that?

P   Usually gives us help on . . .

DH And then when you've done that, what do you do next?

P   Usually start on the questions.

DH Say you got a question on . . . something about 'How civilization got to Egypt'. How do you find the answer?

P   You go to the resource centre.

DH What do you do when you go there?

P   Well if you don't know where the books are, there's a little booklet which has all the names of the books. Then you have a code number beside it, then you go to the shelf, that'll say so-so number, then you look on the shelf until you find the book.

DH Do you ever look on the first-year project shelf?

P   Yes.

DH Or do you get most of your books from somewhere else?

P   Well, I found I got most of my books from the project shelf.

DH What books have you looked at from the resource centre for your project on Egypt.

P   I think there's one . . . *Daily Life in Egypt* and *The Pharoahs*.

DH These were both on the first-year project shelf? What do you do when you go in the resource centre and you look at a book? What do you do?

P   You look up in the book and get the information out that you need.

DH How do you do that?

P   You read the part that you want, then you write down things in your rough book.

DH How do you write them down? Do you see a sentence and put that down or what?

P   You usually read it first and put down the ideas and a bit more information to go with them.

DH Yes, so you probably wouldn't write sentences, but just write words or little bits?

P   Little bits and . . .

DH Then what do you do when you've got all these? Do you sometimes look at other things apart from books?

P   Yes, there is a shelf with theme boxes in.

DH What are they?

P   They are boxes with drawings, pieces of newspapers and magazines.

DH Do you look at those? Did you look at them this time?

P   No. I looked at them for 'Old and New Stone-Age Man'.

DH Do you ever look at any of the slides? Or the strips ... filmstrips?

P   Yes.

DH Have you looked at any this time? Which ones have you looked at?

P   Yes. *The Rise of Egyptian Civilization.*

DH What was that? Filmstrip?

P   Filmstrip.

DH How does that help you? What does it tell you when you've looked at your filmstrip?

P   It has pictures and then underneath there might be a bit of writing. And I think on the filmstrips they have a booklet which will give a passage.

DH So there's a bit of reading and looking at it as well and that gives you more ideas does it? When you've got all your ideas down in your rough book, what do you do?

P   I come down and start writing it out on the table.(!)

DH Do you like doing Integrated Studies?

P   It's all right.

DH Not very keen. What don't you like about it?

P   Well I prefer to do things of today.

DH What do you mean? Tell me.

P   Coal and how they actually mine it out.

DH You mean you don't mind going and reading on your own and answering questions, but you don't like the sort of things you're reading about. Or would you prefer it if you had a class lesson and the teacher taught you and you worked together as a class? Would you prefer that?

P   Well, usually with science you're doing a certain thing, but with this there's a lot of questions and the fast people they shoot off and the slow people they ...

DH What I mean is, do you mind answering the questions, is that the bit you don't like or is it just the sort of things you're having to look at you don't like?

P   Usually the actual topic itself.

DH Then you don't mind ... If it was on coal you wouldn't mind going off to the library and looking up on your own about that? Why don't you like doing the ones you're doing now then? Just because they're a long time ago?

P   Yes, I prefer the things of today.

DH What do you like best about ... is there anything you like about IS? Is there anything you like about it?

P   Yes, I think I preferred Egypt to the rest of the topics.

DH Why is that?

P   I think, there's a bit more to it than the others.

DH Have you any idea what we're doing?

P   Are you to do with ITV or BBC?

INTERVIEW WITH LAURA

DH What school were you at before you came here?

L   (Child names school.)

DH When you were at your junior school, did you used to do topics?

L Yes, we did it on police and things like that.

DH How did you do it?

L Well, find out what police did, you know, and we have this printing pad and we had to put our fingers on it.

DH Did you do it all together as a class?

L No we did it in a little group.

DH Did the classteacher help you or did you do it on your own or what?

L No, we did it on our own and found our own information.

DH When you were here and started to do Integrated Studies, was that like the topics you've been doing . . . the way you do IS here?

L No, because you find out more for yourself and it's more interesting.

DH Why is it more interesting?

L Well, you've got the resources to use and you've got all the books and information sheets you see and you haven't got a teacher telling you what questions to do because you've got a sheet to read it from.

DH Did the teacher used to tell you before?

L Yes.

DH What sort of resources have you got to use? When you're doing your topic, what sorts of things do you find in the resources centre?

L I don't know really. I just find the information that I need.

DH Are you doing Ancient Egypt?

L Yes.

DH Have you been to the resource centre this time?

L What today?

DH No, I mean while you've been doing Ancient Egypt.

L Yes.

DH What have you looked at when you went there?

L Um for noblemen, peasant and Pharoahs.

DH And what did you do? Did you look in a book?

L Yes.

DH What book did you look in or was there more than one?

L Oo, I looked at more than one.

DH Can you remember what they were called?

L I used one down in the classroom, *Out of the Ancient World*, and I can't remember any I used in the resource centre.

DH How many did you use in the resource centre.

L About two or three.

DH When you go to the resource centre, have you ever used the theme boxes?

L Yes.

DH When did you use those? Not this time?

L When I was on 'Evolution' and 'New Stone-Age Man'.

DH And have you ever used the slidestrips or the slides?

L I've used the slides; that was for 'Old Stone-Age Man and New'.

DH How do you use those? What do you do with them?

L Well, you have like your own slide thing with its own screen and you work it yourself.

DH Are they useful?

L Yes.

DH Why?

L   Because um on the bottom of the slide you get all this writing and you can make it from your own notes and put it in your own words.

DH When you're reading a book, and you're after the information, how do you get the information? What do you do?

L   Well, I look at it you see, and if there's a sentence to make it ... you know how I think.

DH I see. So if you've got a page on ... I don't know ... civilization and how it got there, would you sort of put all that was on that page into sentences of your own?

L   Not everything. What I thought was most interesting.

DH And what would that be? Into your rough book?

L   Yes, I put it into my rough book and then I bring it back down to the classroom then I put it into a piece of paper.

DH Do you just copy it straight out of your rough book as it stands?

L   No.

DH What do you do then?

L   Because sometimes in my rough book I don't get it into good enough sentences, so I put it better.

DH Oh, I see, sometimes you just put notes down.

L   Yes.

DH Do you like doing IS?

L   Yes.

DH What do you like about it best of all?

L   Well, it's more interesting. You can find out your own information. You haven't got teachers to tell you what to do.

DH You like doing that do you?

L   Yes.

DH Smashing. Is there anything you don't like about it? Anything that could be improved?

L   How do you mean?

DH Well, is there anything that you think ought to be changed in Integrated Studies to make it better or do you like it as it is?

L   I just like it as it is.

DH Have you any idea what we're doing?

L   No.

DH No idea at all? Wouldn't you like to guess?

L   I think you're working out who's good at something and who's best. What we do and the information we find out.

5 The report-back session

The report-back sessions provided evidence as to what the pupils gained from their efforts. Their quality varied, as any classroom work varies. There are successful lessons and unsuccessful lessons. However, a complete account of a typical session is given below. It begins with an extract from an observer's diary, and transcripts of recordings of the pupils' presentations follow.

A REPORT-BACK

Three girls started with a report-back on Egypt. They used the 'board and chalk' technique for a difficult name they wished to bring to everyone's notice. They produced a chart illustrating the Tutenkamen death mask and the next girl to speak referred to the exhibition at the British Museum held a few years ago. Then the girls gave a short play showing the death of a nobleman and another depicting the superstitions of the Egyptians connected with gods and life after death. One girl explained what the play had been supposed to tell us afterwards!

(All this time the children watching and listening continued to concentrate well, even though we heard a teacher in the next base shouting at a child quite clearly.)

At the end of the first report-back, the teacher commented on the amount of factual information which had been gathered, saying that he was pleased with the effort the girls had made, but he suggested that they could have made illustrations of the various gods they had chosen.

Three boys then offered to speak about Rome. (David 1, D1: David 2, D2; Keith, K; Teacher, T.)

Transcription of report-back by three boys

D1 David, Keith and I are going to talk about three very important things that were very important in Rome.

K I'm going to talk about basic Rome.

D1 I'm going to talk about the Roman Army.

D2 I'm going to talk about Hadrian's Wall.

D1 As usual, Keith will start us off.

K The population of Rome today is 2,560,000 and it started from a small village on the banks of the River Tiber. (Moves to the blackboard and draws the river and village plan.) So it started there (pointing to drawing) and as time went along, it started to spread—wider all the time 'till it got to the total of 2,256,000. In the sixth century the Etruscans conquered Rome and they came in from here (illustrates direction on the blackboard) and they attacked Rome. In 509 B.C. the Romans kept them back (draws arrows on blackboard opposing the advance) and then after they'd driven them back again, Rome became a Republic. (Writes RUPUBLIC on the board.)

T A what?

K A republic, sir ... oh, I've got it ... I've spelt it wrong. (Alters it to REPUBLIC.) And republican Rome was ruled by two elected consuls, chosen by the citizens called the patricians. They, they helped to govern the different assemblies and the most important assembly was the Senate. Now, a little later than this there was a civil war, and out of the civil war arose Julius Caesar and when he was alive he wanted to take the throne but the people of the Senate didn't want him, so he was assassinated, and his nephew who was called Octavian, he got to be the First Consul of Rome and his name was Augustus when he was

Emperor. Now religion grew up at the end of his reign and Christians were persecuted until A.D. 313 when the Emperor Constantine set the Christians free. Now David will talk about armies.

D1   Well, the Roman Army established a reputation for success on the battlefield. A soldier had to be ready for anything, ready to fight the enemy. They'd go into battle with two javelins and a sword. A javelin is rather like a spear, about six foot. It is made out of wood and iron. Often the iron end would be fastened on by a pin, so that when it struck something ... when it struck something, say this is a wall (moving to blackboard and drawing) like the end part would fall off so that the enemy couldn't use it against them. Romans used many weapons and here are some of them; (poster held up by the other boys, consisting of illustrations by David), here's a sword ... a shield and there's a spear I've just talked to you about, a catapult and a ram. A soldier marched long distances every day ... so he had to wear stout shoes so he wore heavy sandals and armour underneath with a cloak on top. He wore a metal hat with feathers sticking out the top and it looked like this (another poster)—there's his cloak, there's his armour, and his shield and helmet. When the Romans started conquering countries they got groups of men who wanted to join their army, so the army got bigger and bigger and grew. Now David will talk about Hadrian's Wall.

D2   Hadrian's Wall was built between A.D. 122 and A.D. 128. It was built when the Romans invaded England and captured most of England and Wales, but Scotland wasn't and Scotland attacked England so the wall was built to stop them. The wall stretches from Newcastle to Carlisle, which is about eighty miles. There was a 27 feet wide ditch and 6 feet deep ditch in front of it. The wall itself was 10 feet high and 16 feet wide. This stopped the Scots from getting over. The first forty-five miles of it were made out of stone and this came out of Carlisle, and the last thirty-five is made out of mud and turf. Along the length of the wall there are mile-castles. These mile-castles were ... these mile-castles came every mile. These were where the soldiers slept. (Illustrated by drawing on blackboard.) Sixteen mile-castles were added to the original plan. In the mile-castles, the soldiers stayed there and when somebody was attacking, they would send a message by fire. And there are still parts of the wall left today—you can walk on them. And here is a picture of Hadrian's Wall (pointing to blackboard), here is a mile-castle and that's part that's still being built and that's already been built.

T   O.K.? A good attempt ... I'm a little bit disappointed that you didn't go into resources and use some of the posters, because there's some very good stuff on Roman Britain—several very large posters which illustrate what you've been talking about, about Hadrian's Wall, the depth of the dyke, the height of the wall, how it was built, the mile-castles, in fact you could have had a couple of posters up on the board and just talked, just about those two posters. If you had've used a little bit of this, saved you a lot of time. Right? So next time you prepare a talk, go into the resource centre, look at what slides they've got and what posters they've got, because you've just missed a very good opportunity there of using some really good visual illustrations.

Right? But apart from that it was very good: I thought it went down very well.

IV Discussion

1 Introduction

A Language for Life contains an analysis of the development of reading for learning. It suggests that in the middle and secondary years:

1   Pupils should learn methods by which study becomes more effective. (para 8:10)
2   Pupils should become accustomed to applying strategies which give them access to appropriate materials. (para 8:13)

With reference to 2, our study had shown that a group of pupils with a rudimentary knowledge of how to search for sources chose to ignore the advice they had been given. They went their own way, and followed their own strategies for learning.

It is easy to condemn the pupils. They did not do as they were told, so they must have been stupid, wayward, or lazy. Equally one could bewail the quality of the teaching and conclude that reading, like other activities that come under close scrutiny, 'is the worst-taught subject in schools'. These responses do not get us very far. It is more productive to seek reasons for the behaviour that was observed and arrive at some conclusions concerning guidelines for future policy and action. That is the intent of this discussion.

2 Perspectives

It is possible to describe an ideal strategy or set of strategies which define how an expert reader should behave. One can then make judgements about the manner in which particular students set about the task of reading for learning. But if one judges actual performance against an ideal, one is likely to be over-critical.

The students observed in this study were not undergraduates. They were twelve-year-old children. One is not surprised to find that when judged against an ideal picture of efficient reading they were inefficient readers. This should cause no surprise. It is important, however, that we should seek to understand what the children were doing and then pose two fundamental questions:

1   Does the observed behaviour of children illuminate our thinking about reading for learning?
2   Does an analysis of the observed situation offer any suggestions for appropriate teaching methods and styles?

Further, it must be recognized that a teacher has aims and objectives beyond the acquisition of effective reading. It would be unwise to consider the project we observed only in terms of an exercise to improve reading. No doubt the teachers were seeking a means to encourage cooperative learning; perhaps they wished their pupils to acquire specific facts; possibly they had in mind the fostering of enthusiasm for learning. Hence, it would be improper to criticize or condemn just because the goal of achieving more efficient reading was not sought more systematically.

This raises another fundamental question: In the middle years could the teaching strategies thought to be necessary for improving reading stand in opposition to the strategies adopted by teachers for enabling their pupils to acquire factual knowledge? Put another way, in the project we observed, the teachers could have intervened more frequently to counsel pupils about reading techniques and strategies. If they had done this would the pupils have learned more about reading but less about 'The Birth of Civilization'?

3 An analysis

It will be recalled that the pupils we observed were set to answer questions from their Pupils' Guide. They were directed to school-produced materials and the library/resource area to find answers. In the main, the pupils found it easier to work from the teacher-written sources than the reference books. This material had been produced with the set questions in mind; the books were less concise, and less 'topic-orientated'. Hence, it is reasonable to assume that the pupils avoided books for reasons of efficiency. They chose a simple rather than a complex path.

Then, when they did have recourse to books, they were more interested in sampling than in studying. Certainly, they had a question in mind when they sought books, but they were easily distracted by pictures and illustrations. Perhaps the range of available materials was overwhelming; perhaps the question that had to be answered was not sufficiently compelling. Whatever the reason, the fascination of books for the pupils we observed rested in a search for anything, rather than a search for 'what I have been told to find out'.

This perusal of materials was supplemented by talk. The operation of small-group cooperatives has already been described, and within these groupings the essential business of finding answers to questions was not overlooked. No doubt there were occasions when the dominant member of the group merely informed the others, but serious discussion also took place. One way and another, the children talked about finding answers.

For some pupils, talking within the group was a substitute for reading. They got the information they needed from their friends. For others, it was an opportunity to prompt their memory, test out their suggestions, or rehearse their written prose. In many ways their behaviour was similar to that of a group of undergraduates during a coffee break.

Talking for learning, then, played a major role in arriving at answers, and this should not be ignored. The results of our observations could be interpreted as indicating either that children find discussion more productive than reading, or that they found reading for learning difficult and sought ways of avoiding it: if they had been better readers there would have been less need for discussion.

If one accepts the former then the implication for teaching is that some retreat from print is justified, but if the latter is preferred then greater emphasis should be placed on teaching, counselling about and giving practice in, reading for learning. However, it may well be that reading for 'talking about reading' is both a stage on the road to 'reading for learning on one's own' and a valuable part of a total learning situation that comprehends thinking and discussion as well as reading.

When one turns to a consideration of the written outcomes of the topic work one cannot but note the amount of copying or near copying which took place. The reaction of teachers is also relevant. No one seemed surprised. The result was expected and a number of suggestions were put forward to point to possible explanations. Let us consider the following hypotheses:

1 The pupils were incapable of restructuring the information they obtained.
2 Copying was evidence that little or no inferential or evaluative reading took place.

The first of these propositions should be tested against the evidence of the report-back sessions. Capability is revealed in one performance. That it was achieved once is sufficient to show that such achievement is possible. The oral performance of the twelve-year-old pupils indicated that they were capable of transforming their study into a lively and informative presentation. They had learned something in spite of their inefficient methods of study, and were able to communicate their learning in a way that held the attention of their peers. Therefore the hypothesis that the pupils were incapable of restructuring the results of their study must be rejected.

In examining the second hypothesis we need to consider the constraints of the situation. The pupils were studying ancient history which is far removed from their personal experience. The information they sought was the result of inference and evaluation carried out by people trained to sift historical evidence, and the pupils accepted the information on trust. What else could they do? Sometimes learning must be an act of faith. Many readers of this report must accept our assurance that we have brought our own critical abilities to bear on the problems we faced. Others who have had direct experience of handling research questions may adopt a different stance.

Of course there is uninformed comment, and this was the only kind of evaluation open to the twelve-year-old pupils who were studying the topic we observed. Set this alongside the fact that they were answering—not posing—questions, and their reasons for copying become evident. It was the simplest and quickest way of meeting the demands of the situation. A teacher, or an author, had already composed the required answers. Their prose was superior to that of the pupils, their knowledge greater. Under these circumstances the urge to avoid inaccuracy can be more demanding than the exhortation 'do not copy!' Some theses produced for higher degrees are not free from a similar kind of writing. This is not entirely a fault of training; it is also a response to demands and pressures.

V Conclusions

All of the foregoing observations relate to one section of the work of a single school in one particular area and over a limited period of time. Also they are confined to a single age-group. It might therefore seem dangerous to attempt to derive from them conclusions of any generality. Nevertheless, by luck or by judgement, the work we have reviewed constitutes an admirable illustration *in vivo* to illuminate any discussion of the role of reading in learning. By any reasonable standard, the teaching we have described is good teaching, and it has resulted in useful learning. Also, by contrast with much of the work reported in Chapter 5, it is learning and teaching in which reading and learning from reading play an important part. Above all, and doubtless for these reasons, it raises most of the key questions which must occupy the mind of any teacher who wishes to teach children to learn, and to learn from written material.

1   To begin with, we note that there may be a conflict between aims. Education is concerned with the transmission of knowledge and skills. But it is also concerned with transmitting a love of knowledge and the skills that are required for the independent pursuit of knowledge. If one considers the process of education as a whole, the two aims are complementary. But whenever one is thinking about a particular group of lessons, one is bound to make a choice of emphasis. In the present instance, the emphasis is not clear, but perhaps one would be right in concluding that the team was more concerned to give their pupils a frame of reference about ancient history. The experience of finding out was perhaps a secondary aim, though nonetheless important. Almost certainly the experience of collaborative endeavour was a third aim.

1.1 Our interest is chiefly in the second aim. We would suggest that this aim has been least realized. Yet it has not completely failed.

1.2 We would hazard a guess that when a teacher is most concerned with learning to learn and less with learning, he should select a topic less remote from the pupils' own experience. Such a topic would enable them to frame their own questions more easily. They would be less inclined to restrict their inquiry to 'answering the questions', and they might be less tempted to stray from the path upon which they first set out (as when they are beguiled by an interesting story—Romulus and Remus, or an arresting illustration—the Roman Forum).

2 These children evidently gained from their reading: their report-back was (sometimes) informative and well-organized (bearing in mind their age and the remoteness of the subject), and it was largely based on what they had learnt from written material. But most of what they learnt was drawn from a single predigested source: the Teachers' Guide.

2.1 Most of the children who were interested had a verbal knowledge of how to select a book, and how to find what they wanted in the right book once they had located it. Almost certainly, the knowledge was inadequate. They could not use it in real life (i.e. when they found themselves in a familiar but well-equipped resources centre). We conclude that children need help and guidance in a real context to convert the verbal knowledge to behavioural competence.

2.2 Although the material was used in a topic setting, and questions were not set as a comprehension exercise, the reading that occurred was largely of a similar type: reading to answer questions. A different sort of preparation (and perhaps a different sort of topic) would be required to encourage children to 'read to learn' in the fullest sense: first surveying the material to gain an appreciation of it, then reading an appropriate passage—having thought about it and formulated some expectation about what they might learn, then perhaps thinking it over again and studying some particular paragraphs, and finally copying out extracts or making appropriate notes.

3 Much of what was supposed to be note-taking was in fact copying. Here a number of points are in order:

3.1 There are occasions when a faithful copy of a well-phrased summary is preferable to any paraphrase. The well-trained advanced student will acknowledge the quotation. That is all.

3.2 The more one knows and the better one's judgement, the more selective and apt will be one's use of quotations.

3.3 Children can be helped to make these selections. The group discussions that were observed are obviously a useful step in this direction.

3.4 A paraphrase is not superior to a quotation unless it is either more succinct, i.e. a sort of précis, or it is couched in language more congenial to the writer and reader, and more consistent with the context in which it is set.

3.5 Children need to be taught how to paraphrase and how to précis—preferably in a real context.

3.6 There is little recent research bearing on what stages one may legitimately expect in note-taking, especially in the context of mixed-ability work of this kind in the secondary school. Clearly, there is scope here for further research to build on the pioneering work reported by Howe (1972).

4 The children we observed spent as much time in discussion as they did in reading. We regard this as entirely good. It is through spoken language, discussion, that we come to terms with written language. When the matter is difficult for us, it is only in the process of talking and writing about it that we can overcome what is compact or opaque in the printed word. Chapter 9 is directed to the consideration of various techniques which can help to exploit these possibilities.

4.1 Often, if not always, what is done in and by a group is largely determined by the strongest personality in that group. The wise teacher will bear this in mind when allocating and reallocating pupils to groups. (The strongest personality is not always the ablest pupil.)

8

Reading Laboratories

Roy Fawcett

I Introduction

It has been said in Chapter 1 that programmes of reading instruction are rare in British secondary schools, except in the work of remedial departments whose concern is limited to work with backward students. This is in quite marked contrast to what one finds in America, where it is generally accepted that all students can benefit from specific tuition in study skills, including reading comprehension. There the teaching of reading continues after the student has achieved mastery in the basic skills of decoding.

There are two ways in which this can be organized. The school can either make separate curricular provision for the teaching of reading, or else the study of text and of how to learn from reading may be included as part of the tuition provided for each subject. The two are not mutually exclusive, although curricular pressures will generally preclude any major investment of time in both kinds of work.

There are also two ways in which the instruction can be given. One is by means of teacher-directed activities, often designed in such a way as to capitalize on the potential for mutual help and enhanced motivation inherent in various kinds of group work. The other is through individualized programmes of study, made possible by the existence of a rich and well-prepared bank of instructional material, the reading laboratory, from which each student can draw what he needs, with minimal guidance from the teacher once he has been shown how to use the material and how to select the parts that are right for him.

We have felt it incumbent upon us to carry out some investigations of our own in both types of programme. The first mode, which is teacher-directed and group-oriented is explored in Chapter 9. The second, which is geared to individualized learning, is also better known and more popular in the USA. The effectiveness of this kind of programme has been shown in a number of studies. But for the most part these inquiries were undertaken in the context of other school systems. Would the use of reading laboratories prove equally effective in the context of our own primary and secondary schools?

In the course of the first part of the national survey described in Chapter 10, it was found that many secondary schools possessed reading laboratories, although quite often they were little used, or used only by remedial departments. Of the various laboratory and workshop materials on the market the SRA *Reading Laboratory* was by far the most common in these schools. For this reason it was decided to concentrate our inquiry on the usefulness of the SRA material. The main part of this chapter describes a large-scale experiment in which the effectiveness of SRA work is compared with the English department's normal programme for the promotion of comprehension in reading. In addition, however, a smaller inquiry was also mounted comparing the SRA material with the Ward Lock Educational *Reading Workshops*. Finally, the chapter includes a brief account of a small pilot inquiry in which the SRA material was combined with the group work described in Chapter 9.

It should be added that the design of reading laboratories is such that they do not lend themselves to specialized work on reading within the various subject areas. Therefore the present studies are directed only to the first kind of organization mentioned earlier: work that is separately timetabled or carried on under the auspices of the English department.

II Background

1 Rationale

The SRA *Reading Laboratories* are a fairly highly-structured means of developing competence in literacy and reading comprehension. They use a multi-level approach with the expressed aim of getting an individual into 'top-gear' relative to his own learning rate and capacity. The intensive or 'booster' programme lasts about a term.

Its aim is to develop a wide range of related abilities such as a greater vocabulary, an understanding of more complex sentences and structures, the use of contextual clues, and the development of comprehension in the areas of order, detail, global understanding and inference. The programmes also foster an appreciation of word structure, a faster rate of reading for scanning and other purposes, the use of index and dictionary and the development of greater listening skill.

This is done by means of power builders, rate builders and listening-skill builders, together with the extensive use by the children of the SQ3R[1] (i.e. Survey, Question, Read, Review, Recite) study-skill technique for developing more purposeful reading. Each child

---

[1] SQR for junior-school children.

carries out an intensive programme at his own particular level and rate during the first third of the year. It is claimed that the skills which he has developed can now be effectively applied in all the relevant fields of literacy, such as the reading of literature, topic work, individual research or any other form of content reading.

The Laboratories encourage the use of what they call 'reading-thinking skills' as against mere memorization, by reminding children to look back before making decisions. They also emphasize the importance of learning from mistakes. There is considerable stress on self-evaluation at each stage: pupils mark their own work on completion. This provides for the immediate reinforcement of correct responses as well as creating the conditions for effective learning through the diagnosis and correction of errors. Working out percentages and maintaining progress charts sometimes creates difficulties for younger children to begin with. But it is essential for motivation and self-evaluation. As the work is finely graded, most children usually achieve high success rates fairly soon. Only a few errors need correction and morale is nearly always high.

Short talks followed by discussions take place in the first week of the programme to introduce such topics as the importance of reading today compared with twenty or thirty years ago, the advantages of a book over television, individual differences in physical and mental capacity and how to measure one's own achievements. It is the improvement of a child's own performance which is stressed.

During the initial period, the students are also introduced to a study-reading technique (SQR or SQ3R) as a means of developing a systematic and therefore more effective way of reading. This method is constantly stressed in the hope that it will become automatic and transfer into other content reading in general school work.

This preliminary work slows down the introduction of the Laboratory, but it is considered to be an integral part of the course, and one which will provide benefits later on.

2 Previous studies

In the course of a thorough review of all published accounts of experiments dealing with the use of reading laboratories, the writer found about twenty which were of some importance. These are reviewed more fully elsewhere (Fawcett, 1977). Many of these studies involved quite small numbers. Others were lacking in one or more necessary controls. Some give insufficient information about such matters as the length of teaching, the training of teachers, the tests that were used to measure progress, or even the name of the

---

[1] Dr Neale was then Superintendent, Special Services, Education Department, Government of Western Australia. A summary of this study will be found in Mortlock, 1959.

laboratory material that was being tested. Nearly all are based on experiments carried out in North America or in Australia. However, there are some studies which merit a brief note here.

The first is a large-scale inquiry carried out in Western Australia by Doctor Wallace Neale.[1] This involved seven schools, thirty-six classes and nearly 1000 pupils. These were taken from the first three grades of their secondary schooling. The programme lasted three months and the teachers concerned were given adequate training beforehand in the use of the SRA material. Immediate post-tests given at the end of the one term of instruction showed that, on average, all pupils had achieved gains amounting to 13.4 months in an age-related test of comprehension. While the retarded pupils made the greatest gains, all but the most advanced showed mean gains of more than ten months. However, this experiment had several defects: there was no control group; the same test was used in pre-testing and post-testing, and little information is given about its validity; also there was no follow-up. One is therefore left wondering whether the gain was short-term only, how far it was due to practice effect on the test, and how far it was due to a 'Hawthorne' effect, i.e. the fact that these pupils had been singled out for instruction in how to read.

The second is an inquiry carried out in Brownsville, Texas, involving fourth-grade children (ten-year-olds). It was on an even more ambitious scale (forty-five 'sections'). This too was an assessment of the effects of an eleven-week crash course. Two forms of a standardized comprehension test were administered, one as pre-test, the other as post-test. Thirty-eight of the forty-five sections achieved gains of more than the three months to be expected, and the overall mean gain of seven months was more than twice the expected figure. Once again the report of this inquiry[1] gives insufficient information but it is clear that there were no control groups and no attempt at a long-term follow-up to establish whether the gains achieved were durable or transitory.

The third is again an Australian experiment, carried out in New South Wales, and involving 800 fifth-graders (eleven-year-olds). This inquiry is one of a number in which the progress of children who were taught through SRA was compared with that of control groups who followed the standard curriculum. Pre-tests and (immediate) post-tests in verbal intelligence, word knowledge and reading for meaning showed significant advantage to the experimental groups. These were more marked in the average group. Above-average children apparently made significant gains only in verbal intelligence and

---

[1] 'Study of the measured results while using SRA *Reading Laboratories* in the fourth grade for an eleven-week period' by Dr L. X. Magnifico (Superintendent of Brownsville Public Schools) Brownsville, Texas, USA, spring 1963 (unpublished). Available from Don H. Parker, Multilevel Incorporated, Alta Mesa Professional Center, 335 Eldorado, Monterey, California 93940, USA.

below-average children only in the area of word knowledge. Once again, there was no long-term follow-up, and the key test of comprehension, Schonell R-4, was used both as pre-test and as post-test, and was therefore highly susceptible to practice-effects.

Before turning to the British scene, mention should be made of Patterson's experimental work in Canada in 1964. He was particularly interested in the effect of the Laboratories on the development of secondary school pupils of below-average ability.

He had three groups, including a control and two experimental groups, which had different programmes. One underwent the standard intensive course while the second one used the material twice weekly. Both experimental groups made significantly more progress than the control group. Somewhat surprisingly it was the less intensive programme which produced the more impressive gains (sixteen months), while the standard crash-course produced a gain of only twelve months, although this was still well above that achieved by the control groups.

Of the research undertaken in this country, the most interesting are the Aberdeen experiment in 1963, the Midlothian project of 1964, Donald Moyle's Cambridgeshire experiment in 1965 and finally the ILEA study of 1969. Unfortunately, the experimental design of the Aberdeen experiment has serious defects and the Midlothian project was on a small scale and made questionable use of tests. In addition, both were confined to children at the primary level. Moyle's experiment was interesting, but it was on a very small scale, using two junior-school classes.

The ILEA project was an ambitious one involving large numbers of children. Many of the features of the experiment were admirable and one can mention the care taken in the selection of schools, the balance of control and experimental groups in respect of ability, socioeconomic and other factors, selection of appropriate material and the training of the teachers.

However, certain matters do cause concern. Although the experiment involved junior and secondary pupils, no control groups were used in the latter, and at this level the work was restricted to remedial pupils. The schools were also given too much freedom in deciding how much time should be allocated to the use of the materials.

The results of this project provided no evidence to show that the use of SRA *Reading Laboratories* had any marked effect on the development of reading ability, other than a suggestion that it would be useful at the secondary-remedial level.

It will be clear that each of these inquiries is open to serious criticism. Also, the only large-scale British inquiry produces results which are in conflict with nearly all the remainder. Only one (in Australia) extends to the average and above-average pupil in the secondary school. Taken by itself, our search of the relevant literature does not permit us to pronounce on the relevance of laboratory material to the improvement of reading in secondary school pupils in Britain.

III The main SRA experiment

1 Design of the inquiry

This inquiry was designed in the hope of producing a rigorous and reliable assessment of the effectiveness of the SRA material in the context of the middle years of British schooling. Like the observational study recorded in Chapter 5, the inquiry was repeated with three age groups: fourth-year juniors, first-year secondary and fourth-year secondary pupils. Five schools participated at the junior level while three large comprehensive schools were involved at the secondary level. Within these schools, each of the groups which took part in the SRA programme was matched by a parallel group to serve as its control. These control groups completed the whole of the testing programme, but received no special tuition in reading beyond what was included in the normal curriculum as it obtained before the experiment was mounted. The SRA programme itself was the recommended one-term intensive course, and this was given to the experimental groups in the autumn term of 1974, using whatever Laboratory was most appropriate for each of the groups concerned. The testing programme was ambitious: several different tests of comprehension were used and some of these were replicated, using parallel forms, on three occasions: in September 1974 as pre-tests; in the period December 1974—January 1975 when they served as 'immediate' post-tests; and finally in June 1975 as 'late' post-tests to assess the stability of whatever gains had been achieved. Altogether there were 1018 children who participated in the inquiry (423 juniors, 322 first-year secondary and 273 fourth-year secondary students). About half this number were in the experimental groups, the remainder serving as controls.

2 Subjects

The three secondary schools which took part in the inquiry are situated in different outlying areas of Nottingham. One was formerly a secondary modern school, but in 1974/5 its intake in the first two years was fully comprehensive. The upper school was housed in the old building, and the teaching here was almost wholly subject-based. First- and second-year pupils, however, were taught in a purpose-built lower-school unit, with a well-equipped resources centre and excellent facilities for group work, topic studies, craft work and so on. The second was again a secondary modern school with a comprehensive intake in the first year only (in 1974/5). The school building here was more modern, but there was no lower-school unit. The teaching in the upper school was somewhat less compartmentalized here than it was in the first school, especially in English and humanities, where the heads of department concerned had agreed on a close and fruitful collaboration. The teaching in the lower school was perhaps a trifle less innovative, due in part to the lack of comparable facilities. The third school was formerly a grammar school. Upper and lower schools were housed in separate buildings. At the time of the inquiry, the staff of this school had to cope with problems of physical communication as well as problems of adjustment to a comprehensive intake. The teaching here was, predictably, more traditional and compartmentalized, but this should be taken as a statement of fact and not a value judgement. Taken together, the three schools provide a not-unrepresentative cross-section of the schools which one might find in any of our conurbations.

Each comprehensive school was asked to provide two experimental and two control classes from both the first- and fourth-year children, with the proviso that each experimental group had a control group of similar ability. One of the schools could only agree to allow two fourth-year classes to be used, but in other respects the requests were met by each school. This meant that 10 fourth-year and 12 first-year classes were used, half of them as experimental and the remainder as controls. At the upper end, the sample included O-level students; at the lower end it included near-remedial (but not remedial) groups.

Three of the five junior schools were 'feeders' to the second comprehensive. One had about 370 children and was generally innovative, with team-teaching in the upper classes. The second was a C of E school, with only 280 children, and more traditional in outlook. The third was a large and reasonably progressive school (450) with three large, unstreamed fourth-year classes each of forty pupils. Two of these served as experimental groups and one as a control.

The other two junior schools were feeders for the third comprehensive. One of these, with 650 children, was able to provide two experimental groups and two controls. This school was organized on fairly formal and rigid lines, with a detailed timetable and a traditional curriculum. The last school, which was neither avant-garde nor traditional, had about 400 pupils and contributed two parallel fourth-year groups, one as experimental, the other as control.

Thirty-five groups participated altogether, as shown in Table 8.1 (p. 200).

None of the teachers of experimental and control classes in these

Table 8.1 Number of groups involved in project

Type of class	Experimental				Control				All subjects
	Groups	Total boys	Total girls	Boys & girls	Groups	Total boys	Total girls	Boys & girls	
4th-year secondary	5	54	81	135	5	65	73	138	273
1st-year secondary	6	81	79	160	6	79	83	162	322
4th-year junior	7	117	118	235	6	101	87	188	423
Totals	18	252	278	530	17	245	243	488	1018

schools was previously known to the researcher and the allocation of classes was arranged either by the headteacher or by the head of the English department. No special requests were made to them. It was hoped that as thirty-five classes were involved, the overall pictures that emerged would not be distorted by variations in the characteristics of the teachers concerned. In practice this worked out well, the more so as the attitude of the schools was neutral. As far as they were concerned, the experimental material was very much on trial. For this reason, they made a conscious effort to balance staffs, thus ensuring that there was a fair mixture of experienced and inexperienced teachers within each method, as well as a reasonable balance between men and women teachers.

In the secondary schools, three heads of department or senior teachers took an experimental as well as a control group. Clearly this could not happen in the junior classes, but in one school the experimental group was under the control of the deputy head, while in a second, the equivalent person had charge of the control class. In addition, there were probationary and other young teachers involved, as well as more experienced personnel.

3 Procedure

The essential details of the conduct of this inquiry are set out in Table 8.2 (p. 203), which gives details of the programme of special tuition given to the SRA groups, together with the testing programme which was common to all groups.

The 3A and 2A SRA Laboratories are recently revised international laboratories with English spelling and much more European material, while the other Laboratories used, although having been recently revised, are still American editions using American spellings and idiomatic expressions. The only one not to have been recently revised is the 3B.

In nearly every case, the *Reading Laboratories* were introduced to the classes by the researcher. The exceptions were three groups where the class teacher had had previous experience of them or where a senior teacher was particularly keen to do it himself. In practice this meant that the first four or five sessions, and an additional one or two later on to introduce the rate and listening-skill builders, were taken by the researcher. This was achieved through careful timetabling and staggered starts to the programmes during September. It made it possible for standard procedures to be adopted, for a high degree of motivation to be developed and for the groups to use the material in fairly similar fashion throughout the programme.

The tests that were used in the inquiry were selected after an intensive examination of tests of comprehension, speed and vocabulary. The main criteria were that the tests should be reliable and valid, and that where possible, they should be available in parallel versions to reduce practice-effects.

The *Gates-MacGinitie Reading Tests*, published by the Teachers' College Press of Columbia University, New York, were selected as the first set of measures. They are available at different reading levels and the appropriate ones for the research project were Survey D for the fourth-year junior and first-year secondary children and Survey E for the older pupils. In each case, the paper consists of three sections: the first yields separate scores for speed and accuracy; the second is a test of vocabulary; and the third is a measure of comprehension. Two sessions of twenty-five minutes were found to be sufficient to examine these four aspects of reading.

All pupils were also given comparable British tests. At the secondary level the best available test was found to be the *NFER Reading Test E-H*, which consisted of three separate papers: vocabulary, comprehension and speed in the accurate reading of continuous prose. The inclusion of this test allowed an additional post-test to be included in the programme.

Since these tests were unsuitable for junior-school children, the youngest group were given *Reading Test BD* and *Reading Comprehension Test DE*, also published by the NFER. The first is a multiple-choice sentence-completion test. The DE test uses six passages each followed by a set of comprehension questions. The passages cover a variety of themes, ranging from poetic material to popular science, and the questions are varied in scope.

Finally, the testing programme included two of the tests described in Chapter 3. *Brighty* was used as a pre-test and the parallel test *Alistair* as a post-test.

It should be noted that, with the exception of *Brighty* and *Alistair* which are unstandardized, only the Gates-MacGinitie tests exist in parallel versions. It was for this reason that they were chosen as the main instrument, with separate forms being used as pre-test, post-test and late post-test.

Table 8.2 (p. 203) includes details of the timing of these tests. It will be seen that late post-testing was carried out in two phases, the NFER tests being given in the spring, while the final testing was completed in June.

To ensure uniformity in testing, all tests were conducted by the researcher, who is glad to acknowledge the generous cooperation of all the schools concerned. The extent of this is perhaps better appreciated when one adds that arrangements were made to enable nearly all the children involved in the experiment to take all of the tests. Often three or four visits were necessary to complete a testing session. Nevertheless it was felt that the sampling should be exhaustive. Almost certainly, the exclusion of absentees would have meant excluding a disproportionate number of pupils who were in

Table 8.2   Timetable of SRA inquiry

	4th-year secondary	1st-year secondary	4th-year junior
Pre-tests September 1974	Gates-MacGinitie Survey E, Form 1 (a) speed (b) accuracy (c) vocabulary (d) comprehension NFER Reading Test E-H (a) vocabulary (b) comprehension (c) continuous prose *Brighty* test of comprehension	Gates-MacGinitie Survey D, Form 1 NFER Reading Test E-H *Brighty*	Gates-MacGinitie Survey D, Form 1 NFER Reading Tests (a) BD (b) Comprehension DE *Brighty*
Programme autumn term 1974	SRA Laboratory 3A or 3B	SRA Laboratory 2C	SRA Laboratory 2A or 2B
Immediate post-test December–January 1975	Gates-MacGinitie Survey E, Form 3 *Alistair* test of comprehension	Gates-MacGinitie Survey D, Form 3 *Alistair*	Gates-MacGinitie Survey D, Form 3 *Alistair*
Later post-tests (a) March–April 1975	NFER Reading Test E-H	NFER Reading Test E-H	NFER Reading Tests (i) BD (ii) Comprehension DE
(b) June 1975	Gates-MacGinitie Survey E, Form 2	Gates-MacGinitie Survey D, Form 2	Gates-MacGinitie Survey D, Form 2

any case below average, with consequent distortion of the true picture.

The fact that the writer was personally involved in the administration of all tests was doubly useful. It allowed him to stress the importance of the tests and of the reading programme for all of the children involved, including the control pupils. Even the older age-groups who had served as controls were willing to give of their best in the knowledge that they were participating in a 'genuine experiment', the results of which could prove helpful to others. This is even more true of the teachers, who were being asked to put up with a great deal of inconvenience and to set aside three to five periods a week[1] for a whole term (for the experimental groups) for a method of teaching which they tended to view with some suspicion, preferring a freer, more exploratory and more imaginative approach to the teaching of literacy. Nevertheless, what emerged from far-ranging and serious discussions was a feeling of mutual respect. These were teachers who were not easily seduced by gimmickry or innovation *per se*. Some were more attracted to the SRA approach than others. But all were prepared to use the material in the recommended manner, and all were satisfied that the only way to assess it was to put it to the test of a fair and rigorous experiment.

4 Results

Separate and parallel forms of the Gates-MacGinitie test were used on three occasions respectively: in September as pre-test, in January as a test of immediate gains, and in June to assess how far these gains had been retained. These tests provide separate scores for speed, accuracy, vocabulary and comprehension. Because a different form was used on each occasion, the results are uncontaminated by the effects of test-specific learning. It is these measures that afford the most reliable index of the effectiveness of the experimental treatment.

It will be recalled that a number of previous studies have indicated that one may expect the use of laboratories to be especially effective with students of lower initial ability. It was therefore thought desirable to present the results separately for students whose initial performance was above the mean and those who fell below the mean.

Figure 8.1 (p. 205) is a graphic presentation of the data obtained from the experiment in junior schools, with separate graphs for the two ability-groups. Each of the four indices is treated separately. The vertical bar on the left of each diagram shows the mean and standard deviation found in the initial test. This may be read as a scaling device to show the importance and to indicate the statistical significance of

[1] Five periods were required in each of the first six weeks of the programme and three in the remaining six weeks.

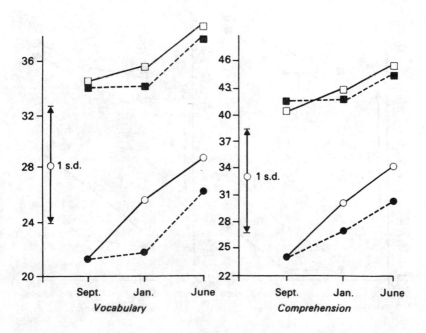

Figure 8.1   *Results on Gates-MacGinitie: 4th-year juniors*

Figure 8.2   *Results on Gates-MacGinitie: 1st-year secondary*

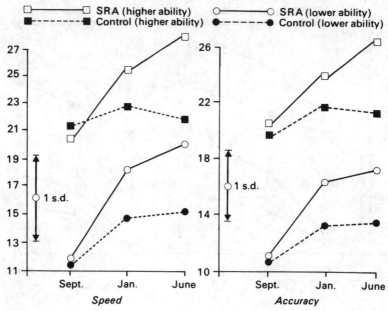

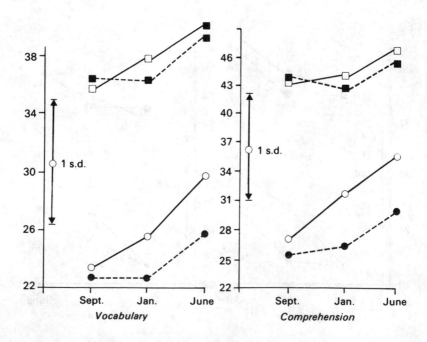

Figure 8.3   *Results on Gates-MacGinitie: 4th-year secondary*

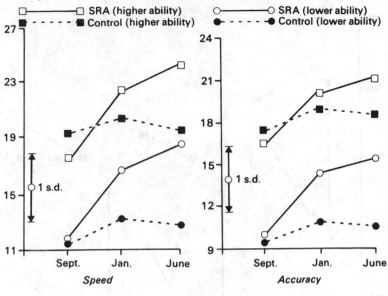

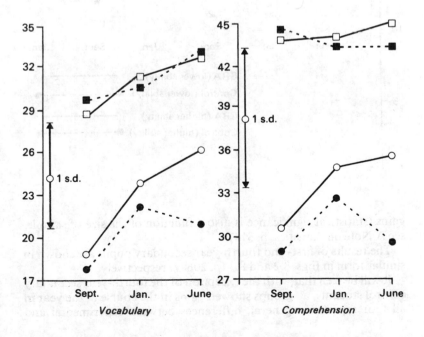

Figure 8.4   *Results on Waite tests (*Brighty *and* Alistair*)*

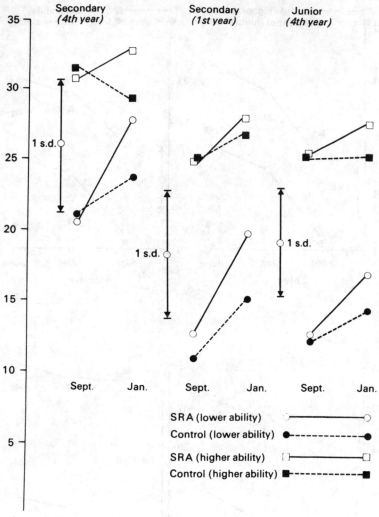

gains (statistical significance is also a function of the size of sample, see A Note on Statistics, p. 314).

The results of first- and fourth-year secondary pupils are shown in similar form in Figs. 8.2 and 8.3 (p. 206–7) respectively.

It will be seen that, with the exception of the fourth-year secondary control students, all groups showed gains in the course of the year in all four aspects. In general, differences between experimental and control groups were uniformly small on initial testing, and none was significant. By contrast, several of the differences found in January and, especially, in June were considerable and clearly significant.

In all three figures the widening gap in speed and accuracy is immediately apparent. The relative improvement of the experimental groups on these two measures is nearly as great in the high-ability range as it is in the low-ability range. Taken together, these two scores may be thought of as an index of the efficiency of reading short-test passages. The student who is fast and accurate can get on with the job (under test conditions) and produce an immediately acceptable result. In the light of these findings there can be little question of the efficiency of the SRA Laboratories in bringing about an improvement in this aspect of reading.

The differential effect of treatment on gains in vocabulary is less consistent. It is generally small in the higher-ability range, but more marked in the low-ability range. Although the analysis of word meaning is one feature of laboratory work, improvement in vocabulary is best thought of as a spin-off of reading. It is the least direct measure of reading itself.

The fourth set of graphs shows gains in comprehension. Within the limits of the test, this is the best measure of the student's ability to derive maximum profit from his reading: to think about what he is reading and its implications and, in the final analysis, to learn by reading. Each of the experimental groups has made more progress at the end of the year than its own control. But these differences are appreciable and significant only in the case of the lower-ability groups. However, one may note that two of the three high-ability comparisons show a cross-over: initially the control groups are marginally superior; by June the advantage is to the experimental groups.

Perhaps the most unexpected feature of the results is the fact that the gains that were achieved in the first term, when the Laboratories were used, were not lost in the ensuing six months. The experimental groups retained their advantage and in many cases actually increased it. This is particularly apparent in the fourth year of the secondary school, where one is led to conclude that for pupils below average the feeling of success that is associated with the experiences of using the Laboratories was sufficient to offset the fall off in motivation which is so familiar to their teachers.

Figure 8.4 (p. 208) shows the results of the test *Alistair*, taken in January, compared with the parallel test *Brighty*, taken in September. With one exception (the lower-ability groups at first-year secondary), differences at pre-test (*Brighty*) are minimal. None is significant. All six graphs diverge for the post-test (*Alistair*), showing marked differences in favour of the experimental groups in five instances and a small difference, albeit in the same direction, in the sixth (higher-ability groups at first-year secondary). As indicated in Table 8.3, the sixth difference is the only one that does not reach significance.

These results are particularly noteworthy because the tests in question do not measure literal comprehension alone. They were specifically constructed to tap a broad range of tasks requiring careful reflection about the passage that was read (Chapter 3). In the light of these findings, it is not easy to argue that, in the above-average range, the effect of laboratory experience is limited to the more superficial aspects of comprehension (speed and making some sort of immediate sense). For it appears that the advantages are manifest in all aspects of comprehension and throughout the ability range.

The results of the NFER tests were less impressive, especially in relation to comprehension. However, these are likely to be contaminated by previous familiarization with the passage, since the same tests were used as pre-test and post-test.

To test the significance of differences in gains made by the experimental and control groups, it was essential to partial out the effect of initial differences between subjects (children who start lower have more to learn). We therefore calculated the correlation between initial and final scores for each age group, and hence obtained a statistical prediction of the most likely scores for each student on each post-test on the assumption that such differences were due only to initial differences and variation in experience has no effect. By subtracting these predicted scores from the actual scores, one can then find residual scores which represent (within the limits of measurement error) the effects of the differential experiences undergone by each child. The most important differential experiences are, of course, the treatment built into the experiment (SRA Laboratory versus normal curriculum in English). After calculating the means and variances for each group on each test, using residual scores, tests of significance (t-tests) were applied to determine the likelihood that differences between experimental and control groups were due to chance.

The results of this procedure are summarized in Table 8.3 (p. 211). The entries in this table cover the results of separate analyses for boys and girls, as well as those for the NFER tests. The table also includes entries in respect of the breakdowns illustrated in Figs. 8.1–8.4. Where differences are not significant, the entry E or C denotes which of the two treatment groups obtained the higher means. Where they are significant, the symbol ** denotes an advantage to the experimental group which was significant at the .01 level, while the symbol * shows a lower level of significance, .05. None of the analyses produced a significant advantage to the control groups.

Table 8.3 Results of main inquiry showing significance levels only (see text)

		September–January					January–June					September–June					September–March (NFER)				
		Boys	Girls	HA	LA	All	Boys	Girls	HA	LA	All	Boys	Girls	HA	LA	All	Boys	Girls	HA	LA	All
4th-year secondary	S	**	**	**	**	**	**	**	**	**	**	**	**	**	**	**	**	**	**	**	**
	A	**	**	*	**	**	**	**	**	**	**	**	**	**	**	**	**	**	**	**	**
	V	E	E	E	E	E	E	E	E	E	E	E	*	E	E	E	*	E	E	*	*
	C	E	E	E	E	E	E	E	E	E	E	E	E	E	E	E	*	*	E	E	**
	B-A	**	**	*	E	**	E	E	E	**	**										
1st-year secondary	S	**	**	**	**	**	**	**	**	**	**	**	**	**	**	**	**	**	**	**	**
	A	**	**	*	**	**	**	**	**	**	**	**	**	**	**	**	**	*	**	**	**
	V	E	E	E	E	E	E	C	C	E	E	E	E	E	E	E	E	C	C	E	
	C	E	E	E	E	E	E	E	E	E	E	E	E	E	E	E	**	E	E	E	
	B-A	*	E				E	E	E	**	**										
4th-year junior	S	**	**	**	**	**	E	*	E	E	**	**	**	**	**	**					
	A	**	**	*	**	**	E	E	C	C	*	**	**	**	**	**					
	V	*	E	*	E	**	E	C	C	C	C	E	E	E	E	E					
	C	*	E	E	**	**	E	E	E	E	E	E	E	E	E	E	E	C	C	C	C
	B-A	**	**				E	E	E	**	E						E	E	E	**	**
	BD																E	E	E		C
	DE																*	E	E	**	**

S speed, A accuracy, V vocabulary, C comprehension, HA higher ability, LA lower ability.
In all blocks except the fourth (NFER) the significance levels for S, A, V and C refer to the Gates-MacGinitie test. B–A *Brighty* and *Alistair*, BD and DE are NFER tests.

IV Subsidiary inquiries

Two additional inquiries are reported in this section. The first is an account of a small-scale experiment to compare the SRA Laboratories with an alternative but similar set of materials produced in this country, the Ward Lock Educational *Reading Workshops*. The second is a pilot study to explore the effectiveness of following-up laboratory work with a discussion approach, as described in Chapter 9.

1 The SRA and Ward Lock Educational experiment

During the spring of 1975, when the experimental work of the main project had been completed and all that had to be done was to administer the last two post-tests, it was decided that it would be interesting to organize a second and smaller project in which comparisons could be made between the value of the American-produced SRA *Reading Laboratory* and its English equivalent, the Ward Lock Educational *Reading Workshop*. Although both had many points of similarity, there were differences which might make a comparison useful. The Workshop work and speed cards were the equivalent of the SRA power builders and rate builders, but the Workshop had no listening-skill builders. A further difference was that after an initial test, children using the Workshop began using the individual work and speed cards immediately. There was no initial programme to heighten interest, to introduce reading strategies or to help with early problems of organization and administration of the programme, which it must be said was more straightforward.

Again, when using the Workshop, children were expected usually to work through all the cards of a colour before moving onto the next level. By contrast, when SRA Laboratories were used, this became a matter for discussion between teacher and child, with reference to the progress charts. The number of cards of a particular colour to be completed varied from four to twelve, dependent on circumstances and rate of progress. There were also differences arising out of the way that the two programmes were produced. The American policy was to consider the nature of reading and the necessary skills and ability that required developing, and to grade the steps very finely and scientifically. Having done this, they looked for suitable material which would fit these requirements. By contrast, the selection of material for the Ward Lock Educational Workshops was essentially intuitive and the progression of steps is less carefully worked out.

The experiment was carried out in three junior schools situated in the same region as those involved in the main project. Each of these schools agreed to offer two parallel third-year classes[1] for an

---

[1] Fourth-year pupils were now in their last term at the school.

Figure 8.5   *Comparative gains of groups taught by SRA and Ward Lock Educational*
(significance of difference shown in brackets)

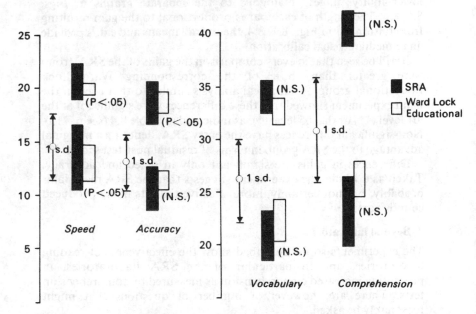

Lower extremity of each bar shows mean initial score, upper extremity shows mean final score. The upper diagrams represent comparisons of pupils whose scores fell above the mean at initial testing (HA), the lower diagrams to the complementary groups (LA).

intensive programme of one term, one to work on the SRA material, the other on the Ward Lock Educational. The allocation of classes to methods was left to the schools, but all the six teachers involved were experienced and very sound, they were equally keen to join the experiment and happy about the particular material given to them. Six sessions were spent with each group by the researcher and, in his view, the effect of the teachers on the eventual results of the experiment could be considered as minimal as is possible under experimental conditions in schools. All the SRA groups used the *2A International Laboratory*, while the Ward Lock Educational groups used the *9–13 Workshop* supplemented by some cards from the *6–10 Workshop* in order to give a greater range of material. Altogether there were exactly 100 children in each of the two groups.

The conduct of the experiment was similar to the main inquiry, save that only the Gates-MacGinitie tests were used in the pre-tests and immediate post-tests (Forms 1 and 3 respectively), and there was no late post-test.

The results are shown graphically in Fig. 8.5 (p. 213). The base of each column corresponds to the mean pre-test score and its summit to the mean post-test score. Separate bars are given for the upper-and lower-ability ranges, analogous to the separate graphs in Figs. 8.1–8.4. The length of each bar is proportional to the gain resulting from tuition. As in Figs. 8.1–8.4, the overall means and s.d./s provide an immediate visual calibration.

It will be seen that in every comparison the gains of the SRA group were greater than those of the corresponding Ward Lock Educational group. A statistical analysis similar to that used in the main experiment showed that these differences were significant at the .01 level (**) or the .05 level (*), as indicated in Table 8.4 (see p. 215). Non-significant differences have the entry SRA, denoting a marginal advantage to the SRA group in terms of residual post-test scores.

Differences in gains are significant only in speed and accuracy. Taken as a whole, the experiment suggests that the SRA material is probably, but not certainly, more effective than its home-produced counterpart.

2 Beyond laboratories

The experiments so far described show the effectiveness of reading laboratories, and in particular of the SRA Laboratories, in promoting increased comprehension as measured by comprehension tests. There are, however, a number of questions that might reasonably be asked.

1   It was argued in Chapter 3 that comprehension tests offer only an indirect measure of the efficiency of reading. Moreover, the questions themselves, if put by an outsider (the test setter), distort the nature of the reading. The reader reads not to inform himself, nor yet to obtain a vicarious experience or an aesthetic experience, but simply to answer the questions (Rothkopf, 1966). A request to summarize the passage as a whole constitutes a more demanding and also a more realistic task, at least in relation to the first of these purposes. Would the SRA experience be equally effective in improving the quality of such summaries—despite the fact that summary writing is not one of the tasks used in the Laboratories? If the conclusion of Chapter 3 is correct, i.e. that comprehension is mainly a matter of reflection, then they might well achieve this end also. But the point cannot be settled *a priori*.

2   Laboratories were not intended to be used as the sole ingredient in a reading programme, but rather as a booster device, to give experience of certain techniques (especially SQ3R), and to be supplemented by a more varied programme of reading for enjoyment and learning. While the present researcher was testing reading laboratories, other members of the project team were piloting the use of group discussion in relation to reading, a technique which is freer

Table 8.4   Significance of differences between gains of SRA and Ward Lock
Educational groups

	Boys	Girls	HA	LA	All
Speed	*	*	*	*	**
Accuracy	**	SRA	*	SRA	**
Vocabulary	SRA	SRA	SRA	SRA	SRA
Comprehension	SRA	SRA	SRA	SRA	SRA

HA higher ability   LA lower ability

(more open-ended) and also potentially more far-ranging (see Chapter 9). Would the combination of the two approaches bring about additional gains, over and above those achieved by the laboratories alone, especially in, say, summary writing?
3   Laurie Thomas has recently developed a device, the Reading Recorder, which enables one to assess the quality of reading more directly, in terms of variations in the reading speed, and the incidence of pauses for reflection and of backtracking to check on a previous point. The text to be read is mounted on a roller and viewed through a window which exposes three or four lines at a time. The reader turns the roller on when he wants, and he can also turn it back if necessary. These movements of the roller are an index of variations in reading style. They are recorded automatically by a pen which traces a graph of roller movements in one axis and time elapsed in the other (see Fig. 8.6, p. 219). Would such a device offer more direct evidence of change in reading style resulting from practice with laboratories?
4   More generally, what evidence is there for variation in style of reading as a function of reading purpose in children as young as this? Thomas and Augstein (1972) and Thomas and Harri-Augstein (1976) found ample evidence of such variation in sixth formers and adults.

The following inquiry is no more than a preliminary attempt to explore these problems. Indeed, shortage of time and the small numbers prevented any direct investigation of (3). The experiment was carried out in 1975–6, after the previous experiments had been completed. The subjects were thirty-four children in vertically-grouped third- and fourth-year classes taken from the writer's own school. The design involved four groups of nine children, but two children left the school during the year. During the first term, two of these groups worked with the SRA *Reading Laboratory 2A* while the remaining two acted as controls. In January 1976 one of the SRA groups was taken through a programme of group discussion in relation to text for a period of six weeks, as was one of the control groups. The remaining SRA group continued with further laboratory work, while the second control group continued with normal school work, serving as control throughout the experiment. Thus the four groups were: SRA + group discussion; SRA + SRA; control + group discussion; and control. All the experimental teaching (SRA and group discussion) was carried out by the experimenter himself.

A series of tests were given to the children on three occasions: in September (pre-testing); in January (immediate post-test following the initial experiment, bearing only on the effects of SRA); and in March (bearing on the total programme for each group). The coverage of these tests was deliberately extended beyond the battery used in the main inquiry and consisted of the following: the Gates-MacGinitie tests, Survey D; the Waite tests (Chapter 3); and six passages similar to those used by Waite. The latter were included to allow for comparisons between summaries and objective questions under various conditions. In all cases, parallel versions of similar tests were used on each occasion of testing.

Two of the six additional passages were used on each occasion. For all passages, children were required to write a summary and also to answer a series of objective questions. The conditions were varied, however. For certain passages they were warned they would be asked to answer questions but the summary was an unexpected request (Objective Test 1, Summary 1), while for others the summary was expected but the questions were not (Objective Test 2, Summary 2). This was done following a design used by Thomas and Augstein (1972), who found that in adults the request to summarize led to better performance overall. As a further departure from standard comprehension-test procedure, the passage was removed while the summaries and questions were being worked. In most cases, the reading of the passage was monitored by the Reading Recorder.

The first grouping of the children (SRA versus control) was carried out by matching pairs on the basis of the Gates-MacGinitie scores in vocabulary and comprehension (pre-test). Subsequent partitioning into four groups was done in a similar way, using the immediate post-test scores. Results were analysed in the same way as those of the main inquiry, by first eliminating the effect of initial differences and then using residual scores to test the effect of treatment on group means.

The first analysis, carried out in January, adds little to the information already gained in the main inquiry. The SRA group achieved superior gains in the adequacy of their summaries as well as in answers to objective questions, although these differences were not significant. However, it should be noted that when numbers are small, differences need to be fairly considerable to offset variance within groups (see A Note on Statistics, p. 314).

The results of the final analysis are set out in full in Table 8.5 (p. 217). These are based on a comparison of pre-test scores with those gained at the conclusion of the experiment in March. Each cell in the table contains the pre-test means and post-test means for each of the

Table 8.5 Comparison of results for pre-test and final test for four treatment-groups

	Speed			Accuracy			Vocabulary			Comprehension			Waite Tests		
	P	F	R	P	F	R	P	F	R	P	F	R	P	F	R
SRA+ GD	17.00	21.89	0.77	15.56	21.22	1.42	30.11	38.33	2.35	35.78	44.33	2.47	17.33	24.67	3.33*
SRA+ SRA	19.75	25.25	2.01	16.63	21.88	1.21	28.38	34.75	0.03	35.75	40.88	-0.97	18.88	21.25	-1.03
Control+ GD	16.75	19.50	-1.43	14.75	17.75	-1.41	27.25	32.63	-1.28	33.75	40.25	-0.43	17.75	19.88	-1.71
Control+ Control	19.00	21.00	-1.66	18.14	20.29	-1.59	29.57	34.00	-1.59	38.71	42.00	-1.58	18.43	20.86	-1.15

	Summary (1)			Objective Test (1)			Summary (2)			Objective Test (2)		
	P	F	R	P	F	R	P	F	R	P	F	R
SRA+ GD	10.22	14.22	1.24	18.11	28.56	3.77*	10.00	17.33	5.12*	30.67	26.78	2.07
SRA+ SRA	7.25	11.38	0.09	15.00	22.75	-0.69	11.50	12.50	-0.07	27.00	22.63	-0.42
Control+ GD	7.75	10.00	-1.57	16.50	20.50	-3.59	11.25	9.25	-3.26	25.00	20.75	-1.39
Control+ Control	6.57	11.00	0.10	16.86	24.29	0.04	11.14	9.71	-2.77	25.71	21.86	-0.60

Key
P pretest F final R residual GD group discussion
* Significant at .05 level.

four groups as well as the residuals used in the calculation of significance.[1] It will be seen that for all tests except speed (when SRA alone seems to have been most effective), the order of improvement was the same, with the greatest gains being associated with the combination of SRA and group discussion, followed by SRA with additional SRA. A short period of group discussion was not effective by itself, and this group made less progress than the group that acted as control throughout. The differences between the groups showing the greatest and least improvements are significant for the Waite tests and also for Objective Test 1 (test expected) and Summary Test 2 (summary expected).

Because of the very small numbers (7–9 in each group), these results should be treated with caution. They are indicative rather than conclusive. However, they suggest that hypotheses (1) and (2) are probably true. The benefits of the Laboratory extend to the more searching summarizing task as well as the ability to answer questions on the passage (from memory). Also, and more important, the gains of laboratory work are best exploited when this experience is followed by (or perhaps associated with) an imaginative and varied programme designed to promote critical thinking in relation to the reading of any passage. The lack of success of the group discussion taken by itself is doubtless due to the relatively short duration of this part of the programme. In any case, the small size of sample prevents one from attaching much weight to this negative finding.

Because of the small numbers and certain difficulties of administration associated with the tight timing of the experiment, it was not found possible to make any adequate test of hypothesis (3), that the observation of SRA-trained readers would reveal differences in reading style. However, the experiment did show the anticipated effect of reading purpose on reading style (hypothesis 4). Figure 8.6 (p. 219) based on Thomas and Augstein (1972), shows seven characteristic tracings made by the Reading Recorder. They illustrate a progression in the degree of reflection shown by the reader, beginning with a quick

Table 8.6   Reading style and reading purpose (%)

	Style					
	1	2	3	4	5	6
Objective test expected	21.1	33.6	13.3	28.1	3.1	0.8
Summary expected	0	12.5	4.7	78.2	4.6	0

[1] Because four groups are involved, these calculations were based on analysis of variance, followed by comparison of means using Tukey's test for differences between means of more than two groups.

skim and extending to a slow read with pauses for reflection and occasional backward movements to check on a previous point. In this inquiry, when the children were preparing to answer questions or to summarize a passage, the passage was presented on the recorder. The percentages shown in Table 8.6 (p. 218) are based on the second and third testing sessions, when the tracings were no longer affected by the novelty of the apparatus.

These figures show a clear shift to a more thoughtful reading style when the children are told they will have to produce a summary of what they have read. 'Double reads' (style 6) are still rare at this age,

Figure 8.6   *Patterns of reading*
(after Thomas and Augstein, 1972)

1. Rapid read, indicated graphically as:

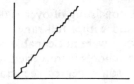

2. Rapid read with stops or hesitations at certain words or phrases:

3. Slow read:

4. Slow read with stops or hesitations:

5. Double read (generally one of the reads would be a quicker one than the other):

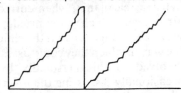

6. Regressed read (reference back to a previous section):

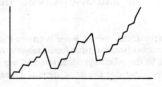

7. Double regressed read (not achieved in this research):

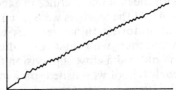

and regressions (style 7) are totally absent. Nevertheless, the table leaves little room to doubt that quite young children can alter their reading style to suit their purpose. One is led to suspect that the Laboratories are effective because their use encourages children to adopt a more reflective reading style. But this last point is conjecture, and points to the need for further experimental work.

V Evaluation

1 Effectiveness of the SRA Laboratories

All of the above results show that quite significant gains were made by the groups using the SRA material when compared with the control groups. These gains were evident in all aspects of reading considered and they were present at all age levels.

In the main inquiry the sample was large, consisting of over 1000 children from three different school years and with a full range of ability (excluding a few remedial children who were not capable of using or benefiting from the material). The schools were varied in organization, grouping, methods and, to some degree, general philosophy. Because the schools were selected from two nearby county education authorities, the variety in sampling was achieved with the minimal sacrifice in experimental rigour.

All of the teachers were given systematic training in the use of the Laboratories. Initial sessions with all children were taken by the researcher who first introduced the material and thereafter maintained a close supervision throughout the experimental period. Each school was visited, on average, two or three times weekly for two terms. The intensive programme was therefore carried out according to the makers' instructions.[1] Finally, all the testing and marking of scripts was carried out by the one researcher.

It was clear that, when correctly used, the material produces an atmosphere which is organized, purposeful and motivated. The work was well arranged so that the children were clear about their tasks and the way in which they could assess their own development. They were involved in this personally by charting their own results and occasionally discussing them with the teacher. The multi-level cards allowed all of the children to find material which was appropriate, acceptable and generally interesting. The purposes of the work were made clear for the child through discussion and involvement, and

---

[1] Had the procedure not been standard, the experiment would have been invalid. Nevertheless, it was appreciated that when the teachers became more familiar with the material, they would probably make adjustments to the official programme and use it more flexibly, adapting it to their various needs, but retaining the basic ideas and plan.

motivation was generally at a high level throughout.[1] In general it appeared that the experimental groups were more organized than their controls and could work with greater purpose.[2]

The results of this inquiry show that the effect of a highly-structured reading programme was not limited to an immediate gain in reading proficiency. The children were also able to work more effectively when they returned to normal curricular activities. In other words, a structured programme devised to develop certain aspects of reading enables the student to deploy his newly developed or acquired abilities in the context of an open-ended style of teaching. It can well be said that freedom does not exist in any real sense unless one has the skill and techniques as well as the ability to use it as fully as possible. It was apparent that the SRA *Reading Laboratories* had much to offer in this respect.

Finally, the present results do not support the assumption of most of the secondary schools who use reading laboratories that they are suitable only for use with remedial classes or groups. Significant gains were found among children at all levels of reading ability and, although the below-the-mean SRA groups benefited most of all, these were not remedial groups, but children in ordinary classes with less reading ability than the average. The ability range of children in these groups was considerable.

We therefore conclude that the SRA *Reading Laboratories* have been shown to be a valuable tool for promoting the effectiveness of reading across the ability range and at all ages considered.

2 Limitations

In considering the limitations of SRA *Reading Laboratories*, one must begin by stressing certain dangers which arise if the material is not used correctly. This happens frequently and there are a number of reasons for it.

The first is that teachers do not bother to read the handbook and simply use the cards as occasional material. It is fair to say that the handbook is written in a rather tedious and sometimes pretentious way and its style is typically American, but despite its weaknesses it

---

[1] In one school, it was felt that the fifteen-year-old pupils were well motivated for seven or eight weeks but then began to lose some interest, and it was suggested here that a six- to eight-week programme might be more suitable for older children. While fourth-year secondary children in the other schools were motivated throughout the term, the suggestion from the first school is of interest and it may well have some substance.

[2] One of the incidental findings was that the fourth-year secondary control-group actually regressed in reading performance between January and June, which suggested that once the effect of beginning a new school year with new curricular options had worn off, interest in the work as a whole was diminished. One may guess that the trend is not unconnected with the problems associated with the raising of the school leaving age. But whatever the reason for the regression, it deserves close investigation to see whether it is widespread, and if so how it can be overcome.

gives clear instructions on how to start the programme and how to continue it. Once this has been mastered, the teacher can adapt it flexibly to his own requirements and use examples and language which are more meaningful to his own pupils. If the children are not given the initial programme, which is devised to motivate them, and if the procedures are not carefully explained during the first week, there are likely to be real problems. But once this groundwork has been thoroughly covered, there are few problems of procedure or organization.

A second malpractice is that of using the *Reading Laboratories* as 'Friday afternoon' material, where the pupils select any of the cards and work on them for about three-quarters of an hour. As the children are then choosing their own material from any colour of card, much of the work will be too easy or too difficult, real purpose is missing, motivation is lacking and the work is fragmented. This is a gross misuse of the Laboratories.

Both of these errors are associated with failure to appreciate the true potential of laboratories and the importance of the structural features which they embody. However, there are equally real dangers in an over-reliance on laboratories. We believe that the SRA *Reading Laboratories* should not be thought of as a complete reading programme. To use them as if they were is not only limiting but damaging. It has been shown that the use of laboratories can develop a number of aspects of reading ability. However, some of the attributes which are deliberately built in and necessary for their effective use, are also limiting in a wider sense. For example, an integral part of the programme is the self-marking principle: it enables pupils to find their errors immediately and 'learn' from them because of the immediacy of the correction. It also allows pupils to chart their progress and to organize their own individual programmes with occasional guidance from the teacher. All these factors do much to create a learning atmosphere where motivation can be high because of the involvement of the pupil and his interest in the programme and his own progress. Nevertheless, for this to be possible it is necessary to make extensive use of multiple-choice answers, particularly in the comprehension section. This means that although a real attempt has been made to provide experience of comprehension questions at all levels, for example by demanding inference and some degree of evaluation as well as recall of facts, the use of multiple-choice answers tends to restrict the range of questions that can be asked. Questions of this sort are usually less searching than a request to summarize a passage or discuss what has been read. This extra depth is crucial to the development of reading and must be catered for.

Therefore it is not claimed that reading laboratories are complete reading programmes, but that their use will help to promote effective reading. They do so by increasing the power of vocabulary, giving greater understanding of word structure, developing the effective use of contextual clues allied to the use of word-attack skills, developing the relevant use of speed in reading, giving practice in the use of dictionary and other skills, and developing within children the ability to understand more fully what they have read, not only because they have a wider vocabulary, but also because they have been trained to appreciate the importance of the order of events in the story or account, to isolate the main points and to gain an overall understanding of the passage.

3 Follow-up

These considerations suggest that the benefits of laboratory work can be fully realized only if they are accompanied and followed by study programmes which call for individual- and group-work on topics in geography and history, scientific and natural history studies. No less important is the opportunity and challenge of literature where one can, as it were, communicate with the author, feel at one with the characters, reflect on what is read and relate it to what one knows of life. It is only in an enlightened atmosphere of this kind that really effective reading development can take place, by using a well-organized and structured programme, while at the same time allowing freedom to use developing abilities (see Chapters 7 and 9).

If this development is important, and if to make provision for this a programme which includes most of the activities described above is necessary, regular time is required throughout the school years. Time for an intensive laboratory programme, individual research work, the reading of literature and the use of the suggested group techniques will make inroads into the timetable, especially as it is being suggested that they become permanent features of it. It could well demand the use of two periods weekly over the first three or four years of the secondary stage of education. The same would also be true in the junior school, but here one can see problems of time being more easily overcome because of the greater flexibility of the timetable together with the general practice of having one classteacher for all or most aspects of the curriculum.

4 The way ahead

To ensure the necessary allocation of time, teachers in the primary section need to be convinced that the teaching of reading needs to be continued and that it is of vital importance to spend time in the ways outlined in order that the use of reading can be made effective, for there is little doubt that many primary and indeed most secondary teachers consider reading to be a 'once and for all' achievement which is largely the responsibility of the infant and lower-junior teachers.

At the secondary level the problems are compounded, for here there are many teachers in different departments who will argue that the responsibility for reading development must be in the hands of the English department. For their part, teachers of English will quite properly say, 'How can we give up two periods weekly for several years for reading development of the type outlined, when we also have the other aspects of our work to cover?' It is indeed difficult to see a permanent solution to the problem until all teachers are prepared to recognize that the development of effective reading is a responsibility not only of the English department but of everyone, as advocated by the Bullock Report. It is essential to work in all areas of the curriculum, whether it be English, the humanities, science, mathematics, music, art or religious education. Perhaps, then, it is unfair to expect the English department alone to give up the necessary time for its development. If the arts and sciences gave up one period weekly each, the time would be readily available and a programme could be formulated on the lines indicated.

But mere acceptance is not enough. One has to be realistic and accept that there is a dearth of teachers with sufficient expertise and interest in this field. Certainly the fact that a teacher is a head of an English department in a secondary school is no evidence of his or her ability to formulate and carry out an effective reading programme. What is urgently required is an appreciation and recognition of the generality of the problem. *A Language for Life* (DES, 1975) is surely right to recommend the appointment of specialists in this field to all schools as soon as possible. In an enlightened school one would hope that this person would strongly influence and advise other teachers on how to tackle and reduce the problem of ineffective reading. But once again, one must be realistic and appreciate how long this might take. In the intervening years, there is a very strong case for a common course which is less demanding in terms of teacher-education.

5 The Bullock Report

One part of the brief of the Bullock Committee was to inquire into the teaching of reading in schools and at the same time to express its views on the use of various materials and methods as means of developing effective reading. Its main views concerning reading laboratories are to be found in Chapter 8 of *A Language for Life*, which deals with 'Reading: the later stages'. Here we find the following view expressed:

> Associated with the notion of the specialised teaching of reading both in the USA and here, is the commercially-produced programme, sometimes called the 'reading workshop' or 'reading laboratory'. Again on the face of it such programmes appear to offer a ready-made route to the development of reading skills. However, the fact that a pupil can become adept at completing the reading tasks in this rather narrow context does not mean that this ability will automatically transfer, and that he will be able to apply

it at will in his reading. Moreover, we have seen little evidence to support the view that there is any long-term value in 'booster' courses using these programmes. Scores on reading tests are certainly raised in the short term, but gains do not appear to be sustained over a longer period. This does not necessarily mean that the kinds of experience provided by 'reading workshops' or 'laboratories' are of no value. Though the skills in which they offer practice will not *automatically* transfer, the teacher could take steps to ensure that they were applied to other reading tasks, notably within the subject areas. However, any real gain in reading development must come through the generation of a strong motivation, and this means reading to satisfy a purpose. This is more likely to arise from the wide-ranging opportunities of the curriculum than from the arbitrary stimulus of 'laboratory' materials. We therefore believe the real possibilities are to be found in the second of the two approaches we identified earlier, namely the extension of skills in and through normal learning activities. (p. 117)

Although *A Language for Life* was not published until mid-way through the project, the researcher was aware that the sentiments expressed in the passage just quoted were widely held by many authoritative experts in the field of reading. One would agree that the real possibilities for the effective development of reading lie in the 'extension of skills in and through normal learning activities'. But this recognition is of little value, unless we have teachers with sufficient skill and knowledge to develop and implement programmes through this medium. At present, there is no evidence to show that this is so, and therefore it appeared important to continue this project. It was essential to *test* the value of a laboratory or workshop approach. For such an approach is less demanding of the teacher but is nevertheless based on a scientific consideration of the development of reading. Programmes such as SRA are an attempt to structure a satisfactory course to cater for successive stages.

The evidence of this research is clearly at variance with the views expressed in the Bullock Report, for it was found that children, having used a laboratory, continued to develop their ability in the normal school curriculum, thus suggesting the long-term value of the 'booster' course and indicating that some transfer took place. With reference to the sentence which says that reading development must come 'through the generation of a strong motivation, and this means reading to satisfy a purpose', one can only agree with the sentiments expressed, while noting that the motivation is created and the purpose satisfied by the use of a laboratory.

In a later paragraph, *A Language for Life* has this to say about reading laboratories and comprehension:

Comprehension work is standard practice in schools, and for most pupils it occupied a place in English lessons for the greater part of their school life. Much of this work is from textbook exercises designed for the purpose, and in recent years there has been an increase in the use of reading 'workshops' or 'laboratories' to which we have already referred in general terms. In our view, exercises in English textbooks or in kits of one kind or another are inadequate for developing comprehension. They provide too restricting a context and do not take account of the fact that reading should satisfy some purpose on the part of the reader. This may be to derive pleasure, experience or information: it may be serious or relatively trivial. But whichever it is, the individual will read most rewardingly when he has a personal reason for reading, for he will then carry his own attitudes and values into the text and not simply respond passively to it. The declared 'purpose' of so many of these exercises is to improve particular skills of comprehension. But even if there *is* any such result, the improvement is so specific to the situation, that it is unlikely to transfer to other reading tasks. ... Another shortcoming of exercises in many English workbooks and kits is that they tend to give undue emphasis to literal comprehension, doubtless because it is much easier to frame multiple-choice items at the literal level. The use of multiple-choice items does not, however, represent a realistic approach to the development of comprehension even at this level. For it is one thing to match multiple-choice items against the text but quite another to identify the relevant section of text without the aid of such pre-selected alternatives. (p. 120)

In the light of the present results, these strictures appear to us to be too strong. First of all, it is stated that kits are 'inadequate for developing comprehension'. In the fullest sense this is true and it has been made perfectly clear in this account that a laboratory must be considered in the context of a complete reading programme. However, this research project has clearly demonstrated that properly used a reading laboratory can have a beneficial effect on the development of comprehension.

Second, the point is made that reading must satisfy some purpose, whether this be 'to derive pleasure, experience or information; it may be serious or relatively trivial'. It is false to assert that the student can find no purpose in the reading associated with laboratory material. The introductory sessions, the individual programmes and the responsibility given to each pupil through self-marking, charting and evaluation all give real purpose to the work and ensure that in most cases motivation is high and that a child has a personal reason for reading.

Third, there is a critique of multiple-choice items. Such items are widely used in order that the self-marking can be achieved. That this sets certain limits is undisputed. Questions of this kind cannot test the depth of understanding that can be shown through discussion or perhaps summarization. Nevertheless, it is unfair to suggest that undue emphasis is given to literal comprehension because quite deliberate attempts have been made to include all aspects of comprehension and, within the limits of multiple-choice items, quite successfully.

The final criticism is that any improvement resulting from laboratory work is specific. The evidence of this research project suggests that this is far from the truth and that there are good grounds for considering that its effect on the general and wider reading of the pupils is beneficial.

VI Conclusions

This chapter reports an intensive and large-scale inquiry on the use of SRA *Reading Laboratories*. It is the only inquiry in this country which has been especially concerned with secondary-school children of average and above-average reading ability. We conclude:

1 The evidence clearly indicates that children of ten, eleven, twelve and fifteen years of age benefited at a highly significant level in developing speed and accuracy of reading, wider vocabularies and greater understanding of what they read, from the use of the SRA *Reading Laboratories*.

2 Teachers and other educationists need to recognize what a laboratory can and cannot do. When laboratories are used, there must be some provision for other reading experiences of various kinds.

3 Provided that teachers familiarize themselves with the laboratory procedures thoroughly, use the material properly and recognize its values and limitations, its wider use must be recommended to schools in general, for not only were substantial immediate gains made, but these were maintained and even increased over a longer period. Although below-average readers made greater gains than did those of more ability, substantial gains were made by both, relative to their respective controls. As a means of ensuring the effective development of reading ability, the reading laboratory can play an important part in a balanced and carefully-planned programme for all children in the middle years of school, at least up to the age of fifteen.

9

Improving Reading through Group Discussion Activities

Terry and Elizabeth Dolan, Vic Taylor, John Shoreland
and Colin Harrison

I General introduction

One of the most important undertakings by the project was to
examine current approaches to the improvement of pupils' reading.
The survey of classroom practice reported in Chapter 5 presents
details of a range of lessons and activities in which children had to
read, sometimes to practise their reading but more usually to
complete learning assignments. Chapter 8 presents an examination of
the effectiveness of the SRA *Reading Laboratories*, a 'study skills'
programme specially designed to improve comprehension. An effort
will be made in this chapter to assess the usefulness of an interesting
approach intended to lead children to flexibility in their reading of
texts and passages encountered in the different subject areas.
Essentially the approach involves small groups of children in a range
of activities which call for members of the groups to read in order to
solve problems and to reflect not only on the results of their reading
but also on the thinking and strategies used in arriving at decisions.

Teachers are well aware of the increased involvement of children
who are placed in game situations in which they are set communal
problems. The reading-extension activities described in this chapter
capitalize on this phenomenon. A range of reading activities which
lend themselves to this approach has been developed over the years
but these were implemented by very few teachers, and only on
occasion. Recently, however, a change of emphasis has seen the
development within many schools of systematic language-extension
programmes and here the inclusion of the reading activities has
excited considerably interest. Movement in this direction received
added impetus with the publication of *A Language for Life* (DES,
1975).

In the course of the present project, teachers in one school wished
to investigate the potential application of the activities across the
curriculum, both at the level of extending reading competence and as
a means of adding variety to the learning situations in different

228

subject areas. Some teachers, in cooperation with the project team, tried out activities in the school with a view to refining techniques and producing formats which would be appropriate to secondary curricula. Three teachers (a deputy head, a head of faculty and a head of department) have collaborated with Terry Dolan to report their experience in the second section of this chapter.

First, however, some comment might be helpful on the rationale for using the group situation to improve reading.

Many readers will have participated in the practice of 'group reading' when they were learning to read: children of similar reading ability listen and follow a text while one of the group reads aloud. An interesting extension of this situation is reported by Stauffer (1969) who demonstrates how children may acquire critical reading through variations of the group-reading situation. As part of a 'language-experience programme' which he had developed, young children were engaged in what Stauffer terms 'directed reading-thinking activities'. Using their readers, pupils were directed by their teacher to predict what was likely to follow in the text on the basis of evidence gleaned from isolated sections of the text, titles, subheadings, illustrations and so on. Children were asked to read to themselves, then to draw upon what they had read as evidence to justify their predictions and to substantiate previous speculations. Judgements were tested by the group and this immediate feedback was used by the teacher, who acted as a catalyst to stimulate insight and to guide decision-making.

These group activities were introduced only when children had acquired foundation reading skills and the ability to read at first-reader level. Stauffer's language-experience programme is extensive in scope and eclectic in its construction, embracing a range of 'best' practices noted by its designer over a number of years. Its effects have been investigated using matched populations and on a longitudinal basis (Stauffer, 1970). Although superiority was claimed for experimental groups over children who had followed the usual basic-reader course, no attempt was made to establish the independent contribution of the group activities. However, it was pointed out that teachers who had tried the approach were 'evangelistic' in their enthusiasm for the activities.

Stauffer's deliberate grouping of children for reading served an entirely different purpose from the grouping of children by age, grade or ability for administrative convenience. He claims that the group setting is very conducive to learning when it operates under 'favourable' conditions. In *The Language-Experience Approach to the Teaching of Reading* (1970) he lists these conditions:

1   All in the group examine the same material.
2   Each pupil reacts in terms of his own private stock of experience and knowledge.

3   Because pupils share ideas and the spirit is competitive and fosters the will to do, it *motivates*.
4   The information extracted and the assumptions made are compared and contrasted and likenesses and differences are noted.
5   The activity itself provides the means for the creative use of ideas.
6   Each pupil's personal integrity is at stake.
7   Each pupil's educated guesses must be defended, proved or disproved.
8   Available evidence must be presented to the group for acceptance or rejection. The group is the auditor, jury, and judge.
9   Pupils learn to have the strength of their convictions and not to be dominated by loud verbalizers.
10   Pupils learn to respect the thinking of others, to study how they examine evidence and how they prove points.
11   Pupils learn to temper their emotions in the crucible of group interaction, to be enthusiastic without being obnoxious, to rejoice without being offensive, to accept mistakes without being stifled.
12   All this is done under the direction of a prepared teacher. She knows the content, the important concepts to be attained, and how to promote thinking in others without putting words in their mouths. She knows the desired *effect*.

Stauffer's work has been exclusively concerned with 'reading' lessons and although there is variety in the literature read by the children, there are no reported investigations into whether or not pupils are able to apply their 'reading-thinking' skills to new situations and across different school subjects.

Abercombie (1960) has investigated the generality of skills gained in group discussion situations. She was concerned that students who were able to solve problems presented in a familiar format were frequently perplexed when problems were presented in a slightly new way. In an effort to develop 'mental flexibility', she initiated a course of group discussion sessions during which students considered various problems. She reported that when students who had covered the course were compared with students who were otherwise similar, the experimental group were notably superior in four areas:

1   the ability to discriminate between facts and opinions;
2   the ability to contemplate and then resist false conclusions;
3   the ability to generate and consider alternative solutions to problems;
4   the ability to regard each problem as if it were new, and to be less adversely influenced by previous experience which was now inappropriate to tackling the problem in hand.

Abercrombie's study lends powerful support for group discussion as a technique for improving objectivity and flexibility of thinking. However, it has to be pointed out that her sample consisted solely of medical students of high intellectual ability. On the other hand, Stauffer's efforts seem largely limited to six- and seven-year-olds and to using only one reading situation as the stimulus for discussion.

Christopher Walker bridges the gap to an extent by describing in his book *Reading Development and Extension* (1974) three group-discussion reading activities (group prediction, group cloze, group SQ3R), and by suggesting that the techniques are suitable for all children who have finished a reading scheme and are in need of practice in extending and applying their reading.

The first activity, 'group prediction', is similar to the type of prediction exercise described by Stauffer. However, Walker suggests that school texts may be supplemented by specially-prepared separate instalments of passages for use as reading material, and that passages may be selected from books used across the subject range.

Entire passages, booklets and books may be used in 'group SQ3R', a second activity outlined by Walker. The SQ3R method was introduced as an educational technique by Robinson in two publications (1961, 1962), since when it has undergone various adaptations, most notably by Parker (1963) who incorporated the technique as an integral component of the SRA *Reading Laboratories*. The formula stands for 'Survey, Question, Read, Recite, Review'. The mechanics of the technique, described in operation in the second part of this chapter, engage children's attention and focus on chapter headings, subheadings, illustrations, introductory and concluding paragraphs. From reading and discussing the information gained from these, the group is encouraged to formulate the main ideas and salient points in the text. The technique allows for considerable flexibility in the activities involved and is suitable for use with texts from most subject areas. Aukermann (1972) has produced an extremely useful book on the use of the SQ3R technique by individuals using reading matter from across the curriculum.

The third activity which is advocated by Christopher Walker is described as 'Group Cloze'. This is a technique which involves children in supplying words in order to complete sentences from which words have been systematically deleted. Teachers have used the 'gap-filling' technique for years, usually as a vocabulary exercise. However, by systematically deleting words (say every tenth word) considerations of a variety of different aspects of grammar and language arise. The use of cloze procedure to test comprehension has been raised by Vincent and Cresswell (1976), has been examined by several researchers in the USA (principally Bormuth, 1969), and is currently the subject of inquiry at the National Foundation for Educational Research.[1]

There are obvious similarities between Walker's 'teacher-directed oral group activities' and Stauffer's 'directed reading-thinking activities': children are asked to read in silence; no written work is

[1] NFER research project Reading Level Tests, directed by Dr R. Sumner. An experimental version of a test using cloze procedure to arrive at an estimate of pupils' performance has been produced by the NFER (Sumner, 1976).

involved; discussion is teacher-led; children are grouped according to homogeneous reading ability in groups of 8–12; pupils only take part in activities when they have a fair standard of reading; the accent is on reading in the wider context of language; and it is clear that teachers who lead groups need to be very familiar with the reading matter and with the abilities of group members.

Many readers may have observed that the activities which have been described are certainly not new to classroom practice. Indeed, it is possible to list textbooks from several years ago which contain exercises similar in content to those mentioned in this short review. The essential difference is to be found in the manner of execution of the exercises, the changed emphasis being on using what has been read for scrutiny of arguments raised in group discussion and for justifying attempts at solutions to assigned tasks. The procedures which are used in two of the activities not mentioned so far but described in section II, owe their origin to exercises carried out by children on an individual basis from textbooks. Thus 'group sequencing' is based on a well-known intelligence and comprehension exercise while group discussion of reading for different purposes' is derived from activities in the Scott Foresman *Reading Systems Programme*.

The potential of group interaction as an aid to reading development would appear to merit further exploration. Numerous questions need to be resolved: How adaptable and suitable is the general strategy to helping children read specialist books from various subject areas? Will children actually transfer newly-gained ability to other situations? How do the activities influence the learning of what is read? Do the activities lead to gains which can be measured in terms of increased reading comprehension or is their value largely a social one?

It was beyond the scope and brief of the project to provide definitive answers to these questions. However, in an effort to clarify some of the issues and to obtain the opinions of a range of experienced teachers, a series of workshops has been held since the autumn term of 1974 with teachers in schools, at the University and in teachers centres. The project has been fortunate in having the opportunity to cooperate with teachers in a project school in constructing an experimental reading, language and learning course. Members of staff in the school, a medium-sized comprehensive in a suburb on the outskirts of Nottingham, cooperated closely with the team in designing the programme, agreeing to implement it on a systematic basis for a minimum period of one year. Several of the activities already mentioned were included in the scheme. We are particularly indebted to teachers in Pilot School 1[1] for the advice offered on the actual conduct and organization of activities, their

---

[1] Christ the King Comprehensive. By the time the project was completed in 1976, other schools were also participating in piloting the techniques.

application across the curriculum and their uses with classes of mixed-ability children.

The classroom potential of the activities has been further investigated by a group of twenty-four experienced teachers who attended an extended in-service course on English, Language and the Curriculum at Nottingham University. Workshops run during the course by members of the project team were supplemented by seminars and demonstration lessons by members of staff from Pilot School 1.

Half of the teachers were from infant or junior schools, and half were based in middle schools, secondary schools, or further education colleges. Teachers agreed to try out the activities with their classes over a period of one school term, and to base the reading tasks on passages which they had chosen and prepared themselves. The decision to ask teachers to prepare their own materials was not made in order to simplify life for the team; one of the advantages of the activities is that they can be based on content which is related to the normal work of the class or group. This contrasts with the essentially arbitrary content of most reading laboratory assignments or textbook comprehension exercises.

Reactions from the teachers who took part were collected using a questionnaire. The teachers were asked to try to specify which aspects of language competence seemed to benefit from each group discussion activity and to comment on general problems encountered as they ran the activities.

The following section is an account of work carried out in Pilot School 1 in the first year of the reading, language and learning programme. Details are presented of the various problems faced by staff in the school as they attempted to supplement the school's general approach to reading and language development by introducing the activities into the timetable. Descriptions of the activities and the way in which they were developed in Pilot School 1 are then provided, together with transcripts of discussion arising during activity sessions. Comments on the usefulness of the activities, fed back to the team by members of the study group, are added after each activity has been outlined. A note on difficulties encountered in the preparation of materials is followed by an evaluative discussion of the programme and its effects, and an indication of future action in Pilot School 1 in the light of the year's experience in the venture.

II A programme for improving reading, language and learning

1 Background to the establishment of the programme

When the invitation to participate in the project was accepted by Pilot School 1 in September 1973, many teachers did not really grasp the aims and objectives of the project. A number of teachers believed that the centre of interest lay in basic reading and it was some time before it was generally realized that the chief concern was with the application of reading in all areas of the curriculum. As it became clear that one of the foremost concerns was to improve reading comprehension and language, it was then imagined by many to be an effort by 'English' teachers to influence other members of staff in the school. The recommendations of the Bullock Committee had led some members of the staff to an increased awareness of the role of language in learning and to accept some measure of responsibility for extending children's use of language in all its forms. It is probably true to report, however, that this genuine acceptance of responsibilities was accompanied by feelings of inadequacy, particularly in teaching children to cope more effectively with the reading demands made in lessons. It was in this connection that the project's activities attracted special interest.

Many teachers reflected on their own language in lessons, especially when dealing with children of different ability levels and when work was directed through worksheets and cards. Teachers with responsibility for timetabling and curriculum planning became concerned that children were apparently spending some days completing worksheet after worksheet, with only the content changing. This led to a desire for the provision of a variety of lesson activities in an effort to preserve motivation and interest.

Group discussion activities seemed admirably suited to the school's purposes. The techniques were tried out by a few teachers who had taken part in workshops run by the project team in the school and at the University. Although some teachers, particularly from the English department, recognized the potential value of the activities, others were less convinced and doubted whether the outcome of the activities would justify the input in terms of effort and time.

Recognizing that the group activities were relatively untried in the area of secondary education, Pilot School 1 was understandably reluctant to apportion too large a section of the timetable to their development. Several issues needed to be resolved before the activities could be given any general seal of approval. How would the activities work with mixed-ability groups of secondary children? Would it be possible to organize sessions so that one teacher could satisfactorily supervise and control an entire class divided into groups, each following a quite different activity? And of paramount importance, would children call upon ability developed in the reading sessions when they were faced with work in subject lessons, and would teachers detect any improvement in children's performance?

In view of these hesitations, the scale of the programme was not extensive. Children in the first three years had one lesson every week, whilst fourth-year children had one lesson per week for three weeks in every term. In addition to allocated time, some teachers tried the activities from time to time in lessons across the subject range.

2 Classroom organization and conduct of the programme

The organization of the programme was similar for all four year-groups but was most intensive and consistent in first-year classes. This was deliberate policy. On the one hand, it provided a link with the primary-school reading lesson (a 'prop' which many children seem to miss on transfer), and, on the other, it provided a foundation for further development in subsequent years and in other areas of the curriculum. All lessons took place during time scheduled for English.

Each class was divided into three mixed-ability groups of 8–10 children. These groups rotated through a set of activities over a three-week period, one activity being completed by each group each week. Although parents, students and other members of staff were often present, the activities were arranged so that one person could cope if left alone. Activities were sited in the same room in the school, using the same furniture plan, with reading equipment and material clearly labelled and easily accessible to pupils. Because of the set routine, the pupils came into the room and 'got on' with a minimum of fuss, although there was variety within the structure.

One group read school library books which they brought to the room and which could be changed in the nearby library during the lesson. A second group was directed from a cassette audio-tape on which the teacher had recorded instructions which led the children through an activity (usually group SQ3R). This group used a group-listening set of headphones so that there was minimum distraction between groups. Tapes were programmed and bore signals which told the child in control of the tape recorder when to switch off the tape. Children then removed the headphones and discussion ensued. After discussion, the child in charge of the recorder restarted the machine and the giving of directions was resumed. Thus the teacher was left free to direct the third group in one of the other activities.

3 Group discussion activities
(i) GROUP CLOZE

Children are faced with a text from which words have been deleted, the task being to think of words which may be inserted so that meaning is restored. A paragraph is left intact at the beginning of the passage, or a few sentences, in order to set the scene and to portray the writer's style. Thereafter, words are systematically deleted in a regular numerical pattern, say every fifth to twelfth word, depending on the difficulty of the text and the ability of the group. Occasionally, the regularity of the pattern may be broken so that words which are likely to promote discussion are deleted. The activity concentrates on developing the ability to read in units of words and thoughts, instead of individual words, by establishing linguistic relationships such as collocation, grammatical links and word patterns.

In the example which follows, the group was given the passage and the teacher briefly introduced the topic. The group was then broken down into pairs, and the children were asked to read through the entire passage before attempting to find 'words which fit'. Pupils were asked to suggest words and to justify to each other the suitability of any words selected. The extract transcribed presents the discussion that took place between two twelve-year-old girls, both of average intelligence and reading ability and in their first term in a mixed-ability class in year one of the school. Only one section of the passage is presented here: the entire passage is given in the Appendix (p. 265).

I can hardly believe it's true. I'm almost exactly on my route, closer than I'd hoped to come in my wildest dreams.

The southern tip of ____! On course, over two ____ ahead of schedule, the ____ still well up in ____ sky, the weather clearing! ____ circle again, fearful that ____ wake to find this ____ phantom, a mirage fading ____ mid-Atlantic mist. But ____ no question about it. ____ detail on the chart ____ its counterpart below; each ____ feature on the ground ____ its symbol on the ____.

The girls have read through the passage once to themselves and now read aloud. The discussion is picked up shortly after the selection of words has begun.

Ann	The something still well up in . . . (pause)
Sue	That's THE . . .
Ann	Yeh.
Sue	. . . something sky, the weather clearing. Something circle again, fearful that . . .
Ann	(interrupting) . . . The AEROPLANE still well up in the sky. 'Cos he's in an aeroplane, isn't he?
Sue	Yes. Well . . . (Pause as the girls decide to retrace their steps now that they have a start.) The southern tip of some . . . er . . .
Ann	IRELAND?
Sue	IRELAND. On course over two . . .
Ann	Can't get that.
Sue	Two . . . (long pause)
Ann	(tentatively and in a quiet voice) TWO MINUTES?
Sue	Something ahead of schedule. (pause) The aeroplane still well up in the sky, the weather clearing . . . (Both girls read silently around the deletion they are struggling with.)
Ann	I reckon that's a number . . .
Sue	Um . . .
Ann	(continuing) . . . two HUNDRED or two something . . . (Her voice peters out and another long pause follows.)
Sue	I think it might be two MINUTES . . .
Ann	(agreeing quickly) Yeh, ahead of schedule . . .

Sue	... ahead of schedule. The aeroplane ...
Both	still well up in the sky ...
Sue	... the weather clearing ... (Long pause as the children consider the next word.)
Ann	WE? (answering herself) No ...
Sue	No ...
Ann	We circle ... (quickly) Yes, WE circle again, fearful that WE wake to find this ...
Sue	(interrupting) I know, but there's only one person, isn't it? It says 'Now *I* am ...' ...
Ann	(conceding) Oh, yes.
Sue	... So it's only one person. (Sue retraces her steps and repeats the version agreed so far, while Ann puzzles on the one word.)
Sue	The weather cl ...
Ann	(breaks in) *I* circle again, *I* circle ...
Sue	Fearful that ...
Ann	I wake to find this A phantom?
Sue	Yes, A phantom, a mirage fading ... IN mid-Atlantic mist ...
Ann	(agreeing) Yes, IN mid-Atlantic mist ...
Both	But THERE'S no question about it. (Pause as they meet the new delection.)
Sue	THE detail on the chart ... er ...
Ann	WITH its counterpart below?
Sue	(considers the suggestion then agrees) ... Er, I think so. With its ...
Both	Counterpart below. Each ... (pause)
Sue	Each ... Each something feature on the ground ... (long pause) Each SMALL?
Ann	Wait a minute, where are we? (finds Sue's place) Oh ...
Sue	Each SMALL feature on the ground.

This discussion continued for another fifteen minutes, after which the pairs of children were called together and the group reassembled. Frequently in lessons, we allow one pair to discuss their proposals with another pair before the whole-group discussion ensues, but in this case there was only enough time for the whole group to discuss the passage. Six children were in the group. The transcript of the discussion which took place is, as in the case of the two girls, from the same section of the passage. The children gathered round a table so that they faced one another, and the teacher read the passage aloud from the beginning with the children following the text. On reaching the 'task part' of the passage, the teacher read the passage and stopped at each deletion. The children were then invited to volunteer answers. The lengthy transcript allows an interesting insight into how the preparation completed by the two girls assists them when they enter into discussion with the entire group.

Teacher, The southern tip of ...?
(Chorus of voices 'IRELAND'.)
Teacher   Yes, and how do we know it's Ireland?
(a babble of voices, each giving an explanation, including)

Betty	It says so on the top.
Joe	Miss, it says the southern coast of Ireland.
Sue	It says, well (she reads from the card) The southern ... He's crossed over the southern ... (loses her place)
Ann	Yes ...
Teacher	Yes. So, he's on course and he's over two ...?

(Various answers are given but the dominant answer is 'THOUSAND'.)

Joe	TWO HOURS ...
Teacher	Hours? Well, you said thousand. What ... why?
Sue	We said MINUTES ...
Teacher	How would he ...
Ann	No, because it doesn't fit ...

(Several voices are heard at the same time but the general theme is one of reciting the words 'two THOUSAND ahead of schedule' and saying that they don't sound right and that it doesn't fit.)

Teacher	It doesn't fit?
Chorus	No!
Teacher	(agreeing) No. And why would it be hours and not minutes do you think?
Joe	Because ...
Ann	(interrupting) because it doesn't take minutes ...
Elizabeth	Because, only, he's only just over Ireland ...
John	(breaking in) It wouldn't sound right if it said 120 minutes ahead of sh ... sc ... (struggles with the word)
Teacher	(supplies word) Schedule.
John	On schedule. It wouldn't sound right. He'd say, he'd just say 'two hours' ...
Joe	Well, if it was only two minutes, he'd just as well be on schedule ...
Betty	And, if you're just over Ireland, you must have a long way to go ...
Teacher	I think Joe's right, though. Yes, (in answer to Betty) it is a long way to go. If it was just two minutes, he wouldn't remark that he was so well ahead of schedule. So, what about this next bit though? The something still well up in ...
Ann	The AEROPLANE ...
Sue	The AEROPLANE still well up in the sky ...
Teacher	Yes. Is he just concerned with the aeroplane being well up in the sky, though? Think of how long ago it was. How would he manage to find his way, do you think, so many years ago? ... What ... seventy years ago? (an impetuous overestimation in the heat of the moment)
Joe	The CLOUDS well ...
Betty	Would he have a map of England?
Teacher	He'd have a map, but what would he need ...
John	He'd probably fly under the clouds ...
Betty	(quietly) COMPASS ...
John	(continuing) ... so he could see the landmarks.
Teacher	Yes ...
John	They'd give him a chart of landmarks.

Teacher	That's right. So, he needs to be able to see his way. So, what does he still need still well up in the sky?
Joe	The CLOUDS?
Teacher	Oh? They'd block his view wouldn't they? (The teacher immediately realizes that the answer 'CLOUDS' was acceptable, but before she can take back her objection, the child agrees with her and another child offers another line of answer.)
John	He'd need a light day, a bright day ...
Teacher	A light, yes. So, what's still well up in the sky?
John	The SUN.
Teacher	The SUN still well up in the sky, the weather clearing. Now ... circle again, fearful that ...
Betty	I circle.
Teacher	I, why I? Why do you know it's just 'I' circling?

(A babble of voices is heard as children draw attention to previous mentions of 'I'.)

Betty	Miss, because he's telling the story.
Teacher	Yes, and does he have any companions with him?

(chorus of voices answer 'no')

Teacher	No. He's all alone isn't he? I circle again fearful that ...

(Chorus of voices answer 'I'.)

Teacher	I wake? *I* wake? (pause) ...
Liz	I'LL wake!
Teacher	I'LL wake to find this ...?
Joe	PLANE?
Sue	A PHANTOM?
Teacher	(agreeing) A phantom. A mirage fading ...

(Numerous children now offer answers, all either IN or INTO.)

Teacher	IN or INTO? You say IN. You say INTO. Who wants to give me a reason for their choice?

(Numerous children reply, each drawing attention to the fact that it doesn't 'sound right' if 'IN' is used.)

Teacher	It doesn't sound as right, doesn't it? So, you agree on INTO, then? INTO mid-Atlantic mist. But ...
Liz	THERE'S.
Teacher	(quickly accepting answer) THERE'S no question about it. Yes, we use that don't we. Now, here's a difficult one ... Something ... (she hears a child faintly mouthing the answer) Oh, yes Joe. What?
Joe	EACH detail ...
Teacher	Each detail on the chart. Now what do you think of that?
Sue	Well, it could be EVERY detail.
Teacher	It could be EVERY detail on the chart, yes. Well, shall we perhaps decide ...
John	SOME? (answers himself) No, it couldn't be SOME.
Teacher	No? Why could it not be SOME?
John	There's not an 's' on the end of detail.
Teacher	Yes, that's right. So, EACH or EVERY detail on the chart. Now, this space here ... its counterpart below.
Ann	SHOWS? (teacher fails to catch this suggestion)

Teacher   Supposing we had EACH detail on the chart ...
Sue   HAS its ...
Teacher   (agreeing) HAS its counterpart below. Would that be the same
             for EVERY detail on the chart? ... HAS its counterpart below? Is
             that right?
(Several children chorus affirmatively.)
Teacher   Yes. So, look at the second half of that sentence. What word
             does it begin with?
Joe   EACH. (agreement from various children)
Teacher   So, which do you prefer? EACH detail on the chart, or EVERY detail?
Sue (and   EVERY.
others)
Teacher   EVERY? Why?
Sue   Well, it's not very good if you say ... we ... if you're going to
             start with 'EACH detail on the chart' and then carry on when you
             come to it with another 'each'.
Teacher   Hm. Hm. You don't like it?
Sue   No. It doesn't sound right.

The above discussion illustrates the fact that, in group cloze, there
is no fixed idea of 'right' or 'wrong' words, only those which the group
deem suitable after reasoned argument. (Sometimes, however, the
author's original choice of words is disclosed and discussed.) It is
interesting to note how the teacher tried to rectify her 'dogmatism'
when she later dealt with the argument over 'each' or 'every'. In fact,
the author had used 'every' in the original text, but the teacher
preferred 'each'. She did not pursue the discussion, preferring to
accept the choice of word agreed on by the children in the group.

The procedure seems to have great potential for the teaching of
technical vocabulary and terminology in context. Teachers may work
from a class textbook, or have children tackle a summary
of information about a topic taught over various stages of time.
When used in the latter manner, group cloze seems an excellent
revision exercise.

Once children have some proficiency in a foreign language, the
passage may be presented in that language with subsequent
discussion carried out in English. (With children of poor foreign-
language ability, the teacher may also present the passage on an
audio-tape to supplement the text. This technique is also used as an
aid for children of very poor reading ability.)

Comments and reactions of the study group
Group cloze involves the participant in discussions about meaning
and content of the passage as a whole, but since the task is to replace
individual words which have been deleted, the focus is generally at the
word or sentence level. There is little doubt that this is a fairly taxing
activity which needs careful handling, but it was felt by many teachers
to offer a fascinating insight into the level of a child's comprehension

of a passage. One teacher who tried out group cloze with sections from science textbooks was shocked to find that there did not appear to be a book in his department which third-year grammar-school girls could cope with successfully. There is a good deal of interest in trying the activity with modern-language groups, and some English teachers found it an ideal tool for encouraging a response to poetry and to literary criticism with O- or A-level groups. One teacher felt that to use cloze merely as a reading comprehension technique is to miss valuable educational opportunities. Among the spin-offs he mentioned were 'a springboard for critical analysis of style; a readiness to think into authorial intention and purposes; a practical illustration of pupils' native understanding of grammar'. This teacher certainly explored several possibilities for cloze procedure. The technique seemed to lend itself to examining writing at many levels: 'I have found it a fascinating way in for kids to analyse their own writing,' he says, and, 'We had some good times with two scientific passages where the activity raised for attention some interesting (and daft) features of scientific writing.' This teacher, along with several of his colleagues who took part in the study, had perceived the adaptability and flexibility of cloze to teachers' styles and usage. One teacher commented that the activities as a whole ought to be techniques for improving the 'reading kids are doing at the time rather than as a throwaway line or a completely separate programme'.

(ii) GROUP SQ3R

This activity incorporates into the group situation techniques used for individual learning by Francis Robinson in the 1940s, and later by Parker for the SRA *Reading Laboratories*. Booklets or documents may be specially prepared for the activity, or children may read a chapter or section of a book. In most lessons in Pilot School 1, the activity is controlled through instructions presented on a specially-prepared audio-tape which gives directions to the children to discuss this or that point. A child is selected to act as 'leader' and has the responsibility for switching off the recorder in response to signals on the tape, and for restarting the machine once discussion is completed. A group-listening set with individual headphones for each child is sometimes used, although this is merely an effort to reduce distraction for children in other groups and is not essential for the exercise.

In the course of the activity, the children survey (S) the title, subheadings, illustrations, and first and last paragraphs. They aim to gain as much information as possible in a couple of minutes. An integral part of the activity is the encouragement of the children to raise questions (Q) about the content during the surveying process. At each stage, directions are given and the points raised by the children are discussed. Questioning is followed by a reading through (R1) of the text, reviewing (R2)—that is picking out the salient points and making sure that they are understood, and finally reciting (R3)— a consideration of the implication or application of what has been read, and a testing of recall.

The tapes have been carefully graded from the first 'survey-question' tapes to ones which involve note-making, dictionary work, cross-referencing and a range of other assignments arising from the content of the passage.

In the transcript which follows, the instructions on the tape had taken a group of eight first-year pupils to the point where they had almost finished the S–Q assignment of a specially-prepared booklet entitled *Return*. Children had examined and discussed a map which had several cities circled in red; they had discussed the title and the fact that it was written by David Attenborough; they had been told beneath the title that the passage was an extract from a book *Zoo Quest to Guiana*, and had just read the first and last paragraphs. The transcript begins with a comment from the teacher.

Teacher	Now, we've looked at the map, the title, the first paragraph and the last paragraph. Tell your leader what you think this extract is going to be about. (Signal)
Joe	I think it's going to be about ... he's after some animal and eventually he's found it, some type of a pig because pigs eat swill.
John	I think it might be ... you wouldn't shout at a pig to come, though, would you? So, I think it might be sort of a dog, you know, that he's found. Or it might be that cat that he mentioned.
Liz	It says 'paddock' in it. I think it might be a horse or something.

(One child signals agreement with John. However, most seem to agree with Liz. Nevertheless, John persists.)

John	It might be a vicious dog and it might be, you know, it might be a bit dangerous so he put it in a paddock, 'cos, you know, it's not going to get out of a paddock too easily.
Joe	And horses don't eat swill!
Ian	No.
James	It must be rather an intelligent animal if he called it.
John	Yes, that's what I say ...
Joe	But it ignored him though didn't it?
Ian (the leader)	Has everyone said what they want then?

The group went on to follow the entire passage as the teacher read it, then split up into pairs to follow instructions which led pupils to dictionary and reference work in a school resource centre. For this exercise the teacher left the group entirely to themselves, but on other occasions a teacher, a parent or a student teacher 'sits in' to chair the discussion.

(iii) GROUP SEQUENCING

Several consecutive sections of the same passage, poem, set of instructions, workcard or a child's account of an event experienced by the group are prepared. Working in pairs, the children have to arrange the sections into an order which makes sense. Once an agreed order has been arrived at, one pair joins another or the group reassembles and discusses the respective orderings. Children frequently decide that several orderings are acceptable without the overall meaning being materially altered. The author's original order is usually revealed to the children and discussed. In performing the task, children may focus on punctuation and typographical clues, syntax constructions, units of meaning, the logic of the author's argument and the direction to which the passage is pointing.

A ready supply of duplicated sets of material has been found in multiple copies of newspapers and 'colour supplements'. Sets of material produced from these have been used in sequencing, children seeming very interested in items of local interest, in reports of football matches and in well-known advertisements.

The passage below was prepared for a lesson in school. The 'bits' of the passage were typed onto separate cards and covered with plastic film for greater durability. Each section was numbered with a key which indicated to the teacher the original structure of the passage. A group of eight children undertook the exercise. Children were paired off and asked to sequence sets of cards, then the pairs were asked to join another pair of children and to compare the orderings. The transcript is from discussion which took place when two boys and two girls met to inspect and comment on their decisions. The major part of the discussion during the first partnering of the boys was undertaken by Joe, and it is interesting to see that during the discussion with the girls it is John, the less intelligent of the two boys, who makes the greater contribution, advancing the very arguments put forward by Joe. (N.B. The passage appears in the correct order.)

8 Marcia was deaf. She had always been deaf. She had seen people walking but she had never heard their footsteps. She had watched her sister playing the piano but she had never heard the music.

3 Marcia had looked up at the sun and seen the bright rays of light coming through the trees. She'd seen the shadows on the ground. She'd felt the warmth from the sun. 'The sun is wonderful,' she thought. 'Of all the sounds in the world, I wish I could hear the sound of sunlight coming through the trees.'

9 Marcia wondered. Bright sunlight coming through the trees was such a beautiful sight. She could imagine the beautiful sound that it made.

1 She tried to imagine the sound of the sunlight. 'It must be beautiful,' she thought. 'It must be one of the most beautiful sounds.' And then she did imagine what the sounds might be.

5 The next day Marcia saw one of her deaf friends. Marcia moved her

hands and fingers in sign language which her deaf friend understood. 'Do you know what sound the sunshine makes when it comes through the trees?' she asked. 'No,' the friend signalled with her hands.

7 Then Marcia went to her teacher. 'Can you tell me the sound that sunlight makes as it comes through the trees?' she asked.

4 'It doesn't make a sound, Marcia,' said the teacher clearly so that Marcia could read her lips.

2 'No sound? But I can imagine the sound,' said Marcia. 'I can hear it in my imagination. You told me the wind makes a sound. You told me that the rain makes a sound. The sun should too. It should make the most beautiful sound of all.'

6 The teacher saw that Marcia was disappointed. 'You know, Marcia, you shouldn't be upset,' she said. 'You're really a very lucky girl because you can imagine a very beautiful sound that no one else can hear. I can only see the rays of light coming through the trees. But you can hear them too. And that's a wonderful thing.'

Teacher	Now you've got no. 9 before no. 1. Why's that?
John	Well it says, 'I wish I could hear the sound of sunlight coming through the trees. Marcia wondered' ...
Teacher	Um. (indicates to child to continue)
John	She was thinking about it ... 'Bright sunlight coming through the trees was such a wonderful sight. She could imagine the beautiful sound it made.' She was thinking about it.
Teacher	She was thinking about doing it then?
John	Yes.
Teacher	I see, yes. And so you've put no. 9 first. Well why is it different to no. 1? Because it mentions her thinking about it then?
John	(reads) 'She tried to imagine the sound of the sunlight.' Well, she *thought* there (points to card no. 1) and she's *trying* now.
Teacher	Yes. And what about the last sentence on that card? What do you think of that?
John	'And then she *did* imagine what the sound might be.'
Teacher	So, she actually did it?
John	Yes.
Teacher	(turning back to the two girls) So what do you think now then? Which one would you like to have first? No. 1 or no. 9?
Pat	No. 1. (firmly)
Teacher	No. 1 still?
John	I think no. 9.
Pat	No. 1.
Liz	(has now changed her mind) I think no. 9.
Pat	I think no. 1.
Teacher	I think you're outvoted.
Pat	(conceding) Well ...
Teacher	Let's put that there then. (Places cards in the newly-agreed order.) All right?
John	(volunteers answer) No. 9.
Teacher	And then what have you got?
John	No. 5.
Teacher	No. 5? 'The next day Marcia saw one of her deaf friends'?

John	Yes.
Teacher	Yes. (agreeing)
John & Joe	7.
Pat	But she's got to ... say ... 'She could imagine the beautiful sound that it made.' But she's got to try to imagine it before she can imagine it.
Teacher	Ah yes. But, what does 'could' also mean apart from 'doing it'? It's not she 'can'imagine it; she 'could'.
John	Hope we've got this right. We've never got it before.
Teacher	I think that means that it was possible for her to do it if she tried.

(Children signify that they've taken the point.)

Pat	Yes, I see.
Teacher	So then you've got her ... what? (looks at children's sequence) Imagining it? Yes, and then you've got to no. 5, is it?
Joe	5.
Teacher	What? 'The next day Marcia saw one of her deaf friends'?
John & Joe	Yes.
Teacher	And what have you got after that?
All children	No. 7.
Teacher	'Then she went to her teacher'? (considers the reply for a time) Yes, and then what after that?
All children	4.
Teacher	That's her teacher speaking to her. Ah, what about no. 2? Who's Marcia answering there, do you think? Her teacher or her friend?
Pat	Her teacher.
Teacher	Definitely her teacher? What would happen if you put no. 2 after no. 5 do you think?
Liz	I don't think ...
Pat	Well it says there, 'You told me that the wind makes a sound'. Well, the friend's deaf, too. So her friend wouldn't know.
Teacher	Ah.
John	No, no. I think we're right still.

The teacher then read through the agreed version, which in this instance happened to coincide with the author's original. The group then discussed the passage and its resemblance to a previous passage on Helen Keller.

Comments and reaction of the study group
In group sequencing, as the title of the activity suggests, the emphasis is on the order of events or thoughts in a passage. Many teachers have observed that children take some time to learn that there may be a better way of writing than simply to put down thoughts in the order they happen to occur to the writer. Group sequencing offers a framework for discussing why one paragraph ought to be placed before another. Most fluent readers will tend to recognize a general introductory paragraph or an epigrammatical final paragraph

without fully realizing the features they have analysed in doing so. Children tackling the activity, on the other hand, have to find ways of explaining why they have decided a certain segment is appropriate as an opening paragraph when their neighbour has decided it belongs elsewhere. A number of teachers pointed out that this activity is by no means novel, and cited English textbooks from the 1930s in which a series of numbered paragraphs have to be given a logically-acceptable ordering. This one must accept, although the point should be made that having the passage cut into sections which can be manipulated represents a crucial departure from the textbook exercise. It allows the reader to try out a number of different approaches without being committed to any one initially, and offers a much more worthwhile basis for discussion between pupils. This discussion is a crucial aspect of the activity. In the original textbook exercise children would no doubt read and respond on their own, and receive no feedback until their responses had been assessed as 'right' or 'wrong'. In group sequencing the active discussion of choices is much more important than approximating to the author's original order. Passages vary, but quite often children will suggest perfectly coherent alternatives to the author's order; they may even improve on it.

Group sequencing drew mixed comment from the study-group teachers. Some considered that the exercise was quite a novel way for children to examine the structure of written material. Comments drew attention to 'how much pupils bring to reading situations', and 'insight into how children are actually reading'. Subject teachers in particular seemed pleased with the exercise both at the level of discussion of texts and of studying content. However, English teachers who had used the technique primarily as a comprehension activity noted that there is a danger of superficiality in the venture. It was reported that some children if asked to 'decide on an order' settled for just that and arranged the instalments almost at random. More seriously, without an expressed purpose and objective, children were in a position to 'do it well (i.e. articulate furiously and get a logical order), and have nothing more than a vague understanding of what the passage was about'. One teacher was hesitant and wanted to know exactly what was gained from the activity: 'children who it was thought would use reading skills did so, and those who could not were not particularly helped by the activity'. It is interesting to see that the same teacher noted that the group seemed subsequently more contemplative about their writing. Two teachers drew attention to the fact that in this activity more than in any other the dogmatic child tended to take over. Whereas with cloze several words are 'correct', and with prediction several speculations may be in the air at the same time, sequencing seems to offer less room for manoeuvre. Perhaps this situation would suggest that teachers need to be sensitive to the dynamic structure of groups and to partner children with some care.

(*iv*) GROUP PREDICTION

In this activity instalments of a passage or story are distributed one at a time to a group of up to ten children. The children read the instalment, discuss its content with the chairman and try to predict what is likely to happen in subsequent instalments. After each section has been discussed, the chairman (usually the teacher) summarizes the discussion, then gathers in the instalments so that children may no longer refer back to previous information. Pupils have to justify all predictions and comments, the general aims being to evoke judgements about the text and to develop the ability to support, to defend, to modify and to rethink judgements in the light of comments from others in the group and of further evidence from the passage. Discussion is most lively and predictions most forthcoming when there is a short unusual story which has an unexpected but plausible outcome. Such a story provides an opportunity for the teacher to heighten the suspense and to encourage the group to generate new ideas and to hypothesize developments. This is not to say that the activity lacks application in other areas in the curriculum. The technique has been used with some success in a variety of subjects, including history and French unseen.

The prediction lesson from which the extract below is transcribed was with a mixed-ability group of first-year children and took place only six weeks after they had entered the school. It was the children's second prediction exercise. The six sections of the passage are given in the appendix, but here the transcription is of the discussion which occurred after the children had read the fifth instalment. Previous discussion had been lively and two main concerns had emerged: First, was what was happening to the person in the story real, or was it a nightmare as the title of the story (*Nightmare*) would suggest? Second, would the person survive?

> 5 Slowly, he emerged from the nightmare. This was no dream! He was drowning! Only that stunning blow on his head had prevented his realizing it before. The painted lady of his confused state was the figure-head of the sailing ship *Pandora* in which he had been serving. She had foundered on the rocks near the Cornish coast and was now plunging down for the last time.
>
> Before drifting once more into unconsciousness, he made an effort to see if any of his shipmates were still alive.

Children raised the point that it was now more likely that it was a real happening, and not a dream. Several weaker children actually read from the text such evidence as 'slowly he emerged from his nightmare' and the part which indicated that he hadn't realized it before due to 'the stunning blow on his head'. The teacher then swung discussion to consider whether or not the person in the story would be saved. Children drew attention to the point that survival was possible because the ship was aground on rocks near the Cornish coast, but that it was not guaranteed because the person in the story was 'drifting once more into unconsciousness'.

> *Teacher* And what about any other survivors? Do you think that's likely?
> (Several children now speak but the teacher signals to David, a boy who hadn't said too much so far, to talk.)
>
> *David* It says he looked around to see if any of his shipmates were still alive.
>
> *Carol* I think some of them are still alive ... because there were muffled voices. There were muffled voices ... (pause)
>
> *Teacher* Yes, muffled voices ... so? (indicating to child to continue)
>
> *Carol* So somebody must still be alive to hear muffled voices.
>
> *Teacher* And does anything else happen? ... that makes you think that perhaps there was someone else surviving?
>
> *David* When er, when er the man on the log came.
>
> *Teacher* So he was still alive, wasn't he? But, do you think they will survive long enough either to be rescued or to be washed up on the coast or ...
>
> *Jeremy* I think, I think he may survive but I don't think his shipmates will survive.
>
> *Carol* I don't think actually ... I think the man in the dream, the man was in the dream, it was just a dream and that man in the log was in the dream. He was dreaming that his shipmates were still alive.
>
> *Teacher* Ah, I see. So, we've all sorts of possibilities there. But there are two main questions we want to decide on, I think. Is he going to survive? Is he going to get saved? Who wants to say yes then? Who thinks there's evidence to show that he probably will?
>
> (Only a few children raise hands to indicate agreement.)
>
> *Teacher* Oh, the rest of you think he's going to drown?
>
> *David* Maybe, I don't know ...
>
> *Teacher* You don't know?
>
> *Ian* I'm not sure either.
>
> *Teacher* You're not sure.
>
> *Jeremy* I think he may survive because he's the 'star' of the story!
>
> *Teacher* That's as good a reason as any.
>
> *Carol* No, I think he'll die because it says 'he was drowning' ...
>
> *Anna* Not necessarily. (in answer to Jeremy)
>
> *Teacher* ... it says 'he was drowning' ...
>
> *Ian* It's a cheerful thing, Miss, because I've only just said, er, in this, Miss, he's the star of it, so he can't die. Miss, but, he can die, because I've seen it done. So I think, Miss, it is real, and he is going to die.
>
> *Anna* Spartacus was the hero but he died in the end.
>
> *Teacher* So, you still don't know? You're not going to come out and have the courage of anything you've said so far? (pause) Oh all right then.
>
> (Teacher collects in the instalments and hands around the next one.)

On completion of the final instalment, the group were led by the teacher in a discussion of the story and its ending. The group was divided in opinion about the suitability of the story's ending, with some children thinking it 'a funny ending' while others considered it a good ending.

It is interesting to contrast the general discussion in this activity with discussion transcribed from the cloze and sequencing sessions. The level of discussion is much more general, children say more and the individual contributions are lengthier. At the same time, the teacher needs to be very careful in framing questions so as to open up discussion and not to close it.

Comments and reaction of the study group
Group prediction was judged to call upon a number of skills. The reader has to examine each section carefully, setting it in his own mind against earlier instalments and the predictions made from them, and must draw new inferences if possible. He must find a way to express aloud what he feels is happening and is likely to happen, working on the basis of partial information. If the activity is to have any real value, pupils must be able to respond critically to the statements of others in the group. With younger children the critical response may relate mainly to statements of fact; someone may have ignored, overlooked or forgotten a vital piece of information. With older pupils the discussions might relate to the logical or temporal order of events, to what is artistically consistent, and to the extent to which personal anecdotes can be accepted as evidence. If all this sounds rather like an academic rationalization of the obvious, perhaps one should stress the point that these insights are those suggested by teachers who have tried group prediction exercises with children from the ages of six to eighteen. What any particular group can gain will be determined by certain key factors: the passage chosen for discussion; the language competence of the group; the familiarity of the teacher with the passage and individuals within the group; and above all by the teacher's ability to draw out and stimulate purposeful discussion.

On the whole, there was enthusiastic support for group prediction. An experienced teacher felt that one of the main attractions was the very novelty of the situation, '... gets away from the wearisome business of isolated language study'. The informal conversation-like discussion also appealed to other teachers, and some felt that they had unexpectedly gained insight into the ability of members of the group. One teacher felt that she was witness to 'mental activity in the raw' and was struck by the variations in the pace of reading. She noticed that the pace of reading increased as children gathered purpose and momentum. Another teacher, an English teacher working with fourth-year secondary pupils, spoke of 'a real breakthrough' with the group. Immediately on completion of their first prediction activity, '... the group demanded another lesson like this and seemed galvanised into constructive discussion about it among themselves'. One teacher went as far as saying, 'should be made compulsory by DES circular!'

(v) GROUP READING FOR DIFFERENT PURPOSES

A complete class or a group share common reading assignments. Subgroups are given different tasks to complete, the general objective being to devise a set of questions for the class as a whole. These may consist of:

1 listing three statements of fact and three of opinion then asking the class to determine which is which;
2 listing the important points in the passage and asking the class to say which four are the key ones;
3 presenting two arguments to support alternative explanations to points of issue and asking the class to determine which argument is the stronger;
4 devising a set of questions which can only be answered through reference to several paragraphs in the text;
5 carrying out a critique then subjecting it to class scrutiny;
6 testing a writer's assertions by reference to other sources;
7 listing three salient points which are not affected in their importance by the order in which they are presented in the text, and three with a sequence of presentation which is crucial. The points are randomly presented and the class has to arrive at the group's categorization.

Discussion takes place within groups, and the outcomes are presented in a class or total group forum. The questions are posed by each group in turn and the group as a whole have first to try to answer the questions, and second to comment on the suitability of the questions.

4 A note on material used in the activities

There was no material published specially for the activities when the reading, language and learning programme was initiated, so it was necessary for Pilot School 1 to produce its own resources. Once a passage or text had been found successful, it was duplicated and transferred onto a more robust backing card and covered with plastic film for greater durability. Sets of material were then stored in clearly-labelled boxes and catalogued. Master tapes were kept so that worn tapes might be replaced, and copies of texts were filed for future reference.

Members of the project team have been pleased with efforts made by agencies such as teachers centres in acting as central libraries for materials which teachers have found useful. Once materials are catalogued and added to a central library, they may be copied or borrowed for use in school.

Almost every member of the study group mentioned the difficulties of finding suitable material for the activities, especially of obtaining passages with structures appropriate for group prediction. Since group cloze does not tend to involve very lengthy passages no one reported difficulties in preparing these, but two teachers did describe sequencing as 'laborious' to prepare, and another noted that it was not easy to pitch passages at the appropriate level of difficulty for a group. A passage might seem very straightforward for one group but unapproachable to another, and this would lead to an absence of useful discussion in the former case and wild guessing in the latter. Another interesting insight has been that having very brief segments (for example one sentence each) was felt to make the task of sequencing more difficult rather than easier. This is because the reader has less information available on which to base a judgement about where the segment comes in relation to the passage as a whole. Only one teacher in the study group tried out group reading for different purposes and he reported that preparation was simple for this activity. Pupils were given a range of different passages and stories, all from sets of books used in the school. It is interesting to report that one teacher has modified the latter activity to concentrate on developing skilled listening in the children in his classes. He either reads out the passage or presents it on audio-cassettes. Children formulate their comprehension questions, listen to the reading once more, then present their questions to the rest of the class or group.

The preparation and production of material was a considerable chore for the first Pilot School 1 teachers who ran the reading programme. However, when several teachers helped to devise and prepare material the task was easier. Each set of material has been used repeatedly with different groups of children and is now having a second 'outing' with the new first-year.

5 General comments on the group reading activities and the reading programme in Pilot School 1[1]

Initial reading during the activities is silent as pupils read the text and search for clues, but they soon voluntarily extract phrases to read aloud in order to support or refute arguments. The level of reading ability of individual children is not revealed during silent reading, so no embarrassment or frustration is caused as in 'reading aloud' lessons. Knowing that discussion is to follow, pupils adjust their reading speed to ponder information which they feel may be

---

[1] Sections 5 and 6 were produced by Elizabeth Dolan, Vic Taylor and John Shoreland, all teachers in Pilot School 1.

important and cut quickly through parts which do not add to or influence decisions. This silent reading involves an implicit, silent personal conversation as well as ongoing questioning and prediction. We feel strongly that these processes help form the interrogative reader.

Writing does not take place during reading activities when they feature in the structured programme. This is quite deliberate in an effort to discourage the attitude that the reading games, while enjoyable, are only a pleasant prelude to the inevitable chore. In cloze procedure, particularly, we have found that when children have been invited to 'write in' the words, discussion seems limited thereafter with children usually concentrating on a single choice of word rather than holding several suitable alternatives in mind to be considered alongside those suggested by other children. So that its application may become more apparent, there is a small amount of writing occasionally in group SQ3R, but this writing only features after children are familiar with the basic routine of the activity. It is encouraging to note that some teachers have commented on the usefulness of group sequencing to children in planning writing. Indeed, one hopes that all of the activities will lead children to reflect on the choice of words to convey their ideas and to express themselves both in speech and writing.

It is essential that the children know and understand why and to what purpose these activities take place: that they are taught from the start to distinguish different reading situations; that they are able to assess the efficacy of their reading; and, most important, that they feel confident that what they are doing is vital and relevant for present and future study.

The activities are essentially game situations which are interesting and enjoyable while calling for intense and careful reading. In order to evaluate and discuss a text, children must know it thoroughly, and the main idea or ideas, supporting details and peripheral points must all be distinguished. Formal comprehension exercises do not always call for such manipulation of ideas. Only answers given in a format dictated by the stereotyped 'style' of the question are required. Questions are often read before the text, and many children hope to pick out pieces without either reading, remembering or understanding the text as a whole. (Undoubtedly, this strategy may lead to success in completion of some comprehension exercises and, as such, it ought to be taught. However, it is quite inappropriate in most learning situations and, even in many comprehension exercises, may lead to failure.) In formal comprehension exercises, children may not know for days if the answers they have given have been marked right or wrong. By contrast, answers offered in discussion activities are considered immediately and children may extend, modify or rephrase answers, and these in turn may be subjected to the same cycle. In many of the activities there may be several acceptable answers to a problem. And in cloze procedure, the offered word may improve on the one which has been deleted. It is imperative that teachers who are leading the discussion really know the text so that all responses may be given careful consideration. If teachers were magically given the benefit of an 'action replay', they would see just how often they reject children's answers, answers which are perfectly correct if somewhat unexpected, unusual and seemingly inappropriate. It is also vital that teachers using the techniques know the children well enough to anticipate how individual children are likely to react in the course of activities. Experience in Pilot School 1 would suggest that, even with the best of teachers, several 'pilot runs' may be necessary before teachers have sufficient expertise to get the most out of the activities.

When the techniques were introduced on the timetable, several members of staff showed an interest and decided to try out the activities in their lessons. Initially, success was limited. There had been little piloting of the techniques on any scale with children in the secondary school—at least, not to the knowledge of the writers—and teachers had little to guide them. The activities soon broke down when tried out with too large a group, or the whole class; teachers had a tendency to build in a writing component; discussion was too teacher-dominated; material was not always suitable and stimulating, sometimes being too long and sometimes too short; and the activities called for very skilful use of open questioning. With the cooperation of members of staff and the audio-visual technicians in the School of Education at the University, some lessons were video-taped for training purposes both in and out of school. These tapes have proven most useful in promoting deeper understanding of the mechanics of the techniques and in illustrating the outcomes of the activities.

To a large extent, children direct their own activities, they raise their own questions and make their own decisions as to the merits of the various answers suggested. They are encouraged to question one another's findings, to justify their responses, to explain what they have understood and to outline the course of their understanding. This greater involvement produces optimum learning conditions in which children may offer solutions in a friendly, unthreatening atmosphere. We would agree with Stauffer (1969) that the informality of the group situation, in which everyone is able to have a say, is an ideal setting for stimulating motivation. As the lack of motivation amongst average and below-average secondary pupils is a serious problem, this aspect in itself is surely a weighty argument in favour of using group activities.

In the group situations, children work through all aspects of language, reading, discussion, and especially listening, to explore and examine the reading material and to make inferences beyond literal comprehension. They share difficulties and insights instead of thinking in isolation.

To read critically and to gather information, one needs to exercise judgement on a text in order to be aware of the author's intentions. In the discussion, a crucial component of the activities, pupils learn to modify, reject or develop their own views and to weigh their judgements against those of others. It is hoped that, arising from discussion associated with the reading, children will acquire an open and impartial approach to the written word and will recognize ill-founded and unreasonable conclusions. All these abilities are needed in objective assessment of the relative merits of alternative texts and are so necessary for topic work, or for tasks which require children to consult several sources for information.

The above implicitly endorses the recommendations of the Bullock Committee that reading is a major strategy for learning and that a systematic provision is necessary for the growth of reading competence. At the same time, we feel that the activities help children at all age and ability levels in the secondary school. Small-group discussion involves all abilities from the least able, who may merely rephrase the ideas of others, to the most able who are constantly challenged and therefore 'forced' to put their case clearly and logically. It has been found that less able children are in a position to contribute to the discussion and to offer judgements. Children of very poor reading ability need never read aloud but may follow the open discussion, using this as an aid to understanding the text. The self-concepts of these children seem to have been enhanced since pupils are placed in a situation which credits them with expertise from the start, and which does not continuously draw attention to weaknesses. It is interesting to report that on occasions when groups assemble to thrash out their conclusions, less able children may feature prominently in the discussion, often advancing argument reached through the help of an abler child. On the other hand, the brighter child is taxed particularly, since his views are open to immediate scrutiny and evaluation by an interested and questioning audience. What about times when some children don't appear to be contributing much—at least in terms of actual participation? Admittedly there are such occasions, but this ought not to be taken to signify that silence means non-involvement. Some children may not have overtly taken up discussion but may have closely followed the discourse and would probably be able to recount the discussion and argument if so requested. This may be no mean achievement when participation in group activities is compared with participation in many class lessons.

Many secondary school teachers complain that pupils do not know how to gather information or to evaluate the merits of various books or pieces of information. They feel that pupils do not know how to make notes for future use and are unable to use reference and index systems. They insist that they do not have time to teach anything other than the content of their subject. By making sure that all teachers in the school are aware of and familiar with the framework of the reading programme, we hope to provide a basis on which to build. We would hope that the techniques used in the activities find their way into 'non-reading' lessons and that teachers will set tasks which call upon children to exercise and practise the abilities being developed in reading lessons.

6 Evaluative comments on the reading programme in Pilot School 1

The training and experience gained in the programme was intended to transcend discipline and subject boundaries through the process of transfer of abilities, and through using a wide range of reading material. Children apply their experiences to all sorts of situations and the inventiveness they display can surely be an inspiration for those who are trying to improve learning. Nevertheless, it is difficult to see at present how evidence of transfer is to be objectively evaluated in the absence of control groups. For instance, a scheme was run recently with lower-school groups in science where pupils were encouraged in the effective use of the school's resources centre to produce an extended piece of work. The resultant improvement was probably due to such a multiplicity of influences that the contribution of the reading programme was not able to be independently assessed. However, it may be taken as a measure of our opinion of the reading programme that we are reluctant to try to assess the impact of the activities by setting up experimental control groups in which children are denied the benefits of the experience.

It has not as yet been possible to evaluate objectively the programme and its effect. Suffice it to report that the teachers involved consider progress so far to have been most encouraging, so much so that the scale of the programme is to be enlarged in the next school year. A subjective spotcheck on reading competence across the curriculum after a term of group reading activities hinted that most children had certainly not been hindered in other subject areas by the activities, and some, notably in the range recognizably just above the traditional 'remedial' category, had improved especially. Opinion (again subjective) sounded in the third term suggested that this trend had continued, that some children who were also on limited withdrawal for remedial work were improving in and through group activities, and that the high-flyers were better able to contribute to work and thereby refine their own competences.

In general terms, the activities seem to generate involvement in reading as a social activity that is central to learning. When backed up by reminders of the similarities between listening and reading as learning procedures, one sees an improvement in listening ability in all concerned, teachers and pupils alike, especially through something like group SQ3R and reading for different purposes. Group prediction in particular seems to encourage a development of speech patterns. Discussion, given point in the activities, seems generally to have improved, and has attained specific importance in the mixed-ability teaching of writing, where a common task now takes on an individual significance when the preparation for the writing is broken down by small-group decision-making or solution-posing. There seems also to be a spin-off in techniques like punctuation from group sequencing, and in creative thinking about words from cloze—the spin-off supports the feeling of many teachers that many writing skills depend on reading habits. All these abilities combine in what is seen as better reading, not necessarily we feel just because of the precise implementation of the programme's ideas, but because the deeper implications of them for better learning, especially in a mixed-ability set-up, have been imperceptibly absorbed by teachers and children.

The children's response to the activities has been good: the degree of involvement has been high: performance in the activities has become astute and efficient: and there has been assiduous reading of novels when it has been the turn of a group for 'reading for pleasure', regarded as an important part of the reading programme and not merely as 'filling in the time'. While enthusiastic about the activities, we do not see them as a panacea for all ills, or pretend that there is 100 per cent involvement for 100 per cent of the time. We would merely claim that the level of purposeful involvement is higher than in most other reading situations encountered by participating members of staff. By building on the efforts of teachers in our feeder primary schools in the area to foster attitudes towards reading and the printed word, we hope to lead children to believe in the desirability of being able to read effectively when the occasion demands, and of enjoying the pleasure of reading for leisure. At the same time, by using material which is wide in subject content and by calling for a variety of responses, we hope that children will not see the work they do in the sessions as an amusing interlude between serious lessons. Rather, we hope that children will grow more sensitive to the occasions when they read, both for pleasure and as part of a lesson, so that they will recognize when it is appropriate to use the strategies developed in the activity sessions. Furthermore, by gradually diffusing the activities into the content areas of the curriculum, we hope that abilities initiated and developed in the activity sessions will be nurtured and regarded by the children as integral parts of the techniques used to study the subject in question.

One certainly sees an increased sensitivity in some teachers to the importance of language activities for the development of thought and reading competence, but one has to be wary of giving the impression of a general staff awareness of this aspect of education. There is still a feeling among some teachers that 'language across the curriculum' is a term that implies condescension by the English department towards others—and, no doubt, approaches to learning through specific reading activities come within this misapprehension. People hesitate and ask: reading development for what? If one is to improve reading, this should be in context, they say, and if one is to find reading material for the group activities that links with the literature stimulus in the normal course of lessons, one risks the danger of looking within literature only for material that serves a certain limited purpose. In other words, one may merely have a reading-activities-based alternative to thematic learning; and both may be forms of stultification if over used.

Allowing for mistakes, whether through caution or clumsiness, which have been made in learning how best to implement the activities, it is clear that the activities have a high probability of success because they involve a high degree of enjoyment by the children, and that in itself is a very important aim in education. At present, children encounter pretty explicitly the importance of language in learning across the curriculum: the activities contained in the programme seem a good way in for teachers to become fully aware of it as well.

Progress in the first year of the programme has been sufficiently impressive to warrant an expansion of the scheme. Consequently, it is proposed to continue with the scheme as it stands with children from year two upwards and to take all first-year children through a programme of activities designed to enable them to develop an awareness of their capabilities and limitations in learning. It is proposed to extend the range of activities to include practice in indexing, interpretation of graphic and pictorial representation, note-making and other activities recommended in the Scott Foresman *Reading Systems Programme*. In addition, all first-year children will follow a course prescribed by the SRA *Reading Laboratories*. In our concern to take steps to relate the programme to the efficient use of all school resources, we intend to site the activities in one of the school's resource areas and to use facilities and materials provided there.

To obtain an efficient and effective use of resources, a system of in-service training for both staff and pupils is envisaged. The time allocated for the programme is one hour per class each week, with three groups of twenty-five children being taken simultaneously in the resources area by three teachers, one of whom will be the teacher responsible for running the programme in its first year. The other teachers will come from the various subject areas. One hopes to see a proliferation of group activities into the routine learning experiences in a wide range of lessons across the curriculum. The school librarian is to play a prominent part in running the activities and assistance has already been offered from students in local teacher-training establishments. The hope too is that parents of pupils will also be available to help in much the same way as they have helped in leading groups of children in the reading lessons.

The overall impact of the reading programme on the school curriculum has been both subtle and marked. Children and teachers are growing more sensitive to using reading more strategically in learning. The programme has certainly earned its place in the timetable outside the time allocated to individual subjects and disciplines. Finally, there is more variety in the type of learning situation with an upsurge of group work and children learning with and through each other.

III Evaluation studies

Most teachers need little persuasion to try for themselves techniques which promise to facilitate life in the classroom, especially if only a little extra effort is all that is needed to produce quick and impressive results. The task of the curriculum-innovating agency is fairly straightforward in these circumstances, and consists chiefly of finding effective means of disseminating information. Teachers are understandably more hesitant to commit themselves when they are not clear whether the extra expenditure of effort will be justified in terms of results, particularly when there is little empirical evidence to support the approach being advocated.

It would not be honest for the members of the project team to claim that they are in a position to itemize with certainty all that is attained by participants in group discussion activities. Furthermore, there is no conclusive evidence that the techniques in their present state of development are worth the effort of introduction into subject areas of secondary school curricula. The team has repeatedly stressed this point whenever courses have been held to explain the activities. But this has not deterred the many teachers who have been excited by merely observing the responses which children make during the activities, nor those teachers who have mastered the techniques. 'I don't need any further proof to convince me,' said one teacher who had just been introduced to the activities by watching a video-tape of a group prediction exercise, 'I can see for myself. It's obvious!' Such enthusiasm, while encouraging, is quite properly insufficient to entice busy teachers to try out the activities.

Nor would it be truthful to claim that the very real difficulties reported by teachers in preparing suitable materials for the activities have been overcome. Individual teachers and isolated groups are working away at this problem in a number of schools without any central agency to coordinate efforts and to enable some sharing of experiences and resources. Plans to develop the techniques within subject areas in the secondary school have been drawn up to initiate curriculum development work in Nottinghamshire, Derbyshire and Lincolnshire. However, for the moment there are only the subjective reports of a handful of teachers to support group discussion activities, alongside evidence from a few small-scale investigations.

Some of the teachers on the in-service course mentioned in section II were invited to cooperate in carrying out a pilot examination of the effects of the activities on pupils' learning. Individual teachers carried out separate experiments, each study being unsupervised and involving materials and assessment tests produced by those teachers concerned. Procedure was similar in every case. Two groups of children from the same class were matched for general reading ability. One group completed a group discussion activity on a passage, while children in the other group, working individually, read the passage and had a comprehension test on it. A fortnight later, both groups were given the comprehension test which had been previously given to one group only, but on this occasion the children were not allowed to refer to the passage. The relative performance of both groups of children was noted, then the entire procedure was repeated using a second passage. This time the group tasks were interchanged so that the group which had previously examined the passage through a comprehension exercise now completed a group discussion exercise, and the other group now tackled a comprehension test. Results were again examined.

Teachers who carried out the investigations were quick to point out that there were serious flaws in the design and conduct of the inquiry. They emphasized that a test comprised mainly of factual recall is hardly the criterion they would have chosen to establish the worth of techniques which have the explicit aim of encouraging a broader evaluative response to reading; the preponderance of questions in the comprehension tests were at a literal level and merely called for recall of isolated snippets of the passage rather than for general inferential ability; finally, the interval between testings was so short that children who had been examined only a fortnight earlier could easily remember previous answers.

In spite of these deficiencies, the 'comprehension' groups performed generally no better than 'activity' groups. It would be entirely redundant at this point to introduce numerous tables to emphasize the parity in performance between groups. However, by way of illustration, Tables 9.1 and 9.2 (p. 260) present results obtained in two schools, one junior and one secondary.

It can be seen from Table 9.1 that children in groups which had seen the test before performed slightly better than those who had not, but not significantly so in statistical terms.

It may be seen in Table 9.2 that the secondary school children in the

Table 9.1   Mean 'no passage' comprehension test scores (junior children)

	'Activity' group		Comprehension test group	
Passage 1	(Group A)	6.3	(Group B)	7.6
Passage 2	(Group B)	6.6	(Group A)	7.8

Group A: n = 10   Group B: n = 10
(scores out of 10)

Table 9.2   Mean 'no passage' comprehension test scores (secondary children)

	'Activity' group		Comprehension test group	
Passage 1	(Group A)	7.7	(Group B)	7.3
Passage 2	(Group B)	7.2	(Group A)	5.8

Group A: n = 8   Group B: n = 8
(scores out of 11)

activity groups were slightly better than children in the comprehension test groups, but again the differences are not statistically
significant.

These results were obtained using very small samples and do not
really indicate the possible value of the activities. Nevertheless, any
school which wishes to assess for itself one aspect of the activities
could easily follow the above procedure (heeding, of course, the
advice to extend the interval between tests and to provide
comprehension questions at different levels).

A more carefully controlled investigation has been carried out by
Clarke (1977). A science teacher in a very large comprehensive school
in Nottinghamshire, he was interested to discover the effect of group
discussion activities on children's reading and understanding of
worksheets in chemistry practical lessons. Three A-stream forms in
the third year had chemistry lessons, one per week, over a three-week
period. Children were required to follow information and instructions presented on worksheets in order to carry out laboratory
experiments using apparatus and chemicals. The usual procedure in
lessons in the school is for pupils to read worksheets carefully for five
minutes, asking questions as necessary before starting experiments.
All three classes followed this procedure in the first week of the
inquiry.

However, in the second week each form tackled its assignment in a
different way: one group followed the usual routine, read the sheet
then started the experiment; a second group of children also followed
this routine, but in addition inspected copies of tests they were to be
set at the end of the lesson; children in the third group were handed

Table 9.3 Total number of questions asked and errors noted during lessons in weeks 2 and 3

	Questions about:			Errors in procedure
	procedure	facts	understanding	
Normal lesson (control group)	9	8	0	7
Sequencing group	4	0	1	10
Comprehension preview group	8	2	1	11

worksheets which had been cut into 11–13 pieces and their task was to work in pairs to reassemble individual worksheets into a satisfactory order before carrying out lesson assignments (several orderings were appropriate). Performance was assessed in three ways:

1   an observation schedule was used by a colleague of Clarke's to monitor the incidence of occasions when children had to seek information from the teacher, and of the errors made during the sessions;
2   an attitude test was given at the end of the entire investigation to test response to the activities;
3   a written test was given at the end of lessons, one aspect measuring pupils' recall of what they had done while a different aspect tested children's understanding of the principles of chemistry brought out during the experiments.

One week later the entire procedure adopted in the second week was repeated but, whereas the first group still followed the usual routine (control group), the two experimental groups now exchanged places so that the group which had previously sequenced the worksheet now had prior information of test questions, and the other group now carried out the sequencing activity.

Although results were obtained from a sample of only fifty-five children, they are nevertheless quite informative.[1] Turning first to children's behaviour during the sessions (observation schedule), it is interesting to note that over the three-week period children grew familiar with the format of lessons and they needed to ask fewer questions. Table 9.3, above, presents a general summary of the

[1] Clarke discussed performance in relation to only those children who were present in all three lessons. Hence, the overall population was reduced to fifty-five children.

number of times questions were asked, together with details of the number of errors of procedure recorded in sessions. Information for week 1 has been omitted as there was nothing in the general achievement to separate groups and the first session served mainly to establish baselines for attainment.

Although there is little to choose between the 'preview' groups and control groups when it came to procedure ('What do I do now, Sir?'), children who had sequenced the instructions seemed much more certain of what to do and asked half as many questions. Having a preview of the test dramatically reduced the number of 'fact' questions ('Is that what I have to record?'), as did the sequencing experience; the control group's behaviour was much more in line with what chemistry teachers might expect, with children asking many questions which could easily have been answered by careful reference to worksheets.

Despite the fact that at least one group of children knew during each assignment that they were to be questioned about understanding chemistry, only one question was asked by children about this in the three lessons. Clarke reported that it was as if all children were treating worksheets as they would an instruction manual, and that neither experimental activity overcame this tendency. He was struck by the notion that the format of the worksheets probably encouraged this trend and that he would have to try to avoid this in future. Although it would appear that the control group made fewer errors of procedure, it has to be borne in mind that this was almost certainly due to the fact that children in the group questioned the teacher much more on matters of procedure.

A science teacher with no training in the teaching of reading might be expected to question the value of starting a chemistry practical lesson with a reading activity. However, Clarke felt that this would be justified if children were to end up with a clearer grasp of worksheets giving instructions and directions in chemistry experiments. He predicted that the extra few minutes required to perform a reading activity would be compensated for. On the basis of recordings on his observation schedule and from his impressions of the lessons, he concluded that this hypothesis was correct. He felt that pupils who had sequenced and discussed worksheets had a better overview of the assigned tasks and a clearer realization of the continuity of the separate stages in the procedure.

Children's attitudes to the activities were gathered using a questionnaire. Pupils were requested to try to gauge how much they had been helped by the activities (both sequencing and previewing the tests), and to rate how enjoyable and useful they had found the activities. Although children felt that participating in the sequencing helped them to follow the procedure, they were divided on its usefulness. A small number of children definitely disliked sequenc-

Table 9.4 Average differences between scores predicted on the basis of performance in week 1 and scores actually obtained in weeks 2 and 3

		Week 2		Week 3	
		mean	s.d.	mean	s.d.
Group 1	Recall	−0.23	1.80	−0.92	2.92
(n = 20)	Understanding	−0.14	2.45	−1.50**	2.67
		Normal		Normal	
Group 2	Recall	0.36	1.92	−0.49	2.49
(n = 15)	Understanding	0.71	2.92	2.06**	2.77
		Sequencing		Test Preview	
Group 3	Recall	0.05	1.46	1.29*	2.21
(n = 20)	Understanding	−0.39	2.21	0.05	1.17
		Test Preview		Sequencing	

*$p < .05$ **$p < .01$

ing; they felt that it was an unnecessary burden and a waste of time—practical chemistry is a favourite lesson, and sequencing reduced the amount of time available for experimentation and using apparatus. On a closer analysis of results, Clarke found that this disfavour had been expressed mainly by intelligent boys. While the latter considered sequencing an encumbrance, girls, and especially the less intelligent, thought sequencing was very enjoyable and useful in promoting understanding of the worksheets and the steps which needed to be followed during the experiments.

Scores obtained in the first week were used to predict performance in the second and third weeks. Predicted scores were calculated using a regression analysis and then the differences between these and the scores that were actually obtained were calculated (residual scores). The average residual scores for recall and understanding for each group are presented in Table 9.4. Negative scores indicate poorer performance than predicted, while positive scores tell of better performance. The results may be summarized as follows:

1 *Testing of recall of procedure and facts in week 2*
  Differences between children's performance in the three groups are not statistically significant (one-way analysis of variance). The performance of children in the sequencing group was slightly better than predicted, and a little better than that of children in the other groups.
2 *Testing of understanding of principles of chemistry in week 2*
  Differences between children's performance in the three groups

are not statistically significant. Children in the sequencing group did rather better than predicted while children in the other two groups achieved less than predicted.

3   *Testing of recall of procedure and facts in week 3*
Differences between children's performance in the three groups are statistically significant at the .05 level. Performance of children in the sequencing group is significantly better than predicted (.05 level), whereas that of children in the other groups was worse than predicted.

4   *Testing of understanding of principles of chemistry in week 3*
Difference between performance of the three groups is quite significant (.01 level). Children in the test-preview group did significantly better than predicted (.01 level), while children in the control group did much worse (.01 level). Children in the sequencing group performed almost exactly as predicted.

Although the results of this study show only marginal advantage to those children who had approached practical work by discussion of worksheets, conduct in the lessons seems to support Clarke's claim that pupils had been surer and more positive in following instructions.

IV Conclusions

It is clear from the response to the work in Pilot School 1 that, when teachers have the opportunity to see these comprehension activities being operated over a period, they are impressed by what they take to be their potential and they are anxious to try them out for themselves. It is also apparent from the reports of the study groups that when they do so they are generally not disappointed. Lessons usually go with a swing, despite the reservations noted on page 253, and the pupils ask for more. Above all, there is whole-hearted involvement and the stronger pupils are stretched as much as the weaker.

Against this we have to concede that, so far, we have little positive evidence that group discussion exercises lead to significant improvements in reading comprehension as measured by tests or, more importantly, as assessed in the context of the normal work of the curriculum. On a priori grounds, we would expect such an improvement because of the role of reflection in reading which we emphasized in Chapter 2. Well-chosen exercises make the pupil think, and the discussion sessions seem to prove to him that he can think. But such a priori argument is not proof.

There is a second important limitation to the work reported in the present chapter. For the most part these exercises were carried out on a fairly small scale. They were new to the pupils and often new to the teachers. Was the enthusiasm no more than a natural response to the stimulus of novelty? The more protracted experience of Pilot School 1 suggests that it was not. Nevertheless, even here the experience is too short to allow one to say what importance should be attached to these techniques in successive years or how they can be integrated for use in the context of different subjects.

In this context the interest of Clarke's study is considerable. The sequencing was devised and executed in the context of a science lesson. It was brief and it was relevant. Far from detracting from the value of the practical work and its impact, it led to an actual improvement in results—by comparison with the control lessons. Results in the post-test were indeed comparable with those gained by students who had actually seen the test itself before, and who therefore knew what questions to expect. Finally, children who had had the sequencing experience asked fewer questions during the practical work that ensued and were evidently more positive in following instructions.

Clearly more work needs to be done. It is an indication of the interest aroused by the pilot work carried out in this project that the Schools Council have readily provided funds for a further inquiry in the course of which it will be possible to extend all of the work reported here.[1]

Appendix

Sample passages used for group discussion activities

Group cloze: extract from *New York to Paris* by Charles A. Lindbergh

Now I'm flying above the foam-lined coast, searching for prominent features to fit the chart on my knees. I've climbed to 2,000 feet so I can see the contours of the country better. The mountains are old and rounded, and farms small and stony. Rain-glistened dirt roads wind narrowly through hills and fields. Below me lies a great tapering bay, a long-bouldered island, a village. Yes, there's a place on the chart where it all fits—line of ink on line of shore—Valentia and Dingle Bay, on the south-western coast of Ireland. I can hardly believe it's true. I'm almost exactly on my route, closer than I'd hoped to come in my wildest dreams.

The southern tip of ____! On course, over two ____ ahead of schedule, the ____ still well up in ____sky, the weather clearing! ____ circle again, fearful that ____ wake to find this ____ phantom, a mirage fading ____ mid-Atlantic mist. But ____ no question about it. ____ detail on the chart ____ its counterpart below; each ____ feature on the ground ____ its symbol on the ____. The lines correspond exactly. ____ spiral lower, looking down ____ the little village. There ____ boats in the harbour, ____ on the stone-fenced roads. ____ are running out into ____ streets, looking up and ____. This is earth again, ____ earth where I've lived ____ now will live once ____. Here are human beings, ____ a human welcome. Not ____ single

[1] Reading for Learning in the Secondary School.

detail is wrong. _____ never seen such beauty _____, fields so green, people _____ human, a village so _____, mountains and rocks so _____ and rocklike.

Group prediction: *Nightmare*

1   It was no use! The painted lady wasn't going to save him. Desperately, Midge clutched at her wavy hair but it was hard and slippery, a tawdry gold like the mane of a roundabout horse.

His inside felt full of water. It must be sweat brought on by the nightmare he was in. He was dreaming that he was drowning and bodies floated around him.

2   He had got to break out of this nightmare, got to wake up. He wanted to shout out to the painted lady but another great gush of salt water made him shout and splutter. As for the painted lady, all she could do was to stare blankly as if she too had been hit on the head. She heaved up and down and if Midge had not been choking he would have begged her to keep still.

3   Swimming as best he could, fighting his way through the surging water, he struggled to get clear of the wreck. He knew that if he did not he would be sucked down by the ship. Worn out though he was, his lungs choking, he made a frantic effort. He was vaguely aware of a figure thrashing helplessly near him. Muffled voices were shouting wildly. A great baulk of timber came charging past him. A man was striving to cling to it and at the same time held out a hand to the boy as he too tried to grab a hold.

4   The sea rose and severed all contact between them. Midge sank suffocatingly below the surface. He fought his way up again and saw another baulk of timber. The huge log bore near and somehow Midge managed to hoist himself onto it.

He was chilled to the bone, drenched, half-stunned, aching in every part of his body. Face pressed to the heaving timber, he allowed himself to be swept on in the bruising sea.

5   Slowly, he emerged from the nightmare. This was no dream! He was drowning! Only that stunning blow on his head had prevented his realizing it before. The painted lady of his confused state was the figure-head of the sailing ship *Pandora* in which he had been serving. She had foundered on the rocks near the Cornish coast and was now plunging down for the last time.

Before drifting once more into unconsciousness, he made an effort to see if any of his shipmates were still alive.

6   'My dear parents,' Midge wrote, 'I was lucky beyond words. I was washed unconscious, onto some rocks and rescued by local fishermen. They have cared for me and soon I will be well enough to make the journey home. It seems a miracle that I survived but today I heard the news of another survivor who was found further up the coast. I'm sure he feels as I do, that we are both very fortunate fellows.'

10

What the School Can Do: Instances of Current Practice

Eric Lunzer[1]

I How the survey was conducted

What can be done in the secondary school to improve the quality of learning across the curriculum? What should be done?

Both these questions are central to the present inquiries. They are not at all the same. The first may be answered in terms of the outcome of psychological and pedagogical experimentation in the widest sense. It is about what we can teach, how we can set about teaching it, and with what expectation of success. The second is a question of cost, especially in terms of curriculum-time. If we elect to provide instruction and experiences of the sort that will help our students to inform themselves about science or history (say) by choosing and reading appropriate books or pamphlets, we must be prepared to allocate time for these purposes. Is it time well spent? Very early in the course of our inquiries, we noted that many teachers were unconvinced. Senior teachers of science and mathematics in particular were apt to argue that reading is not a very reliable way to introduce a topic, nor was it an especially effective way of acquiring information for most children of school age.[2]

The first question, what can be done given the will, is of course very pertinent to the second. Suppose it could be shown that certain sorts of approach to learning through reading result in a marked enhancement in motivation, in a noticeable increase in self-informing of all sorts, for instance through television, and in consequent gains in the quality of learning in a particular subject. A teacher who was aware of the potential of these approaches would surely be willing to 'spend' more of the available teaching time on them than one who was ignorant of them or sceptical of their efficacy.

There is no tried and tested approach to learning through reading which can be recommended without reservation. Nevertheless, there

[1] With the collaboration of John Cole, Terry Dolan, Keith Gardner and Colin Harrison.
[2] Cf. Chapter 2, p. 7.

267

are a number of ideas and techniques which are currently being developed in schools, and while one cannot make definitive judgements about their effectiveness and their implications, one can at least outline their rationale: what some teachers hope to achieve and why. Nor is it difficult in particular to discover something about the cost: why the methods that are approved by some are neglected by others.

In order to enable the teacher to arrive at informed interim decisions (pending the results of further experimental work in schools) about what can be done and what should be done, it seemed to us essential to establish what were the solutions presently being adopted by schools, and, especially, to report on what was being achieved or attempted in schools where the headteacher and staff were particularly sensitive to the potential value of reading. (The resources available to us were too limited to allow us to carry out a full survey of reading for learning in a representative group of schools across the country.)

Thus the present chapter has the limited aim of giving some indication of the state of thinking and practice among forward-looking teachers in 1974–5 (i.e. immediately before the publication of the Bullock Report).

All local education authorities in England and Wales were written to in May 1974 with an invitation (a) to report on the degree of interest in reading for learning among the schools in their authority and (b) to provide a list of schools which they knew to have a special commitment to reading and whose work might be of interest to the team. Between thirty and forty replies were received, of which fifteen stated that they were unable to nominate schools that stood out in the way indicated. After careful examination of the remainder, it was decided to visit only a few areas, to allow sufficient time to visit more than one school in each area, to talk to several teachers in each school, and to see examples of their work. In the event, seven such visits were made, including a total of fifteen schools. Had our own request not coincided with local government reorganization, we might have obtained more positive returns. Perhaps, too, the LEAs concerned would have been more aware of the total picture within their authorities.

It should be emphasized that all possible steps were taken to enhance the probability that the schools we visited would be representative of that minority—and it certainly was a minority—for whom the role of reading in the pupil's learning appeared to be especially important. Whenever a school had been specifically named by one of the selected authorities, that school was included in the programme of visits—unless the relevant work was confined to the use of laboratories, which was to be the subject of an independent report (see Chapter 8), or to imaginative work with poor readers (specifically excluded from our own terms of reference), or it was apparently duplicated in other schools that had already been visited. The many exchanges we have had both with teachers and with inspectors since the completion of the inquiry tend to confirm the impression that, before the publication of the Bullock Report, few schools were prepared to recognize that the need to enhance the effectiveness of reading is one which cuts across most subject boundaries if not all. Those that were visited were certainly among the most concerned, and they were probably fairly representative of such schools.

The remainder of this chapter consists of five sections.

Section II is an overview of the impressions gained from visits to the fifteen schools referred to above, and especially from discussions with the staff of these schools. This is followed by a more detailed statement and discussion of a general policy as formulated in one of the schools concerned.

In Section III we present a few select examples of worksheets, since it was found that in the majority of schools it was the worksheet which best embodied the policy of reading for learning.

Section IV is short, and describes some of the more systematic attempts to teach study skills, efforts which were usually confined to work with sixth-form students.

In Section V we reproduce two interviews taken in a single school in Derbyshire, one which was found to be sufficiently enterprising and innovative to merit singling out in this report, especially in relation to the steps that were taken to implement the policies of encouraging individualized learning through language across the curriculum.

The last section presents a summary of the whole together with a few concluding comments and some reservations bearing on the particular time at which the survey was made.

II Reading across the curriculum

1 Teaching comprehension or bypassing it

Chapter 2 contains a fairly lengthy discussion of the problems of comprehension in reading: why do some readers find it difficult to come to terms with some of the texts they encounter or even with most of them?

Because oral communication is usually face to face, the situation is partly under the listener's control. He can ask questions and have things repeated or explained. A page in a book cannot be changed nor can it easily be augmented—though one can come back to it as often as one needs. To anyone who is unused to learning by reading, the printed page is sometimes a difficult medium of information. If one wishes to encourage pupils to make more use of printed material, one must be prepared to help them to cope with the problems they will encounter. One must therefore be aware of those features of text that contribute to its difficulty: technical and semi-technical vocabulary, abstract ideas, density of presentation, imperfect matching between the importance of an idea and the amount of space devoted to it, and so on. And of course one must have resources to help pupils overcome these obstacles.

In the course of the present survey, it was apparent that a number of schools were alert to these problems, albeit a minority. One of the most striking instances was a small secondary modern school in Norfolk. Teachers here were aware of the difficulty experienced by fluent 'decoders' when asked to learn from text. In particular, they had noted the problems often experienced with the language of Nuffield Science texts. There was also a substantial number of children who could apparently cope with the reading demands of other subjects but who were often unable to make sense of their reading in mathematics. Because they were aware of these difficulties, teachers in this school would frequently attempt to iron out problems of understanding in a given text before requiring their pupils to read it and use it in their work. Preliminary work of this kind was especially frequent when worksheets were used to supplement printed texts.

There were other instances where the use of reading for learning was promoted in some way throughout the pupil's schooling and in several subjects. Such was the case in a school in Cornwall where the methods chosen ranged from SRA Laboratories to instruction in note-taking. In discussing the problems with the visiting team, the Deputy Headmistress herself suggested the importance of distinguishing between three types of reading response, all of which needed to be encouraged: a surface level, a logical level and a critical level. The distinctions she had in mind were clearly akin to those that were embodied in our own tests of comprehension (Chapter 3) and especially to the distinction between literal comprehension and word meaning on the one hand and inference or evaluation on the other.

The same teacher, like a number of others, expressed the belief that laboratory materials are perhaps more useful in promoting literal comprehension than in encouraging thinking. To achieve the latter, she advocated an insistence on planning in the preparation of written work. It will be recalled from the last two chapters that the research team favoured, additionally, the use of group discussion and the preparation of summaries, whether oral or written.

It was clear that in this school, the enthusiasm of the Deputy Headmistress was communicated to several other members of staff. One of these was the Head of History who was convinced of the importance of reading in her subject, and especially of the differing demands of reading in literature (response to text) and in history (extracting factual information).[1]

At this point it should be noted that it was rare to find uniformity in any one school. More often, even in those schools which stood out for their interest in the problems of reading for learning, only a few teachers had elaborated their own techniques for reducing some of these problems. Thus in one school in Kirklees, the Head of Biology was particularly alive to the importance of language both as a mode of acquiring information and as a medium for its expression. He had constructed his own worksheets for teaching mixed-ability groups, drawing on experience gained in a previous post when he had been assisted in this task by members of the English department.

In the same school, however, the present Head of English was by no means committed to a policy of extending the use of reading for learning. Like many other teachers of English to whom we spoke, he believed in encouraging children to read, but this was mainly in the context of his own subject, as was apparent from his advocacy of a reading-improvement workshop based on good literary material.

This teacher was not in favour of SRA, for he found these materials too restricting. But he had little to offer in its place, and even gave it as his opinion that children learned note-taking by taking notes—a view which would doubtless be correct if taken as a description of what actually transpired, not just in this school, but in most schools in Britain at the time of this survey.

At the same school, the Head of Science expressed the view that reading as a means of learning is neither efficient nor effective. Instead he insisted on the importance of experiment in the learning of science. Few would question this emphasis, but here it was apparent that the potential of the written medium as an aid to learning in science was largely unrealized. Also in this school, the Head of Maths eschewed the use of textbooks and so was able to report that language problems did not arise. By contrast, the Head of History was insistent that the use of document extends the pupil's thinking as well as his awareness of language. Reading in history frequently presented problems to the average and even to the able pupil, but these problems were seen as a worthwhile challenge.

Uniformity of view is perhaps undesirable. It was nevertheless a little surprising to find so much disagreement about the importance of reading and its role in promoting learning even in schools which had been signalled as particularly committed to just such an emphasis. Thus, whereas in several schools the headteacher and the head of English were both concerned about the role of reading across

---

[1] Yet, disappointingly, while note-taking was encouraged, it was not taught, since this was thought to be a skill which appeared as a function of general intellectual development.

the curriculum, there were an equal number in which the emphasis within the department of English was limited to promoting reading of any sort, without special regard to the needs of colleagues in other departments, or even deliberately confined to the reading of fiction. Similarly, while no less than five schools advocated the use of SRA either in the first year, or in the fourth year (as an aid to note-taking), or both, at least an equal number of English departments were critical of this approach. Few, it should be added, were able to offer anything substantial in its place, confining themselves to a generally supportive attitude and, in one case, grading all books in the school for readability.[1]

2 Reading in science

Among heads of science to whom we spoke, two were thoroughly convinced of the need to teach the language of science in its widest sense and were also aware of the initial and continued difficulty posed by ignorance of this language. Because these teachers and their colleagues were dissatisfied with the books available, their commitment to learning through reading, alongside observation and experiment, led them to make up their own worksheets. Some examples of worksheets will be given in the next section, together with some considerations governing their construction and use.

At this point it should be added that the problems posed by the language of science are not confined to vocabulary or to the difficulties of coming to terms with an impersonal 'register' (see p. 21). Difficulties include the need to adapt to a language of instructions (e.g. what steps are needed to assemble a particular bit of apparatus), which is generally a great deal more dense, i.e. less predictable than most narrative styles. They also include the need to recognize when the sequence of what is written parallels a necessary sequence either in the events that are described or in the steps that are prescribed, and when that sequence is of a 'rhetorical' or stylistic nature. Examples of the former class might be a description of the life cycle of some organism or a statement of the steps that must be taken to set up an experiment. A fairly common instance of the latter might take the form: statement of principle, followed by restatement (often in less rigorous terms), as an aid to interpretation, followed by one or more examples (Becker, 1965).

Difficulties of vocabulary are not restricted to 'pure' technical terms like *centimetre, pipette, alkali,* or *chlorophyll,* all of which are necessarily taught. Most have both a technical and a non-technical connotation, e.g. *salt, gravity, mass, force,* or are best thought of as semi-technical, e.g. *control, hypothesis, increase, rate.*

[1] The limitations of this approach, as noted previously, are that the same book often incorporates wide variations in readability (in the strict sense of Chapter 4) and also in what might be termed comprehensibility (in the wider sense of the present chapter).

The last four examples could serve as a reminder that while some ways of stressing language in teaching science are in fact counter-productive, in that they attach an exaggerated importance to the repetition of verbal formulae, this is not true of all such approaches. Thus any attempt to teach the meanings of words like *control* and *hypothesis* is likely to entail a move away from the rote-learning of experiments and towards an appreciation of scientific problems and scientific methods, at least at an initial level. The difficulty of the principle of controlling variables in experimentation is well attested by subsequent research since the problem was first signalled by Inhelder and Piaget in their work on *The Growth of Logical Thinking from Childhood to Adolescence* (1958). There are similar problems in coming to terms with the relations between trends in two variables, for example (especially) proportionality, with rate of increase, and later with change in rate of increase, etc. In cases such as these, in the extent to which one can resolve the language problem, one will perforce have tackled the problems of conceptualization.

3 Reading in mathematics

Most teachers of mathematics to whom we spoke tended to avoid reading as far as they could, although there were a few exceptions. Thus the majority were highly critical of the SMP numbered series, because its presentation was felt to be too verbal. More specifically, the series is too abstract in its choice of examples and its language is too formal to be acceptable to more than a minority of pupils in a comprehensive secondary school. A number of teachers preferred the lettered series, while others had chosen to rely on the Scottish mathematics material or on SMILE, which is a workcard approach in which the use of language is held down to a minimum.

This was the approach taken in the school featured in section V of this chapter where the Deputy Head, himself a mathematics specialist, was not only concerned about the role of language in science as well as mathematics, but was actively engaged in trying to find ways of making language a facilitator of learning rather than a barrier. We were able to observe a double period of mathematics during which the pupils were working on their own on different assignments, and also to talk to the Head of Mathematics. In the first years, and also more generally for poorer readers, he aimed to reduce the amount of language and also to simplify it. Instead of using a formal language to define the concepts and operations in any topic or structure, concrete situations were introduced so that the pupils would be able to work through the material. In so doing it was hoped they would come to at least a practical understanding. While this teacher recognized that mathematics could not progress without the construction of a precise notation system and an equally careful meta-language, it did not follow that these should figure prominently at the initial stages. Therefore, at least until the third year, formal language was deliberately eschewed.

However, a somewhat different emphasis was noted in a school in Yorkshire where the Head of Maths deliberately incorporated a large language element into the course which he had developed for pupils not entering for public examinations. His concern was to bring out the mathematical content inherent in real situations. Thus, when dealing with the theme of travel, the materials he used included technical magazines, AA books, timetables, brochures, and maps or atlases. The children would be challenged to interpret the material, to find out what it meant in terms of what a traveller must do to reach his destination, then to establish the relevant mathematical relations, and finally to complete the necessary calculations to resolve any outstanding questions. If this teacher thought that any mathematical terms were alien and off-putting, he still made it his business to teach such terms if he thought that they were mathematically important.

Both the teachers described were outstanding not merely as teachers of mathematics but also in their concern for the role of language in mathematics learning. The solutions which they adopted differed radically. But it may be that, paradoxically, what separates them is not so much their attitude to language but their attitude to mathematics: what each sees as most important, especially for the less able and less motivated student. The first teacher stresses the use of concrete apparatus to support an initial coming to terms with pure mathematics, while the second is more concerned with inculcating an appreciation of the relevance of mathematics. What they share is a concern to avoid a formalized language and a formal approach.

4 Reading in the social sciences

While teachers in this area were understandably more favourable to learning from books than teachers of mathematics, they too showed a wide range of practice and beliefs. Thus, attitudes of history teachers varied from those who thought reading purposes in history were indistinguishable from reading purposes in English through those who insisted on the importance of giving children access to primary sources, to one who was quite explicit about the importance of providing a variety of materials at all levels. He was Head of History at a school in London to which reference has been made earlier. Here the teaching of social studies was planned in such a way as to make the fullest use of a wide variety of resources. Typically, pupils would work in groups and every group would visit each of four 'stations' in the course of a sequence of lessons: a slide/tape station, a tape/headphone station, a reading/workcard station, and a discussion station at which the teacher was also present. Workcards were provided to give purpose to the activities at each of the stations. The use of workcards in connection with the utilization of reading resources was advocated by more than one teacher in this subject group. One example was a history teacher in a Cornish school who had found that children could be helped to acquire skill in making notes by having their attention directed to salient points.

This last point is clearly valid in a general sense. Making notes is an open-ended task. For without an adequate comprehension of the whole, the reader would be unable to select key sentences and phrases. It therefore requires a high degree of comprehension. It may also involve paraphrasing key sentences, or substituting a juxtaposition of key concepts for the sentence form, or even making a diagrammatic representation of the relations between such key concepts. Finally, it may involve rearranging the points that have been selected. Workcards do offer the pupil a more structured task. Most of these things have either been done for him or (rightly or wrongly) they are not required in the finished product. This means that the pupil has to do just a few things instead of many. It also means that he is pointed in the right direction for doing each thing.

The question remains: what can we as teachers most usefully require the pupil to do at any given point in his learning of a particular topic, having regard both to his knowledge of the area in question and to his general competence as a reader and as a learner? This question cannot be answered with any assurance without purpose-directed research. As yet, there is no set of rules that are well founded on valid research and at the same time sufficiently practical to commend themselves to the teacher-user. There is thus a clear case for a programme of research aimed at establishing just how we can best promote the competences which students would require to enable them to inform themselves from whatever resources are to hand, including especially the printed word, without constant intervention and direction from the teacher. What are the props that the teacher needs to supply to begin with, and in what order may they be removed?

As at present, such questions can be answered only at the level of intuitive hunches. But even a hunch is better than nothing. And it has indeed been shown experimentally that students are better at recalling those features of any complex which they have actually used in solving a problem. For instance, given a set of pictures, for example a knife, a horse, an apple, a book, a pear, a church, children who are asked to categorize them into three groups are more likely to remember the items than other children who are simply asked to memorize them (Smirnov and Zinchenko, 1969). So if we ask pupils to supply the key word in each of ten sentences and if these sentences and the gaps in them have both been selected in such a way as to isolate just those things that are most central to the purpose of the lesson concerned, our teaching method is not without theoretical and experimental justification. And in practice it works quite well.

Just the same, we might ask: would it not be equally possible to give the pupil a set of propositions (in the form of sentences or parts of sentences) and ask him to knock out the least significant ones, then the ones which contribute least thereafter, and so on, until he arrives at the list of sentences which we, in the other exercise, have preselected? Might not such a procedure lead to a more general kind of learning—even at the cost of some sacrifice in the specific theme concerned (in that the pupil's selection might be less ideal than that of the teacher)?

Even this last procedure presupposes that the teacher has preselected various sentences from which the deletion is to be made. But the cutting-up itself is a challenging task, and this too is one which brings the student right up against the problem of reflecting on the material and identifying what it contains that is new and significant and what revision he should make to his thinking in the light of that understanding.

There is therefore a wide range of questions that one can ask the pupils just as there is a wide variety of passages which one can set before them. For it is obvious that a task which is demanding in relation to one passage may be easy in relation to another, either because the passage is easier or because the reader is more familiar with the topic. These considerations suggest that the variety of tasks used in workcards and worksheets might possibly be increased, but that careful thought should be given to the question of what task should be appropriate at any point in the pupil's learning. At least one instance of this sort of planning was found in our sample and this will be reported on below.

5 A policy for a school

In concluding this section, it is of interest to reproduce a written policy statement produced by one headteacher[1] as a first stage in establishing staff investigation of the implications of a reading policy across the curriculum.

LEARNING TO READ AND READING TO LEARN

1 *Philosophy*

1.1 One of the major causes of our educational difficulties lies in the very low reading standards of the large bulk of our pupils, whether judged by nationally standardised tests (for all their limitations) or by the nearer and sharper test of our pupils' inability to cope with much of even the simplest written material we put before them. The ability to handle language competently is necessary for a large part of learning, and conversely, the large part of learning is itself a vehicle for the pupil to extend his or her personal language. We are concerned not only with our pupils' learning to read, but also with the fact that they need reading to learn.

[1] Mr Michael Marland, Headmaster of Woodberry Down School, London.

1.2 The ability to read at the highest possible level is essential to the individual's personal growth in the modern world, his ability to benefit from most of the learning opportunities at school, and his ability to take his place in society. The school must therefore take the teaching of reading and language very seriously.

1.3 Behaviour and adjustment problems not only lead to difficulties in learning to read, but, and this is less widely realized, the reverse is also true: reading difficulties are a frequent cause of difficulties of behaviour.

1.4 Pupils having difficulty with language must have the unhampered opportunity in those subjects in which reading and writing play a lesser part. On the other hand, it is unfair to ask the English teachers to carry the entire burden, bad psychology to encourage the pupils to think that good writing matters only in English, and a pity to miss the opportunity to help pupils learn in other contexts.

2 Complementary approaches

2.1 The over-riding concern of the English Department is for the quality of language. Teachers of English should include in their work the methodical extension of their pupils' handling of language at all levels. (This is picked up, to some extent, in the sixth form by the General Studies team.)

2.2 The specialized and intensive work of the Remedial Department is carried out in smaller groups with approximately the least able 15 per cent. This is picked up in the middle school by the 'support' options.

2.3 Individual help is further given by the Reading Centre to selected pupils outside the group helped by the Remedial Department.

2.4 The fourth approach is potentially most important: only a whole-school policy can hope to succeed significantly. The teaching of speaking, reading, and writing is therefore an important part of every teacher's responsibility, including his or her tutorial role. It is the job of every teacher to ensure that a pupil understands what he teaches, and therefore if he uses any print material, it is his responsibility to make sure that it is understood from the text (i.e. not merely by the teacher's shortcircuiting the text by alternative verbal explanation).

3 Classroom procedures

3.1 Reading—We must not react to low reading standards by retreating from print. Essentially we should see all pupils, from the youngest and least able struggling with the first steps of letter recognition to our oldest sixth formers making out a closely argued historical text or a Nuffield A-level Science base, as part of the same teaching problem. It is therefore important not to cut off the teaching of 'backward readers'. Similarly it is important to realize that all the pupils in a secondary school need some degree and some kind of 'teaching to read'.

For the sake of simple analysis, reading can be regarded as having a hierarchy of skills:

(a) Primary skills
(i.e. recognizing separate letters, groups of letters, or whole words; associating sound or words with letters.)

(b) Intermediate skills
   (i.e. the ability to grasp sequences.)
(c) Comprehension skills
   which can further be subdivided into a number of kinds, e.g.
   i.   literal comprehension (the ability to make out the overtly stated sense);
   ii. reorganization (the ability to analyse and synthesize and to select and rearrange);
   iii. inferential (the ability to interpret significance, and to 'read between the lines');
   iv. evaluation (the ability to judge the adequacy of what has been presented);
   v.   appreciation (the ability to react to aesthetic effect).

There is, however, no fixed sequence of 'learning order' or even order of difficulty. Indeed it is important that the whole hierarchy should be taught simultaneously, and that the comprehension skills that are sometimes thought of as 'higher-order skills' (e.g. evaluation) should be taught from the first. Furthermore, pupils frequently have difficulties with all levels simultaneously. Thus a sixth-form student may need help with (a), (b) and (c) iii when reading material in General Studies in exactly the same way as a first-year pupil in 'Man' though at a different level of complexity.

At the level of 'comprehension skills' the different subject areas have to some extent different problems and need somewhat different teaching approaches. Thus reading in each of history, science, maths and literature, for instance, requires markedly, though obviously not completely, different comprehension skills. Clearly, therefore, it is impossible to teach 'reading' in isolation. Indeed, a good teacher of, say, science is also a teacher of reading in and through science.

The teaching of reading relates to the need to be taught and to have practise in the 'study skills', from finding your way around a book (e.g. using the index), through note-taking (however simple), to the storage and retrieval of ideas and information. There is then a parallel with the previous paragraph: the good teacher of, say, geography, is also a teacher of study in and through geography.

Whenever reading material is used in any subject, teachers are asked to assist the individual, the group or the class to understand it. This is very necessary in all subjects, even those with few written words like mathematics. General guidance might include:

(a) telling the pupil(s) the general aim of the passage first so that they know what to expect;
(b) writing on the board, pronouncing syllable by syllable and explaining any key difficult words;
(c) drawing the pupils' attention to key words which carry the argument forward, e.g. 'Since ...', 'As a result ...';
(d) in discussion asking pupils to read out the sentence(s) which give them a particular idea or piece of information;
(e) encouraging pupils to comment on how clearly or effectively a point is made in whatever is being read.

3.2 *Writing*

(a) Require a *variety of kinds* of writing including personal accounts even in 'factual' subjects.

(b) Suggest a *variety of real audiences* whenever possible, e.g. other pupils, other classes, displays, other teachers, the Headmaster, friends of the school, other schools.

(c) In 'marking' any written work, try hard in your comments to stress your reaction to the piece of writing as a communication, rather than merely grading it.

The document is of interest in that it focusses attention on most of the issues raised by the present project, and does so in the context of a single school. The various procedures indicated in section 3.1 are especially noteworthy. The author shares with the present team the view that all aspects of reading should be taught simultaneously, and in particular, that higher-order skills need to be taught from the first.[1] What is less certain is whether the advice to subject teachers is sufficient and self-explanatory. In the absence of detailed examples and a well-articulated plan, it seems likely that many secondary school teachers would not pay more than lip-service to statements of general policy. Even in the present section, enough has been said to indicate that the beliefs which are shared by the present authors and the writer of this document are by no means universal among secondary school teachers.

But it is also certain that the position has altered since 1974, when the statement was first issued, and the ground for its acceptance is now more fertile.[2]

It has been the impression of this team that innovation in a school requires the active support of a nucleus of teachers which should include the headteacher. The existence of such a group is important because innovation often demands more planning, more concrete effort, and a greater variety of expertise than can be expected of any one individual teacher. We will return to these issues in the following sections.

[1] We have been led to question the view that higher-order skills can be carefully differentiated from others, at least in terms of test results and of diagnostic individual prescription.

[2] Michael Marland writes: 'This initial document did indeed prove far too brief. It was later taken under the wing of a staff working party that looked at the whole question of a general "language across the curriculum" policy. That working party produced a much fuller document, though it is noticeable that the original points were retained as the skeleton of the recommended procedures. However, even after the publication and discussion of that fuller version, the continuing working party share my worry that the difficulties of implementation are very great indeed. It is easier for a teacher to "circumnavigate print" by explanation than it is to help the pupil cope with the print.'

III Worksheets

It has been seen that in many schools and in departments within schools, the role of reading for learning was most prominent when the text to be read took the form of a worksheet. Worksheets have a number of advantages to the teacher who wants to individualize learning or to break the lockstep of class-based teaching. Worksheets, workcards or workbooks (all of which are variants of the same category) are a school- or class-product and can therefore be tailor-made to suit the aptitudes and interests of specific groups or individuals within the school. In particular, the text can be simplified to enable poorer readers or the less able generally to occupy themselves in profitable learning activities without the constant intervention of the teacher.

But it does not follow that the worksheet is always or even usually superior to published material in the form of books. Printed or duplicated resources need to satisfy a number of criteria if they are to be a valuable asset in the school situation.

1   They should be challenging, yet not too difficult.
2   They should be interesting and stimulating.
3   They should be clear and well produced, with good illustrations where needed.
4   They should, normally, be part of a programme which is sequenced in difficulty or in demand for previous knowledge or both. The programme should cover a recognizable block of the relevant curriculum; in other words it should itself form a whole.
5   If the worksheet material is to function as an aid to the acquisition of skills for self-informing (study skills and note-taking skills), then the material must not itself take the form of ready-made notes—although it can include such notes, by way of example.

It must be borne in mind that any publishing company is in a position to bring a wealth of resources to bear on the production of teaching materials. The materials will always be read by other teachers and often by readers who are expert in some relevant field (usually the content area concerned, sometimes experts in layout). But the mass-produced series is aimed at a broad section of the school population. The potential advantage of the worksheet is that of the small bespoke tailor over the large manufacturer. But the small tailor is usually expected to have a great deal of skill and moreover he will be working full time at tailoring. Not all teachers have the skills of accomplished writers and few have the time required to produce materials of a high standard. It seems to follow from these considerations that useful worksheets will usually be the product of team-work within a school. This is certainly the case of the best examples featured below.

Example: Fold Mountains

FOLD MOUNTAINS

These are the main types of mountains on the earth's surface:
a) Fold Mountains
b) Block Mountains
c) Volcanic Mountains

These types have been formed in different ways. You have learned how the Volcanic Mountains were formed.

'Fold Mountains', in fact, form the highest mountain ranges in the world at present (e.g. Everest in the Himalayas, and other ranges include the Andes of South America, the Rockies of North America, the Alps of Southern Europe and the Atlas Mountains of North Africa.)

Fold Mountains were formed from vast thicknesses of sediments that were deposited in the seas.

The sediment was trapped in huge basins (or hollows) in the earth's surface called Geosynclines.

On either side of the basin were two continental land masses (or plates) which slowly began to move towards each other. The effect of this tremendous pressure was to push up the sediment so that it slowly appeared above sea level. Many of the seas would be trapped while some would flood elsewhere. After many millions of years, the pressure would have compacted the sediment into sedimentary rock and it would form vast 'up' folds (anticlines) and 'down' folds (synclines) in the earth's surface.

Before weathering and erosion some of the peaks on the earth surface may have been as much as 50,000 feet high—that is another 20,000 feet on top of Mount Everest today!

The first example, *Fold Mountains*, formed part of a second-year head-lesson in environmental studies in a school in Derbyshire. Surprisingly, the readability level of this was only 13.00 (Fry Graphs). Despite this it will be immediately apparent that this type of text is more appropriate as an *aide memoire* to the teacher than as a learning source for pupils: the text is intolerably dense, and in addition it incorporates assumptions about the existing knowledge of the reader which are unlikely to be realistic for more than a very few students.

Example: Working in the Mill

WORKING IN THE MILL

Jimmy Haslam worked in the *carding room* in a mill near Bolton. In this room the raw cotton was treated with special equipment to remove dust, seeds and leaves. Then it was passed through rollers, straightened out, and wound onto bobbins ready for the spinners to spin it into thread.

It was in this great carding room, fifteen feet high, that Jimmy worked as a 'scavenger'. He emptied the trays filled with seeds and dust; he cleaned the rollers of the carding machines with hand-cards. He loaded the bobbins into trucks and wheeled them to hand-lifts, which dispatched them to the spinning room above. He had to trim the candles and run errands.

The atmosphere of the carding room was heavy with dust, and shreds of cotton wool floated like wisps of smoke across it. The smell of the oily cotton was sickening and the heat oppressive. Ten boys and girls worked here with him and, although this was Jimmy's first week in the mill, they had taken him to their hearts and most were good friends. Being strong and well cared for, he pitied those whose clogs were too worn to keep out the rain, and he was especially careful of one girl who limped badly as she moved round the room and of a boy who was thin, tiny and ill-fed.

Dan Robinson, the overseer in the carding room, always checked the arrival of his boys and girls, both in the morning and after dinner. Anyone late was fined $\frac{1}{2}$d. from his weekly wage, which might average 2s. 3d. Dan kept a strap on the wall. He rarely needed to use it, for the children feared his gruff voice, rasping tongue and scowling face. Dan would not allow pranks or play in the carding room because the machines were not fenced. A boy could easily have a sleeve caught by a belt and be whirled helplessly round the machine.

A rough wooden stairway led from the carding room to the spinning room on the floor above, where Anne and Mrs Haslam worked. The spinning room was a large, bleak room running the whole length of the mill with windows on either side. Rows of tall, solid iron pillars supported the ceiling.

At half-past seven each morning work at the mill stopped for the breakfast break. It was Anne's duty to listen for the parish clock chiming the half hour and then to tug the rope which operated the clapper of the mill bell. Equally promptly, at eight o'clock, Anne rang the bell for work to resume. Mrs Haslam, Anne, and Jimmy had breakfast together, sometimes in the spinning room, sometimes outside on the river bank. They ate slices of bread and dripping or sandwiches or bread and jam. After two hours' work they were glad of rest and food.

Questions
1 What jobs did Jimmy have to do in the mill?
2 Why was it unpleasant working in the carding room?
3 What was the punishment for being late?
4 Why was it dangerous to play around in the carding room?

Working in the Mill is again taken from a worksheet designed for second-year pupils. It is far less dense than *Fold Mountains*, and at the same time has a greater interest appeal for most pupil-readers. One notes, too, that the questions sometimes demand inference on the part of the reader. Regrettably, the standard of production of this worksheet was poor.

Example: The End of the Open Field System

THE END OF THE OPEN FIELD SYSTEM

After 1750 more and more land was enclosed and by 1850 open fields and strips had disappeared except in a few places.

Many of the larger landowners realized that the new methods of farming could be used only on enclosed land. So they began to fence land which had previously been farmed by the villagers.

The first step was to ask Parliament to pass a law enclosing the village land. Parliament then sent officers, called commissioners, to divide it amongst farmers who could prove ownership.

Anyone who could not prove ownership lost their land. If a man could not afford to pay the heavy legal fees or the cost of fencing he had to sell his share to one of the larger farmers.

Staking out boundaries.

Some of the farmers sold their land and rented farms from the landowners as tenant farmers. Others became farm labourers and worked on farms they had formerly owned.

Many of the villagers lost their old right to graze cattle on the commons and waste lands. Squatters saw their homes pulled down.

There were riots in some villages particularly when the landowners tried to fasten the enclosure notice to the church door.

Villagers attacking landowners.

Life became even more difficult for the villagers when mills and factories made goods which they had formerly spun and woven in their cottages. Many had to leave the countryside to find work in the towns.

SUGGESTED WORK

Questions
1 What happened to most of the open fields and strips between 1750 and 1850?
2 Why did landowners fence the land in the villages?
3 What was the first step to enclose land in the villages?
4 Who were the commissioners?
5 Which people could not prove ownership of land do you think? What happened to their land?
6 Why did some people have to sell their land to the larger farmers?
7 What did these people become?
8 Why were there riots in some villages?
9 Where did people who left the countryside go to find work?

By contrast with *Working in the Mill, The End of the Open Field System* is well produced. The information is, on the face of it, clearly presented, and the questions seem to be searching and well thought-out. Nevertheless, this example, taken from the work of a school in the north-west, does have some features which give cause for concern. Consider the passage:

> The first step was to ask Parliament to pass a law enclosing the village land. Parliament then sent officers, called commissioners, to divide it amongst farmers who could prove ownership. Anyone who could not prove ownership lost their land.

What is the background of existing knowledge which the pupil can bring to bear on these three sentences? What is or was Parliament? What is meant by the words 'to pass a law'? What importance attaches to the name 'commissioners'? How do you prove ownership?

No doubt some of these points would have been treated in lessons or in other worksheets. But it is difficult to resist the impression that the presentation here is too succinct. Excessive economy of words makes it hard for the inexpert reader to supply meanings. Nor do the illustrations themselves convey information. As a result, this example seems to incorporate some of the faults of *Fold Mountains*. Clearly there would have been a strong case for a more extended but at the same time more informative presentation—perhaps in the historical-fiction mode of *Working in the Mill*. This could be supported by a simulation exercise.

All this takes time. But whenever pupils are asked to accept a verbal formulation for which they are unable to supply any useful meaning, a formulation which either does not communicate with their existing knowledge or one which merely serves to blur whatever structure this possesses to begin with, the learning is in fact counterproductive. One is inadvertently teaching children the short-term advantages of unthinking repetition. This is surely too high a price to pay for the saving of time.

A combined-science course: worksheet and policy statement

The next example was taken from the same school. It was one in which a great deal of thought had gone into the development and improvement of an integrated science course, one which would be firmly based on practical experiment, observation and inference[1], but at the same time consolidated by verbal discussion and verbal formulation. For the whole of the first three years, all members of the teaching group were engaged together in observing or conducting the experiments. The circus technique[2] was not used until the fourth year. It was deliberately avoided to allow the fullest opportunities for discussions and argument and to bring out the cogency of inferences made from experimental observations. Worksheets and allied material were not seen as a separate strand to the teaching of science, running parallel to the practical work and discussion, or simply as background reading. Instead they were closely dovetailed to the lesson material, as is clear from the worksheet *A Further Look at Heating Copper Sulphate Crystals*.

A FURTHER LOOK AT HEATING COPPER SULPHATE CRYSTALS
You know from earlier experiments when you heated many things, that Copper Sulphate Crystals, when heated, turn white and give off a vapour (gas) that condenses to give a clear liquid that looks like water. If water from the tap is added to the white powder it turns blue.

Procedure
We heated some blue copper sulphate crystals in a test tube as shown in the diagram below. White powder was left. The vapour given off condensed (changed to liquid) as it cooled in passing down the condensing tube. Clear liquid was collected in the test tube.

Diagram

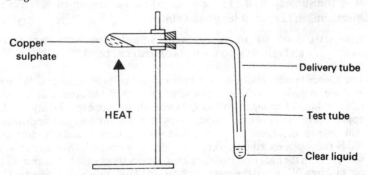

Copper sulphate

HEAT

Delivery tube

Test tube

Clear liquid

---

[1] As the scientist gains in sophistication, so the order of these may change, often to: observation, inference, experiment.

[2] A teaching technique in which a series of experiments, often related to a single theme, is divided into a number of stations and a group of pupils (or individual pupils) allocated to each station. The pupils move on from station to station until they have all completed all the experiments.

Results
Before we could say the clear liquid was water we had to decide on some tests. Say what these were and what results we got. _____

_____

_____

_____

Conclusions
From the results of our tests we can say that the clear liquid is _____
Note
1 When you added a little water to the white copper sulphate did you expect it to get hotter or colder? _____
2 Did it get hotter or colder? _____
3 Explain why _____

_____

_____

This worksheet is one which incorporates a number of features that clearly attest to a great deal of careful planning. These include such details as supplying everyday equivalents of technical terms, clear and economical diagrams, and thoughtful questions like those at the bottom of the sheet.

The Head of Science at this school was asked to supply us with a brief statement of the teaching policy which they had evolved. The following extract gives some indication of the variety of reading materials used, especially in worksheets. At the same time it provides an admirable illustration of the way in which a carefully thought-out teaching strategy can use reading to enhance the quality of learning within the subject itself. There is clearly no question of sacrificing subject aims in favour of language aims.

THE AIMS AND METHODS OF THE SCIENCE DEPARTMENT WITH PARTICULAR REFERENCE TO LANGUAGE AND READING
General discussion
The science taught to all pupils is firmly based on practical work. We see, and use, practical work as a prime motivator of children. Further the relationships of thought and language with the concrete reality of the apparatus or material being used means that the concepts and knowledge that arise are more real for the pupil. However, the practical bias does not imply that open-ended discovery is the primary method. On the contrary, we believe, in the light of experience, that that method leads to frustration in our children. We avoid the mere verification of previously-stated facts. The general method adopted is one of guided discovery or even stage-managed heurism—putting the child in the position of inevitable discovery. This leads to a variety of teaching situations in some of which language and reading are of vital importance.

Often the oral directions of the teacher complement those on a written worksheet. This is part of a deliberate policy, relating spoken word to written instruction for a procedure that the child is well motivated to follow.

To assist the children during lessons a variety of forms of worksheet are used. They serve the important function of preparing pupils for the worksheets associated with more complex experimental procedures later on. They also offer a tool for refining language and reading skills.

(i) *Simple table of results*
Such sheets are the simplest form that was used. They consist of a ruled matrix with headings. Within the matrix the pupil has to record his observations. Without it many children fail to organize the recording of their observations or alternatively take too long over it. With it they can contribute more easily to the class discussions and the derivation of conclusions.

(ii) *Combined table of results*
Like the 'Simple table of results', these sheets contain a matrix for pupil-observation and results. They also contain a brief introduction, a set of instructions, and a space for conclusions. The instructions on procedure complement those that have arisen during discussion or have been given by the teacher. They are particularly valuable where there are several stages to the procedure to be followed. The instructions are kept fairly simple in terms of syntax and vocabulary. An example is given below:

BURNING SUBSTANCES IN OXYGEN

1   Place a little of each of the substances shown in column 1, in turn, on to a combustion spoon. Heat in a bunsen burner and see if it burns in air. If it does burn in air, describe how it does so in column 2.
2   Re-heat, and then remove the cork from a tube of oxygen and plunge in the heated surface. If it burns in oxygen describe how it does so in column 3.
3   Remove the combustion spoon and its cork from the tube, quickly add some water, return the cork and shake the tube of water up. Add *two* drops of universal indicator and write any colour change in column 4.
4   If there is any colour change to the universal indicator find out what the pH is and put it in the last column.

1 Substance	2 Burning in air	3 Burning in oxygen and product if any	4 Colour change	pH
Wood splint				
Carbon (wood charcoal)				
Iron (iron wool)				

(iii) *The simple record* (See *A Further Look at Heating Copper Sulphate Crystals*, p. 285).

This is essentially a description of the experimental procedure in the traditional way with headings such as 'apparatus', 'method', 'results' and 'conclusions'. It is not issued until after completion of the experimental procedure and the drawing of conclusions in discussion.

Its function is to serve as reinforcement of the procedures and concepts that have been the objectives of the lesson. It also serves a language and reading function. Words missed out in the description are often 'scientific' words, representing procedures, concepts, material, that had a place in the lesson.

The conclusions for the experiment are left blank for the pupil to complete in full sentence form.

(iv) *The sequential worksheet*

This is the most complex form of worksheet used in the first two years. The instructions supplement the oral preparation given by the teacher to the extent that the sequence of procedures cannot be followed by the pupils without their reading the sheet. Consequently such sheets are very carefully designed and laid out. The written instruction is complemented and reinforced, wherever possible and appropriate, by drawings and diagrams. The presentation, together with the motivation of the pupil to want to do the experiment, is vital to these worksheets which are directly related to the type the pupil will have to use in later years in circus situations. The reading requirement is seen as a vital contribution to the pupils' development of that skill, related as it is to the concrete nature of experiments.[1]

(v) *Information sheets*

These are issued to pupils very occasionally in year 1 and 2. They serve to consolidate and broaden the pupils' grasp of the concepts and content that have arisen in practical work. They are written with simple syntax but do not neglect scientific terms. Initially they are read by the teacher with the help of the children, and with the children following the text. Needless to say the teacher needs to stop regularly to clarify points and confirm understanding. If appropriate, illustrations are incorporated into these instruction sheets and great care is taken in their layout.

These sheets, like the others discussed, become part of a child's folder. We find that many children often reread their worksheets (of all types). This greatly assists consolidation of concepts, procedures and basic body of knowledge. These different formats of worksheet are used in about 40 per cent of lessons in the first two years. They do much to give our pupils basic confidence in language and reading.

(vi) *Other sources*

In the same way that school science can assist in language development, so too can it contribute to the pupils' confidence and interest in using books.

---

[1] The reference is clearly to the non-redundancy of 'the language of instructions' as used in certain work-cards, but also in recipes, on medicine bottle labels, etc!

In their second year pupils are required, as homework tasks, to produce 'projects' related to the topic they are studying practically in class at that time. They are given a series of headings to find out about, by reading, and then write up. To start them off the children are given access in class to background readers, carefully chosen for the purpose, and the contents of resource boxes containing pamphlets etc. related to the topic. The pupils are directed to the school and public library for further resources. The school library contains books specifically ordered to assist the children in doing these homeworks. The response is pleasing. Of course there is, initially at least, much plagiarization evidenced in the writing. However, before the child can plagiarize he has to read, and the topics are broken down so that no one book, or even two, is likely to provide all the information required. From a science-education viewpoint the headings of each topic are selected so as to broaden the child's outlook and reinforce the relevance of the material being taught.

IV Sixth-form programmes

However desirable it may be for schools and departments to elaborate a well thought-out sequential programme for promoting independent learning by reading and study, such programmes were in fact rare. Indeed, the science programme described above, extending as it did to the upper forms of the school, with increasing demands on the pupil as he gained in age and experience, was practically unique in our survey, the only parallel being the school treated in section V.

Much more commonly, teaching of study skills was sporadic and *ad hoc* in years one to five. Even in the most forward-looking schools, it was usual at the time of the survey for a fuller use of reading and instruction in note-taking to be reserved for sixth formers. In the sixth form itself the pattern varied, but it is instructive to consider at least one such programme in a little detail despite the fact that the team were more specifically concerned with teaching and learning up to the age of fifteen, since the reader may well feel that similar procedures could be modified for use lower down the school, or simply taken over, with different materials.

The programme in question was being implemented in a large comprehensive school in north London and was the work of a teacher who was in charge of sixth-form students for the school as a whole. She had arranged to spend one session each week with all sixth formers. Lessons were generally given to groups of approximately twelve students with several different options represented in each group, for example English, maths, biology, economics and history all figuring in a single group. In one lesson which was observed by members of the project team, each member of the group first studied a topic in one of his A-level subjects. He was then required to reproduce as much as possible of what he had read in a very brief period (3–5 minutes, timed with a stopwatch). Following the summaries, the students worked together asking questions, commenting on significant points, possible deletions, etc. As in another school where similar work was noted, the pupils find themselves under severe pressure but are nevertheless appreciative of this type of lesson, and they themselves are convinced of its efficacy.

It should be added that the lesson observed was only one example of the instruction given, which also included instruction to improve reading speed, guidance in note-taking and assistance in examination technique. The main suggestions for the improvement of reading speed are contained in a handout from which the following paragraph has been reproduced.

METHODS OF IMPROVING READING

Practise reading faster

Spend 15–20 minutes *each day*—at a time when you will *not* be interrupted—preferably before going to bed.

Start with fairly easy material, e.g. newspaper articles, magazine or weekly paper articles etc.

1 Read each article as quickly as possible without sacrificing comprehension.

2 Time yourself for each article and work out your rate of reading in words per minute (estimate number of words in article by multiplying the number of lines by the average number of words per line).

3 Keep a chart or graph of your reading rate—keep this up for a fortnight and note the increase in speed.

4 Progress to more difficult material. Test your comprehension of the passages/articles read.

Remember

(a) Technical books may have to be read relatively slowly, whereas texts in English or history may usually be read at a faster rate. Therefore keep separate records.

(b) Be careful not to read so fast that you fail to get the full meaning.

Improve vocabulary

by reading widely in your field of study—try to use new words in your own writing and speech.

It should be recalled that these notes were addressed to sixth-form students and that they were strengthened by regular counselling sessions. Younger pupils could not be relied on to decide without aid whether or not they were sacrificing comprehension. They would also need far more guidance in the selection of materials. Even sixth formers or older students should be warned that there are often very wide variations in difficulty within the same text (Stokes, 1978). However, the emphasis on comprehension before speed is well placed.

V Case study

Few schools were operating a consistent policy to increase the use of reading for learning across the curriculum. While section III contains at least one outstanding example of what can be done, this was largely confined to science teaching. It also includes a policy statement from an innovative headteacher, but at the time of the inquiry, the policy had yet to prove itself in practice. Of all the schools known to the team or made known to us in the course of the inquiry, the one that came nearest to the idea of implementing a general policy, emphasizing the use of language and reading, was a school in Derbyshire.[1] This was a school where the view advocated in the present chapter was shared by the headteacher and several members of the staff. The following interviews are of interest both as a description of what was being achieved and for the insights that they afford about the difficulty of translating policy into practice.

1 Interview with headteacher

Would you agree that this school is one which anticipated the recommendations of the Bullock Report in developing a language policy across the curriculum?
No, that would be going too far. We don't have a language policy but we are trying to develop one. We do this in an *ad hoc* way by getting all the staff to share their insights and experience in any particular field. But the staff were not specially selected. Most of our teachers stayed on when the school was formed out of the amalgamation of three existing schools. I don't suppose the idea of a language policy across the curriculum would have been much canvassed in these schools. As a matter of fact our first attempts to put over the ideas of Jimmy Britton and others met with scepticism or frank hostility. But when we advertised for a head of English I asked for an interest in language across the curriculum. This is because I believe that although the idea is not confined to English as a subject, it is one which has occupied the minds of English teachers for the past ten years.

So now you have one ally in advocating a brand new policy?
Not just one. As well as the Head of English, we've recruited others with wide interests. One is second in the English Department. Then there is the Deputy Head who worked with English and science teachers in our last school. They've managed to interest others and we have had a number of exploratory meetings involving scientists and other teachers.

What sorts of things came up at these meetings?
Well, they've alerted members of staff to a number of things we think are important. For instance, we had some discussion of worksheets which started as just a discussion on worksheets, and to begin with we talked

---

[1] We are grateful to the headmaster and staff of Belper High School for permission to reproduce these edited interviews.

about things like layout. But that led to a discussion of the language in our worksheets and there was pretty general agreement that a lot of our worksheets are bad because the language we've used is inappropriate. Now that was a very helpful discussion because it made teachers more aware of what we do when we talk to kids and especially when we write things for them. We begin to take less for granted.

What sorts of things?
Some teachers are reminded that the kids don't always understand the jargon we use. Now I'm sure that's not enough. For instance it does not mean that we ought to talk down to children. What it means is often you have got to be more explicit, and that's not easy to put across in a general and systematic kind of way. But the Head of Resources can do a great deal by assisting with particular problems as they arise.

How does he do that?
Well, he is in a very commanding position. He sees the worksheets that the departments produce, he sees the kids who come to the library with questions to answer, and he sees the syllabuses which teachers are preparing, because they often want him to provide them with the right material. That means he is engaged in a great deal of on-the-job discussion with other teachers. Also the Deputy Head has been spending a large part of his time helping people to develop Mode 3 syllabuses for presentation to the CSE Board. So he, too, is involved in discussions with other teachers, and he often visits their classes to find out what the kids are actually doing and how they are coping. That's one reason he is doing some science teaching in the lower forms this year. That way he can take a share of what's going on and influence the planning of the department, trying to make it less rigid.

Can you tell me a little more about that?
Yes. At the moment a lot of the science teaching in the lower school is just a body of verbal knowledge, represented by a set of definitions and things that you can learn almost by heart. We want to change that, make science more exploratory. And things are beginning to move. For instance we had one teacher who used to be a very straightforward science specialist going to town on the subject of the human skeleton. This resulted in some very lively and amusing child-centred summaries of what had been learned, presented in cartoon form. The cartoons included jokes to bring out certain human bone characteristics and their functions and what would happen to people if these hadn't evolved the way they did.

In some of our own work we have tried to combine this sort of child-centred approach with an emphasis on group discussion. Do you find when children work together they learn from one another and the poorer students are helped by those who are stronger?
Yes, I think that is so. We have tried to insist also that every department also has to do its own remedial work. In the lower year when the kids arrive, which is at thirteen plus, they all follow a common curriculum. So they go to all departments and everybody has got to offer them something. This something has been quite helpful in a way because it has enabled us to

push back to the subject teachers the responsibility for solving some of the reading and writing problems of the weaker children. I think you would need someone with specialist knowledge to teach them the things that they need to do, say in science. I know it's very easy to say and very hard to do it. But it does often mean that we don't stick to using printed sheets or printed books. Instead, you encourage children to discuss and to talk to one another and to work with one another and you have to go and talk to them, instead of just instructing them as a class. I think this has probably been helpful to all the departments in the long run. We encourage children to write and talk more about what they do when they are doing things like environmental study and science. Now I think in social sciences this is pretty common, but teaching biology, physics, and chemistry used to be the transmission of knowledge. You learned it and then you were tested to see if you had learned it. Then you went on to the next bit. Now there are more occasions when students can speculate about what they are doing and discuss things with one another, and I think that is quite important. Mind you, I don't think we have gone very far over this. We are hampered by exam requirements and when students come at thirteen they only have just about a year before they make choices.

A lot of teachers have told us that they can't expect the average child to learn by reading, so they rely on talking to them. Do you agree?
Well, I would have thought that talking to children could be just as good a preparation for intellectual activity of one sort or another as reading, and sometimes the other way round. But at the same time I feel there is an awful lot of anxiety that reading is going to be boring and that you mustn't bore children. In a sense that is perfectly true, but I also think that by and large we don't demand enough of children in the school because we are too anxious about being boring. Now that is partly because a lot of reading material that we offer children is not intrinsically worthwhile. I would like to see a wider use of things that aren't in textbooks, more imaginative presentation of different aspects like the ones you find in the Penguin *Extensions*. These may be a little highbrow, but, for instance, although Tinbergen's book may be a little bit hard for average children, it is nevertheless the sort of things that interests them because it deals biographically with someone's work. I myself would have thought this a suitable subject for study, whereas many science teachers' inclinations would tend to abstract from such a writer's work a set of biological facts and summarize them in note form and then make the children learn them. I don't like that approach. I believe that a lot of the interest and value for the kids would be to see how the scientist did what he was doing and why, rather than just what he did and what he found out at the end. I think the same is true in history and I know that there are many history teachers who do this, and who take a more imaginative approach in which they get children to reconstruct things or to read novels with historical figures and backgrounds and so on. When we provide this kind of material I don't think we are pandering to the child. I think it's the sort of material that appeals to the child, material that builds on his existing interest as a child, and that can take him further on the way to becoming a scientist or an historian.

2 Interview with Head of English

I suppose from the point of view of the English Department, reading across the curriculum is largely a matter of reading comprehension. How do you go about that side of it?
Well, ideally we like to think of language learning as a progression. We want every child to extend his reading potential from whatever level he has reached at any given moment.

Writers vary. So presumably this means in part having to disentangle material that was not well put to start with?
Right. And we don't always deal with things that are immediately enjoyable. From time to time we try to present everyone with things that are difficult, or things that are awkward and need organizing. What's more I'd want to relate these organizing skills to writing. For instance, right now we've got a group writing argumentative essays. That's not new, but it is very difficult because it involves collecting ideas, putting them in order, and saying things at length and not just in one sentence. So I start by actually giving them an argumentative essay, which helps them to acquire the skill of reading and that is associated with the skill of writing it. They see how the essay is structured and why this paragraph comes before that paragraph, this example is backing that point and so on. So I look for a constant movement back and forth from reading to writing. Hopefully, I'd like to find materials and tasks for each kid to take him on from where he is. If we do our job properly and there is this extension of ability, then he ought to be able to cope with anything which he meets up with later on.

But even when you teach for learning across the curriculum, you've still got to function some of the time as a teacher of English, haven't you?
Yes, indeed. But one weakness of traditional English teaching is that it tended to concentrate on the interesting and the lively and the mythical, if I may use that term. We didn't deal much with opinion, with fact, with information. So I for one would want to ensure a much greater spread of reading, with less emphasis on fiction than a lot of other English teachers. But then again I don't see these two as necessarily mutually exclusive.

Can you explain that a bit more?
In our upper year we have a system that we call the unit system. This means we divide the children into groups which are reorganized every half term. Every half term they meet with a different teacher, and they stay with him for all that half term. That gives us all sorts of advantages to do with the way we teach English in general, but in terms of reading it means that the teacher knows in advance that he will have half a term on one particular area, so he has to have materials to sustain interest and occupy him with a wide range of ability. So instead of dealing with what you know well in a programmed way, we use a much more flexible approach. For instance, in the first half of this term I had a group that had chosen to do sport. Part of this was fairly traditional, and I'd read them an exciting sport story and get them to write one of their own, and so on. But we also spent a lot of time analysing newspaper reports, and we use a wide variety of these. Some reports would be used with some kids just for finding facts, but we also use

the same materials and others for getting children to talk and to write about what people might talk about after coming away from the match. And others would use the report as a literary study looking at similies, metaphors and so on, the sort of thing you might find in a sports report in the *Guardian*.

Does that mean you build up your own materials?
Very much so. It started as an idea with us and all we need now is time and money to build up a wide range of materials in all sorts of areas. That allows you to suit work very personally for every individual. For instance, I have been making up cards to suit a particular child in a group, but once a card is made up it stays as part of the system and it can be used again with another child. Right now may be the thing isn't too impressive. But that's only because we have not been going long, and I am sure the idea is one which can be carried out a lot further.

Tell me, when you were appointed it was with an explicit aim of involving yourself with language across the curriculum and not just English. Does that still occupy much of your time?
Well, yes, but there has been a change because we now have a Head of Resources who was once the second in my department, and he does more in that area than anyone else. But we do work pretty closely together.

Is he the librarian?
Yes, in a way, but we couldn't get the sort of librarian we wanted. But he can do that job and he also does part of the job he used to do in the English Department before he was appointed to his present post. That's largely a matter of changing the work that you are doing, since there were several things that were going wrong.

What sorts of things?
In many subjects there were many teachers who were throwing vast amounts of print at kids who simply could not take it in, and we had to find a way of drawing attention to this without being smug and superior. So we persuaded them to look at what they were doing and change it if they felt it should be changed. This is mainly a matter of cutting down the contents. I think what teachers have got to do is to make fewer things the minimum. As I see it every teacher of a mixed-ability group has a minimum that he wants everybody to do, but that minimum has been too high. What the teacher says to himself is, 'Well, they will all do this and if they are very bright they can go on and read and if they are struggling they can have an extra workcard.' I think they need to cut down on the minimum for all children, and that means increasing the amount of variety open to people when they have completed the minimum. But of course that means a lot of extra work for teachers and it is a long-term process.

I take it that means you are only just beginning to get round to that sort of problem. Can you tell us a little bit more about some of the other ways in which you managed to influence the use of language and of reading across the curriculum?
Well, we've managed to raise questions of the sort you were talking about

to the Head. Questions about variety. We had a very useful joint meeting with the Science Department and I would say that of all departments in the school, we have been of most use to the Science Department. At our last meeting we talked about their lower-year course and what they felt was going wrong with it in terms of language. We dealt with the wording of worksheets and also with the amount they had to read. Then we went on to deal with the invariable demand they made at the time that all experiments should be written up in a particular way. We tried to inject a more creative element into what they were doing, so that instead of the writing up of experiments you could have presentation, displays, tape recorders and even dramatisation. So far this hasn't affected the material which they provide for kids but it has affected what the kids themselves produce. I think of the discussion between two gods about the design of the human body which the Head talked about. Now the teacher who had that piece of work was delighted with it, so I'd like to bet that she will have that duplicated or taped and that means it will be available next time, and so it will become part of the material put in for next year's work study. As things stand, I think much of the material we provide is too factual and assumes a commitment to science and to investigation which maybe the kid hasn't got.

These two interviews are of interest both as testifying to an achievement and as an account of what problems were met and how they were overcome.

As regards the achievement it will be apparent that there is no sacrifice in the content of learning and, above all, that the object is to make the learning more meaningful, less formula-bound, by making the teaching more flexible and at the same time more self-critical. As to the problems in securing these goals, we would stress the evident importance of team-work. In order to secure change in the character of the worksheets used in various lessons, the Head of Resources went into classes to observe, to teach, and of course to collaborate more effectively in the preparation of materials. So too, the Deputy Head, a mathematician, elected to teach in the Science Department so as to learn the problems at first hand and, hopefully, to initiate a collaborative effort designed to improve the quality of the pupils' learning.

The apparent success of collaboration in one school does not imply that comparable results might not be achieved elsewhere by individual teachers working in isolation. But it is by no means obvious how one might bring about changes in well-tested habits and expectations in an entire school without breaking down some of the barriers between teachers.

VI Conclusions

The survey upon which this chapter is based was carried out before the publication of the Bullock Report had made any impact on the practice of teachers of English and other subjects. Also in the last few years, an ever increasing number of teachers have completed the Open University course on Reading Development, and this will have given them ample opportunity and encouragement to extend their understanding and to experiment with new methods of teaching. Finally, it is apparent to the writers that many teachers and advisers have been made aware of the work reported in the present volume, especially the ideas contained in Chapter 9, and this too has affected practice in schools. Thus there can be little doubt that since these visits were made and these contributions were received from schools which were in the forefront of changing attitudes, others have adopted similar methods, and some will have gone beyond.

Nevertheless many of the conclusions of this survey retain their validity and some would appear to have important implications.

1   Some departments in some schools were beginning to give increasing attention to problems of vocabulary and of 'register'. Discussion of words as well as arrangement often led to a fuller understanding of the underlying ideas.

2   Not infrequently, workcards and worksheets are used to supplement oral presentation and practical experience. Sometimes these were used in conjunction with published materials (books) rather than replacing them. Properly designed and programmed, such material can provide pupils with incentives and opportunities to acquire a more critical approach to their reading (e.g. by well-designed questions) as well as some techniques of independent study.

3   At the time of the survey, it was not unusual to encounter resistance to the suggestion that reading should receive more emphasis in all subjects. Younger pupils, it was argued, learn more effectively by practical work or by oral communication. Others, including the present writers, were of the opinion that the written word offers the greatest support for critical thinking because it is permanent and can therefore be referred to continually as required by thought or discussion or the well-chosen exercise. Thus an extended use of reading in science would reduce the tendency to memorize experiments without appreciating their significance. Such arguments should not be pushed to the point of absurdity: reading cannot replace experience, experiment and observation, nor should it supplant the spoken word. But a judicious policy for reading across the curriculum can reduce the need for teacher-talk.

4   At the time of the survey, the teaching of study skills was often postponed to the sixth form. It is apparent that there is scope here for an extended programme of research designed to establish viable ways

of promoting individual and group learning based at least in part on written materials, to cover the first five years of secondary schooling. Until this work has been done, the bases for effective change remain too problematic.[1]

5   In the experience of the team, a policy of extending the use of reading for learning across the curriculum is most effective when (a) it has the support of the headteacher in a school and of several senior assistants, preferably including the head of English; (b) there is team-work at least within subjects and often across subjects. The visible output of such team-work may take the form of quality worksheets etc., but the input may well include sitting in on lessons, team-teaching and discussions with students involving more than one teacher.

[1] The Schools Council is currently funding just such a programme of research at Nottingham University under the title *Reading for Learning in the Secondary School*. The project covers the first three years of the secondary school and is under the direction of the present editors.

11

Summary and Conclusions

Keith Gardner

I Introduction

At the inception of the project it was decided that the main efforts of the team should be concentrated on four areas of inquiry:

1 an investigation of the nature of reading comprehension;
2 a description of existing classroom practice across the curriculum;
3 an evaluation of methods of improving reading for learning;
4 an analysis of measures of readability.

The intention was to provide teachers with a clear concept of reading comprehension; to obtain a general picture of the extent to which reading for learning is used across the curriculum; to establish guidelines for classroom action; and to establish, if possible, a simple means for assessing the difficulty of reading materials.

In the event, the four studies were extended to eight, and it is interesting to note that this extension was determined by practical considerations. Classroom practice, as it was originally conceived, provided only a partial picture of total reading behaviour. It proved necessary to examine reading for homework, and reading in an integrated-studies course. Also, the evaluation of contemporary methods had to cover two distinct approaches which could not be encompassed within one inquiry. Thus, the final form of the project has been determined partly by issues and considerations which arose as our work proceeded.

Each of the eight studies which comprise our inquiry into the effective use of reading has already been described. What remains is to relate the parts of the total presentation, and assess to what extent we have been able to achieve our original intentions.

II Reading comprehension

So far as the study of reading comprehension is concerned (Chapter 3), two important findings were established. First, reading comprehension cannot be broken down into a number of distinct subskills. Instead, the evidence pointed strongly to a single aptitude. Second, we found no support for the hypothesis that some pupils might 'possess' lower-order skills but not higher-order skills.

From this it seemed reasonable to conclude that individual differences in reading comprehension should be thought of as differences in the willingness and ability to reflect on what is being read. This, of course, is not a simple characteristic. Nor is it innate. It is the outcome of many factors including reading fluency, intelligence, and interest. Also, it can be enhanced by appropriate reading strategies.

The implications of this for the teacher are far-reaching. In searching for ways and means of improving reading comprehension, it would appear that a prime consideration should be the involvement of pupils in their reading. At the heart of the matter is the willingness to reflect. This is simple to state, but more difficult to achieve. Teachers of English are engaged in a constant search for texts that capture the imagination of their pupils and there is a great deal of thought given to methods of presentation. What is less obvious, however, is the situation of the subject teacher whose concern is more with content than appreciation. How does one create a willingness to reflect on a physics text or an historical treatise? Yet it is in the subject areas that reading for learning could play a major role.

Interest in a particular subject is a personal preference. Enthusiastic subject teachers consciously and unconsciously attempt to pass their own enthusiasms to their pupils. What more can be done?

It is clear from the results of other aspects of our project that there are approaches to reading which increase the involvement of pupils in thinking and reflection (Chapter 9). These will be discussed later. For the present, it is sufficient to draw attention to three relevant issues. First, the study of readability (Chapter 4) indicated instances where texts in the content areas would present severe problems for the average reader. When a pupil starts out with the intention of finding something out but finds himself constantly pressed by textual problems, frustration rather than learning is a likely outcome. Therefore, reading for learning in the content areas could be made more effective by a more careful selection of reading material. Second, the incidence of 'short-burst' reading reported in Chapter 5 indicates a serious lack in the provision for continuous reading in the classroom. While it cannot be argued that all 'short-burst' reading is non-reflective reading, it seems that pupils in our classrooms have only a minimal opportunity to dwell on a substantial piece of reading. Third, the investigation of project work (Chapter 7) showed that reading to answer questions can result in a passive absorption of facts rather than reflection or evaluation. It seems, therefore, that in organizing the purposes of reading across the curriculum, teachers need to balance 'getting information' with genuine inquiry.

All this relates to creating the conditions for 'a willingness to reflect on what is being read'. The matter does not end there. Given the initial willingness of pupils to reflect, steps need to be taken to improve the quality of this reflection.

In this respect two quite different issues need to be considered. On the one hand the quality of reflection rests on our existing knowledge and the nature of our existing concepts relative to what we are reading. Quite simply, the phrase 'a black hole in space' will provoke different responses from an astronomer and a twelve-year-old pupil in a secondary school. On the other hand, there are methods of study which refine our purposeful search of the printed text. Our behaviour, when we read for learning, can become more skilled. The former of these considerations relates to the total curriculum of the school and the individual learning of pupils both in and out of school: the latter relates to the guidance and instructional procedures that are built into the curriculum of any particular school.

Thus a broad framework for evolving a policy for promoting effective reading across the curriculum should include:

1 reading situations designed to foster a willingness to reflect on what is being read;
2 a structure of instruction, guidance and reading practice which improves the quality of reflection;
3 a perusal of methods and materials aimed at creating the optimum opportunity for pupils to use reading purposefully.

Such are the conclusions that emerge from the work on the nature of reading comprehension. The seven remaining areas of inquiry provide a commentary on these fundamental issues. The contribution of each of these studies to our understanding of the issues involved in promoting effective reading for learning will now be examined.

III Readability (Chapter 4)

The general conclusions of Chapter 4 were:

1 Many pupils learn less than they might because some of the texts they meet present difficulties, not just in terms of conceptual content, but because of the way in which they are written.
2 Special attention needs to be given to content areas where the pupil's intrinsic motivation is likely to be low, and to those textbooks, worksheets and workbooks which give instructions for a task.
3 The areas of science and social studies make particular demands on pupils, especially in the lower years of secondary schooling.

4   Readability measures can be of value to teachers in assessing the difficulty of texts, provided certain precautions are observed.

It is evident, therefore, that a relatively simple means is available to teachers whereby they can monitor the suitability of reading materials for certain age groups. However, other considerations should be brought to light at this point.

The study on readability was designed to test the validity of certain measures as predictors of textual difficulty, and the limitations of this approach should be recognized. For instance, it is not suggested that pupils should never study a text that presents undue difficulty. There is a sense in which we learn only by overcoming the problems posed by certain tasks. Much depends on the situation. What is suggested here is that the difficulty of personal, unaided reading needs to be monitored. Where the support of a teacher is available different considerations apply. It is important to note, however, that our study indicated that texts read by pupils unaided were slightly more difficult than those read under supervision. This is clearly unsatisfactory.

Further, there comes a point when simplifying a text destroys the substance of a message. Certain ideas or concepts cannot be transmitted by a writer without imposing demands on the reader.

Chapter 2 includes a detailed theoretical examination of the precise nature of the difficulties that face a reader. It is clear that further empirical work is required in this field. For the present all we can do is to suggest that for some learning reading may be inappropriate, but where reading is appropriate, then pupils should be spared the frustration of attempting to read the unreadable.

IV Classroom observation data (Chapter 5)

This area of study was designed to provide data concerning classroom activities in those subject areas where reading for learning might be expected to have a significant role. It was intended that such data would provide some objective evidence concerning current classroom practice.

An important finding was that there were distinct differences in the pattern of lessons between top-junior school classes and first-year secondary school classes. These differences were signalled by:

1   a decrease in individual tuition and an increase in 'teacher informing' at first-year secondary level;
2   a significant increase in pupil time spent 'listening' at first-year secondary level;
3   a marked increase in the use of textbooks in all subjects except mathematics at first-year secondary level.

While such differences were not unexpected, we have been able to indicate the extent to which the use of language in the classroom changes on transfer from junior to secondary education. Briefly, in junior schools reading, writing and listening are fairly evenly distributed, but in secondary schools listening predominates.

This in itself cannot be taken as direct evidence of a discontinuity in the development of the reading process, but some weight is given to the Bullock Report recommendation that there should be greater cooperation between junior and secondary schools. At present it seems apparent that there are wide differences both in teaching styles and in the use that is made of written texts.

In addition, it must be recognized that where 'teacher informing' is the major means of instruction, the role of reading tends to be very subsidiary. Certainly, our observations indicated that a pupil in a junior school is likely to have more opportunities for personal reading than his counterpart in the secondary school. Thus one may surmise that reading for learning does not figure prominently in the pupil's mind in the early years of secondary education, and this would have a bearing on his 'willingness to reflect on what is being read'.

It seems possible, therefore, that whereas the less-able reader becomes increasingly conscious of his disability, the average and above-average reader finds less use for his reading and relegates it to an inferior position. A 'reading' homework becomes a soft option, not a challenge.

The incidence of 'short-burst' reading in the classroom was another important finding, and some of its implications have already been discussed. For the purposes of the present argument, however, there are some additional issues to consider. First, the fact that more than 50 per cent of all reading across all subjects is of 1–15 seconds duration is a clear indicator of the extent to which the written text is used to control classroom behaviour. Pupils read a set of instructions from a textbook, from the blackboard, or from an assignment card, and then set about working. This is probably the major purpose of reading in many classrooms during many lessons. Second, whatever the purpose of 'short-burst' reading, it is difficult to justify the substantial part of classroom reading it occupies, if the development of reading is a serious objective.

It appears, therefore, that the pattern of many existing lessons does little to offer an opportunity for the improvement of reading for learning. Teachers shape their instructions so that pupils acquire information, learn and apply processes, find solutions to problems. We believe that we have been able to show that the printed word can be used as a stimulus for reflective and critical thinking (Chapter 9). Instead of being passive recipients of information, students can be taught to approach the material in the role of interrogators and discussants. Reading for learning then becomes a 'conversation' with the text in which the student asks his own questions, finds the answers, and makes his own comment. But such an approach does not come easily. It must be learnt through guided experience and practice. In the measure that this is acquired, one may say that the student has learned how to learn and this, surely, is a more valuable acquisition than mere factual knowledge. To use a metaphor from economics, the teaching of reading is a capital investment, and justifies the sacrifice of some consumer goods.

V Reading for homework (Chapter 6)

Our analysis of reading behaviour in the classroom led to the conclusion that many lessons outside of English provided little opportunity for reading for learning. When reading for homework was considered, a balancing situation was anticipated and partially confirmed.

It was found that continuous reading is required frequently in homework tasks. The demand varied from subject area to subject area but it appeared that while most English and social sciences homework contained a substantial amount of reading, mathematics demanded comparatively little. Between these extremes, some form of study reading was a characteristic of more than one-third of work set in science.

While the classroom data (Chapter 5) cannot be compared directly with the homework data (Chapter 6), chiefly because in one instance the information was obtained by direct observation and in the other by questionnaires and interviews, it is reasonable to conclude that reading does play a larger role in homework than in classroom activities. Moreover, reading set for homework is more likely to demand 'study'—in the sense of memorizing, making notes, preparing summaries and the like—than many of the reading situations observed in the classroom. However, it should not be forgotten that the pupil at home is usually isolated from peer discussion, which is a source of information in topic work (Chapter 7). In a word, homework is likely to make greater demands on the reading ability of pupils than many of the classroom situations we observed, but the pupil working at home has no immediate access to professional guidance.

This is a matter which teachers should consider. If the reading set for homework requires a complex and sophisticated response, then pupils need adequate preparation for the task. It is a major finding of this project that study reading can be improved, but only if specific attention is given to this particular activity. Leaving reading ability to develop as an outcome of normal classroom work is not enough (Chapters 8 and 9). Therefore, the fact that practice in study reading is provided through homework rather than classroom procedures does not indicate a balance has been achieved in the total educational situation. On the contrary, the lack of classroom action to promote effective study reading in many schools is a positive factor in reducing the value and the outcomes of work set for homework. We would stress the view that for reading homework to be fully successful, pupils should have the support of a reading development regime in the classroom.

VI Reading in topic work (Chapter 7)

The scale of this inquiry does not permit broad conclusions to be made, but some useful information was gained concerning the methods adopted by pupils to meet the demands of their assignments.

It was found that even though the pupils concerned had been instructed on the use of a library/resource area and could recall advice concerning the use of indexes and chapter headings, few of these pupils used the approved strategies. In scanning books they were readily distracted from the purpose of their search; information was often transferred direct from text to notebook. We noted that pupils preferred to work in small groups, and talking played a prominent part in arriving at answers to set questions. We also gained the impression that while nearly all of these pupils had experienced project work in their junior schools, they were somewhat bewildered by the resources of a secondary school.

Certain important questions are raised when our observations of topic work are analysed. For instance, it might be argued that the individual or group assignment which involves pupils in researching written texts is the ideal situation for encouraging 'a willingness to reflect on what is being read'. Many teachers, especially those from the primary school, believe quite strongly that project work motivates children to read in a way that can rarely be achieved in traditional lessons. We would suggest that such a view is over-optimistic. The pupils we observed were, in fact, generally interested in, and even enthusiastic about what they were doing. For the most part they were highly motivated and willing to work. The important point is, however, that they were willing to find answers to set questions, or to produce presentations for report-back sessions. What we did not observe was a willingness to reflect on what was being read. The reference book was treated more as a treasure trove of sentences and paragraphs which could be stolen and marketed again in another setting.

This comment is made without any criticism of either pupils or teachers. It is a firm impression that brings into focus a real practical problem. Promoting effective reading involves more than creating interest and turning pupils loose on resources.

Once again the conflict of aims and objectives is apparent. A project designed to provide pupils with a background of knowledge may not, in fact, be effective in enabling pupils to develop reading for learning. Indeed, one is forced to conclude that those occasions when pupils deliberately set themselves to study from printed texts in a systematic way are very rare.

It must therefore be emphasized that children absorbed in a task that involves reference to printed texts are not necessarily children who are using, and developing, reading for learning. On the other hand, the potential of the topic-work approach cannot be denied. It provides pupils with the essential freedom to use sources, discuss findings and evaluate results. But there are several factors which are critical for reading for learning. These include the nature of the topic and the opportunity it provides for informed pupil comment, the suitability of the texts used for the pupils concerned, and the quality of teacher intervention which is specifically designed to promote efficient study.

VII An evaluation of SRA Laboratories (Chapter 8)

The commentary on the work carried out and described in Chapters 4–7 has been confined largely to a discussion of how certain aspects of current practice tend to limit the acquisition of effective reading for learning. In this section we analyse one specific procedure which is designed solely to improve reading ability. The distinction is important because the teacher has many concerns and responsibilities. Reading is but one of a host of issues that jostle for priority in the classroom. Hence, in evaluating a specialized approach, using normal classroom routine as a control, there is a strong expectation that the specialized method should be superior with respect to reading improvement. The fundamental issues do not revolve around a simple question—superior or not? Rather, it is necessary to consider the extent and permanence of any gains, and also any limitations which the specialized procedure might impose on the wider scope of classroom work.

In fact the research, substantial in its sample and rigorous in design, indicated that highly significant gains in reading comprehension were obtained, and that these gains were sustained during a reasonable post-test period. Moreover, on some measures the gains increased after the use of the specialized procedure had ceased.

During the interim dissemination sessions organized by the project, these findings have been subjected to greater scrutiny and more questioning than any other aspect of our work. The project team became aware that there existed a strong 'anti-laboratory' lobby.

It must be emphasized that our research was not designed either to please commercial interest or to confirm contrary prejudices. We set out to obtain objective data and these we have reported. The plain truth is that SRA *Reading Laboratories*, used systematically by a teacher conversant with the system, contributed to the reading ability of most average and above-average readers. If this conclusion is to be attacked, then evidence must be produced to show where our experiment was defective.

In interpreting the results of this particular research we have also stressed the limitations of reading laboratories. They can be, and are, misused. Most important, however, we consider that they should not be thought of as a complete reading programme. Indeed, we have stated that 'the benefits of laboratory work can be fully realized only if they are accompanied and followed by study programmes which call for individual and group work ... (in literature and the content areas)'. The fact that laboratories have been and are being misused provides grounds for rethinking, not an argument for not using laboratories under any circumstances whatsoever.

In considering when laboratories should be used, and in what context, we need to deal with a number of possible objections to the research itself.

First, one may argue that laboratory work was evaluated against normal classroom practice which admittedly does not include significant attempts to improve reading ability. If therefore such practice was revised it is possible that gains in reading ability could be obtained which would dispense with the need for laboratory work. This argument ignores two facts. The revision of classroom practice is a slow process, and the inefficient reader inhabits the classroom now. Therefore, we suggest that one means of effecting improvement immediately should not be ignored just because other procedures may produce similar results in the future.

Second, it is generally held to be true that a reading policy across the curriculum will necessitate a wider awareness of the principles for promoting effective reading among the total teaching force. In a sense, laboratory work may be seen as an escape route which prevents teachers of all subjects from gaining direct experience of dealing with reading problems. However, we do not suggest that laboratory work should be used as the only solution. We specifically recommend other programmes. If this advice is followed, then all teachers will be engaged in procedures which will result in some measure of self-education through face-to-face work with pupils, and the evaluation of such work.

Third, it may appear that the improvement in reading ability effected by the use of structured materials contradicts our findings related to the nature of reading comprehension. On the one hand we claim that reading comprehension is a unitary competence, and on the other we establish that a 'skill'-based procedure is beneficial.

There is in fact no contradiction. One effect of the laboratory situation was to produce 'a willingness to reflect on what was being read'. This was supported by regular, systematic, purposeful reading.

In other words, some of the conditions set out in our description of a viable reading programme were met by the laboratory work.

In addition, we were careful to emphasize that laboratory work should be complemented by a more open-ended approach. We have also produced some evidence to support such a combination. It has been shown that the laboratories produce significant gains for each of the age groups at which they were tried. But it does not follow that schools can be recommended to introduce a separate laboratory course each year. To begin with, the most effective mix might well include one term of laboratory experience at the beginning of the first year and a second at the beginning of the third. As teachers gain experience with alternative approaches, it is possible (but not certain), that laboratory work can be phased out altogether without loss.

Fourth, it is often said that researchers have little practical advice to offer teachers. The opposite is true in this instance. We have a clear and unequivocal recommendation which can be implemented. It has been a salutary experience to discover that our advice has met with intense opposition. But if research is to be meaningful, its findings must at least receive genuine consideration. It cannot survive if acceptance of its work is limited to those occasions when personal opinion is confirmed.

VIII Improving reading through group discussion activities (Chapter 9)

The reading laboratory is the instrument most extensively used by schools to effect an improvement in reading ability, but the project team also carried out an assessment of other procedures. At the time when our investigations were being carried out these approaches were not common in secondary schools. Our interest was aroused partly because the work on the nature of reading comprehension (Chapter 3) stimulated an effort to explore means of creating 'a willingness to reflect' within the reader, and partly because in project seminars the idea of harnessing reading to pupil-centred discussion seemed to merit further study.

In the event, five different ways of presenting a written text so that corporate reflection or prediction might accompany or follow reading were selected for pilot work. These were:

1 group cloze
2 group SQ3R
3 group sequencing
4 group prediction
5 group reading for different purposes.

These activities have been described in Chapter 9, so no further explanation is offered here. What must be emphasized, however, is that it was impossible to apply to this inquiry objective measures of assessment of the same scale and rigour that were applied to the reading laboratories.

There were many reasons for this. Most important, perhaps, was an error of judgement in the early stages of the project. Given the benefit of hindsight, and assuming a new project was being designed now, what we as a project team would be compelled to do would be to concentrate a major portion of time and resources on exploring discussion approaches to reading for learning. Time had passed and resources had already been allocated before we fully realized the importance of the approaches now under discussion. Then, reading laboratories were in existence and were already being used. The task of finding schools willing to devote classroom time to our experiment, of setting up the necessary groups within schools, and of carrying out training and testing was accomplished without undue difficulty. In the case of the group discussion procedures, however, the approach was novel for most teachers, and a great deal of pilot work had to be carried out. The vastness of our brief, to consider effective reading across the curriculum, involved delicate negotiation with subject specialists. There was even a dearth of proven materials suitable for the work we envisaged. Thus, behind the bald account of what we achieved lies a story of gathering teachers together for practical workshops, following-up work which emerged from these sessions, proving or discarding materials, discussing difficulties as they arose.

The work undertaken by Pilot School 1 was the most significant outcome because in this instance a number of procedures were developed in a variety of situations, and a viable method of assessing the results was evolved. We owe a great deal to the enthusiasm of the staff of this school, who accomplished more within the setting of a single school than we anticipated would be possible.

Thus, although what we achieved in the end was perhaps no more than an initial survey of the field, at least we were able to study one situation in which the integration of discussion procedures into the school curriculum was attempted on a considerable scale.

Our conclusions are brief, but important:

1 The procedures have been proved at the level of practicability. They can be used in the classroom given that the teacher is adequately prepared.
2 The pupils we have worked with have responded well. They appear to enjoy using set reading for discussion.
3 The pupils revealed an ability to think about their reading in a way that is not evident when only the written outcomes of reading are considered.

4   Teachers have noted an improvement in the quality of pupils' reflection as confidence in using the procedures increases.

At this point it is important to note that we have some indication that the competence of pupils to reflect on their reading is greater than their performance on written work might indicate. Some sections of this report have tended to a pessimistic view of the ability of pupils to use reading for learning, but in the setting of the group discussion activities, what the pupils achieved allows for greater optimism. Even to produce hope within the minds of teachers is gain, but there is more to the matter than that.

Our judgements of children's performance as intelligent readers have often been made from their responses to closed questions given during or after a piece of set reading. The teacher ascertains if the pupil has 'learned' this or that. The group discussion activities, however, are designed to stimulate questioning within the reader, and we have some grounds for putting forward the suggestion that children are quite alert readers when we judge their performance on the quality of their predictions or their 'psycholinguistic guesses'. Therefore, on the basis of starting where the children are, a reading programme should include opportunities for talking about reading in the structured way implicit in the discussion procedures.

We can now return to the vexed issues of the relationship between laboratory work and the more open discussion activities. In the main, the laboratory is concerned with overt reading behaviour. The student is guided in a particular way in order to achieve determined goals. The discussion activities are more related to covert reading behaviour—what goes on in my mind as I process what a writer has written. While this is an over-simplification, it points to the two aspects of 'the ability to reflect' suggested in our review of Chapter 3 above. In the laboratory situation the reader learns the rules of the game that help to make his behaviour skilled. In the discussion situation the reader is being invited to practise reflection with immediate oral expression and immediate response, with the expectation that the individual exercise of reflection in solitary reading will also become more skilled.

Reference should be made here to the thesis put forward in Chapter 2, where the differences between spoken and written communication were considered in detail. There is a real sense in which the group discussion activities serve to minimize some of these differences. In particular, a situation has been created where immediate responses can be aired and argued out. The reader is no longer left to his own internal thoughts. The assumptions of the writer can be questioned and explanations offered, thus making more explicit the communication between writer and reader. We believe this process is a stage on the way to becoming an efficient solitary reader.

It is inevitable, perhaps, that the question will be raised again: which is best—the laboratory or the group discussion? The question itself is ill-conceived. One might as well ask: which is the best for health—an apple or a piece of cheese? We are not comparing like with like, but a total diet of either is likely to be insufficient.

One advantage of the discussion activities is the information they provide for teachers about the thinking, knowledge, level of conceptualization, and reading difficulties of their pupils. They are diagnostic as well as teaching procedures. Given new data about the response of their pupils to reading, teachers can modify their teaching, and become better teachers of reading. This can be achieved to a certain extent merely by applying general teaching principles without any recourse to expertise about learning to read. Hence, the discussion activities can be, and should be, learning sessions for teachers as well as pupils. We consider that where these activities can be implemented across the curriculum a means has been created for teachers in the content areas to become teachers of reading.

A defect might be that discussion activities do require careful preparation and sensitive handling. We must be careful here to avoid the conclusion that such means should, therefore, be limited to teachers with special gifts, with the corollary that laboratories are for the rest! A teacher faced with unexciting outcomes of reading day by day in the classroom may find greater incentive if introduced to procedures which open up new possibilities, and the discussion activities certainly do this.

IX Visits to schools (Chapter 10)

It is not proposed to summarize our programme of school visits again. Rather we shall detail a few key issues.

1 Our visits did not confirm the most pessimistic prediction that no work on reading development is taking place in our secondary schools. Like the Bullock Committee we were introduced to instances of 'good practice'. It is impossible, however, for us to comment on the extent of such practice throughout the country as a whole. We merely visited those schools to which we were invited.

2 We gained the impression that whenever a school introduces the development of reading into its programme, whatever the nature of the measure or measures considered appropriate, some benefit accrues. This is confirmation of the belief that the development of effective reading demands some form of direct intervention on the part of teachers. It cannot be regarded as a byproduct of a liberal education.

3 In many cases, efforts to improve reading for learning within a

school stemmed from the enthusiasm of a single member of staff. It was inevitable, therefore, that the innovative approach was often limited to one subject department, or one group of pupils. We would comment that such work is likely to fail in its objective if it is not supported across the curriculum, and extended along the age range. Hence the need for some form of language policy throughout a school is underlined.

4   We observed many arrangements within schools which would extend our own concept of viable action to make reading for learning effective. Within the project we concentrated on laboratory work, group discussion activities, and the editing of texts. We would now wish to add:

(a) means for improving the 'search' techniques available to pupils;

(b) attention to note-taking and note-making, together with other ways of recording information and ideas;

(c) efforts to promote a wider use of both literature and information texts in private reading;

(d) arrangements for individual or group counselling concerning study methods.

Thus, our programme of visits served a dual purpose. On the one hand we were able to observe at first hand the work of committed teachers, and this has been reported. Also, we have been reminded of the limits of our own inquiry and have been encouraged to widen our own perspectives.

X The way ahead

The task of teaching reading lies mainly in the hands of teachers. It is proper therefore, that this report should conclude with a statement that summarizes our findings in so far as they bear upon policy, organization and teaching method within schools.

1   We must emphasize that the reading ability of average and above-average pupils in the 10–15 year age range can be improved. Of this, we are in no doubt whatsoever. Substantial proof was obtained from the inquiry into the effectiveness of reading laboratories; more subjective yet convincing evidence came from the work with discussion activities; further support for the conclusion was forthcoming from our visits to schools.

2   The common factor which underpins such improvement is the insertion of some form of special attention to reading, or study methods, or both into the school programme. Reading improvement can be effected by attention to reading and its allied skills; we have found no evidence that a similar improvement can be brought about by treating reading as a byproduct of normal classroom practice. It

must be pointed out, however, that we cannot claim to have sampled schools on a wide scale. Our conclusion is based on observations within the limits of the project.

3   While it might appear that almost any action which stresses reading or methods of study is likely to benefit pupils, there are some clear indications as to the most effective line of action. The outline of a programme to improve reading for learning should include:

(a) the use of reading situations designed to foster a willingness to reflect on what is being read;

(b) a structure of instruction, guidance and reading practice which improves the quality of reflection;

(c) arrangements to monitor methods and materials across the curriculum in order to create the conditions under which pupils may use reading purposefully.

We have arrived at this formulation by considering the nature of reading comprehension, and by examining a variety of routines and approaches which are presently available to teachers.

4   Throughout this inquiry our attention has been focussed on reading. Yet from time to time, we have found it necessary to examine other language activities—listening, speaking and writing. Our concern with the total pattern of language work illustrates the fact that reading can rarely be considered in isolation.

A Language for Life stresses the unity of language and we would endorse this emphasis. It is important however to appreciate the implications of accepting that listening, reading, speaking and writing are, in some way inter-related: the four modes of language are components of learning through language, and such learning is enhanced when more than one language mode is employed. In particular, the link between reading and discussion is crucial.

The effective use of reading always involves thinking as well as reading. At its best, it is a conversation with the text. An emphasis on reading can and should coexist with an equal emphasis on spoken exchange. When they are used together in the same setting, reading may provide the stimulus to thinking; spoken language gives it reality and sustains it; finally, writing crystallizes the product.

A Note on Statistics

Keith Selkirk

The first aim of statistics when faced with a set of data such as those obtained from administering a test is simplification. The first statistic used for this purpose is the *arithmetic mean* (also known as *average* or *mean*) which should be familiar to readers. The arithmetic mean is a measure of the central position of the scores, but it is insufficient in itself as a complete description of them. We also need some measure of how spread out the scores are, and the statistic which is commonly used for this purpose is called the *standard deviation*.[1]

Test scores can be plotted on a diagram called a *histogram* whose outline is usually approximately bell-shaped. Three such histograms are shown in Fig. S.1 (p. 315): all have arithmetic mean 100, while standard deviations are respectively 5, 10 and 15. The shape of such histograms is frequently close to the shape of a mathematical function known as the *normal distribution*. The normal distributions with the same arithmetic means and standard deviations as those of the histograms in Fig. S.1 are shown in Fig. S.2 (p. 316). Provided the number of scores plotted is reasonably large (say over fifty), the standard deviations of distributions such as these will probably be about one-sixth of the difference between the greatest and least scores.

In many situations, especially where mathematical manipulation is used, it is convenient to use the square of the standard deviation; this is known as the *variance*.

We often wish to know how well the mean value obtained in administering a test estimates the true mean value of the underlying population. The accuracy of the estimate depends on two things; a set of scores with a low standard-deviation will be more accurate than a set of scores with a high one, and accuracy will increase with the number of scores measured. In general the probable error in the

---

[1] The standard deviation is the root mean square deviation of the scores from the arithmetic mean. We shall ignore considerations of degrees of freedom in what follows.

Figure S.1   *Examples of histograms with total frequency 100, mean 100 and various standard deviations*

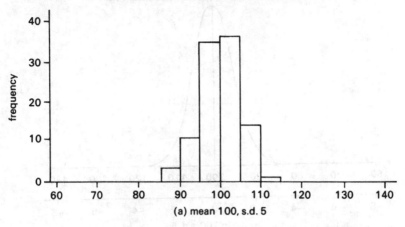

(a) mean 100, s.d. 5

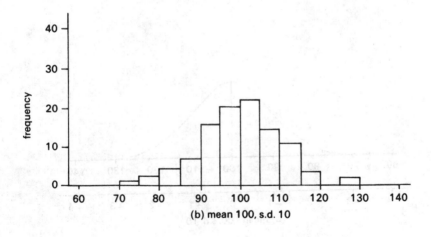

(b) mean 100, s.d. 10

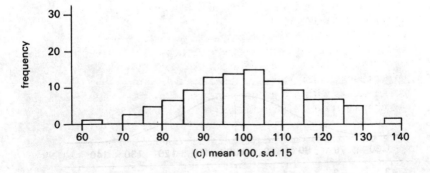

(c) mean 100, s.d. 15

Figure S.2   *Examples of the normal distribution with mean 100 and various standard deviations (lower scales give standard or z scores)*

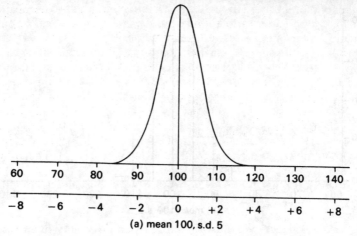

(a) mean 100, s.d. 5

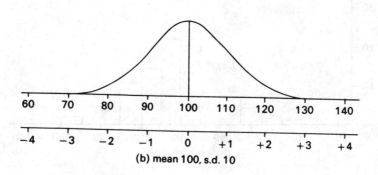

(b) mean 100, s.d. 10

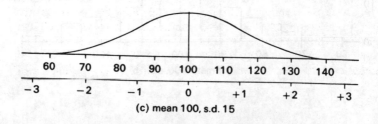

(c) mean 100, s.d. 15

measured arithmetic mean is proportional to the standard deviation of the scores, and inversely proportional to the square root of the number of scores used. This quantity, which is the standard deviation divided by the square root of the number of scores, is called the *standard error* and gives a measure of the accuracy of the experimental mean as an estimator of population mean. Approximately, there is a 95 per cent chance that the true population mean lies within two standard errors of that actually obtained. For example, if a set of twenty-five test scores has mean 100 and standard deviation fifteen, then the standard error is $15 \div \sqrt{25} = 3$, and we can be 95 per cent certain that the true mean lies between $100 \pm (2 \times 3)$, that is, between 94 and 106. If there are 100 test scores, the corresponding range of 95 per cent certainty is 97 to 103. The latter corresponds to the distribution in Fig. S. 1 (c).

If simplification is the first task of statistics, the second is drawing logical inferences. No statistical inference is ever completely certain, because even the most improbably extreme results could have happened by chance. We must therefore risk a possibility of a result which we call *significant happening by mischance*. In educational statistics we are usually willing to have a 5 per cent or a 1 per cent chance of being wrong, and we test our results according to whether the chances of being wrong are less than 5 per cent or less than 1 per cent. Conventionally these 0.05 and 0.01 levels of significance are often denoted in reports by one (*) or two (**) asterisks respectively.

The simplest situation which we wish to test in this way is whether the means of two sets of scores are sufficiently far apart for the difference not to have occurred by chance. To do this we standardize the difference between the means by dividing it by the combined standard error of the two sets of scores (we shall not go into the method of obtaining this combined standard error). The resulting quantity is tested by using the t-distribution and is known as a *t-test*. Values for t which are significant depend on the number of scores tested, but for values over about 30, the t-distribution is almost identical to the normal distribution. Figure S.3 (p. 318) shows some pairs of distributions which are just significantly different at the 0.05 level. Notice that (a) and (b) are for very small sample sizes, and that the shape of the distribution is only given approximately by normal curves.

When more than two tests are being compared, the t-test cannot be used and a more general technique known as a one-way *analysis of variance* must be employed. (The abbreviation *anova* is often used.) The analysis of variance technique will tell us whether there are significant differences, but if we also wish to know between which sets of scores the differences lie, a variety of additional tests is available. The one used in this research is known as *Tukey's* test.

When tests involve two-way comparisons, such as when sex and

Figure S.3   *Examples of normal distributions where the differences between the means are just significant at the 0.05 level*

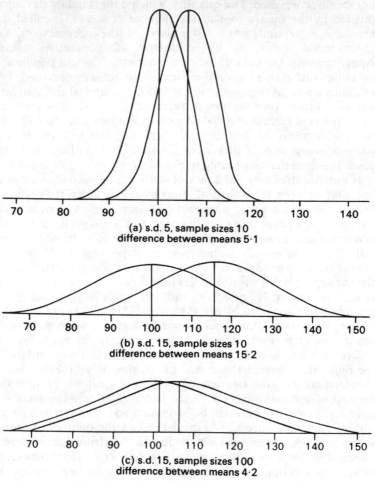

(a) s.d. 5, sample sizes 10
difference between means 5·1

(b) s.d. 15, sample sizes 10
difference between means 15·2

(c) s.d. 15, sample sizes 100
difference between means 4·2

ability levels are both being compared, the anova technique can be extended to cover more than one variable. The *two-way* anova is used in Chapter 8.

Returning to the field of descriptive statistics once more, when we want to compare distributions which are approximately normal, then we must measure them from a common base-level. We do this by transforming the scores. If our scores have, for example, mean 100 and standard deviation 15, we subtract the mean (100) from each score, so that scores below the mean are negative, and the new set of scores then has mean 0 and standard deviation 15. We then divide

Figure S.4   *Examples of the correlation coefficient, r, for samples of size 10*

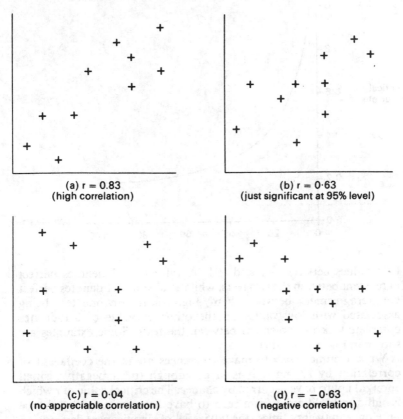

(a) r = 0·83
(high correlation)

(b) r = 0·63
(just significant at 95% level)

(c) r = 0·04
(no appreciable correlation)

(d) r = −0·63
(negative correlation)

each score by the standard deviation (15), so that the whole set of scores has mean 0 and standard deviation 1. Such transformed scores are known as *standard scores* or *Z scores*, and scores expressed in this way can be compared on a common basis. In Fig. S.2 the lower set of horizontal scores on each diagram gives the appropriate Z scores for the distribution.

If the same subjects are given two different tests, then we may measure the degree of agreement between the tests by multiplying the standard scores for each subject and then dividing by the number of subjects; that is taking the average product of standard scores.[1] This gives a quantity known as the coefficient of *correlation* which measures the degree of agreement between the two sets of scores. The coefficient of correlation is usually denoted by the letter r, and can

[1] Strictly we should divide by one less than the number of subjects.

Figure S.5   *Critical values of r at the 0.05 level of significance*

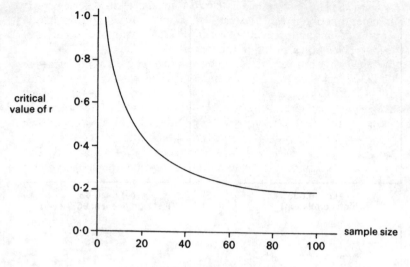

take values between −1 and +1. A value of +1 denotes perfect agreement between the two tests, while a value of −1 denotes perfect counteragreement between them, high values on one test being associated with low values on the other. A value of 0 indicates complete lack of agreement between the tests. Some examples are shown in Fig. S.4 (p. 319).

We sometimes wish to make inferences about the coefficient of correlation by asking if it is large enough (or if negative, small enough) not to have occurred by chance. The critical value of r which is sufficiently different from zero to have been exceeded by chance only once in twenty times (the 0.05 level of significance) depends on the size of the sample, and its theoretical values are shown for positive r in Fig. S.5 above. The negative critical values are, of course, obtained by changing the sign of r. For a large sample a value of r quite close to zero may nevertheless be significant: for a small sample a value of r close to +1 or −1 may be needed. Figure S.5 shows that, for a sample of 10, values of r greater than 0.63 or less than −0.63 are significant at the 0.05 level, while for a sample of 100 the corresponding values are 0.20 and −0.20. In Figs. S.4(b) and (d) examples of sample of size 10 where the values of r are just sufficiently different from zero to have been exceeded only once in twenty times are given.

The coefficient of correlation can also be obtained from the raw (untransformed) scores by calculation of a quantity called the *covariance* of the scores. To obtain r, the covariance must be divided by the standard deviations of both sets of scores, which compensates for the non-use of standard scores in the calculation of the covariance. The covariance is thus a measure of the degree of agreement between the two sets of scores, but is comparatively meaningless in comparisons between different examples because of the lack of standardization of the scores.

When a large number of tests are given to a set of subjects, r may be calculated for every pair of tests and a table or *matrix* of correlations built up. By extracting the common features of sets of tests which have a high correlation, the concepts common to those tests can be identified; these are known as *factors*, and the whole process known as *factor* analysis is an important technique of considerable complexity. This technique has been used in Chapter 3 of this research, but its detailed explanation is beyond the scope of this note.[1]

[1] Interested readers might refer (*inter alia*) to Fruchter, B. (1967) *An Introduction to Factor Analysis* New York: Van Nostrand.

Bibliography

ABERCROMBIE, M. L. J. (1960) *The Anatomy of Judgement* London: Hutchinson

ALLARD, J. A. (1946) Difficulty of poems commonly presented to elementary school pupils (abstract of Doctoral Dissertation) *University of Pittsburgh Bulletin 42*, 9–18 (cited in Klare, 1963, p. 222)

ARGYLE, M. (1969) *Social Interaction* London: Methuen

AUKERMANN, R. C. (1972) *Reading in the Secondary School Classroom* New York: McGraw-Hill

AUSUBEL, D. P. (1968) *Educational Psychology: A Cognitive View* New York: Holt, Rinehart and Winston

BARNES, D., BRITTON, J. and ROSEN, H. (1969) *Language, the Learner and the School* Harmondsworth: Penguin

BARTLETT, F. C. (1958) *Thinking: An Experimental and Social Study* London: Allen and Unwin

BECKER, A. L. (1965) A tagmemic approach to paragraph analysis *College Composition and Communication 16*, 239–42

BELLACK, A. A., KLIEBARD, H. M., HYMAN, R. T. and SMITH, F. L. (1966) *The Language of the Classroom* New York: Teachers' College Press

BERNSTEIN, B. (1961) 'Social class and linguistic development: a theory of social learning' in A. H. Halsey, J. Floud and C. A. Anderson (Eds.) (1961) *Education, Economy and Society* New York: Face Press

BERNSTEIN, B. (1971) *Class, Codes and Control: Volume I Theoretical Studies Towards a Sociology of Language* London: Routledge and Kegan Paul

BLOOM, B. S., HASTINGS, J. T. and MADAUS, G. F. (1971) *Handbook on Formative and Summative Evaluation of Student Learning* New York, London: McGraw-Hill

BORMUTH, J. R. (1966) Readability: a new approach *Reading Research Quarterly 1/3*, 79–132

BORMUTH, J. R. (1967) Comparable cloze and multiple choice comprehension test scores *Journal of Reading 10*, 291–9

BORMUTH, J. R. (1968a) Cloze test readability: criterion reference scores *Journal of Educational Measurement 5*, 189–96

BORMUTH, J. R. (1968b) The cloze readability procedure *Elementary English 45*, 429–36

BORMUTH, J. R. (1969) 'Empirical determination of the instructional reading level' in J. A. Figurel (Ed.) (1968) *Reading and Realism* Proceedings of the International Reading Association Newark, Delaware: International Reading Association

BRITTON, J. (1971) What's the use? A schematic account of language functions *Educational Review 23*, 205–19

BRITTON, J., BURGESS, T., MARTIN, N., McLEOD, A. and ROSEN, H. (1975)

The Development of Writing Abilities (11–18) (Schools Council Research Studies) London: Macmillan Education

CALLAWAY, W. R. (1970) *Modes of biological adaptation and their role in intellectual development* P. C. D. Monographs 1, cited in E. J. Gibson and H. Levin (1975), p. 277

CARROLL, J. B. (1971) *Learning from Verbal Discourse in Educational Media: A Review of the Literature* Princeton, New Jersey: E.T.S.

CHALL, J. S. (1958) *Readability—An Appraisal of Research and Application* Columbus, Ohio: Ohio State University Press

CHOMSKY, N. (1957) *Syntactic Structures* The Hague: Mouton and Co.

CHOMSKY, N. (1965) *Aspects of the Theory of Syntax* Cambridge, Mass.: M.I.T. Press

CLARKE, P. A. (1977) Reading in science lessons Unpublished M.Ed. dissertation, University of Nottingham

DES (1975) *A Language for Life* (The Bullock Report) London: H.M.S.O.

DALE, E. and CHALL, J. S. (1948) A formula for predicting readability *Educational Research Bulletin 27*, 11–20, 37–54

DAVIS, F. B. (1968) Research in comprehension in reading *Reading Research Quarterly 3*, 499–545

DAVIES, A. (1968) Some problems in the use of language varieties in teaching *Educational Review 20*, 107–22

DAVIES, A. (1969) 'The notion of register' in A. Wilkinson (Ed.) *The State of Language, Educational Review 22*, 64–7

DOWNING, J. and THACKRAY, D. (1971) *Reading Readiness* London: University of London Press for United Kingdom Reading Association

EYSENCK, H. J. (1953) *The Structure of Human Personality* London: Methuen

FARR, J. N., JENKINS, J. J. and PATTERSON, D. G. (1951) Simplification of the Flesch Reading Ease Formula *Journal of Applied Psychology 35*, 333–7

FARR, R. (1969) *Reading: what can be measured?* An International Reading Association Research Fund Monograph for the ERIC/CRIER Reading Review Series Newark: Delaware

FAWCETT, R. (1977) The use of reading laboratories and other procedures in promoting effective reading among pupils aged 9–15 Ph.D. thesis, University of Nottingham

FILLENBAUM, S., JONES, L. V. and RAPAPORT, A. (1963) The predictability of words and their grammatical classes as a function of rate of deletion from a speech transcript *Journal of Verbal Learning and Verbal Behaviour 2*, 186–94

FLANDERS, N. A. (1970) *Analyzing Teaching Behavior* Reading, Mass.: Addison Wesley

FLESCH, R. F. (1948) A new readability yardstick *Journal of Applied Psychology 32*, 221–33

FUNKHOUSER, G. R. and MACCOBY, N. (1971) *Study on communicating science information to a lay audience, Phase II* Report based on a study funded by the National Science Foundation (NSF GZ-996) Institute of Communication Research, Stanford University

GAGNÉ, R. M. (1965) *The Conditions of Learning* New York: Holt, Rinehart and Winston

GIBSON, E. J. and LEVIN, H. (1975) *The Psychology of Reading* Cambridge, Mass.: M.I.T. Press

GILLILAND, J. (1972) *Readability* London: University of London Press for United Kingdom Reading Association

GOLDMANN-EISLER, F. (1958) Speech analysis and mental processes *Language and Speech 1*, 59–75

GOODMAN, K. S. (1967) Reading: a psycholinguistic guessing game *Journal of the Reading Specialist 6*, 259–64, 266–71

GUNNING, R. (1952) *The Technique of Clear Writing* New York: McGraw-Hill

HALLIDAY, M. A. K. (1970) 'Language structure and language function' in J. Lyons (Ed.) (1970) *New Horizons in Linguistics* Harmondsworth: Penguin

HALLIDAY, M. A. K. (1975) *Learning how to Mean: Explorations in the Development of Language* London: Edward Arnold

HALLIDAY, M. A. K., MCINTOSH, A. and STREVENS, P. (1964) *The Linguistic Sciences and Language Teaching* London: Longman

HARRISON, C. (1974) *Readability and School* Schools Council Project discussion document, University of Nottingham School of Education

HARRISON, C. (1977) 'Assessing the readability of school texts' in J. Gilliland (Ed.) (1977) *Reading: Improving Classroom Practice and Research* London: Ward Lock Educational

HERRIOT, P. (1970) *An Introduction to the Psychology of Language* London: Methuen

HILSUM, S. and CANE, B. S. (1971) *The Teacher's Day* Windsor: National Foundation for Educational Research

HOWE, M. J. A. (1972) *Understanding School Learning: A New Look at Educational Psychology* New York, London: Harper and Row

INHELDER, B. and PIAGET, J. (1958) *The Growth of Logical Thinking from Childhood to Adolescence* London: Routledge and Kegan Paul

JOOS, M. (1961) *The Five Clocks* New York: Harcourt, Brace and World (Harbinger Books)

KAISER, H. F. (1970) A second generation little jiffy *Psychometrika 35*, 401–15

KLARE, G. R. (1963) *The Measurement of Readability* Ames, Iowa: Iowa State University Press

KLARE, G. R. (1974–5) Assessing readability *Reading Research Quarterly 10*, 62–102

KLARE, G. R. (1975a) A second look at the validity of readability formulas Paper read to annual meeting of National Reading Conference, St Petersburg, Florida, December

KLARE, G. R. (1975b) Judging readability *Instructional Science 6*, 55–61

KLARE, G. R., SIMAIKO, H. W. and STOLUROW, L. M. (1972) The cloze procedure: a convenient readability test for training materials and translations *International Review for Applied Psychology 21*, 2, 77–106

LENNON, R. T. (1962) What can be measured? *The Reading Teacher 15*, 326–37

LUNZER, E. A. (1960) *Recent studies in Britain based on the work of Jean Piaget* Occasional Publications No. 4 Windsor: National Foundation for Educational Research

LUNZER, E. A. (1965) 'Problems of formal reasoning in test situations' in P. H. Mussen (Ed.) *European research in cognitive development* Monographs of the Society for Research in Child Development 30, 2, 19–46

LUNZER, E. A. (1978) 'Formal reasoning: a reappraisal' in B. Z. Presseisen, D. Goldstein and M. H. Appel (Eds) *Topics in Cognitive Development Volume 2: Language and Operational Thought* New York, London: Plenum Press

LUNZER, E. A., DOLAN, T. and WILKINSON, J. E. (1976) The effectiveness of measures of operativity, language and short-term memory in the prediction of reading and mathematical understanding *British Journal of Educational Psychology 46*, 295–305

LUNZER, E. A., WILKINSON, J. E. and DOLAN, T. (1976) The distinctiveness of operativity as a measure of cognitive functioning in five-year-old children *British Journal of Educational Psychology 46*, 289–294

MACGINITIE, W. H. (1961) Contextual constraint in English prose paragraphs *Journal of Psychology 51*, 121–30

MCLAUGHLIN, G. H. (1969) SMOG grading—a new readability formula *Journal of Reading 12*, 639–46

MCLEISH, J. (1976) 'The Lecture method' in N. L. Gage (Ed.) *The Psychology of Teaching Methods* Chicago: National Society for the Study of Education (seventy-fifth year book)

MCNINCH, G., KASELSKIS, R. and COX, J. A. (undated) 'Appropriate cloze deletion schemes for determining suitability of college textbooks' in P. L. Nacke (Ed.) (1976) *Interaction: Research and Practice for College-Adult Reading* Twenty-third yearbook of National Reading Conference, 249–53

MARTIN, N., D'ARCY, P., NEWTON, B. and PARKER, R. (1976) *Writing and Learning Across the Curriculum 11–16* London: Ward Lock Educational

MELNIK, A. and MERRITT, J. (1972) *The Reading Curriculum* London: University of London Press in association with the Open University

MILLER, L. R. (1974) Predictive powers of the Dale-Chall and Bormuth readability formulas *Journal of Business Communication* winter, *11*, 21–30

MORAY HOUSE COLLEGE OF EDUCATION (1973) *Edinburgh Reading Tests (Stage 3)* London: University of London Press

MORTLOCK, R. S. (1959) Reading improvement among high school students using the SRA *Reading Laboratory Education 8*, 2, 19–23 (Education Department of Western Australia)

MUGFORD, L. (1972) A new way of predicting readability *Reading 4/2*, 31–5

NEW YORK CITY BOARD OF EDUCATION (1964) Reading in the subject areas, Grades 7–8–9 *Curriculum Bulletin No. 6* 1963–4 series. Table reprinted in Melnik and Merritt (1972)

PARKER, D. H. (1963) *Schooling for Individual Excellence* London: Nelson

PASK, G. (1976a) Conversational techniques in the study and practice of education *British Journal of Educational Psychology 46*, 12–25

PASK, G. (1976b) Styles and strategies of learning *British Journal of Educational Psychology 46*, 128–48

PHILLIP, A. (1969) Some notes on the informal study of register *Educational Review 22*, 93–102

POWERS, R. D., SUMNER, W. A. and KEARL, B. E. (1958) A recalculation of four adult readability formulas *Journal of Educational Psychology 49*, 99–105

RANKIN, E. F. and CULHANE, J. W. (1969) Comparable cloze and multiple-choice comprehension test scores *Journal of Reading 13*, 193–8

RANKIN, E. F. (1974) *The Measurement of Reading Flexibility* (Reading

Information Services: Where do we go?) Newark, Delaware: International Reading Association

ROBINSON, F. P. (1961, first published 1946) *Effective Study* New York: Harper and Row

ROBINSON, F. P. (1962) *Effective Reading* New York: Harper and Row

ROTHKOPF, E. Z. (1966) Learning from written instructive materials: an exploration of the control of inspection behaviour by test-like events *American Educational Research Journal 3*, 241–9

RYLE, G. (1949) *The Concept of Mind* London: Hutchinson

SAUSSURE, F. DE (1916) *Cours de Linguistique Générale* Paris: Payot English translation W. Baskin (1959) *Course in General Linguistics* New York: Philosophical Library

SCHLIEF, M. and WOOD, R. W. (1974) A comparison of procedures to determine readability level of non-text materials *Reading Improvement 11*, 57–64

SHNAYER, S. W. (1969) 'Relationships between reading interest and reading comprehension' in J. A. Figurel (Ed.) *Reading and Realism* 1968 proceedings, Vol. 13, Part 1, Newark, Delaware: International Reading Association, 698–702

SKINNER, B. F. (1938) *The Behaviour of Organisms: An Experimental Analysis* New York: Appleton-Century-Crofts

SKINNER, B. F. (1959) *Cumulative Record* London: Methuen

SMIRNOV, A. A. and ZINCHENKO, P. I. (1969) 'Problems in the psychology of memory' in M. Cole and I. Maltzman (Eds) (1969) *A Handbook of Contemporary Soviet Psychology* New York: Basic Books

SMITH, F. (1971) *Understanding Reading: A Psycholinguistic Analysis of Reading and Learning* New York, London: Holt, Rinehart and Winston

SMITH, F. (1973) *Psycholinguistics and Reading* New York, London: Holt, Rinehart and Winston

SPEARRITT, D. (1972) Identification of subskills in reading comprehension by maximum likelihood factor analysis *Reading Research Quarterly 8*, 92–111

SQUIRE, J. R. and APPLEBEE, R. (1969) *Teaching English in the United Kingdom: A Comparative Study* Champaign, Illinois: ACTE

STAUFFER, R. G. (1969) *Teaching Reading as a Thinking Process* New York: Harper and Row

STAUFFER, R. G. (1970) *The Language-Experience Approach to the Teaching of Reading* New York: Harper and Row

STICHT, T. G. (1973) Research toward the design, development and evaluation of a job-functional literacy program for the U.S. Army *Literacy Discussion IV*, 3, 339–69

STOKES, A. (1978) The reliability of readability formulae *Journal of Research in Reading 1*, 21–34

SUMNER, R. (1976) *Reading Level Tests* Windsor: National Foundation for Educational Research

THOMAS, L. and AUGSTEIN, S. (1972) An experimental approach to the study of reading as a learning skill *Research in Education 8*, 28–46

THOMAS, L. and HARRI-AUGSTEIN, S. (1976) *The self-organized learner and the printed word* Report to the Social Science Research Council

THORNDIKE, R. L. (1971) Reading as reasoning Address delivered to American Psychological Association, Washington D.C., September 1971

TUINMAN, J. J. (1973) Determining the passage-dependency of comprehension questions in five major tests *Reading Research Quarterly 9*, 206–23

VERNON, P. E. (Ed.) (1957) *Secondary School Selection* London: Methuen

VINCENT, D. and CRESSWELL, M. (1976) *Reading Tests in the Classroom* Windsor: National Foundation for Educational Research

VAN DER WILL, C. (1976) The wording of spoken instructions to children and its effect on their performance of tasks *Educational Studies 2*, 3

WALKER, C. (1974) *Reading Development and Extension* London: Ward Lock Educational

WASON, P. C. and JOHNSON-LAIRD, P. N. (1972) *Psychology of Reasoning* London: Batsford

WATTS, L. and NISBET, J. (1974) *Legibility in Children's Books* Windsor: National Foundation for Educational Research

WEBER, R. M. (1968) The study of oral reading errors *Reading Research Quarterly 4*, 96–119

WHITEHEAD, F., CAPEY, F. C. and MADDREN, W. (1974) *Children's Reading Interests* Schools Council Working Paper 52 London: Evans/Methuen Educational

WILKINSON, A. M., STRATTA, L. and DUDLEY, P. (1974) *The Quality of Listening* London: Macmillan Education for the Schools Council

WISEMAN, S. (1964) *Education and Environment* Manchester: Manchester University Press

YOUNGMAN, M. B. (1975) *Programmed Methods for Multivariate Data* Nottingham: University of Nottingham School of Education

ZIPF, G. K. (1935) *The Psycho-Biology of Language* Boston: Houghton

List of Tables

Table   *page*
3.1 Reading in the Subject Areas   42
3.2 The four tests: summary of item analysis   50
3.3 Reliability of the four tests   52
3.4 Factor analysis, four tests   56
3.5 Intercorrelation of factors in Table 3.4   57
3.6 Summary of Table 3.4   57
3.7 Factor analyses: two tests   58
3.8 Correlations and factor analysis for subscale totals   60
3.9 The Edinburgh Reading Test Stage 3   61
3.10 Comparative performance on sections of the tests   62
3.11 The process of reading: description   67
4.1 Teachers' mean estimates of readability levels   74
4.2 Flesch formula grade scores for passages   82
4.3 Correlation of assessments of passage difficulty   91
4.4 Means of readability scores over 40 passages   92
4.5 Intercorrelations of variables in cross-validation study   94
5.1 Percentage of teacher's time spent on various activities   119
5.2 Percentage of pupil's time spent on various activities   120
5.3 Types of writing and reading materials in subject areas   123
5.4 Patterns of reading continuity   125
5.5 Activities observed   128
5.6 Activities recorded on RBI   129
5.7 Summary of observed reading   131
5.8 Reading in English lessons   132
5.9 Estimates of continuous reading   133
6.1 Distribution of questionnaires returned   142
6.2 Frequency of assignments reported in interviews   142
6.3 Duration of homework   144
6.4 Duration of reading   145
6.5 Longest period of uninterrupted reading   147
6.6 Homework-reading: purposes given by teachers   150
6.7 Homework-reading: purposes given on teacher-
     questionnaire   152
6.8 Sources of text read as homework   153
7.1 Dominant activities   171
7.2 Percentage of reading time distributed by text   174

7.3   Library/resource area grouping and activities   175
8.1   Number of groups involved in project   200
8.2   Timetable of SRA inquiry   203
8.3   Results of main inquiry   211
8.4   Significance of differences between gains   215
8.5   Results of pre-test and final test   217
8.6   Reading style and reading purpose   218
9.1   Mean comprehension test scores (junior)   260
9.2   Mean comprehension test scores (secondary)   260
9.3   Total number of questions and errors noted   261
9.4   Average differences between predicted and actual scores 263

List of Figures

Fig.   *page*
2.1   The setting of spoken language   12
2.2   The setting of written communication   16
5.1   Reading Behaviour Inventory   113
7.1   Behaviour in library area   173
8.1   Results on Gates-MacGinitie: 4th-year juniors   205
8.2   Results on Gates-MacGinitie: 1st-year secondary   206
8.3   Results on Gates-MacGinitie: 4th-year secondary   207
8.4   Results on Waite tests   208
8.5   Comparative gains of SRA and Ward Lock Educational
      groups   213
8.6   Patterns of reading   219
S.1   Examples of histograms   315
S.2   Normal distribution: mean 100 and standard deviations   316
S.3   Normal distributions: significant differences between
      means   318
S.4   Examples of correlation coefficient r   319
S.5   Critical values of r at 0.05 level of significance   320

Index

Abercrombie, M. L. J., 230
accuracy test, 204, 205–7, 209, 211, 213, 214, 217, 227
Alistair (comprehension test), 45, 46, 50, 51, 52, 55, 56–8, 202, 203, 208, 209–10, 211, 216, 217, 218
Allard, J. A., 84
Applebee, R., 109, 116n, 121
Argyle, M., 13
Assessment of Fundamental Skills Involved in Reading Comprehension (Bezdek), 64n
audialization, 28
Augstein, S., 69, 215, 216, 218, 219
Aukermann, R. C., 231
Australia, reading laboratories studies in, 196–8
Ausubel, D. P., 30

BIDA (Behaviour Inventory Data Analysis), 117
backtracking, 1, 25, 26n, 28, 31, 215, 219
Barnes, Douglas, 34
Beachcomber, 15n
Behaviour Inventory Data Analysis (BIDA), 117
behavioural objectives, 38–9, 66
Bellack, A. A., 109
Belper High School, 291n
Bernstein, B., 2, 8
Bezdek, Anna Miars, 64n
Bloom, B. S., 38
Booth, Vera Southgate, 2
Bormuth, J. R., 77, 85, 88, 97–8, 231
Brighty (comprehension test), 45, 46, 50, 51, 52, 55, 56–8, 70–1, 202, 203, 208, 209–10, 211, 216, 217, 218
Britton, James, 2, 17, 25, 56, 122
Bruner, J. S., 2

Bullock Committee, 2, 34, 108, 136, 137–8, 224, 234, 254; Report (*A Language for Life*), 32, 72, 73, 187, 224–7, 228, 268, 269, 297, 303, 313

CSE, 75, 118
Canada, reading laboratories study in, 197
Cane, B. S., 109
Carroll, J. B., 38, 99
Chall, J. S., 78; *see also* Dale-Chall readability formula
Children's Reading Habits (Schools Council project; director, F. S. Whitehead), 2
Chomsky, N., 8n, 17, 20, 23n
Christ the King Comprehensive School, 232; *see also* Pilot School 1
Clarke, P. A., 260–4, 265
classroom, reading in, 4, 5, 108–38, 302–4
  main observation study, 108–26;
  primary-school study, 126–34
cloze, 88–90, 94–5, 96, 97–9, 275; group cloze, 231, 235–41, 249, 252, 253, 265–6
Cole, John, 116n, 141, 143, 153, 169
communication, 13, 14
comprehension
  definition, 38, 66, 67
  exercises, 31, 159, 252
  literal, 44, 61, 270
  reading, 4, 5, 7, 26, 29–32, 37–71, 84–5, 214, 223, 226, 299–301
  (Davis' study, 40–1; levels of, 37–8, 61–2, 68, 300; project inquiry, 41–62; teaching of, 69–70; unitary or manifold ability, 37–40, 51–62, 63, 64–8)

see also cloze, *Alistair*, *Brighty*, *Grieg*, *Jane*, Edinburgh Reading Scales; New York List (NYL)
comprehensive education, 3–4
continuous reading, 124–5, 130, 133, 134, 136, 137, 140, 143, 146–51 *passim*, 154–8, 300, 304
conversation, 9–14, 15, 24, 30, 31
copying, 137, 170, 171, 176, 189–90, 191–2, 305
Cresswell, M., 231

Dale 3000 word list, 90, 91, 94–5
Dale-Chall readability formula, 78, 79, 83, 87, 90, 91, 92, 94–5, 99
Davies, Sue, 78–9
Davis, F. B., 40–1, 59, 65
de Saussure, F., 8
deep structure, 20, 22, 23n
discussion, 32, 119–21, 129, 135–6, 171–2, 175, 188–9, 191, 192, 226, 228–66, 298, 305, 313
group discussion activities, 214–15, 215–20, 228–66, 292, 293, 303–4, 308–11 (earlier studies, 228–32; evaluation studies, 258–64; generality of skills, 230; project English, Language and the Curriculum course, 233; project reading, language and learning programme, 232–58; and mixed-ability teaching, 254, 256; and remedial pupils, 255); *see also* group activities under cloze, prediction, SQ3R, reading, sequencing
Dolan, T., 55

Edinburgh Reading Scales, 51, 59, 61, 63
editing, 17, 18, 19–20, 21, 32
education, changes in UK, 3–4
Effective Use of Reading Project, 1–6
English, 34, 35, 109, 135, 136, 194, 210, 223–4, 234, 257, 271–2, 294–6
choice of texts in, 83–4, 93, 300
classroom observation study, 114–25 *passim*

homework, 140–58 *passim*, 304
primary-school classroom study, 127–33 *passim*
and readability survey, 75, 80, 82, 83–4, 93, 96
English, Language and the Curriculum (project course), 233
environmental studies, 85, 293
errors in test measurement, 53–4, 58–9
Extending Beginning Reading (Schools Council project), 2n

factor analysis, 51, 53–5, 321
Farr, J. N., 79
Farr, R., 41
Farr-Jenkins-Patterson readability formula, 79, 91, 92
Fillenbaum, S., 89
Flanders, N. A., 109
Flesch, Rudolf, 74, 77
Flesch Grade, 79, 80, 82
Flesch Reading Ease Score (RE), 77, 79, 83, 90–1, 92, 93, 94–5, 96, 99, 106–7
flexibility in reading style, 2, 24–6, 29, 31
Fog readability formula, 79, 91, 92, 94–5
Forcast readability formula, 79, 90, 92
Fry Readability Graph, 92–3

GCE, 118
Gagné, R. M., 38
Gates-MacGinitie Reading Tests, 202, 203, 204–7, 211, 213, 216
geography, 85, 86, 96, 131, 156, 158, 223
Gilliland, Jack, 77
Gibson, E. J., 37
grammar, 7, 8, 17
Great Debate, 3n
Grieg (comprehension test), 44, 45, 46–8, 49, 50, 51, 52, 55, 56–8
group activities, *see* under each activity
The Growth of Logical Thinking from Childhood to Adolescence (Inhelder and Piaget), 273

Gunning, R., 79, 91, 102

Halliday, M. A. K., 2, 7
Harri-Augstein, S., 215
Harrison, A. K., 80
Harrison, Colin, 117
Hilsum, Sid, 109
Hinds, Barry, 93
history, 85, 86, 131, 223, 247, 270–1.
    274–5, 293
homework, 2, 5, 30, 86–7, 137,
    139–66, 304–5
    and classwork, 149, 151, 158–9,
    304
    project inquiry, 139–66 (examples
    of assignment, 154–8; interviews,
    141–3, 144–54 passim, 158;
    questionnaires, 140–1, 142,
    143–54 passim, 158, 160–6)
    teacher support, 30, 140, 155,
    157, 159, 304–5
Howe, M. J. A., 192
humanities, 34, 114, 115, 127, 128,
    131, 224; see also geography,
    history, integrated studies

independent pursuit of knowledge,
    4, 190, 191, 297
individualized learning, 75, 101,
    167, 193, 223, 269
Inhelder, B., 273
innovation, 279
integrated studies, 167–92

Jane (comprehension test), 45, 46,
    50, 51, 52, 55, 56–8
Jenkins, J. J., 79
Johnson-Laird, P. N., 20

Kaiser, H. F., 54, 55
Kearl, B. E., 79
Klare, George, 74, 77, 78, 85, 88, 89,
    101–2

language
    forms, 7
    spoken, 7–8, 9–14, 15–24, 32
    written, 7–8, 14–24, 32
language across the curriculum, 2,
    135–6, 257, 271–2, 276–9, 291–3,

294–6, 297, 298
A Language for Life (Bullock Report),
    32, 72, 73, 187, 224–7, 228, 268,
    269, 297, 303, 313
The Language-Experience Approach
    to the Teaching of Reading
    (Stauffer), 229–30, 231–2
language-experience programme,
    229–30
Lennon, R. T., 41
Levin, H., 37
library, 123, 124, 153, 168, 173,
    174–84, 188, 191, 305
listener (target), 9–14
    compared with reader, 18, 269
    listener-behaviour in reading, 25,
    29, 31
listening, 20, 118, 122, 194, 255–6,
    303, 313
literacy, 3n
Lunzer, E. A., 55

McCall-Crabbs, Standard Test
    Lessons in Reading, 88
MacGinitie, W. H., 89
McIntosh, A., 7
McLaughlin, G. H., 79, 91, 92
McNinch, G., 89
Magnifico, Dr L. X., 196n
Marland, Michael, 276n, 279n
Masterman, Paula, 116n
mathematics, 34, 35–6, 42–3, 54,
    135, 224, 267, 271, 273–4
    classroom observation study,
    114–25 passim, 302
    homework, 140–58 passim, 304
    primary-school classroom study,
    127–33 passim
    readability survey, 75, 80, 81–3,
    84, 89
    and text difficulty, 270, 274
    see also SMP, SMILE
meaning, 5, 7, 11, 19, 20
Melnick, A., 41, 42
memorization, 28, 122, 171, 195,
    218, 275, 304
Merritt, J., 41, 42
Miller, L. R., 97
mixed-ability grouping, 3–4, 35, 75,
    102, 168, 192, 234, 254, 256

modern languages, 142, 143, 241, 247
monotony, 18, 19, 21, 30–2
motivation, 19, 87–8, 89, 101, 107, 195, 209, 221, 222, 225, 226, 234, 253, 256, 305
Moyle, Donald, 197
Mugford, Len, 99
Mugford readability formula, 79, 91, 92, 94–5, 99
multiple-choice tests, 98, 202, 226
music, 128–9, 130, 131, 133, 224

NFER (National Foundation for Educational Research), 109, 231
NFER Reading Test E–H, 202, 203, 210
Reading Comprehension Test DE, 202, 203, 210, 211
Reading Test BD, 202, 203, 210, 211
National Association for the Teaching of English (NATE), 93
National Foundation for Educational Research, *see under* NFER
Neale, Dr Wallace, 196
New York City Board of Education, 41
New York List (NYL), 42, 44–5
Nisbet, J., 76
non-verbal behaviour in speaking, 11, 13, 18
note-making, 37, 86, 149, 170, 176, 191–2, 254–5, 270, 271, 275, 280, 289, 290, 304, 312
Nottingham University, 73, 89, 109, 126, 143, 169, 232, 253, 298n
numeracy, 3n

Open University, 4, 297
Oracy Project (Schools Council project; director, A. M. Wilkinson), 2

paragraphing, 30
Parker, D. H., 231, 241
Pask, G., 24
Patterson, D. G., 79
Patterson, Jean, 197

Piaget, Jean, 49, 273
Pilot School 1, 232–4, 251–8
Pinter, Harold, 15n
poetry, 28, 56–7, 84
polytechnics, 4
Powers, R. D., 79
Powers-Sumner-Kearl readability formula, 79, 91, 92
practice in schools, project survey of, 267–98
comprehension, 269–72
English, 294–6
language policy, examples, 276–9, 291–6
mathematics, 273–4
sixth-form programmes, 289–90
science, 272–3, 285–9
social sciences, 274–6
worksheets, 280–6
prediction, group, 229, 231, 232, 247–50, 256, 266
primary school
classroom study, 126–34
secondary school differences, 118, 121, 134, 136–7, 302–3
punctuation, 18, 30, 256
purpose in reading, 27, 140, 143, 148–58, 218–20

Rankin, E. F., 26
rate of reading, 24, 26, 27, 28, 194, 202, 204, 205–7, 209, 211, 213, 214, 215, 217, 223, 227, 249, 290
readability, 5, 72–107, 301–2
and teachers (implications of project study for, 101–3; workshops, 73–4)
assessing text difficulty, 73–4, 76–9, 86–7, 88, 93, 97–8, 156, 159, 271, 302
formulae, 74, 77, 79, 82, 83, 88–90, 91–102 *passim*
project cross-validation study, 79–80, 87–101
project survey on, 74–87
reader
and listener, 17–18
and permanence of text, 24–9
Reading Behaviour Inventory (RBI), 109, 110, 111, 112–14,

118–24, 126, 127, 129
Reading Comprehension Test DE
  (NFER), 202, 203, 210, 211
Reading Development (Open
  University course), 297
Reading Development and Extension
  (Walker), 231–2
reading ease score (RE), 77, 79, 83,
  90–1, 92, 93, 94–5, 96, 99, 106–7
Reading for Learning in Secondary
  Schools (Schools Council
  project), 265, 298n
reading, group, 229, 250, 251, 256
*Reading in the Subject Areas, Grades
  7–8–9* (New York City Board of
  Education), 41, 42, 44
reading laboratories, 31, 193–227,
  233, 312
  and Bullock Report, 224–6
  comparison of SRA *Reading
    Laboratories* and *Reading
    Workshops*, 212–14
  comparison with group
    discussion, 215–20, 222, 310–11
  follow-up work, 223
  generality of skills, 226–7
  project study on SRA *Reading
    Laboratories*, 43, 51, 57, 58, 59,
    198–211, 220, 227, 306–8
  studies on, 195–8
  teacher opposition to, 306, 308
  see also SRA *Reading
    Laboratories* and *Reading
    Workshops*
reading, language and learning
  programme, 233–58
  background, 233–5
  evaluation studies, 258–64
  generality of skills, 255
  group discussion activities in,
    235–50
  materials used in, 250–1
  organization of programme, 235,
    236, 237, 240, 241–2, 243
  teachers' comments on, 240–1,
    245–6, 249–50, 251–8
reading level, 83
Reading Level Tests (NFER
  research project), 231n
Reading Recorder, 215, 216, 218,
219
reading style, 26–9
Reading Systems Programme (Scott
  Foresman), 45, 232, 257
Reading Test BD (NFER), 202, 203,
  210, 211
'reading-thinking skills', 195, 229,
  230, 231, 234
Reading Workshops, 194, 212–14
receptive reading, 26, 28, 29, 37
reference material, use of, 86–7, 101,
  123, 124, 153, 157, 172–4, 188,
  194, 223, 255, 305–6
reflective reading (critical reading),
  26, 28, 31, 37, 64, 65, 69, 70, 121,
  122, 134, 135–6, 137, 157, 171,
  210, 214, 215, 218–20, 229, 254,
  264, 300–1, 303, 305–6, 307, 310,
  313
register, 19, 21, 297
remedial teaching, 100–1, 193, 197,
  204, 209, 221, 255, 292–3
resource area, 159, 168, 174–84,
  188, 191, 305
Resources for Learning
  Development Unit, 102
'retreat from print', 135, 189
Robinson, F. P., 28, 29, 31, 231, 241
Ryle, Gilbert, 67

SMILE (Secondary Mathematics
  Individualized Learning
  Experiment), 273
SMP (School Mathematics Project),
  157, 273
SQ3R (Survey-Question-Read-
  Recite-Review), 28–9, 30, 31, 32,
  194, 195, 214
  group SQ3R, 231, 241–2, 252, 256
SRA *Reading Laboratories*,
  193–227, 306–8
  comparison with group
    discussion, 215–20, 222
  comparison with *Reading
    Workshops* (Ward Lock
    Educational), 194, 212–14
  effectiveness of, 194, 220–1, 227
  and group SQ3R, 231, 241
  limitations of, 221–3, 227
  project study on, 43, 51, 57, 58,

59, 198–211, 220, 227, 306–8
    studies on, 196–8
scanning, 26–7, 28n, 37, 194
Scheffé test, 117, 119
Schlief, M., 97
Schonell R–4 comprehension test,
    197
Schools Council, 1, 2, 4, 158, 265,
    298n
science, 34, 42–3, 81, 86, 135, 223,
    224, 255, 267, 271, 272–3, 285–9,
    292, 297
    and circus technique, 285
    classroom observation study,
        114–31 passim
    and difficulty of text, 85, 103, 241,
        270, 272, 286, 301
    discussion in, 260–4, 265, 293
    and homework, 140–59 passim,
        304
    language policy in, example,
        286–9
    Nuffield Science texts, 270
    and readability survey, 75, 80, 82,
        85, 96
Scott Foresman, 45, 232, 257
secondary school
    /primary school differences, 118,
        121, 134, 136–7, 302–3
    reorganization, 2–4
    sixth-form programmes, 289–90
    topic work study, 167–92, 305–6
sentence structure and readability,
    18–19, 30, 77, 96, 102, 106
sequencing, group, 232, 243–6, 249,
    251, 252, 260–4
Shnayer, S. W., 87–8
'short-burst' reading, 124–5, 130,
    136, 155, 158, 300, 303
sixth-form programmes, 289–90
skimming, 1, 26, 28, 29, 37, 125, 219
Skinner, B. F., 38
skipping, 1, 31
Smith, F., 28, 37
Smog readability formula, 79, 91, 92
    Smog-X, 79, 91
social studies, 42–3, 135, 274–6
    classroom observation study,
        116–25 passim
    discussion in, 293

and homework inquiry, 140–58
    passim, 304
    primary-school classroom study,
        130, 133
    and readability survey, 75, 80, 82,
        85, 86, 103, 107, 301
speaker, 9–14, 18
Spearritt, D., 40
speech, 7–8, 11, 313
    advantages of, compared with
        written text, 17–24
    differences between spoken and
        written language, 15–17, 21–4, 32,
        269–70
    feedback in, 13–14, 24
    non-verbal behaviour in, 11, 13
    register, 21, 297
    settings of, 9–14
    see also conversation
speed-reading, 37
Squire, J. R., 109, 116n, 121
Standard Test Lessons in Reading
    (McCall-Crabbs), 88
statistics, 314–21
Stauffer, R. G., 229–30, 231–2, 253
Sticht, T. G., 79, 91
Strevens, P., 7
study skills, 4, 37, 193, 194, 280,
    289, 297–8
subject teachers' role, 32, 35, 75,
    136, 160, 223–4, 234, 254–5, 257,
    258–9, 269, 271, 272–6, 279,
    285–9, 292–3, 295, 298, 300, 307
Sumner, R., 231n
Sumner, W. A., 79
surface structure, 20, 23n
Survey-Question-Read-Recite-
    Review, see under SQ3R

teacher
    and implications of readability
        survey, 101–3
    language, 234
    and language laboratories, 223–4,
        225, 227, 306, 308
    and language policy, 135–6, 257,
        271–9, 286–9, 291–6, 297, 298
    and low estimate of reading for
        learning, 20, 103, 135, 137
    response to initial project

questionnaire and interview, 34–6
support with difficult text, 86–7,
159
see also subject teachers' role
teachers' centres, 250–1
The Teachers' Day (Hilsum and
Cane), 109
*Teaching English in the United
Kingdom* (Squire and Applebee),
109
team teaching, 115, 168, 298
tests
accuracy, 204, 205–7, 209, 211,
213, 214, 217, 227
comprehension: *see Alistair,
Brighty,* cloze, Davis, F. B.,
*Grieg, Jane, Reading
Comprehension Test DE* (NFER),
Schonell R-4 comprehension test,
Waite comprehension tests
errors in test measurement, 53–4,
58–9
multiple-choice, 98, 202, 226
vocabulary, 202, 205–7, 209, 211,
213, 217
*see also Gates-MacGinitie
Reading Tests,* Reading Level
Tests, *Reading Test E-H* (NFER),
Reading Test BD (NFER)
text
difficulty of, 26, 27, 29, 32, 68,
270, 290, 301 (assessing, 73–4,
76–9, 93, 97–8, 156, 159, 302;
and legibility, 76; and linguistic
variables, 76–8; and reference
material, 86–7; in science, 85,
103, 241, 270, 272, 286, 301; in
social studies, 85; and teacher
support, 86–7, 159; in vocabulary,
78–9, 240, 270) disadvantages
of, compared with speech, 17–24,
32
permanence of, 17, 24–9
Thomas, L., 69, 215, 216, 218, 219
Thorndike, R. L., 40
topic work, 43, 167–92, 223, 305–6
discussion in, 171–2, 175, 188–9,
191, 192

observation study, 167–87
(interviews with pupils, 176–84)
reference material, use of, 172–4,
188, 191
and reflective reading, 300–1
transactional material, 25, 29, 34,
56–7
transformational grammar, 20, 22,
23n
Tuinman, J. J., 69

UK, reading laboratories studies in,
197
USA, 4, 75, 79, 86, 90, 193, 194, 196,
231

van der Will, C., 84–5
Vincent, D., 231

visits to schools, 5, 75, 269–79,
311–12; *see also* practice in
schools
vocabulary, 7, 8, 35, 77, 78–9, 194,
202, 204, 205–7, 209, 211, 213,
217, 223, 227, 297

Waite, Maurice, 43, 116n
Waite comprehension tests, 43–68,
208, 209–10, 211, 216, 217, 218;
see also Alistair, Brighty, Grieg
and *Jane*
Walker, Christopher, 230–2
Walker, Graham, 78–9
Ward Lock Educational, 194, 212
Wason, P. C., 20
Watts, L., 76
Wilkinson, A. M., 22, 55
Wood, R. W., 97
Woodberry Down School, 276n
worksheets, 84, 85, 101, 124, 149,
153–4, 155, 156, 260–4, 270, 272,
276, 280–9, 291–2, 297, 298, 301
Wragg, E. C., 109
writing, 7–8, 313
in classroom, 108, 110, 111,
118–23 *passim,* 129, 135
editing in, 17, 18, 19–20
group discussion and, 252, 256

in homework, 151, 153, 154–5, 156

permanence of text, 17, 24–9

poetic, 16–17

setting of, 14–15

speech and, 15–24, 32, 310

a summary, 214–15, 216, 218, 222, 226, 289, 304

and topic work, 170, 176, 189

see also note-making

Writing Across the Curriculum (Schools Council project; director, Nancy Martin), 2, 34

Written Language of 11–18 Year Olds (Schools Council project; director, James Britton), 2, 34

Yngve 'word-depth' index, 77

Zipf, G. K., 78